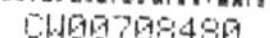

Bruce Foster

James McNeish lives in New Zealand. The author of more than twenty books and plays, he has received a number of awards and scholarships. *The Sixth Man* is the result of seven years of research and writing.

By the same author

NOVELS

Mackenzie

The Mackenzie Affair

The Glass Zoo

Joy

Lovelock

Penelope's Island

My Name Is Paradiso

Mr Halliday & the Circus Master

NON-FICTION

Tavern in the Town

Fire Under the Ashes: A Life of Danilo Dolci

Larks in a Paradise (with Marti Friedlander)

As for the Godwits

Art of the Pacific (with Brian Brake)

Belonging: Conversations in Israel

Walking on my Feet: A Life of A.R.D. Fairburn (with Helen McNeish)

Ahnungslos in Berlin: A Berlin Diary

The Man from Nowhere & Other Prose

The Mask of Sanity: The Bain Murders

An Albatross Too Many

Dance of the Peacocks: New Zealanders in Exile in the time of Hitler and Mao Tse-tung

PLAYS

1895

The Rocking Cave

The Mouse Man

Thursday Bloody Thursday

THE SIXTH MAN

THE EXTRAORDINARY LIFE OF PADDY COSTELLO

V

A VINTAGE BOOK
published by
Random House New Zealand
18 Poland Road, Glenfield, Auckland, New Zealand
www.randomhouse.co.nz

Random House International
Random House
20 Vauxhall Bridge Road
London, SW1V 2SA
United Kingdom

Random House Australia (Pty) Ltd
20 Alfred Street, Milsons Point, Sydney,
New South Wales 2061, Australia

Random House South Africa Pty Ltd
Isle of Houghton
Corner Boundary Road and Carse O'Gowrie
Houghton 2198, South Africa

Random House Publishers India Private Ltd
301 World Trade Tower, Hotel Intercontinental Grand Complex,
Barakhamba Lane, New Delhi 110 001, India

First published 2007

ISBN 978 1 86941 891 5

Design: Elin Bruhn Termannsen
Cover photograph: Paddy Costello
Cover design: Katy Yiakmis
Index: Elaine N. Hall
Printed in Australia by Griffin Press

The Sixth Man

Paddy Costello was a Second World War intelligence officer, a New Zealand diplomat, a linguist, teacher and scholar, a Renaissance man in the breadth and depth of his interests, and — according to his enemies — a Soviet agent during the Cold War. This long overdue biography sets the record straight. It convincingly shows that the slim evidence for the traitor charge was invented, exaggerated and misinterpreted. In fact, when Costello was a diplomat in Moscow the major secret he revealed was to the West: the Soviets had the atomic bomb.

It is now clear that Costello was punished for his pre-war Communist views, which he had trumpeted from the rooftops, and later vilified for being right in his analysis of communism, a victim of the McCarthy period.

This is an important book about a fascinating man who held fast to his beliefs and his humanity at a difficult time in history.

Phillip Knightley, author of *The Second Oldest Profession: Spies and Spying in the 20th Century*

The book draws primarily on letters and diaries, and on interviews conducted over a period of several years. Official documents including declassified New Zealand and American Intelligence files have also been used. The author wishes to thank the late Michael King for a number of British security documents, the so-called Batterbee File, sent to me shortly before he died, the New Zealand Ministry of Foreign Affairs and Trade for help dating back to 1999 and the New Zealand Security Intelligence Service for an informal briefing, following the release of a quantity of declassified material in 2003. A further consignment of forty-one NZSIS documents which arrived in 2007 as this book was going to press has helped to clear up a mystery which has frustrated writers and historians in two hemispheres for forty years.

Conversations where not taken from documents are based on reported speech.

Warm acknowledgement is made to Christopher Costello, Paddy Costello's executor, and his siblings Mick, Katie and Nicholas Costello and Josephine Proctor (née Costello) — and also to Doris Bornstein (née Lerner) and Jack Lerner, Bil Costello's surviving sister and brother — for their unstinting help and generous hospitality. They belong to a richly connected family scattered to Australia and New Zealand, with roots in Ireland and perhaps the sixteenth-century Spanish Armada on one side and, through marriage, the Jewish Pale of Settlement in southern Russia on the other. Their trust and openness to enquiry have made a long labour seem short; and their sometimes critical comments on the text have come without hint of censorship. Without their help and access to the family archives, no book would have been possible.

I owe thanks above all to my wife, Helen, researcher, photographic editor and critic, who has helped more than anyone to disinter Paddy Costello and rescue him from his detractors.

Full acknowledgements appear at the back.

An award by Creative New Zealand enabling me to concentrate on this project and a travel grant by the New Zealand History Research Trust Fund, Ministry for Culture and Heritage, are warmly acknowledged.

— J. McN.

Loved your five "Peacocks". But when are you going to write about the sixth man, Paddy Costello?

— *Letter to author, following publication of* Dance of the Peacocks

I think Costello was pursued by British Intelligence because there was an assumption that it might be an extension of the Philby "ring of five"

— *Sir George Laking, Secretary of Foreign Affairs (NZ) 1967–72*

to

John Bright-Holmes

in gratitude

Contents

Illustrations 12
Author's Foreword 15
Prologue 17

Part One
HOME & AWAY (1912–1940)

Auckland 23
Cambridge 31
Letters 1933 40
"Walking to Olympia" 43
Love in a Bookshop 53
Letters 1936 63
Spain 66
Exeter & the Fyrth Case 74

Part Two
GOING TO WAR (1940–1944)

Letters 1940–1941 83
Prelude to a Battle 89
Battle of Tempe 92
Escape to Crete 99
A Meeting in Cairo 105
The General's Caravan 113
Letters 1941 121
"A Fifth Wheel" 125
Letters 1942–1944 134

Part Three
TO RUSSIA & BACK (1944–1950)

The General's Telegram 141
The First Hardship Post 149
"My Old Man of the Sea" 152
Poland 1945 157
Letter from Stockholm 167
"Moscow! Moscow! Moscow!" 169
Incubus 179
The Paris Peace Conference 185
Letters 1945–1947 193
Tilting at Windmills 196
Doppelgänger 206
The Retreat from Moscow 214
Letters 1949–1950 221

Part Four
A DIPLOMAT IN PARIS (1950–1954)

McIntosh's Folly 227
"A Very Unfortunate Incident" 235
The Unforgiving Mind 240
The Passport Affair 249
Sicilian Vespers 254
Letters 1950–1955 256
"It Was All Very British" 260

Part Five
FULL CIRCLE IN MANCHESTER (1955–1964)

"A Soviet Satellite Going By" 271
A Black Eye in Oxford 279
Dinner with the Freybergs 287
Time's Thief 295

Postscript 305

Appendices 313
Notes & Sources 322
Acknowledgements 388
Select Bibliography 392
Glossary 396
Index 397

Illustrations

SECTION 1 (Auckland and Cambridge)

1. Christopher and Mary Costello, wedding, Melbourne (Woods family collection)
2. The Three Lamps, Ponsonby, 1920s (© Graham Stewart)
3. Paddy Costello at 15, with his Auckland family (Terry Bishop)
4. Costello's favourite sister, Kath, and mother (Terry Bishop)
5. Hunger marchers, Jarrow to London, c. 1933
6. Great Gate, Trinity College, Cambridge (© Helen McNeish)
7. All Saint's Passage, Cambridge, where Maclaurin had his bookshop (© Helen McNeish)
8. Griff Maclaurin, "A Question of Principle", TV2 1976 (© TVNZ)
9. John Cornford
10. Geoffrey Cox in Madrid, 1936 (Alexander Turnbull Library, © *Photo News*)
11. Paddy and Bil Costello, Exeter, 1937 (Josephine Proctor)

SECTION 2 (Greece and North Africa)

12. German tanks crossing the Pinios River during the battle of Tempe, May 1941 (*Die Wehrmacht,* Berlin)
13. General Freyberg during the battle for Crete (Alexander Turnbull Library, © Sir John White)
14. Colonel N.L. Macky, 1941 (Rebecca Macky)
15. Lance-corporal Costello, at sea, 1941 (Josephine Proctor)
16. Costello interrogating Italian prisoner, North Africa, 1942 (Alexander Turnbull Library, © Harold Paton)
17. Costello, 1943, Western Desert (private collection)
18. Dan Davin and Geoffrey Cox with General Freyberg, Italy, 1944 (Alexander Turnbull Library, © Sir John White)
19. Letter to Mick Costello, 1942 (Mick Costello)
20. Dan Davin in Palestine, 1943 (private collection)
21. Vale of Tempe from Ambelakia village (© David McGregor)

SECTION 3 (Moscow and Paris)

22. Chistye Prude, Moscow (© James McNeish)
23. Griboyedov statue, Moscow (© James McNeish)
24. Pasternak's dacha, Peredelkino (© James McNeish)
25. Yvgeny Pasternak with author, Moscow (© Elvina Yerofeeva)
26. Alister McIntosh, c. 1950 (Dr Jim McIntosh, © Leo Rosenthal, New York)
27. Douglas and Ruth Lake (née Macky), Moscow, 1947 (Sarah Lake)
28. Jean McKenzie and Costello, reception in Paris, 1951 (Josephine Proctor)
29. Carl Berendsen, c. 1950 (NZ Ministry Foreign Affairs & Trade)
30. Douglas Zohrab (private collection)
31. New Zealand Legation staff, Moscow, 1946 (Phil & Emilie Costello)
32. Frank Corner with Tom Davin and Richard Collins, upstate New York (© Lyn Corner)
33. New Zealand Legation, Moscow, 1946-1950 (Stuart Prior, © Giraffe Publishing House, Moscow)
34. Peter Kroger's 1954 letter from Vienna applying for passports at the New Zealand Legation in Paris (NZ Security Intelligence Service)
35. Morris and Lona Cohen, alias Peter and Helen Kroger (Neville Spearman, London)
36. Photocopies of the New Zealand passports which enabled the Krogers to enter Britain and pass naval secrets to Moscow (Scotland Yard Crime Museum)

SECTION 4 (Growing Family)

37. Costello in Moscow, "love to Katinka" (Josephine Proctor)
38. Mick Costello with uncles and Lerner grandparents, 1943 (Katie Costello)
39. Paddy and Bil Costello in the south of France, 1938 (Katie Costello)
40-41. Bil with Mick, Exeter (Costello family archive)
42. Bil with Mick and Josie, Exeter (1936-40)
43. Family portrait, Moscow, 1948 (Josephine Proctor)
44. Josie and Katie, Paris, 1953 (Josephine Proctor)
45. Outside the house in Manchester, 1958 (Josephine Proctor)

46. Josie and her father, TB sanatorium, Pyrenees, 1954 (Josephine Proctor)
47. Abba Lerner in America (private collection)
48. Anna Davin and Doris Bornstein, London East End, 2005 (© Helen McNeish)
49. Mick Costello in 1999 (© James McNeish)

SECTION 5 (Last days)

50-51. Paddy and Bil, 1950s (Costello family archives)
52. Costello with Dan and Winnie Davin, Aran Islands, July 1963, shortly before he died (Delia Davin)
53. Paddy Costello, Aran Islands, 1963

MAP

Page 88, Greece, Battle of Tempe, May 1941

Page 192, cartoon of Costello from the *New Hungary* newspaper, Budapest, published during the 1946 Paris Peace Conference
Page 205, Costello's Russian diplomatic pass
Page 238, the New Zealand Legation, Paris
Page 311, this little sketch is from a series of drawings made by Costello when he visited the classical site of Paestum in southern Italy after taking leave of Davin at Cassino in February 1944

Photographic Editor, HELEN McNEISH

Author's Foreword

IT BEGAN WITH Costello being depicted "a falsifier of passports". With time the stories grew wilder. As General Freyberg's Intelligence officer in the war, he had passed on the ULTRA secret; as a seducer of women, he had brought converts to the Stalinist cause; in Moscow he was a disinformation agent, in Paris a tool to bring Czechoslovakia into the Soviet orbit, in England he instigated the Portland naval scandal which helped to bring down the Macmillan government.

The myth-making process was driven principally by three men: the British journalist and conspiracy theorist Chapman Pincher, the Cambridge spy and practised liar Anthony Blunt and, more recently, the Cambridge contemporary historian Professor Christopher Andrew. According to Chapman Pincher who laid the first charge in 1981, Costello was fingered by Blunt as a Cambridge-recruited mole.

In my previous book, *Dance of the Peacocks*, Paddy Costello appears as a secondary figure. When I first heard his name more than twenty years ago, I knew nothing of the spying allegations: I was attracted, through Costello's friend Dan Davin at Oxford University Press, to an enigmatic

New Zealander of infectious joie de vivre who seemed to me one of the last of the great amateur diplomatists of the Cold War. If Davin was to be believed, Costello had rendered invaluable service not just to his country but to the free world. Brilliantly intuitive and analytical, as his reporting of the Russian bomb showed, he was more acutely aware of developments in the Soviet Union than his British or American counterparts in Cold-War Moscow.

The peculiar fact according to documents now available is that the only verifiable charges of actual informing — the Russian possession of the atom bomb being one such case — have to do with Costello passing information not to the East but to the West. Costello is the antipodean counterpart to the American China hands Owen Lattimore and Jack Service, vilified during the McCarthy years for being correct in their analyses of the communist march in history.

Today more than forty years after his death in England Professor Costello's posthumous reputation, mired in myth and innuendo, has him placed firmly in the world literature of espionage as a traitor.

In 1999 Christopher Andrew published his book *The Mitrokhin Archive* which appeared to confirm, for the first time from Russian archival sources, that Paddy Costello had worked for the Soviets. He was, Professor Andrew wrote, a "valuable agent" of the KGB's Paris residency in the 1950s.

After meeting the author in Cambridge, however — we had an extended and entirely amicable discussion — I was unconvinced. Professor Andrew readily admitted that beyond a codename and a brief reference found in Vasili Mitrokhin's notes, he knew nothing more about Costello. After further checking I decided that through no fault or design of his own, he too had become part of the myth-making process.

The most successful spy is the one not caught and, since it is impossible to prove a negative, there will always be a residue of doubt about Costello. Meanwhile we are left with little more than unsubstantiated claims and reports. In press interviews on the publication of his book Professor Andrew named Costello as "the man who transformed the agent Kroger into a Hero of the Russian Federation" and "one of the KGB's top ten".

Fighting words. But if the following narrative is true, they may need to be rewritten.

[April 2007]

Prologue

A MAN CALLED Walter Tongue made the first sighting. Captain Tongue was an amateur soldier in charge of a citizens' rifle company who had been ordered to kill Germans. In professional life he was a funeral director.

Tongue's company had been paid, the men had had tea and were standing to, lounging about the pits with their rifles waiting for the dark. It was not yet dusk. Down on the plain a light mist was forming. It had rained in the morning, drizzle and mist; then the sun appeared. In the afternoon Tongue had noticed some winking lights on the plain, as if reflected from the windshields of moving vehicles. Firing had broken out from the Colonel's Headquarters further along the ridge beneath Platamon castle. Then it stopped. Nothing.

Walter Tongue ran to an observation post at the top of his village. The village he was defending faced Mount Olympus. It was high up, almost in the snowline. Then a runner appeared, a tall gangling man in glasses. Costello. They reached the top together.

"What is it, sir?" Costello said.

Lance-Corporal Costello wore an infantry badge on his forage cap, although he was in fact a signalman. He belonged to Headquarters.

"See for yourself." Tongue handed him the binoculars. Costello shook his head and gave them back. He was short-sighted and mildly astigmatic. "I think they're tanks," Tongue said. "Tanks," he repeated, and gave a sharp laugh, as if he didn't believe it himself.

Costello wiped his glasses and squinted down at the plain. All he could see was a blur of objects drawn up in lines like old-time horse floats. They filled the centre of the plain.

"Tanks?"

"Twenty at least," Tongue said.

"Fifteen." He began to count. "Twenty . . . twenty-five."

Costello felt his diaphragm constrict, and cupped his hands tight. His fingertips were wet against the palms. He opened his hands and cupped them again. It was something he did responding to pressure.

"Thirty-five. Forty. Forty-two . . ." Tongue was still counting.

Costello was thinking of his wife and two children, who were in England. He had joined up the previous summer. He was a new recruit.

"Fifty," Tongue said.

Unbidden, two lines from Housman came into Costello's mind.

He to the hill of his undoing
Pursued his road.

Poetry was something else Costello did. Poetry he found was of great help in some situations, if one suffered from a lively imagination.

The war, when he got up that morning, had seemed far off. They had come from England via Egypt and landed in Greece in time for Easter. Yesterday, Easter Sunday, the Colonel had ordered a church parade. Costello had stood in the fine frosty air with his battalion, thinking how clever of the Colonel to get them posted here, to a part of Greece he had read about as a schoolboy — to Thessaly, in sight of Mount Olympus. Thessaly in the spring. In the ravines violets bloomed, wild strawberries and broom and pink daisies with black centres, and tiny blue hyacinths. In the villages where Costello had gone among the peasants, haggling to buy mules to transport their guns, quince and cherry were in blossom, "and lovely mauve flowers," he wrote to his wife, "which the peasants call kuchiparies."

"Eighty."

Tongue went on counting. When he reached a hundred, Lance-Corporal

Costello descended from the village and returned to battalion Headquarters. It was an hour's walk to the opposing mountainside crowned by a castle where the Colonel had his dugout. Although a mere lance-jack corporal, Costello spoke fluent Greek; as such he enjoyed the Colonel's confidence. He entered the dugout on the side of Castle Hill and knew at once that the situation was deteriorating. The Colonel was saying to the adjutant, "Anyway, I've signalled only fifty. Tongue counted a hundred tanks, he said, but I told him not to go on. No one would believe us anyway. So officially," he turned to Costello, "officially, there are only fifty tanks in front of us."

They were not as it happened tanks, but scout cars and troop carriers. The tanks arrived the next day.

Costello's diary reads:

> 13 April Easter Sunday
> 14 April afternoon. Our guns open on enemy patrol
> 15 April first enemy shell at first light. Shelling all day.
> 16 April Withdrawal to Tempe

The fight for the castle, a fine example of Crusader architecture looming above Headquarters (and Costello's lean-to) had begun at nightfall on the 15th. After the tank and infantry attacks, dive-bombers came over. Costello's account to his wife begins, "Shells are flying so low over my lean-to that the leaves come fluttering down with each shot. I am only a hundred feet from battalion HQ." Shortly afterwards his account breaks off. The Colonel's diary describes the day's activities as "most unpleasant". The Colonel's last message, sent shortly after 10 a.m. on the 16th, reads: "Closing down. Getting out."

So they ran. Officially it was called a fighting withdrawal. They ran nevertheless.

All over Greece at this moment men were retreating and running, pouring south, overwhelmed by superior numbers as the Germans came down from the north. Englishmen, Irishmen, Welshmen, Scotsmen, Australians, New Zealanders, 55,000 of them. The Greek army had collapsed, the prime minister committed suicide. The quixotic "adventure" intended to save Greece — the Allies had come in time for Easter and barely stayed for the Greek Good Friday — was over before it began. Miraculously most of the 55,000 were evacuated by the Royal Navy.

Chief among those not evacuated by the Navy were the Colonel and his seven hundred men making up the 21st Auckland Battalion. When the German commander, Balck, signalled that his tanks had captured the castle on Platamon Hill, the Colonel and his seven hundred retreated like everyone else. But they did not go far. A few miles down the railway track they came to a pass. The name of this pass was Tempe. Here the Colonel was ordered to stand and engage the enemy, "if necessary to extinction".

The Colonel was facing at the time three German divisions, half an army. Like Leonidas and the three hundred Spartans facing the Persian army further south at Thermopylae in 480 BC, he was instructed to hold the enemy at all costs to enable the main force to escape. To make quite sure that the Colonel understood these instructions, all his transport was taken away. So in the Vale of Tempe began an unequal battle — and a feat of arms, we are told, "unsurpassed by any British unit in Greece". The Battle of Tempe however will not enter the history books, although, strange to say, Costello will.

History does not always favour the brave and when a gallant Colonel and his men are left unsung it is quite unfair for a lance-jack corporal with no claim to heroism to be awarded, if not a mention, the only footnote in despatches. All this by way of saying that in AD 1941 (18 April, Greek Good Friday) Costello finally found his war. He had been waiting for it since 1936.

PART ONE
HOME & AWAY

1912–1940

Auckland

"An original mind without job description"

HIS CONFIRMATION NAME was Julius, after Julius Caesar. The significance of this would not be apparent for a further year or two, when Costello wrote a cautionary tale entitled "A Routed Army". The tale was about Xerxes. Xerxes, son of Darius, was the Persian king who invaded Greece in the year 480 BC. The story was in the form of an essay which appeared in the Auckland Grammar School *Chronicle* for 1927, and it described the outcome of a battle where initially the Greek defenders, confronting a superior force — "the most powerful army the world had ever seen" — grew downcast, and retreated.

This retreat occurred at the pass of Tempe — the same place Costello's battalion would be called on to defend in Greece against the invading Germans in 1941. Of course Costello, who was only fifteen when he wrote the essay, could not have foreseen this.

What is interesting about the essay is that the author displays a command of language and historical imagery beyond his years. Hunger, it is said, is the best cook. This is an author hungry for expression, or self-expression. In this fifteen-year-old's account of Xerxes the Immortal, and the fate that awaited him, we are meeting a mind already versed in and in tune with the Ancient World.

"Julius" Costello was born Desmond Patrick Costello in Auckland in 1912. At eight, we are told, or nine, he discovered for himself Lemprière's *Classical Dictionary*. There were a few books belonging to his mother, who had trained as a teacher, in the inner-city tenements where he was growing up in Auckland — first in the grim and gritty Eden Terrace where he was born on the smoky fringe of Newton, then in a small house in the suburb of Ponsonby. The latter comprised a couple of rooms over a shop, which he shared with his brothers and sisters among the sturdy poor of working-class Auckland. But there was no dictionary to engage his imagination to compare with Lemprière. He found it in the local institute library by the Three Lamps, Ponsonby, and soon devoured it, page by page. At fifteen Costello won a junior national scholarship to university but was too young to take it up. He sat for another award, the Lissie Rathbone Scholarship, worth twice as much, won it, and went to 'Varsity. He read Lycias in the original Greek when he was sixteen. At university, encouraged by his professor, he read so voraciously and widely that he began writing Greek and Latin quite naturally. His classics professor, an abstemious cigar-smoking Scotsman named Paterson, taught him Hebrew as well. Costello had already taught himself the Romance languages, according to his brother Phil, and picked up a bit of Gaelic and Yiddish on the side, so it is not surprising to find him described fifty years later in the centennial history of the Department of Classics and Ancient History, University of Auckland (1983) as "probably the most brilliant linguist ever in the department".

Clearly Desmond Patrick Costello was a prodigy of some sort. But what sort? And where was it leading?

It is difficult to get an accurate picture of the young Costello in New Zealand. Except for a declassified security file, there are almost no contemporary records.

> Eyes, blue; hair, brown; height, 6ft 2in. A particularly level-headed student. No communistic or similar views . . .

one reads in his New Zealand SIS (Security Intelligence Service) file. The entry refers to Costello's undergraduate years at Auckland. But this is contradicted by another entry in the file:

> Associated with a group noted for its radical tendencies and communist leanings.

This is confusing, and perhaps misleading, like his reported height. Costello was thin, tall, long-legged as a stork. When he departed for Cambridge he was almost six feet four inches. Yet according to Alex McDonald, another classicist who would precede him to England, at school — on the Auckland Grammar School shooting range — Costello had to be propped up with a pillow before he could see the target.

> He was by far the smallest boy in the school. I was Sergeant Major in charge of Musketry and had to direct the whole school through its shooting practice with .22 rifles. We needed to put a pillow behind Paddy's shoulders.

Evidently he developed physically almost as fast as he did mentally. Yet confusion and uncertainty remain. Until Costello enters Cambridge University in England, we are confronted by a seeming enigma, an original mind lacking in job description. At the University College of Auckland Costello is sociable and witty, but joins no clubs. Alert and athletic but plays no team sport, only tennis. Is not remembered for any debating, artistic or literary pursuits. Indeed in an aviary of literary peacocks — James Bertram, Jack Bennett, John Mulgan, leading lights who will also depart for England — Costello is hardly noticed at all.

Like Costello, these Auckland contemporaries have a feeling for history and language. Also a social conscience. They too are restless and impatient with the furniture of the ordinary world, and just as anxious as he to escape the suffocating conventions and monotony of their New Zealand background. It is a tiny place, the university college where they come to study full time. They congregate under the tower of a fine new arts building, housing languages and classics, in Princes Street. Bertram and Bennett have reserved seats in the library. Picture them, the privileged few, this tiny band of thoroughbreds moving about the half-empty corridors and cafeteria, "and still emptier library, in an unreal building of white fresh-cut stone" (Bertram writes). They know and write about one another compulsively in the university journals. Yet Costello is not mentioned. Apart from a solitary appearance at the literary club, he might be invisible.

It seems he saw himself getting into print. R.A.K. Mason, a poet and a kind of missionary of the Left who frequented the campus, was giving a talk to the club. Costello went along and met him. "Avoid cant," Mason told him. "If you want to write, go and talk to the bargees." If Costello took the advice, the university literary magazines gave no sign. They avoided him and he, them. Apparently it was Costello's only appearance at the literary club.

There were of course social distinctions in Auckland. The average arts student of the thirties was Anglican, middle class and conservative, exhaling an air, if not of sanctity, of comfortable orthodoxy. Anything departing from the norm was suspect. Probably Costello's Irishness and lack of polish set him apart. James Bertram's father for example was a church minister, John Mulgan's a literary editor. Costello's father was a grocer. Costello's "outsider" status, for all that, may be an illusion, more apparent than real.

A family story suggests that the Costellos claimed descent from the "black Irish" who landed off the coast of Scotland from the wrecked Spanish Armada in 1588. But the story is questionable, unconfirmed except anecdotally and by references in Costello's New Zealand security file. His birth in New Zealand was the result of an arranged marriage. Costello's parents were immigrant Irish — his mother from the south, the father from Dublin — who met and married in Melbourne and came to New Zealand on their honeymoon. Here they stayed, for no particular reason that can be discovered, and raised a family. To that extent Desmond, the second born, was an accidental New Zealander.

"We lived in Melbourne," his mother Mary said, speaking of her people who had emigrated to Australia where she was born. She added, "But we grew up in Ireland."

Mary Costello was a fierce little woman with frizzy hair who sang. She sang and he sang — music was a shared passion. She sang operatic arias in the family shop and bequeathed to the second son, he said, perfect pitch. "Can God sing?" Desmond is reported to have asked the local Catholic priest. Desmond, or Des — the Paddy would come later — was an altar boy, aged six or seven. "Certainly he can," the priest replied. The boy shook his head. "No. I mean in tune? Like my ma."

"What made all our family sing in tune," Costello would write later, "was the fact that my mother could, and did." He wrote this during the war in 1941. By now the voice of a boy soprano had metamorphosed into a lilting Irish tenor with a considerable repertoire; by now, a friend records,

"Paddy could ad lib or be persuaded to sing from his repertoire in almost any European language." He seems to have acquired this facility, like almost everything else, by a process known only to himself.

Someone has said that at Cambridge Costello was known as the Irish Nightingale, attributing the phrase to Anthony Blunt. This can't be right, for Blunt and Costello hardly knew each other at Cambridge. Nightingales apart however, mention of Blunt, the future Keeper of the Royal Pictures and Cambridge spy, provides us with a yardstick, perverse as it may seem, helping to pin down an elusive colonial personality. What is unusual about the young Blunt in England, as about the young Costello in New Zealand, is the extent to which their adult interests were already fixed before puberty — two "givens" or constants which would last a lifetime. In Blunt's case, modern art and Poussin; in Costello's, languages and scholarship. We are told by Blunt's biographer, Miranda Carter, that his school career at Marlborough included eight scholarships. Costello when he left for Trinity College, Cambridge, had picked up nine scholarships. The difference is that although he grew up in the core of working-class Auckland with dense housing all around on the slopes of the Ponsonby Road ridge, squashed into a couple of rooms over a shop with three brothers and two sisters, Costello's parents apparently didn't need the subsidy.

At primary school he leap-frogged classes and sat for the coveted Humphrey Rawlings scholarship, open to any child under the age of twelve attending a public school, when he was ten. This propelled him as a Rawlings Scholar to grammar school at eleven, with free tuition, books and an annual £10 maintenance guaranteed for three years. The winner was expected to show that his parents were "poor and needy". Certainly the district was styled poor. But Costello's father was not poor. When he died suddenly in 1923, he left a young widow with six dependants who, though certainly in need, wasn't poor either. Christopher (the father) died of a perforated ulcer when Desmond was eleven; by then the father had acquired property and moved across the harbour to a bigger shop at Devonport; he added on a butchery with flats above and joined the middle classes. There was probably another grocery shop before the one in Ponsonby. Today eighty years later "the shop" itself has come down to Costello's own offspring across the world as a kind of symbol, firing their imaginations in different ways.

Paddy Costello's son Nicholas, who at the time of writing lives in Beijing, recalls:

> I remember that my image of luxury drew on Paddy's tale of growing up in a shop, and his parents being able to go into the shop and take whatever they wanted, even in the evening. In my imagination it would have been a leg of lamb.

The original shop in Ponsonby, oddly adapted to residential use, is still there. One has an image of the young Costello, moving about from grocer's shop to grocer's shop, a crib in one hand, a copy of A.E. Housman in his pocket, coming home from school not to help out behind the counter, as one might expect — unless to give someone the change for a penny that you needed to operate the call phone outside — but to pick up and continue reading the book he had abandoned at breakfast, in order to — to what? To keep on with the game. What game? The game of counting scholarships.

Between the ages of ten and twenty Costello won every scholarship he was entered for, and the mother's hand — her letters demonstrate the bond and complicity, as do his — seems to have been in every one. Other boys played King o'Seni and rounders, collected bamboo pea-shooters and marbles, and read the *Magnet* and the *Gem*; Costello did too; but mostly he played the school piano and the game of collecting scholarships. Scholarship was the Costello Condition.

Certainly young "Des" inherited his competitive genes from the mother. But it wasn't only that.

There were sixty children to a class in the Curran Street primary school Costello attended, built on the site of a Chinaman's garden. But nearby were swimming beaches and — a godsend for a bookworm — a handsome building containing a public library, the Leys Institute. For every down-and-out slumped in pubs like the Gluepot on one corner, there was an itinerant pianist offering bargain-basement music lessons on the other. The vitality compressed into that one square mile of working-class Auckland where Costello spent most of his first ten years generated explosive tensions which were a perfect forcing ground for an Irish romantic.

Costello's mother was née Woods, Mary Woods. The Woodses, she said to him, were a cut above the ordinary. The Woodses, he would say to her after looking them up in Ireland, "are the goodses". Since his mother thought good stories deserved a lot of repetition, Costello got to know more about her side of the family. There is little to be learned about his father,

Christopher, except that he was a widower and twice Mary's age — he was thirty-eight, she barely nineteen — when they married and came to New Zealand. And that he died at fifty-six, leaving her comparatively well off.

In her wedding photograph Mary appears dwarfed by her husband. She is plain-faced, tiny, and unremarkable, except for a mountain of frizzy hair which swallows might nest in. Then one notices the lip. Her upper lip curls down, defiant and insurrectionary. One knows instantly who will rule the household.

In a letter written to her after his first visit to Ireland in 1932 Costello reported on one of the sisters, his Auntie May:

> I told you how impressed I was with Auntie May. She is full of high spirits, using a rather purplish vocabulary in which words with a b —— are noticeably frequent. She is in other respects very like yourself: she has the Woods lip, she uses the same turns of expression as yourself and is easily moved to tears.

Probably it is here, in the nakedness of the heart, that Costello most resembles his mother and that her influence will be felt. Mary Woods was another romantic, naive and idealistic for all her no-nonsense exterior. She will teach Des his first revolutionary songs of Ireland although she herself, born in Melbourne, has never been to Ireland. The romantic son of a romantic mother, he is a true Woods. This too is part of the Costello Condition.

The references in Costello's New Zealand Security file to a student "radical", with all that that implies, contrast quaintly with Costello's role in the famous Queen Street riot of April 1932. This was the moment when university students in Auckland were enrolled as police specials and went out with batons to help quell "the raging mob" in the name of law and order. The incident was a burning issue; nearly 80,000 were officially out of work in Auckland. But once again Costello does not figure. The incident like the Depression itself seems to have passed him by. On the eve of departing for Cambridge, he doesn't seem to have taken sides one way or another.

Trevor O'Leary offers a kind of explanation. O'Leary and the gangling Costello travelled across the water together on the daily ferry. The pair met on weekends and walked round the beaches, O'Leary spouting James Joyce, Costello responding with draughts of poetry from Housman's *A Shropshire*

Lad. Trevor O'Leary was a tally clerk on the Auckland waterfront. Whenever Costello came to see him, he said, it wasn't to go down the stokeholds or learn about working conditions, but to meet Irish stevedores who could sing and talk to him in Gaelic. His interest was linguistic and poetic, not political.

It may be misleading to single Costello out as a sport, distinct from his contemporaries who won scholarships to Oxford. Yet there remains the fact of his Irishness, a fundamental divide. Whereas they, making good going "Home" to England, would head straight for the Oxford colleges where they were enrolled, Costello landing in England would make a beeline for Ireland. It was the first thing he did after his ship docked at Tilbury. Ireland was another constant, saving his soul, just a little, from the anxiety of the expatriate who can never decide where he truly belongs.

Other eventualities lay in wait to test the young Costello. Meantime, having graduated with a double First in Greek and Latin and gained a post-graduate travelling scholarship to Trinity, Cambridge, on a cloudless evening in July 1932 he sailed out of Auckland harbour. New Zealand was receding, almost an abstraction, in some ways a country he had barely known.

CAMBRIDGE

An asylum, in more ways than one

— A.E. Housman

COSTELLO ENTERED TRINITY College, Cambridge, as an exhibitioner in the autumn of 1932. A number of luminaries including the poet A.E. Housman and Wittgenstein the philosopher, besides the future spies, Kim Philby, Guy Burgess and Anthony Blunt, were already there. Trinity was the grandest college in Cambridge, a bastion of privilege which had nurtured six Prime Ministers, besides a tradition of racing around the Great Court before the clock had ceased to strike twelve, an undergraduate romp dramatised in the film *Chariots of Fire*.

At first he was disappointed. If Costello quivered with excitement entering beneath the Great Gate of a college endowed by Henry VIII, or strolling by cloisters in Nevile's Court where Isaac Newton had stamped his foot and timed the echo to calculate the speed of sound, he does not tell us — naturally enough, perhaps, since his head was still spinning from a visit to Ireland where he enjoyed a second baptism with his mother's people in the parish of Mullinavat. They had a farm there.

Costello reached England on 29 September 1932, his ship lying off the mouth of the Thames at 9 a.m. Twenty-four hours later, on 30 September, he was walking up Mullinavat's only street to his Uncle Mattie's place in time for breakfast. The family farm was a reference point and a moral compass; Costello would be drawn into Irish history and debates with the local priest; he was at home there and among cousins in the surrounding Kilkenny countryside. That first term he wrote lyrically about

> Uncle Mattie [who] is, as you know, an angel. Very big, soft spoken, and gentle, and with it all fiercely anti-English. Grandpa is as lovable as anyone I ever met. I can't get over Grandpa, I could talk about him for days on end.

"Did grandpa sing for me?" he wrote again:

> Did he do anything else? He and I used to sing all day together and I heard "Of a Summer's morning I perambled early", and all the ones I've heard you sing.

And:

> They are all clever, and at least Grandpa and Mattie are straightforward with it, though Nicky is an old twister. Still, whenever I happen to think of my breed I give myself a pat on the back.

Trinity may have been the grandest college in Cambridge, it was also in some ways the most impersonal. Scholars read the Latin grace to a standing assembly before dinner, and lessons in a hallowed chapel. Consigned to a remote bedsit in a Victorian terrace on Maid's Causeway, Costello had come at a time when Trinity, like King's, the other plum college, was becoming a hotbed of political ferment and controversy. The Depression was deepening, three million people or a quarter of the insured wage-earning population of England were out of work; even in a semi-prosperous market town like Cambridge, Costello was aware of children looking half-starved. His head was swimming with Grandpa's Irish revolutionary songs. The glory of seven centuries of Cambridge teaching and learning was all around him. In Germany, Hitler was in power, Mussolini's fascists were on the march in Italy, in the Far East Japan had invaded Manchuria. The rush to Marxism, the so-called "honeymoon period of university communism", was about to begin, sweeping Costello along with it. But although he had arrived instinctively facing in the right direction, that is, left, and had joined the growing Socialist Society, he was cautious. Form mattered to him, and academic rigour, as much as fashion. Swept up he may have been, but not swept away. Costello was strangely muddled. His studies were in a mess. He seemed to have fallen among right-wingers. Both of Costello's tutors were reactionary, while his hero, A.E. Housman, whose trade was Latin, was the most reactionary of the lot. For the first time in Costello's life success seemed about to elude him.

It was his own fault. In New Zealand he had won a £40 Exhibition to read classics; then without informing his sponsors he contrived to switch courses and read economics. Once a week, together with a Russian emigré, Count Sollohub, he attended on his supervisor, "a splendid fellow, generally considered to be, after Keynes, the most brilliant economist at Cambridge and hence one of the best in the world". This was Dennis Robertson, a gentle and vulnerable homosexual who, as happened in that world conducive to amours and intrigue, was the man who introduced Kim Philby to Guy Burgess, who "dominated him for the next thirty-five years".

Then a cable arrived from the University of New Zealand ordering Costello to take classics or resign his scholarship. Costello swallowed the pill and prepared to get down to Cicero and Plato again. He wrote to his mother:

> Now as soon as you get this I want you, please, to pack together my Greek and Latin dictionaries (Liddell & Scott, Andrews, and the big English–Latin), Goodwin's Greek Grammar, Mommsen (4 vols), Sidgwick, and the Loebs, like a good girl. Heaven knows what it'll cost . . .

He was beginning to feel he had come to the wrong university. The English, Cambridge people in particular, were impossible:

> It irritates me to see them at hall (dinner) in the evening, with their pink faces and fair hair, their impervious attitude of self-satisfaction, and their outrageous manner of speech. Nearly all the Englishmen I know are sopranos, and they chatter and trill to one another like a lot of birds.

Economics after all appears to have been an aberration. Forced to return to a familiar world of Greek and Latin, Costello now discovered a tutor whom he detested — "possibly the most objectionable person I can yet remember meeting". This was the art collector and classics don, Andrew Gow, who had taught the young George Orwell at Eton. Gow was a friend of Housman, part of an exclusive Trinity set that demanded of the kitchens that fresh raspberries be served at high table with crème brûlée; Gow's rooms in Nevile's Court contained Rodin busts and other Impressionist works he had picked up in Paris for a song. Probably Gow, who would take great pains with some of his students, was more charitable towards Costello than the latter allows. It may have been of Costello that Gow was thinking when he said one day to James Klugmann, a proselytising communist at the college: "Tell me James, why is it that so many of my brightest students seem to be on the left?" "Well, sir," Klugmann replied, "you have to think of the common factor. And that's you, sir."

As it happened the reason Costello had decided to come to Cambridge, rather than Oxford, had more to do with poetry than either economics or classics. According to his brother, Phil,

> Des [i.e. Paddy] was offered places at Oxford and at Trinity College, Dublin, but he chose Cambridge because A.E. Housman, the poet, was there. Housman was also a classics man but Des's great love was poetry.

At Trinity Housman, now in his seventies, was invisible. Few had seen or spoken to the unworldly author of *A Shropshire Lad* since he had taken up the Kennedy Professorship of Latin in 1911, and even someone as distinguished as Dilwyn Knox, one of the Keynes-Strachey set, scholar of Greek texts and a fellow of King's College, "counted himself lucky to receive a glacial few words, now and then, at the Classical Club". Costello burned to meet Housman but wisely kept his distance. He was bucked therefore when, in the Easter term, the reclusive genius emerged from silence to deliver a lecture at the Senate House on poetry, his first public utterance on the subject. Costello wrote to his mother:

> I heard Housman yesterday delivering a lecture on "the Name and Nature of Poetry". He said he had not lectured before in

> public for 21 years (the last occasion was on his appointment to his professorship, when he had to do it) and he will never do so again. So I felt tickled to death I managed to hear him. Of course the Senate House was crowded and many turned away. A.E.H. was very cold, pure and classical, and gave quite a fine address, lasting something over an hour.

Housman's rooms were in Whewell's Court. They were on the same staircase as the philosopher Ludwig Wittgenstein, and a few yards from where Costello would later have rooms as a post-graduate and meet a wealthy young Anglo-American undergraduate, Michael Whitney Straight. Straight's parents had founded an experimental school at Dartington Hall where he lived and where Costello in 1935 would be invited to stay. Straight's rooms, on the same staircase, were directly underneath Housman's; his drinking parties in K5, to which flaunting and brawling homosexuals like Burgess were invited, were famous. These parties usually ended, Straight recalls in his autobiography — improbably perhaps, given the restrictions on noise and night-watchmen prowling — "by standing in a circle and singing 'Arise ye Prisoners of Starvation!'* while poor old Housman gnashed his teeth in impotent rage in his room overhead".

But this was later, in 1936, the year Housman died. In 1933, returning to classics after wasting half a term on economics, Costello found he had fallen behind. He had informed his mother in a fit of modesty that on his record he was "one of the brightest people" the classics department in Auckland had sent abroad. Now he sees his New Zealand education for what it is, "very narrow", and is appalled:

> I have abandoned all hope of getting a First [he writes on 11 February 1933]. The learning of the average student here — chaps who write Latin and Greek verse with ease, who have been learning classics since the age of six — is something alarming.

That first year, at the end of the Michaelmas term and again at Lent, he went back to Ireland. There he hid himself under the hipped roof of the

* Straight's version of the first line of the *Internationale*. Later in America, after Burgess and Maclean fled to Moscow in 1951, Straight would confess to his entanglement with the Blunt–Burgess ring, thus exposing and helping to unmask Anthony Blunt.

Woods farmhouse overlooking the village of Mullinavat, and studied. The oil lamp burning late into the night is still remembered in the parish. Betty Woods, a cousin, says:

> They marvelled at this youth who was always studying upstairs. He'd come down, go outside and run around the paddock with the dog and the goat, and go back to studying. Everyone in the family heard stories about this paragon from New Zealand.

Back at Cambridge, beset by tourists pointing at the natives, Costello affected nonchalance strolling along Jesus Lane or Petty Cury in gown and square. He was nonetheless "working fit to bust".

Cleaving to his Irishness, Costello was also renouncing the Woods family dream, he told his mother, of making money and "getting on". He wrote to her on 12 March 1933, "J.M. Keynes, perhaps the most brilliant man at Cambridge, talks somewhere about 'that goal of mediocrity, a bourgeois independence'. And it's true that only mediocre timorous people do make financial independence their aim. Other people don't bother so much, and they are the only people who ever do anything."

It was in Costello's second — and final — year, 1933–4, that Marxism "hit Cambridge". Miranda Carter, Blunt's biographer, tells of Anthony Blunt's schoolboy friend, Louis MacNeice, returning to Cambridge on a visit in 1936, and being reminded of everything he disliked about Blunt's life. "Cambridge was still full of Peter Pans," MacNeice wrote, "but all the Peter Pans were now talking Marx."

There was already a small communist cell at the university centred on Trinity in 1932 when Costello arrived. Among its early members were the economics don Maurice Dobb who founded the group, and the future spies Donald Maclean and Kim Philby. But Costello was not part of it. The new doctrine which swept away undergraduates and graduate students alike did not take hold until the end of 1933, when two determined young men, John Cornford and James Klugmann, took over Dobb's group and transformed it — Cornford, a first-year undergraduate, Klugmann a post-graduate. The eighteen-year-old Cornford was already a published poet; the soft-voiced Klugmann, genial, roly-poly, prankish, would become the pure intellectual of the Party in Britain. Both were one hundred per cent Bolsheviks. Together they targeted and waylaid sympathetic and impressionable undergraduates deemed worthy of "bringing in", sitting in their rooms, arguing and persuading doubters of the rightness of their cause.

This was not so difficult after the first contingents of hunger marchers began arriving from the north of England. Groups of students, Costello among them, went out to meet the marchers, helping to organise meals and places for them to sleep on their way to London. "Their faces had fallen in and they had ill-fitting boots," noted Margot Heinemann, who would become John Cornford's lover. "It was only a matter of time before I joined the Party." It wasn't only in towns like Jarrow where eighty per cent of the population was unemployed that the Depression cast its pall. It was felt in regions where new industries thrived. Even people not in the least sympathetic to the Left recognised a social collapse in Britain on an unprecedented scale. So many textile mills in the north went out of production that the smut wore off, leaving grimed buildings, to the amazement of the inhabitants, looking clean; former mill owners were reduced to picking up cigarette ends in the street.

As the Slump worsened, left-wing undergraduates, intoxicated by the new Marxist doctrine, began to dominate the traditionally conservative Cambridge Union. Not only left-wingers fell under the Cornford–Klugmann spell.

Julian Bell, Virginia Woolf's nephew, soon succumbed to the "logic" of joining the only organisation that was doing anything about fascism and poverty.

"We are all Marxists now," Bell declared.

Costello knew Klugmann and Cornford. After John Cornford was killed in the Spanish Civil War, Costello would claim him as a special friend (so, it seems, did everyone else). The charismatic student leader who spoke for his generation appears in Costello's early letters as "the head of the Trinity anti-war group and communist movement", a reference to the famous November 1933 peace demonstration. On this occasion Julian Bell drove a car through the centre of Cambridge like a tank, with mattresses strapped to the sides to ward off a swarm of toughs hurling eggs, tomatoes and other missiles. Bell's navigator was Guy Burgess. A tall fresh-faced student studying modern languages at Trinity Hall, Donald Maclean, appears in a newspaper photograph marching in the second rank. Further back, behind a banner:

WORKERS
BY HAND AND BRAIN
UNITE AGAINST WAR

is an equally tall young man in a tie and jacket who, it has been suggested, is Costello. But it is not Costello, although he certainly took part in the peace demonstration.

There is a first-hand glimpse provided by an emeritus professor at Edinburgh, the Marxist historian Victor Kiernan. Kiernan was Costello's contemporary at Trinity. He describes a tall curly-headed figure with a pendulous lip and a slight squint at meetings of the Cambridge University Socialist Society they attended — "a striking personality and impressive physique, valuable when young men with fists were needed to guard doors of buildings where Tory ruffians could be expected to try to break in on our meetings." Costello the Bouncer?

In the autumn term of 1933 he attended a meeting addressed by a trade-union secretary,

> . . . a bird called Brown. He compared the Independent Labour party to the Anglican High Church. He urged us all to join up with the Communist Party. The difficulty is that, postulating I get a job at the end of the year, I should certainly lose it if it became known that I am a communist. Not that I am.

In 1934, the year Cornford and Klugmann are said to have taken over the Cambridge cell, Costello graduated and went down. A friendship with Cornford or Klugmann could be dangerous. A generation later, espionage writers would seize on it, as in the case of Michael Straight, as proof of "recruitment to the Soviet cause". But while it is true that Straight was later brought into the Burgess–Blunt ring, as a probationer-mole, it is also true that Costello was not. By the time the Cambridge five were being recruited by the Russians, Costello had married, left Cambridge and was living in another world.

Despite his friendship with Cornford and Klugmann, Costello seems to have remained largely immune to the solid core of communist ideology. He lacked the intellectual background for a true Marxist, he told his mother. Four terms after coming to Trinity, he had still not read *Das Kapital*.

There is about Costello an unorthodoxy which makes him a difficult target. An Irishman does not easily sell his soul. It is probably unsportsmanlike so early in the piece to decry the later myth, which will be manufactured a generation on, of Costello "the Cambridge-recruited spy". Still, if one is not to fly in the face of facts and common sense, one cannot do less. At Cambridge Costello joins the Socialist Society but is equally absorbed in the Celtic Studies and Hibernian clubs. He is one of those undergraduates who admire Kim Philby, but it is Maynard Keynes's view on "bourgeois mediocrity" which gives him pause and makes him think. He falls for the Russian talkies at the Tivoli Cinema but is equally smitten by the films of René Clair or the sight of Ely Cathedral glimpsed through the mist after a bike ride of sixteen miles.

Innocent of easy solutions, he walks alone like a cat, albeit an Irish-New Zealand cat, bolshie, pink-tied, flamboyant, yet reticent, arrogant, securely insecure in his outsider status. It will be another two years before he decides to join the Party, arriving independently and exemplifying Bunyan's motto, "Every tub should stand on its own bottom".

There were three advantages to be derived from coming to Trinity, Costello told his mother on the eve of his first visit to the Continent in the summer of 1933 — "(a) One can say, 'When I was at Cambridge.' (b) One can wear a Trinity blazer (if one can afford to buy it). (c) One can get a job (perhaps)." There was a fourth advantage, of course. "You meet clever blokes from all over the shop who do you more good than all the textbooks MacMillan ever published."

One of the "clever blokes" was another poor scholarship boy, the future Japanologist and Canadian envoy, Herbert Norman. They met in Costello's second year. Herbert Norman was from Toronto, an emotional convert to communism brought in by Cornford who would devote himself in turn to converting Indian undergraduates at Cambridge. Like Costello, Herb Norman would be hounded by Intelligence agencies in the Cold War. Norman was another troubled romantic, "a tall blond streak with glasses", immensely likeable.

Most of Costello's friends at Cambridge seem to have been Canadians and Americans. Only two were from his native New Zealand, one being the classicist Alex McDonald who had once put a pillow behind Costello's shoulder on the Auckland Grammar School rifle range. The other was a short balding mathematician, enrolled at St John's College. His name was Maclaurin.

From the Letters

1933, Cambridge

25th Jan 1933, My dearest Mother

I don't suppose Grandpa ever sang a song about
As Jack was riding through London City
None of those fair maids did poor Jack pity —
Toodle-eeaddle-eeay-do
Toodle-eeaddle-eaay etc?

He says he always was one for the quare songs.
From your loving son, Des
P.S. Everybody knows me as Paddy here, not Des at all.

12th March
I am entering for a John Stewart of Rannoch Schol. (£40 per year) next term.

10th May
It is with regret that I have to announce my failure to win a John Stewart of Rannoch schol. Trinity Coll. however offers a prize for the best Greek prose. I did not get the prize but my tutor tells me I came so close that the council decided to grant a second prize. It is apparently quite an honour to get it.

21st May
Terms is within three weeks of its close, and I am looking forward to my trip to Spain.

Madrid

12th July
After the [bull] fight we spent the evening singing songs outside the inn seated on benches in the street. Imagine me singing solos in Spanish, English and Irish to an audience of Spaniards, men and women, who applauded like anything and kept us so late we nearly missed our train.

Milano

Monday 21st August
Last night I visited the Exhibition in the huge Parco of Milan. I got there early and secured a seat six rows from the stage. It was an entirely Verdian concert. I was sweating all over when it finished, and the audience, which packed the house, was delirious. The final number was the duet we have from *Aida*, "Rivedrai le foreste imbalsamate". The ticket cost eightpence . . . ,

From your wandering and by now highly Latinized son, Des

Paris

29th August
I have already been five times to the Louvre . . . Last night I met a man just recently let loose from a Fascist prison in Italy, and talked to him till very late. He holds 3 doctorates of science and until 1927 was a lecturer of economics. But unfortunately his knowledge of economics prevents him from supporting the Fascist policy and he was indiscreet enough to let this be seen in his lectures.

Result: he was arrested. I remember Porky Mahon* saying how courteous the Fascists were to his brother when he was in Italy, and how great an improvement Mussolini had effected in that country.

Cambridge

27th October 1933
I wrote to Porky a couple of days ago to tell him how I was getting on. He is a most likeable old man, though I guess he'd be appalled if he knew the direction taken by such eminently bright little fellows as Costello and Maclaurin. I had Maclaurin with me for my last week in Paris.

* Harold James del Monte Mahon, known as Porky, Costello's English teacher and subsequently headmaster, Auckland Grammar School.

"Walking to Olympia"

I only came here to catch a bus for Sparta
— *Costello, letter 1935*

GRIFFITHS CAMPBELL MACLAURIN, known as Griff Maclaurin, was very shy. His ears protruded, he withdrew from physical sport yet was known in his Auckland Grammar School rifle cadets as a marksman. For some reason after he died his Cambridge contemporaries remembered him as "a jolly Australian".

Maclaurin had left New Zealand for Cambridge at the same time as Costello — they were classmates in the upper sixth. They were in the same class at Auckland Grammar School, they learned to shoot on the same rifle range at Narrow Neck, they attended the same university college in Auckland, were capped at the same time, awarded the same post-graduate travelling scholarship, Costello in arts, Maclaurin in the sciences, and they appear to have sailed for England on the same ship as far as Australia, where Costello broke the voyage to see his older brother, Frank, and visit his Irish aunts and cousins in Melbourne. Yet, to judge by Griff Maclaurin's first appearance in Costello's letters home, written from Cambridge — "a most uninteresting little fellow" — it was as if they had never met.

Costello's tongue, it will be apparent, could cut. He liked, on the Dr Johnson principle, "to toss and gore". He was also — it shows in his coming Marxism — a puritan. Costello's put-down of Maclaurin was perhaps due to the fact that on reaching Cambridge, Maclaurin joined the University Conservative Association; then had kindly (read foolishly) thought to invite Costello to a meeting at which Lord Halifax, the future Tory Foreign Secretary, was to speak. Maclaurin was nearly three years older than Costello. He had been taught to raise his cap to his betters and had gone to university taking the tram from the polite Auckland suburb of Remuera, whose windows on the world were impervious to political tremors. However there were other influences in the Maclaurin genes. Griff's father may have planted peas and kumara in straight lines, while treading a sea of compost in his Remuera garden, but he was a Scottish schoolmaster with a feeling for history and he excited his son with tales of his kinsman Robert the Bruce and explorers like Captain Cook; while the mother, Gwladys, who was Welsh, tutored the boy in French. Both parents were teachers, like Griff's uncle, Richard Cockburn Maclaurin (1870–1920). Richard the uncle had gone from Auckland to Cambridge and distinguished himself at St John's College as Senior Wrangler, winning both a Smith's Prize and the Yorke Prize in mathematics; he had then returned to New Zealand as one of the founding professors of Victoria University College in Wellington, before being lured to America to become, at the age of thirty-nine, the President — and virtual founder — of the Massachusetts Institute of Technology.

"Comes of good stock," Griff Maclaurin's Cambridge tutor noted when he came to St John's, following in the footsteps of his famous Uncle Richard. St John's College not unnaturally was pleased to receive him. An Auckland contemporary, Jean Alison, has described Maclaurin as short, slightly balding and not very proficient at games. But his record — he was placed first in the national examinations in applied mathematics and second in pure maths — was excellent; while his New Zealand references — "sober", "industrious, gentlemanly and very reliable", "a gentleman both in instincts and demeanour" — were almost saintly.

One day at Cambridge Maclaurin invited Costello to tea. Costello came, and was shown around. The two colleges, Trinity and St John's, were cheek by jowl. Maclaurin's set of rooms gave on to the river, by the Bridge of Sighs, in the heart of a romantic skyline which had sustained the Cambridge picture-postcard industry for generations. Costello noted Maclaurin's alertness, his enthusiasm for the ghosts of the past, former fellows of St John's like Wordsworth, Lord Palmerston, Brooke Taylor of "Taylor's Theorem", Wilberforce, W.H.R. Rivers, the founder of modern anthropology, Samuel Butler the novelist, Paul Dirac the physicist. He admired Maclaurin's rooms, and said little. But evidently something in Maclaurin's manner, an unspoken distress call perhaps, touched him. Costello's protective instincts were aroused, they parted friends. Maclaurin's reverence for the sixteenth-century Gothic institution which had produced pioneers in almost every branch of human activity could not hide from Costello the fact that Maclaurin was essentially a plodder, and that he was finding the standard of work at St John's beyond him.

At the end of their first year, in June 1933, Costello wrote to his mother:

> Trip[os] and Mays have come and gone and the results are coming out each day. Maclaurin's results in the 1st part maths trip. appeared today. He has already gone down, and I am going down this week (term ended a couple of days ago), and is spared the sorrow of learning he only got a second.*

"I fumbled it," Maclaurin said later. "I was too slow in the examination room."

Costello encouraged Maclaurin to visit Germany in the long vacation; he himself was going to Spain and Italy; they would meet in Paris. Maclaurin's tutor, James Wordie, tried to soften the blow by advancing him funds. Wordie, the polar explorer and geologist who had sailed with Shackleton in 1914, wrote to the Polar Research Unit recommending a small grant for Maclaurin.

> He has not much to go on. He wishes to reach his destination by bicycle. He will be carrying a sleeping bag, as is the custom of New Zealanders in these matters.

---

* Cambridge degrees were divided in two parts, with one part of the tripos normally taken at the end of the first or second year, and Part II — finals — at the end of three or four years. Costello, with a double First from New Zealand behind him, sat finals at the end of his second year.

Maclaurin was an observant young man, and a good mixer. He spent three months in Freiburg, learning German, and moved about, noting Hitler's Brownshirts and anti-Jewish rantings in the New Germany as he went. When he and Costello met up that September, the latter having spent a month in Mussolini's New Italy, they found there was much to talk about.

In Paris Costello introduced him to *Faust*, and a ballet which "recalled those pictures by Degas, the girls in frou-frou short skirts in several layers, and heel-less dancing shoes — a little bit of the Second Empire brought to life."

> After the show [Costello wrote] Mac and I strolled along the Boulevard de la Madeleine towards the Place de la Concorde, singing languishingly "Laisse-moi contempler ton visage" . . . At about two we sat down and drank something in a café, and then walked home through Montmartre. Mac is now as much a lover of France as I am, and is strengthened in his feeling by his stay in Germany which he thinks like Lorie and Bob is the last dam place on God's earth.

They visited Rouen together and returned to Cambridge for the autumn term, Maclaurin by now, as Costello reported to his mother, a somewhat altered character.

Mathematics is generally considered the most difficult subject at Cambridge. Maclaurin had told his tutor after his disappointing start, "I hope to do much better in Part II." In fact he did rather worse. In the final examinations in 1934 Maclaurin was adjudged "junior optime" or the equivalent of third-class, by Cambridge standards a failure.

"At least I didn't get the Wooden Spoon," he joked to Costello, putting a brave face on it.

Costello by contrast, Maclaurin wrote to his mother Gwladys in Auckland, had won a hatful of scholarships and exhibitions. He had "covered himself in glory. But you never saw a man less enthusiastic about his success. He is such a splendid fellow, easily the best friend I have."

Costello had graduated with a First in Part II of the Classical Tripos, with special merit in archaeology, been elected a scholar of Trinity and won a research studentship to study for a year at the British School in Athens.

That August of 1934 Costello's mother received a letter from Gwladys Maclaurin:

> We had not heard that Des was going so far afield. In Griff's letter today he says, "I hope to be able to stay with him and his grandparents on their farm in S. Ireland." This I suppose will depend on whether he gets a position. I expect the two boys will keep well in touch with each other.
> Yours most sincerely
> Gwladys R. Maclaurin

Maclaurin's parents were Presbyterians, their parting gifts to their only son when he left New Zealand were a volume recounting the voyages of Christopher Columbus and a copy of the Bible. Costello, using his mother more and more as a form of diary, wrote to her, saying, "Mac is *not* the type of lad you'd imagined from the tone of the letter his mother wrote you."

> And although his parents' parting gift was a Holy Bible, Mac's thought is not of a biblical type. In fact he shows an alarming sympathy with the points of view of his more "radical" friends.

At this stage, on his way to Athens, probably not even Costello realised how much his friend was changing.

Costello spent six months in Greece, from November 1934 to May 1935. He travelled alone through France, Germany, Italy and Yugoslavia, reaching Athens on 17 November and enrolling at the British School. John Pendelbury, the Cambridge scholar-athlete who had been living at the Villa Ariadne at Knossos near Heraklion and would later become a legend on Crete, was also at the School. He told Costello about the many unrestored sites and digs going on, assuming he would be drawn to one of the excavations. Wasn't that what his studentship was for? Wasn't he planning to work on Clazomenian pots, classifying and cataloguing the stylisations in these vase paintings for posterity? Certainly Costello's security file says so — "Under the auspices of the University of Cambridge", says his New Zealand SIS file, "he was engaged in archeological excavations";

and, also, employed by the British Museum "to collect and classify Greek pottery". Intelligence files are a source of wonderment. Costello did no such thing.

Having arrived in Athens, he visited the Acropolis and stayed there "several hours, simply taking it in". Then he wrote to his supervisor at Trinity saying he had abandoned the idea of archaeology and was going to do something else instead. He did. He took a holiday. That is a small exaggeration. According to the annual report of the British School, 1934–5, Costello undertook a study of Greek economics, "particularly those of the Hellenistic period". Whether true or not, is hard to say. He did travel about and visit some of the classical sites. But he also cultivated a suntan and indulged himself in cafés, smoking inordinately and drinking Samian wine, while pursuing (unsuccessfully) a young woman at the American School. To his mother he posed as a Hellenised spiv —

> I have one Athenian suit and a pair of shoes (very pointy and flashy) and am gradually accumulating a stock of Greek ties, chiefly silk.

Even this is deceptive. In his letters, the sybarite shines through. But so does something else. Beneath the pretence of the beachcomber and wastrel, a thinker is at work. According to his newspaper reading, Costello is veering inexorably towards "the Socialist land":

> All over the city you see hammers and sickles plastered up, and Communist newspapers openly sold, a pleasant change after the prison atmosphere of Germany, Italy and Yugoslavia.

He is teaching himself modern Greek by going every day to a café, buying a communist paper and wading through the columns with the aid of a dictionary. Books arrive that he has ordered from Cambridge with the proceeds of his £5 Greek prize — a Russian dictionary, the correspondence of Marx and Engels, Palme Dutt's *Fascism and Social Revolution,* "and other vaguely Bolshie literature".

But there are competing interests. He is polishing his German by studying the Nazi press, a result of visiting Berlin. He had arrived in Berlin in the summer of '34, en route to Athens, on the day of the famous Nuremberg

Rally, and witnessed on the Nazi newsreels a triumphant Hitler enunciating, ahead of the Nuremberg Laws, the first of his planned brutalities against the Jews. Invited to visit an Arbeitsdienst, one of the Nazi youth labour camps, Costello declined, having persuaded himself — accurately as it transpired — that the camps were a propaganda exercise, a blind intended to build up a secret reserve force in time of war.

At this stage Costello had not joined the Communist Party, nor would he in Greece. The future might "smell of Russian leather" but the times no more propelled him to polish his Russian than his demotic Greek or his German — although his German studies it turned out had a purpose. He had indeed embarked on a study of "the economics and class structure of ancient Greek society" (the annual report was right) for which a proficiency in German was essential. All the necessary texts were in German.

Still, it was 1935. It seems odd that Costello's plans did not include the Soviet Union. Almost everyone who mattered seems to have gone there. H.G. Wells had gone in 1920, three years after the Revolution. And Graham Greene and Muggeridge and the Webbs, Sidney and Beatrice. Malcolm Muggeridge went in 1932, the same year as Bernard Shaw and a questing sparrow from Invercargill named Geoffrey Cox whom Costello had yet to meet. Even the politically indifferent Charles Brasch had been. Brasch had gone with a New Zealand group from Oxford in 1934, just ahead of the most famous group of all which included the future Labour MP Christopher Mayhew, the glamorous Anglo-American Michael Straight, and the man who would manipulate Straight into agreeing to work for the Russians — a drooping homosexual and third cousin to the Queen, the ubiquitous Anthony Blunt. When finally Costello got round to thinking about Russia, towards the end of his Athenian year, it was too late, he had run out of money. The last "good time" to visit the USSR — before the assassination of Kirov* unleashed the first of the show trials and Stalinist purges — was over.

Anyway, he told his mother, "I loathe actual travelling — sitting in trains, dashing to catch boats etc." For someone who complained about the inconvenience of travel, he seems to have gone to a lot of trouble in order to undertake it.

In Greece Costello made several journeys. He excavated no tombs,

* Sergei Kirov, the independent-minded head of the Communist Party in Leningrad and second only to Stalin.

made no finds. He contemplated going to Spain, even at one point America. Only gradually did his research project take hold and begin to concentrate his mind. He would need two more years, he calculated, if war didn't intervene. Through a veil of hedonism and philological enthusiasms, we begin to sense at last the real Costello, a journeyman-scholar who lives in the past as well as the present, a young man whose scholarship dares to compete with a political ideology. We sense an inner conflict, a hidden tension that is a recurring theme. The scholar in his monkish cell striving to overcome the romantic and the revolutionary.

In Greece Costello makes friends but he journeys alone, almost always alone. Meditative, silk-tied, grumpy, merry, occasionally drunk, singular, and solitary.

Towards the end of his stay he goes to Tripolis, in the southern Peloponnese:

> Tripolis, 19th April (Friday)
> I only came here to catch a bus for Sparta [he wrote home], but as it was 8.30 on Wednesday night when I arrived I had to stay the night. Yesterday I reached Sparta about noon, and immediately set out for the old monastery of Mistra, which covers the side of a precipitous rock. At the top of the hill is an old fort, from which there is a superb view of the whole plain of Lacedaemon and the valley of Eurotas. Sitting there on the battlements, smoking a cigarette, entirely alone, one could catch something of that feeling of departed glory. Beneath one are the scores of ruined buildings from the early Byzantine period, in front of me the olive-trees and vines of the Laconian plain, while behind is the huge slab of mountain that is called Taygetus, snow-capped and cloudy.
>
> I went back to the town and then spent an hour or two on the banks of the Eurotas, listening to the shepherds piping as they did two thousand years ago.
>
> I caught a bus at 8 this morning from Sparta and reached this hole again at almost ten. I intend to catch a bus from Andritsena, from whence to make a trip to the temple at Bassae tomorrow (Saturday). I shall sleep at Andritsena on Saturday night and spend all Sunday walking to Olympia.

Costello returned to England.

He left Greece early in May 1935 and got to Cambridge before the end of term, the same month. He wanted to see some friends "whom otherwise I may never meet again". But chiefly he was looking for a job, preferably a job outside England. He had returned via Paris. England, after France, seemed "a land of oafs and philistines". He had failed to visit Russia. His scholarship money was exhausted. Before leaving England for Greece, he had applied for two posts, including one "in the colonies", and been turned down. His mother had pressed him to apply for a Commonwealth Fellowship to America, but he had laughed at her, saying you had to be both extremely clever and extremely *nice* for that, "and in the matter of social graces, I am quite inept". He put his name down in Cambridge with the university appointments board, discovering as he feared that job prospects were slim. Vacancies on university staffs in Britain were "as scarce as icebergs in Borneo". He became despondent and decided to try London, unwilling to admit defeat and consider returning to New Zealand, like Maclaurin.

Maclaurin, he learned, was still in England. He was teaching in York. Griff had first written to him in Greece to say he had landed a job at a state school in Glasgow (but it was temporary), and had applied for a post at a public school in the cathedral town of York. If that failed, he would probably go back to New Zealand. Costello had heard from him regularly while he was in Greece; there was another letter waiting when he got to London. Maclaurin was now teaching in York, he said, but wouldn't be free till August.

Early in June Costello went up again to Cambridge. He was cutting through All Saint's Passage on his way to Trinity when he noticed a sign, "G.C. MACLAURIN BOOKSELLER", over a doorway. The shop was set back, little more than an opening in the passage, dimly lit and crammed with books. Costello entered through a narrow pass between cliffs of tracts and cheap reprints stacked on shelves proliferating on all sides. There were several customers in the shop. Maclaurin was writing in a ledger, his bald patch hidden by a cloth cap tipped forward over his eyes. Above him was a photograph of Lenin. He looked up and gave a shout of recognition. "I thought you were still in Greece," he said.

"I thought you were in York," Costello said.

Maclaurin grinned. He introduced Costello to a young woman who had materialised and who appeared to be his assistant. Her name was Bella Lerner.

Love in a Bookshop

Maclaurin's Bookshop,
the centre of Left literature in Cambridge
— *Eric Hobsbawm*

BELLA LERNER WAS nineteen. She is described on her marriage certificate as "typist". This is misleading. Bella was a scholarship girl denied university who left school and came to Cambridge where she was employed as a shorthand-typist by Pye Radio. She also worked in a jam factory. She was the fifth of eight children born to Russian Jewish immigrants from the Ukraine who had come to England early in the century and settled in London's East End. Bethnal Green, where Bella was born, was at the heart of a square mile of Jewish settlement teeming with persecuted Jews from the Russian empire, squeezed into overcrowded tenements and factories reeking of drains, bugs, pickled herrings and, in the case of the Lerner family, suppressed intellectual vitality. There was a tradition of teaching in the family. Bella's maiden name, "Lerner" (Student), gives a clue. The maiden name of Bella's mother, Sophie, was "Buchman" (Bookman). Further back, her mother's mother's name was "Wahrheit" (Truth). A grandfather had been a rabbi in Bessarabia.

Bella's father, Moishe Lerner, is described on the same marriage certificate as "capmaker". He made ladies' hats. Moishe Lerner was first a "blocker", then became a hat and cap machinist in one of the many factories that operated in the noxious air of a Brick Lane alley squeezed between Shoreditch, Spitalfields, Whitechapel and Bethnal Green. Bella escaped doing piece work for her father, as all the sons did in turn, working as machine-hands, including the only one born in Russia, Abba.

Abba Lerner was an economist, who got out early. Twelve years older than Bella, Abba went from capmaker to machinist to night school to rabbinical school to the London School of Economics, and from the London School of Economics to Cambridge University where he became a disciple of Maynard Keynes, whose economic theories would influence Roosevelt's New Deal in America. Abba Lerner himself went to America where, as a peripatetic, bearded academic in open-toed sandals, he taught in half-a-dozen universities and made a name as a pioneer Keynesian. He went to Mexico to try to persuade Trotsky that Marx's theory of surplus value was incorrect, wrote books and articles on the economics of capitalism and socialism and is said to have contributed to progress in more fields of economics "than any other living economist" (1965)."Lerner's argument is impeccable," Keynes said of him, "but heaven help anyone who tries to put it across to the plain man."

When Abba Lerner first arrived in Cambridge, Keynes was writing his revolutionary *General Theory of Employment, Interest and Money* (1936); evidently the young Abba got so caught up in the Keynesian "circus", writing papers and founding a journal or two, that he sometimes forgot he had a wife and family — he was the father of twins. Which explains what Bella was doing in Cambridge in 1935 when she met Costello. She had come up in answer to an SOS from her brother to help care for his twins.

It is not known how she met Griff Maclaurin. They probably met at a socialist gathering after Maclaurin turned up from York and opened his bookshop. The Maclaurin whom Bella met was no longer a shy mathematician but a fun-loving man who sometimes wore a kilt at parties but more usually a worker's cloth cap and baggy trousers, and was a fully paid-up member of the Communist Party of Great Britain. He told her later that he had found life in York dull and beer attractive, and had been dismissed from his school "after a tipsy frolic". "You mean you were drunk?" Bella said, and he laughed.

He had a jolly laugh, she thought.

Maclaurin's bookshop seems to have sprung up overnight and become, like its owner, immensely popular — its sales, according to Victor Kiernan, who would inherit Maclaurin's stock, "surpassing sales of literature by the Socialist Club". It was Cambridge's first progressive bookshop.

When Bella drifted in, business was already expanding. Bella was an ardent left-winger from a family of left-wingers; she was quick; she could type; she became Maclaurin's part-time assistant, attracted to this jolly and uncomplicated New Zealander from whose lips words like "dialectical materialism" had a mysterious sound, like a conjuror's spell. He took her punting on the Cam. They became, it seems, unofficially engaged.

They might have married, had Maclaurin not one night begun to reminisce about a friend of his, an Irish-New Zealander then in Greece, a linguistic wizard who talked in tongues with a careless fluency and impassioned wit that would make "even Pythagoras blink". Bella listened. She had fine eyes set in an oval face and high cheekbones; she was inclined to perch, like a bird. She was not very tall, nor was Maclaurin. She leaned forward and said in his ear, "Tell me more." Maclaurin did. Bella listened. As Maclaurin talked, she followed him in her mind's eye, "like a starving wolf", like Echo stricken by Narcissus:

And like a cat in winter at a fire
She could not edge close enough

Poor Maclaurin! According to family lore, she was seduced by Costello before ever they met.

Costello walked into the bookshop. He barely had time to say to Maclaurin, "I thought you were in York," when Bella turned and saw him. From that moment, she was in love. Recognition — it came, Costello said later, "like a flash of light" — was apparently mutual. Bella had in her beauty and stillness the sadness of small Jewish towns hemmed in by curses. She wore a loose jacket, tied at the waist. She sat down on a box with her legs crossed, mesmerised by the talk of the tall stranger with bleached hair, his features sunburned, almost black, from the Greek sun.

They met again and talked. They talked of Alyosha in *The Brothers Karamazov*, of Natasha in *War and Peace*, of Housman and Pushkin and he quoted to her his favourite line from Dante, *"segui il tuo corso e lascia dir la gente"* (follow your own path and let the people talk).

They parted.

For a day, two days, a week — who can tell? Costello's schedule after he returns from Greece is bewildering. He is renewing contacts in Cambridge and ostensibly applying for jobs, yet at one point appears to be leaving for Russia ("21 days London to London"). He applies to Trinity for another studentship and gets it; then, re-admitted as a senior research scholar, with rooms in Whewell's Court, he moves to London and takes a flat in Bayswater, in order, he tells his mother, to attend a two-week course of lectures at Karl Marx House. He then takes a room in Bloomsbury and begins a study of Greek inscriptions at the British Museum.

All this occurred in June and early July 1935. Costello returned from Greece on 22 May. The meeting with Bella occurred, as far as one can tell, about three weeks later. A week after that, by 23 June, she had left Cambridge — and Maclaurin — for Costello, and they were living together in London.

> 3, Guilford Street
> London WC1
> 6th September [1935]
>
> My dearest Mother
> I, Desmond Patrick Costello, Student in Arts, did this sixth day of September 1935 take as my lawfully wedded wife Bella Lerner, typist, of 6, Winchester Road, Bethnal Green. What do you think of that? Wish me luck, damn it, and spread the good news. Getting married was for Bil and me a mere formality, as we have been living together for two and a half months.
>
> I am not telling my tutor, as it is just barely possible that I may want to get some money in some scholarship or other which requires celibacy as one of the necessary qualifications. And I'm going out to Greece again —

Costello did not go back to Greece, nor did the planned trip to Russia materialise, although he wrote on 8 June 1935, "I have arranged about my trip to the USSR and hope to leave London for Leningrad this day fortnight." He was not going, he added disarmingly, "to find out whether 'the Soviet experiment' (!) is successful — I know about that already. But people always say 'have you been there yourself?', and it is occasionally a help in arguments to be able to say 'yes'. It is true that £22 is rather a high price to pay for being able to score a point in discussion, but then, there you are, one can't do it for less."

It was his second abortive attempt to visit the Soviet Union. It was beginning to look as if Costello's fate would be the same as that of the sisters in Chekhov's play who lived in the country and dreamed all the time of moving to Moscow, but never got there.

In the meantime, having met Bella and been taken "home" to the East End where her parents and brothers lived, Costello was completing a more fundamental journey. It would be said of Costello after he died, when the finger-pointing began, that his troubles stemmed from marrying "a Russian woman". As if he had become contaminated, having surrendered to her, mind and soul. As if Bil (an adopted name, she had dropped Bella) were the worst thing that could have happened to him. In fact the opposite is true. Bil made him whole, rounding out and helping to complete an educational process in which his emotional, sexual and political development had stuck like a needle on a record at the level of adolescence. Costello's development until then had been entirely cerebral. When they met he was drifting, vacillating between half a dozen competing goals and interests; gravitating, as his letters show, towards the ranks of that most useless and sterile of clan species, the London intellectual. Bil, besides completing his sexual education (he was apparently a virgin when they met), was the best that could have happened to him. She brought with her "a family", moreover a family of tough unsentimental wage-earners who knew about survival.

One recalls that in Auckland Costello had gone down to the wharves but it was not to get his hands dirty or study the social conditions. His goal was poetic. He wanted to listen to the cadences of the bargees, talking in Gaelic. At Cambridge he carried a banner, "POVERTY IN THE MIDST OF PLENTY", protesting at a government policy which dumped tea and coffee in the sea to keep prices up. In Munich he made the provocative gesture of lighting a cigarette from the hallowed Eternal Flame under the nose of its Nazi guard, risking a beating by storm-troopers, while in Paris he documented tales from Italian anti-fascists released from Mussolini's prisons. But all this was literary and political tourism. It was one thing to witness life seen from a passing carriage window, quite another to go into the engine room and meet it at first-hand.

Bil's parents were from *shtetls*, small towns within the Pale of Settlement near the Black Sea: Yiddish-speaking, religious Jews who in London continued to keep the Sabbath. But Bil and her siblings, four brothers and two sisters,* had rebelled and joined the Labour movement. Six became communists, not for ideological reasons only but from a history of exile and persecution.

> I drifted into communism when I was about eleven under the influence of a militant boy named Mickey Lerner [writes Emanuel Litvinoff]. He was thin and undersized, with a chronic cough. His father, a presser, also coughed because his lungs had been rotted by the steaming cloth he pressed ten hours a day. In fact, the whole family coughed. They lived in the sooty air of a Brick Lane alley and had a habit of blinking like troglodytes in full daylight. This made them seem puzzled and defenceless when, in reality, they were a tough and stiff-necked tribe. I was led into Communism more by the misery and toughness of the Lerner family than by anything in my own predicament.

Emanuel Litvinoff, it happens, is not writing of Bil Lerner's Jewish family but of a neighbouring Catholic family. But it is of no consequence. His memoir, *Journey Through a Small Planet*, describes growing up in a Bethnal Green tenement identical to hers; the squalor — the rickety stairs, the pervasive smell of cats — and the anti-fascist struggle were the same. One side of the street where Bil grew up was Jewish, the other side not. Bil joined an experimental theatre movement run by the Pioneers, her brothers joined the Young Communist League (membership dues, sixpence); they got together in a cellar under a tobacconist's shop or in the back of second-hand furniture stores; on the summer's day in 1934 that Chancellor Dollfuss was shot dead in Vienna, Bil and her friend Netta, a tailor's daughter, joined a picket line demanding better conditions in the East End factories.

There is a revealing glimpse of her with a friend — "strange and separate in their zipped lumber-jackets with wide striped scarves around their necks" — in Charles Poulsen's *Scenes from a Stepney Youth*. "I said to Bella once," he writes, "'Don't you find party membership interferes with your college life?' And she replied, as seriously as though she was testifying in a court:

* A younger sister, born in 1918, had died.

'We live in critical times, we work for a Socialist society. Why don't you join us?' 'Well — Bill [Bil],' I replied. She liked to be called Bill, it sounded more proletarian."

At night they went out with chalk and whitewash squads, painting slogans in the streets; by morning their anti-Nazi slogans would be obliterated and replaced by others saying, "YIDS OUT!" and "P.J." [PERISH JUDAH]. Bil's education was punctuated by the cries of hawkers in the streets and scuffles with Mosley's Fascist hoodlums, hurling bricks through the windows of the Jewish shops downstairs. Costello saw some of this, the scuffles and running street battles. Doris Lerner, Bil's sister, remembers a night in 1935 when she and a friend joined a crowd demonstrating outside a public meeting of Mosley's Blackshirts in Kensington. Fascists bayed,

> "Britain awake! We bring a saving revolution,
> We will avenge the long betrayed."

Communists shouted,

> "Hitler and Mosley, what are they for?
> Thuggery, buggery, hunger and war!"

Disorder broke out as Oswald Mosley arrived, saluted by a mass of upraised arms and preceded by ranks of jack-booted Blackshirts bearing Union Jacks and Fascist standards. Knuckledusters and razors were in evidence on both sides, as the Blackshirts began coshing and felling hecklers, throwing them on to the pavement. There was a large police presence. Doris and her friend were suddenly isolated on one of the pavement islands, terrified, she remembers, hemmed in by police on horses — "when Paddy suddenly appeared out of nowhere. He picked us up, one under each arm, and literally plucked us to safety." Doris was twelve at the time.

Bil, seven years older, was exciting, besides physically striking. She was tiny, the top of her head barely reaching to Costello's Adam's apple. She was interested in the theatre, acting, music, literature, and above all — his great passion — in poetry. It was a mutual intoxication and an extension of his Irish–New Zealand roots into a Russian–Jewish hinterland, both a meeting of minds and a liberation.

There was some problem, Costello's son Mick recalls, to do with the head of the house, Moishe Lerner:

> My Mum's father, Moishe, was a religious Jew. He didn't want any of his children to marry out. Grandad had been in the Russian army, as a conscript in the service of the Czar. He spoke Yiddish, Hebrew, Russian and Ukrainian. Paddy already knew Hebrew and a bit of Yiddish, and he won Moishe over with his handwriting. He had beautiful handwriting. Grandad was a sort of lay rabbi, a teacher. Paddy used to do the handwriting for Grandad.

Paddy Costello might protest to his mother that in England he lacked social grace. Evidently he discounted the Irish charm. One recalls the shouted greeting in 1932 from one of Costello's Irish–Australian cousins in Melbourne, when first he clapped eyes on the arrival from New Zealand. "Why it's the snake charmer, bedad," he yelled.

One day Bil took her husband to meet the family in Bethnal Green. The Lerners had graduated from Princelet Street where Bil was born, above a hidden synagogue, to nearby Buxton Street, a turning off Brick Lane which was alongside another synagogue, to Winchester Street where they had a drapery shop. The shop doubled as a front room. When Paddy was introduced to the family, Doris recalls, the shop sold records and there were five of them living there — Moishe the father, Sophie his wife, two sons, Arthur and Nat, and Doris, born in 1922, the "baby" of the family. Doris would later study and obtain an honours degree in Latin-American Studies at the age of eighty. For a time she was a London bus conductor. Arthur would go to the Spanish Civil War and survive capture and imprisonment by Franco's forces, while Nat would die fighting in France after the Normandy landings in 1944. Missing were Abba, Hannah and the youngest son, Jack, who had left home for Calais the previous year, aged fourteen.

Doris describes the house at No. 6 Winchester Street:

> Paddy had to stoop low to get in the door, and then step down into the shop. At the back of the shop was the kitchen where we ate. Four of us could get round the table, three comfortably. The fourth had to stand up when the door opened. We ate in relays. I

> remember Paddy's face when my mother brought the food. My mother put some food on the table. She said to him, "Eat".
>
> I think Paddy's mother must have brought him up to be polite. She attached importance to these things. I met her once. You know Paddy was a mimic? He would have made a good stand-up comic as well. Later he was joking about us one day, taking off the family manners and conversation, and it struck me — you know the Lil' Abner hillbilly cartoons? Our family must have seemed a bit like that. We must have struck him as barbaric and primitive.

It was about this time, the summer of 1935, that Costello joined the Communist Party. The moment was ripe. The cultural atmosphere, according to another convert Arthur Koestler, in *The God that Failed*, "was saturated with Progressive Writers' congresses, experimental theatres, committees for peace and against Fascism, societies for cultural relations with the USSR, Russian films and avant-garde magazines. It looked indeed as if the Western world, convulsed by the aftermath of war, scourged by inflation, depression, unemployment and the absence of a faith to live for, was at last going to

> *Clear from the head the masses of impressive rubbish,*
> *Rally the lost and trembling forces of the will,*
> *Gather them up and let them loose upon the earth,*
> *Till they construct at last a human justice.* (Auden)

A new star of Bethlehem might be rising in the East, but although, by his own account, Costello had grown "two feet taller" on meeting Bil, he would never be an obedient or orthodox Party member. At least not for long. The 1939 Nazi–Soviet Pact and the outbreak of war with Germany a week later would see to that. Nor would Costello join the Party from emotion, like Maclaurin, seeking absolution from guilt at being a member of a privileged class; nor was his conversion a substitute for religion, the result of a sudden intoxication which swept up so many intelligent people at Cambridge and Oxford in the so-called "Pink Decade", including future Cabinet ministers like Denis Healey. Costello's final conversion, three weeks after he met and fell in love with Bil, was an entirely sober affair.

> Last week [he told his mother on 17 July 1935] I finished a two-week course at Marx House; the last two addresses were given by a man whom Phil* at least has read — John Strachey. I had some things that were troubling me on my mind, and it was an excellent occasion to argue them out with a man of Strachey's brilliance. Now you behold me with mind purged of doubts, on the way to becoming quite a fair to medium Bolshevik.

Costello's stay in the Party would be brief. His commitment to an ideal that communism seemed to represent would be strengthened by a number of events which were about to occur, among them Bil's pregnancy and the birth of their first child; the offer of a job as a junior lecturer in classics at the University College of the South West, Exeter; and the outbreak of civil war in Spain. Their first child was a son, Michael. He came into the world during "our first dopy summer together" — not in Cambridge where they had been living but in a London hospital, on 12 June 1936. Five weeks later, on 18 July 1936, the Spanish Civil War began.

* Costello's brother.

From the Letters

1936 Cambridge

15th June

My dear Mother

The chief bit of news is that Bil has just had a baby — a boy. We're going to call him Michael . . .

Say, Ma, if you want to do me a favour and earn my undying gratitude, then listen: please send me the following records:—

Io muoio, confessione Pinza, Ponselle, Martinelli

Caruso & Deluca	Venti scudi
Heta	Te quieto
Caruso	Magiche note
De Gogorza	Preguntala a las estrellas
Crooks	Preislied from Mastersingers

If you will, wrap these records up very carefully with packing, write "Explosives" or something on them . . .

Auckland

10 Grand View Rd. Remuera
July 21st

Dear Mrs Costello
In Griff's letter received this morning he told us of the arrival of Desmond's little son. Desmond was in London at the time of writing. Griff says some measure of his excitement is given by the letter that began in English, suddenly lapsed into Spanish & ended in Italian, with a good German greeting. Griff adds, "when Des writes or talks several languages more or less at once, he is always in a cheerful frame of mind" . . .
Yours very sincerely,
Gwladys Maclaurin

PS I should include Mr Maclaurin's name in this, as he too looks on Des almost as a second son.
It is getting toward the anniversary of their leaving us now. God bless them all and you, dear.

Exeter

University College of the S.W. of England
2nd September

My dearest Mother,
Firstly, Bil & Mike are in the pink. I'm not so bad myself. Living out in this village [Barton] has been very beneficial — good air & a seven mile bike ride every day in & out of Cambridge. But one feels the lack of the amenities of city life, which I fear is not going to be very effectively supplied by our home-to-be, Exeter.

I went down there some time ago to see the necessary people; the junta who interviewed me were a fearful trio: the Classics prof., the head of the Arts faculty, and the Registrar. Anyway they liked the colour of my eyes & they gave me the job. Exeter is in Devon and is a very pretty place with a good cathedral.

Spain

The only hope is that the people
may prove stronger than the fascists
— *Costello to his mother, 1936*

PADDY AND BIL with the baby, Mick, moved to Exeter in September 1936. They had barely settled in and Costello begun teaching when he received a letter from Griff Maclaurin saying he was leaving for Spain. Costello rushed up to London to see him off.

He said later that Maclaurin left England a happy man. He met him at Victoria Station. Griff was with a group of British volunteers, nearly all working class, from whom in his cloth cap, beard, and heavy boots, he was almost indistinguishable. Maclaurin said he had received a telegram from Harry Pollitt, the general secretary of the Party in Britain, and had gone to see him; Pollitt explained that he had received an SOS from Spain saying that machine-gunners were badly needed. Would he go to Spain? Maclaurin said yes. He had closed his bookshop and settled his affairs in Cambridge within forty-eight hours.

He carried a light rucksack. Inside it was a revolver wrapped in a pair of khaki overalls, a copy of *Das Kapital*, his toilet gear and a small chess set. Costello gave him a copy of *Jane Eyre*, his first English prize from Auckland Grammar, to take into the trenches, and a note from Bil wishing him luck.

"It is a finer thing you do than any of us has done before," she wrote, adding "Slay the bastards".

Since the civil war had started, Franco's rebels had captured more than half the country and although Barcelona and the north held out, suddenly the capital, Madrid, was seen to be in danger. This followed the capture of Badajoz where fifteen hundred people were herded into the bull-ring and shot by mercenaries. Spain was convulsed. People were flocking to the government cause. "It's everybody's war," Maclaurin said. Costello nodded. He didn't say that he was thinking of volunteering himself. What was the point? Madrid was "galvanised" and would resist, according to the *News Chronicle*. But everyone knew that three columns of Franco's forces, aided by German tanks and planes and Italian troops, were advancing on the capital. It was only a matter of time before Madrid fell.

"A short life, Paddy, but a merry one." Maclaurin was going to fight "for the revolution and the people of Spain". John Cornford had already left with his own party of volunteers — they would meet up in Paris. Griff was in good spirits. He gave Costello a bundle of letters to post and boarded the night train for Paris. The last Costello saw of him was the copy of *Jane Eyre* which Maclaurin waved, leaning out of the carriage as the train receded into the night.

Back at Exeter, Costello showed Bil the bundle of letters. "Griff wants me to post them for him," he said to her.

"Why? There's no point."

"I've said I'll post them."

"He'll be killed," Bil said. "They'll all be killed." Bil was bitter about the wasted lives. "If he lives, he'll be back. If he hasn't told his mother, it's better she doesn't know."

The letters were addressed to Maclaurin's parents in New Zealand. Griff had written the letters as if from Cambridge, dating them ahead. He had asked Costello to post them for him at intervals.

"He knows what he's doing, Bil."

He tried to cheer her up. At school in New Zealand Costello had watched Maclaurin strip and fire a Lewis gun. "He was good at it," he told her. He was not to know that when Maclaurin reached Madrid and went into action with a French machine-gun company, it would be with weapons they had received only the night before, elderly St Etiennes which had proved unwieldy and inefficient in the 1914–18 war.

Costello did as asked, he franked and posted the letters to Maclaurin's parents. He continued teaching at Exeter. They read the newspapers and waited for news. Costello posted the letters from London, going up occasionally by car. Sometimes he biked. He rode up and back in all weathers. He enjoyed the exercise. The university college where he taught ancient history was in the town, handy to their house in Longbrook Terrace. There were almost no post-graduate students and as a result his lecturing schedule, he told his mother, was pleasant and pastoral. It entailed helping through Lucan and Theocritus the sons and daughters of farmers and shopkeepers from the Devon and Cornwall countryside. He taught "a gaggle of ducks", he said, mostly lame ones.

The news when it did come — that Madrid was holding out and might not fall to the rebels — seemed miraculous. A column of international fighters had been rushed to defend the capital. There was rejoicing at Longbrook Terrace. Bil's young brother Jack was staying with them, and a sister-in-law. An older brother, Arthur, had volunteered for Spain. Arthur would go to the fighting outside Barcelona and be posted missing, though just when Arthur left England is unclear. In November or December came the news of Maclaurin. Maclaurin's departure had left Costello anguished and sick at heart. Now, it seems without saying anything, he went out and put his name down.

Costello's army record suggests he volunteered immediately after Maclaurin left England.

"Have you ever been medically examined for service before?" he would be asked on joining the army four years later in August 1940.

ANSWER	Yes.
QUESTION	When?
ANSWER	Four years ago.
QUESTION	Where?
ANSWER	Exeter.
QUESTION	Were you found fit or unfit?
ANSWER	Fit.

But probably, since Maclaurin died in November 1936 and the news of casualties in Spain usually took a month to reach the press, Costello didn't volunteer until December or the new year, by which time Franco had been fought to a standstill outside Madrid, the Abdication crisis in Britain had broken and Spain had vanished from the front pages. Bil in any case had put her foot down. "Paddy, there's no *point!*" one can hear her saying in a fury. His duty was with his family. She forbade him to go.

He accepted it, and felt a coward.

Spain continued to gnaw at him. Later when Arthur Lerner was captured in Catalonia and then repatriated to England, in an exchange of prisoners, Paddy talked to him. Arthur had joined the International Brigade and been captured while still in training, then imprisoned in one of Franco's jails; every few days they were taken out and stood against a mud wall while the guards shot one in five at random. He remembered Arthur saying that each time he was stood in line with the others, not knowing if his end had come, he found himself shuffling sideways on the muddy turf so that when he died, he might fall on a clean piece of ground.

Maclaurin was reported killed fighting in the defence of Madrid on 9 or 10 November 1936. Costello wrote privately to the parents in Auckland and early in 1937 travelled north and visited Maclaurin's relatives, living near Edinburgh. By then, news had also come of the death of John Cornford.

On the way back to Exeter, Costello stopped in Cambridge. He was surprised to find Maclaurin's bookshop still open. A further surprise awaited him when he went in. There were several people in the shop. Costello waited. The freckle-faced woman at the counter finished serving a customer and came forward, hand extended. "You must be Paddy," she smiled. "Griff never stopped talking of you."

He listened, astonished, as she described her marriage to Maclaurin. She was from the north. She was his widow. They had married shortly before he left for Spain. No, she said. He hadn't told his parents. She seemed not sad but elated and proud that he had done this for Spain.

Afterwards it occurred to Costello that Maclaurin, who had become a communist for emotional reasons, was probably one of those who had married out of principle. One of those who felt it was their duty to look for working-class partners.

It would be some years before Costello would begin to piece together how his friend had died. Geoffrey Cox, a New Zealand Rhodes Scholar whom Costello met later on a troopship sailing to Egypt, would help to explain it. Cox had been in Madrid on the day the first contingent of the

International Brigades arrived, he had rushed out of a shop when the streets suddenly became filled with Madrilenos shouting and cheering, "Viva Rusia!", thinking the Russians had come. Maclaurin was in the ranks, with John Cornford, marching behind the cavalry; Cox could have reached out and touched him. They had marched up the Gran Via in a disciplined formation and gone into action next day.

Cox had been left behind in Madrid when the government fled the capital; he was reporting for a Fleet Street newspaper, the *News Chronicle*.

From the top of the Telefonica tower he had watched the foreigners march towards the front believing it to be thirty miles away, whereas in fact it was a twopenny tram ride, in the rolling woods of the Casa del Campo by the university. He had seen the puffs of smoke from the shells bursting in the university compound. That was all Cox knew.

Later Costello learned more. Griff had spent his first night in the open and gone into action with a French infantry company. He was with three other gunners. The French retreated, surprised by Franco's mercenaries; the machine-gunners stayed to cover their retreat. Four went up, two came back. Maclaurin was found next day, dead at his gun.

"Mac did really well," John Cornford wrote. "Continuously cheerful. It's always the best seem to get the worst." The body of John Cornford, who died at Christmas five weeks later, on the Cordoba front, was never found.

John Cornford was the first Englishman to enlist against Franco. One of the poems he wrote in Spain, published posthumously, Costello would copy out and carry with him in the North African desert, in the back of his army pay book. He would quote it to Bil at regular intervals:

And if bad luck should lay my strength
Into the shallow grave,
Remember all the good you can;
Don't forget my love. ⋆

Bil would fold a photo of John Cornford and his love, Margot Heinemann, to whom the poem was dedicated, into her diary and carry it with her always.

⋆ "[To Margot Heinemann]"— *Poems from Spain, 1936* (John Cornford, *Collected Writings*, Carcanet Press 1986)

After the news of their deaths, Bil became active in relief work and in the Exeter branch of the Communist Party. Costello spent the long vacation of 1937 raising funds for the Republican cause. Somewhere he got hold of a bullet-scarred ambulance. A friend drove him. Equipped with loud-hailer, they toured the West Country under the banner, "BRITISH MEDICAL AID FOR SPAIN", Costello addressing rallies and singing revolutionary songs.

Spain was a central event in both their lives. With the first cries to save the Spanish Republic from Franco's rebels came the forming of the International Brigades, a creation of the Comintern (Communist International) in Paris on the orders of Stalin. Yet even as the siege of Madrid was taking place, the first of the Soviet commissars were arriving from Russia to begin their purges of left-wing volunteers deemed politically "unreliable".

But the people of Madrid did not know this, any more than did Costello. They saw that Russia was the only state that had come to their aid with men and materials; they wove instant legends around the foreign volunteers who were saving their city. In England John Cornford, who died on his twenty-first birthday, was transformed into a demi-god, "a martyr of mythic power" in Denis Healey's phrase. Small wonder that the British government's policy of non-intervention, its tacit support of the Catholic Church and Franco's forces, drove left-wingers to take up arms or, as with Costello, frustrated at being kept on the sidelines, to commit acts of reckless evangelism. Costello's response was to take money to Bombay, headquarters of the Indian Communist Party.

He made the trip in secret that first winter, after learning of Maclaurin's death. Just who paid the fare and/or persuaded him to go — it can hardly have been Bil, given the risk involved — is a matter for speculation. Costello sailed from Marseilles, taking with him five hundred pounds in cash* ($NZ 30,000 at today's value), a gift from the British Communist Party to the fledgling Indian Communist Party. He reached Bombay on the *City of Benares* in February 1937 and left again a few days later. A British police report which reached the Indian authorities about this time described "a courier named Costello, professor of economics, Exeter College, Oxford"[sic]. But by then Costello had been and gone, apparently undetected. The report expresses

* It might have been seven hundred pounds, the copy of the document containing the information is unclear.

some doubt as to whether in fact he did take in money. It seems however that he did. On the voyage to India Costello, travelling third, strolled into the first-class area and struck up a friendship with a young Persian. They played deck tennis and shuffleboard together. His name was Mohammed Reza Pahlavi. The seventeen-year-old Pahlavi, the future Shah of Iran, was returning home from an education in Switzerland, heavily guarded. When the *City of Benares* docked at Bombay, Pahlavi agreed to take Costello's box containing the money through Customs, as part of his own luggage. This was probably done unwittingly, Pahlavi assuming that the box contained drugs or black market goods. A Customs search was thus avoided. Even so, the idea of the heir to the Peacock Throne helping to smuggle money to the outlawed Communist Party of India, with a score of attendants watching, is a choice one.

As Mick Costello remembers his father telling the story, "Paddy did it for a lark. He talked about it over dinner. We laughed. He talked about it quite openly." But the assignment itself, undertaken seriously, was foolhardy. The British IB (Indian Intelligence Bureau) was a highly efficient organisation, sensitive and alive to Russian-inspired attempts to suborn the Indian sub-continent. Some of this courier traffic had its origin at Cambridge University where there was a significant, well-heeled Indian undergraduate population and where, one remembers, Costello's Canadian friend, Herb Norman, was active. It was Herb Norman who put together a small group at Trinity whose job, operating discreetly, was to recruit Indian undergraduates into the Party.

"Groups like ours," wrote Victor Kiernan, who took over the group when Herb Norman left Cambridge, "not only acquired a degree of influence over Indian students, but could do something to give British students and others a comprehension of Indian national aspirations."

Costello's mission to India remains veiled in secrecy. According to the British authorities, it took place in the middle of the 1937 university Lent term. This is a curious fact. Or fable. By some magical process which has never been explained, none of Costello's colleagues appears to have noticed his absence from the college. Not even the college Principal, John Murray, noticed. The local police it seems were not notified. In 1937 the Exeter police were not especially interested in Costello. The year 1937, coming as it did between Hitler's occupation of the Rhineland and his annexation of Austria and the Sudetenland, was a relatively quiet one in England and

France. If the Exeter police had concerns at this stage it can only have been because of Bil, who had become secretary of her local party branch in Exeter, or her young brother, Jack — "a certain Jack Lerner", according to the file — who had been observed delivering the party organ, the *Daily Worker*, in the streets. Jack Lerner, who is still alive at the time of writing, spent two or three years living at Longbrook Terrace with Bil and the family. He used to collect the *Daily Worker* from the railway station, he says, and distribute it around the town on Costello's bicycle.

"But sometimes," he says, "Paddy did it for me. It was easier for Paddy, because the bike fitted him. My feet didn't reach the pedals."

Exeter & the Fyrth Case

He is a Communist!

— *John Murray*

THE UNIVERSITY COLLEGE of the South West of England, Exeter, would later become, with Reading, one of the pioneers of the modern university. But in pre-war years when Costello was a don teaching ancient history the college was small and parochial, still struggling to overcome its birthmark of "the Technical School". The university population of Britain as a whole was stagnant at about 50,000; at Exeter perhaps 250 students from a roll of five or six hundred were reading for a degree, and of these the number of post-graduate students could be counted on fingers and toes. Dons, like the brilliant, well-loved Latinist Jackson Knight, appointed at the same time, were paid no more lavishly than Costello (£250 p.a., only fifty pounds more than Costello's New Zealand scholarship to Cambridge had been worth). Still, though the structure was hierarchical, the college atmosphere was friendly, one or two colleagues complimented Costello on his writings, which were beginning to attract attention, and the New Zealander's way of knuckling down to the drudgery of college life without complaint commended him to the Principal, Dr John Murray. He liked, as Costello said, "the colour of my eyes." So in the beginning it appeared.

John Murray was a former Liberal Member of Parliament. He was the son of a fish curer. Like Costello, he had outstripped his class. Dr Murray was also a classics man. But there any resemblance ended. The Principal is remembered today chiefly for a beautiful speaking voice, his advocacy of "gentlemanliness" as the necessary badge of a university man, and a fierce and intolerant patriotism. Costello tells us that shortly after the war began he went down to the local recruiting depot to enlist, but, on discovering he was expected to sign on for the regular British army and not for the duration of the war, he took advice and decided to wait until he was called up. Few of the college students believed that war with Germany was either necessary or just. There were anti-war protests at the college and in May 1940, when the phony war ended and Hitler's Panzer divisions were pouring through Belgium and the Low Countries, it was only by a small majority that the Exeter guild of students was able to pass a motion of support for the Churchill government. Murray, "a patriot first and a liberal second", was annoyed by the anti-war feeling among the students. When he learned that one of his senior students, a post-graduate researcher tutoring in economics named Fyrth, was about to be prosecuted by the police "for passing naval secrets to the *Daily Worker*", he became enraged and ended by venting his fury on Costello.

Just when the Principal came to suspect Costello's "involvement" is unclear. The college registry was bombed out in the war and the surviving archives, though helpful, are incomplete.

When the war began in September 1939, Dr Murray appears as Costello's enthusiastic backer, providing a testimonial — "A vigorous and illuminating teacher. He has an exceedingly penetrative and rapid mind, a ready gift of decision and resolution" — of fulsome praise. But by May 1940 with France about to fall the relationship between the two was far from idyllic. Murray appears to have been told by the Exeter police that besides addressing public meetings in support of Republican Spain and speaking out during the Czechoslovak crisis, Costello had maintained throughout the winter war, after Russia invaded Finland in December 1939, that Britain must not attack Russia on this issue.

The Fyrth case took place in May 1940. Hubert Fyrth, twenty-two, and his older brother, Patrick, a naval officer serving with the British Expeditionary Force in France, appeared at the Old Bailey in London charged with passing information contrary to the Official Secrets Act.

The charge on the face of it sounded serious. It was in fact trifling. But the case was heard against a background of the Dunkirk emergency, in a climate of near-hysteria. "The college authorities," Costello said later, "were in a fearful state." Even the communist organ, the *Daily Worker*, which initially had been against the war, was moved to declare in front-page headlines:

DEEP ANXIETY FOR MEN OF BRITISH
EXPEDITIONARY FORCE

and

FATE OF COURAGEOUS MEN OF B.E.F.
UNKNOWN

In May 1940 an offence under the Official Secrets Act was taken to mean Fifth Columnism ("some people pronounced it 'fifth communism'", Costello noted). The Fyrth offence was this. Assurances had been given in Parliament by the British war minister, Leslie Hore-Belisha, that anyone serving with the armed forces in France would be able to read the newspaper of his choice, including the *Daily Worker,* which was freely available in Britain. At the same time, in December 1939, the French government issued a decree banning the circulation of the *Daily Worker* among British troops, and it was on this decree that the case — and Dr Murray's fury — turned.

As Costello recounted it, Fyrth came to see him during the legal proceedings and asked for his advice. Fyrth explained that his brother serving in France had sent him a copy of the decree; he had received the document in the post and sent it on to the *Daily Worker* which had published it. Subsequently the Exeter police had raided his lodgings and found the brother's letter. What should he do?

"This was the first I knew of it," Costello said. Costello's version of events, supplied later to the New Zealand government, appears accurate both in broad outline and in detail, and is consistent with the facts now available. It was accepted by the New Zealand government at the time (1945). It was not however accepted in 1940 by Dr Murray. He summoned Costello before the Exeter College Council. "I was invited," Costello wrote, "to give an account of myself and had various questions fired at me.

Any questions that concerned opinions I might hold I refused on principle to answer, and I think it was this attitude that annoyed them. I was not charged with any particular activities that I can remember, and in particular I was not associated with the Fyrth business, though this was the proximate cause of the excitement."

On the eve of the court case, on 27 May 1940, an item appeared in a London newspaper:

> UNIVERSITY SUSPENSION
> Dr John Murray, Principal of the University College of the South West, Exeter, has suspended a member of the college staff.

No name or explanation was given. The newspaper, the *Daily Herald*, reported that the case had not yet been considered by the Senate and the college council.

So Dr Murray moved quickly. He had suppressed any mention of the case in the student newspaper, the *Southwesterner*, instituted censorship and imposed a kind of curfew, forbidding student gatherings. He told a friend that feeling in the town was "inflamed", and "directed against our Communists, real or imagined, and especially against Costello, Ancient History don and a Communist".

At the Old Bailey the prosecutor claimed that the brothers Fyrth were guilty of passing secret information injurious to the defence of the realm, but under questioning the prosecutor retracted his statement and admitted there was nothing particularly secret about the document in question, i.e. the French decree. A hundred copies had been made and distributed, Fyrth's lawyer told the judge. It was a public document. It had no military significance whatever.

"Not by any stretch of the imagination," Fyrth's counsel was reported as saying, "could it be held to be prejudicial to the interests of the state."

The judge listened. Hubert Fyrth admitted passing the document to the *Daily Worker.* The judge said that the Fyrths had disclosed to the world the secret wishes of the French government and sent them both to prison. Patrick, the older brother, was cashiered. Hubert Fyrth was sentenced to six months' imprisonment. Costello, as noted, was sacked.

At their meeting earlier, Costello appears to have told Hubert Fyrth he had acted "very foolishly", but what advice he gave is not known. It seems he simply listened and tried to help. Perhaps he advised Fyrth how to plead. Fyrth was an ardent left-winger. As a friend later put it, "Paddy was congenitally unable to resist aligning himself with any left-wing cause."

Probably, as Costello said himself, his real crime was his intransigence, an inflexible refusal on principle to explain his views when called before the college council. Murray by his own account suspended Costello out of hand before consulting his council. The suspension was duly ratified, not surprisingly perhaps, given the public mood in Britain and panicky fears of invasion after the Dunkirk evacuation. Murray was an autocrat who frequently overrode the objections of his colleagues who, according to the university's historian Brian Clapp, "were just as patriotic as himself but more tolerant". A move by Costello's own colleagues, attempting to have him reinstated, appears to have failed.

However two years later when Costello's replacement Hugh Stubbs arrived in 1942, the public mood had swung again. Fears of invasion had receded. Slogans like "Better Hitler at the Channel ports than Stalin" were no longer heard, nor the voice of the appeasers. Russia was now Britain's ally against Hitler. And although the Fyrth affair was still hush-hush and Hugh Stubbs was conscious, he says, "of being *vocatus in locum mortui* (filling the place of a dead man)", it was now the overbearing Dr Murray, not Costello, who was the object of whisperings and regarded on campus as the villain of the piece.

The case commends itself at several levels. It reveals Costello as a political barometer — his way of finding himself in the eye of a storm not of his making. He is a weather vane for the temper of his times. He is thus a gift to historians, although, having volunteered to enlist in 1939 and been told by his head of department to wait until he was called up, Costello cannot have seen it quite like that. University teaching in wartime was a reserved occupation, something of a sinecure. But now the rug had been pulled out, his credentials gone. Costello was a father of two — a second child, a daughter, had been born to Bil during the emergency — and he had a livelihood to earn. At another level the affair can be seen in retrospect as a stumble (stumble? misjudgement?) which was henceforth to punctuate Costello's career.

Hugh Stubbs, recalling the incident today, uses the term "McCarthyism avant la lettre". And it is true that John Murray's catch-cry "He is a

Communist!" anticipates the Cold War and in particular the witch hunts of Senator Joseph McCarthy by ten years. But it is more subtle than that. In Exeter a police file had been opened. Costello's card was now marked. From now on his dismissal from Exeter and his views will be lumped together in the anonymous catch-all, "pre-war affiliations", to be presented on demand by the mandarins of British Intelligence as evidence of Costello's unreliability and betrayal. The stigma of Exeter would not be allowed to go away.

As to Costello's feelings about the matter, he does not say. We are left in the dark. Apart from an aside in his explanation to the New Zealand government five years later — "John Murray can't stand me" — Costello is silent, though he must have been embittered by his treatment. That said, his encounter with Fyrth in 1940 can be seen, at yet another level, as a kind of blessing. Or if not blessing, at least, like that other more famous meeting between Churchill and Guy Burgess,* as fortunate. For the sacking liberated Costello. He was finally free to enlist where he was wanted. Costello's dismissal at the end of May 1940 coincided with the arrival in British waters of 5000 New Zealanders, troops of the Fifth Brigade, diverted to England from the Middle East to help protect the coastline from invasion.

Over Bil's objections, Costello enlisted and was under canvas in Hampshire in August 1940. He shared a tent with a wool grader, a shepherd and a road-mender who abused him cheerfully as a Pom. He found himself in a completely different world, it was like learning another language. He wrote to Bil, "They're a far better lot of people than I've ever mixed with before."

He entered camp as a private, allotted to Intelligence (signalling), and sailed for the Middle East in 1941.

Until then Costello may be said to have possessed two homes, his Irish one in Kilkenny and his newfound home among the Lerner family. Now he had a third. He was back in New Zealand again.

* In 1938 at the time of the Munich crisis Burgess, as a young BBC producer, visited Winston Churchill at Chartwell and discussed with him a projected radio broadcast. The visit heartened a disconsolate Churchill, still excluded from office, and subsequently helped Burgess, then at the start of his career as a Soviet penetration agent (see Boyle, *The Climate of Treason*, pp. 172–3).

PART TWO
GOING TO WAR

1940–1944

From the Letters

1940, in camp

20th August 1940.

My dearest Bil, My postal address is: "Private DP Costello, 943, 29th Battalion, Dogmersfield, Hants." They have disguised me as a soldier, but the disguise as yet is pretty thin. It's going to take some time getting used to army boots, not to mention carrying one's house about on one's back.

21st

I am attached to Battalion HQ. I have to learn morse and map-reading.

September 1940 Saturday

Now I'll tell you about my tent. Ours has six inmates: Gray Tennant, aged 24, young farmer. Gus Yates, 27, roadworker, resigned a lance-corporalship because he didn't like it: Leo

McCaffery, 35, Irish New Zealander, head shepherd on a farm; Jackson, 23, govt. clerk; Percy Moore, wool-grader. The language here is the foulest you ever heard. If used in England it would be the occasion of fights, but among the NZers the filthiest language is used to indicate affection. Here's a sample: "Oh Christ, here comes that low bastard, Beelzebub Jones" — "Don't talk to me, you offspring of a drunken fuck" (that's a common term) — "Well I don't want to be seen talking to a joker that's lower than a snake's chassis, myself" — I haven't quite got the slang yet, but I'm studying hard.

It's a completely different world from the one I've lived in for the past eight years. Sometimes I feel it might be pleasanter to live in it than here. But this is probably transitory. After all, NZ, earthly paradise though it is, is a life sentence.

7 September 1940

We've just had a big air-battle. It started before lunch. Groups of us stood around on the fringe of the copse where we are encamped. Both pilots baled out and came floating to earth while the planes crashed. They were so close that the chap I was with and I began to run. One of the pilots landed in the next field. You have to keep your tin helmet on during battles, as machine-gun bullets from the planes are liable to hit you. One piece of shrapnel from an AA shell fell three feet away from me.

Priceless, this army talk. Last night Bing suddenly lifts his voice above the murmur of conversation to tell the world, "It was not the Almighty, That lifted her nightie, It was Roger the lodger, the sod." And then followed a stream of limericks, songs and poems that took the boys' minds off the AA shells that were bursting above us. One of his poems was a pathetic piece about a man with a corkscrew tool who spent his life looking for a woman with a spiral passage. And when at last he did find her he fell down dead because her passage had a left-hand thread. Every occasion has its phrase, usually sexual, but I've noticed that these same blokes talking with women are quiet and courteous.

12th November
No sign of my stripes yet.

27 November
Dearest Bil, Would you do me a favour: find that little Modern Greek grammar, the one you learned the alphabet out of that day in Hyde Park, and post it to me, marked Urgent. It's near the top of one of the book-boxes.

30th November 1940
Yesterday it came out in Routine Orders. Pte Costello has been raised to the rank of T. L/Cpl = Temporary Lance Corporal. This is one step higher than Acting L/Cpl. I can draw my extra 3/6 a week right from the start.

1941, AT SEA

Friday 14 February, off Madagascar:
We will be disembarking in Egypt in a fortnight's time. It's unlikely we'll fight in Libya — Greece is my pick.

15 February
My dearest, I heard during the morning of news received by today's radio. Six ships of the convoy after ours sunk! And they say that two of the one just before us have gone west. We cruise along in between, unscathed.

Monday 17th
I am in the signaller's platoon, with good prospects of promotion.

Thursday 20th
I have lost my watch. I would give a lot to get it again. It reminds me of that afternoon in Paris when you met me at the St. Lazare station, you remember, just before we went to Sanary. Some day we'll go there again.

Tuesday 25th
I am able to receive 18 words a minute with practically no errors. 8.30 p.m. Don't know why — I've been thinking about England. I felt a deep nostalgia, recalling the trip Rex and I made to Torquay across Haldon. As you cruise down the moor you look across towards Dartmoor over the valley of the Teign, with little villages and well cultivated fields, all very beautiful. It made me realise why people who have seen a lot of the world are quite content to settle down in England.

28th
Eight weeks today on ship board!

Sunday 2 March
Today's news tells us that the Germans have occupied Sofia. Just what repercussions this will arouse I can't guess. I do know that it means a stink around Salonika, and that is what interests me.

Tuesday 4th March
A bombshell. My battalion will be broken up. I lose the prospects of promotion and shall probably be starting off again from the beginning, in a plain rifle company.
[Suez]
We are disembarking at 6 a.m. tomorrow.

Although on my last 3 nights of duty I have seen the Great Bear and North Star, higher in the sky each time, yet I feel very far away from you and Josie and Mick. It is not so much that there is a big tract of land and sea between us, but rather that between you and me now there is a fierce campaign somewhere in the Balkans (my guess) and it may be harder to come through that than to cross sea. I believe it is quite close now and we are all thinking about it and talking about it, which makes it harder to think of home as something close and real — rather it is far away and unattainable, though warm, not cold like the stars. Goodbye, my darling love.

Wednesday, 26th
Reveille at 2 a.m., breakfast at 2.30. Struck tents and marched to the station at about 4. It was black night when we left, and perhaps because the eye sees things like pictures when one is half-asleep, the departure from camp looked impressive. Our company was halted at the side of the road to allow another lot to pass; just at that point on the other side a fire was still burning, and I stood in that strange half-dazed condition which belongs to those who have missed their night's sleep, and watched the soldiers march into the sphere of light and out again into the dark, each one partly stooped beneath the ninety pounds weight of his full pack and rifle, plodding along senselessly as I had always pictured soldiers going off to war. And this time we were moving up to the front, and I felt quite solemn about it, more with pity for the young men about to face death than for myself personally.

And down the distance they
With falling note and swelling
Walk the resounding way
To the still dwelling.

And so we reached the station, entrained and proceeded to the port for embarkation. That's how they relate it in the official reports. And here we are waiting to go.

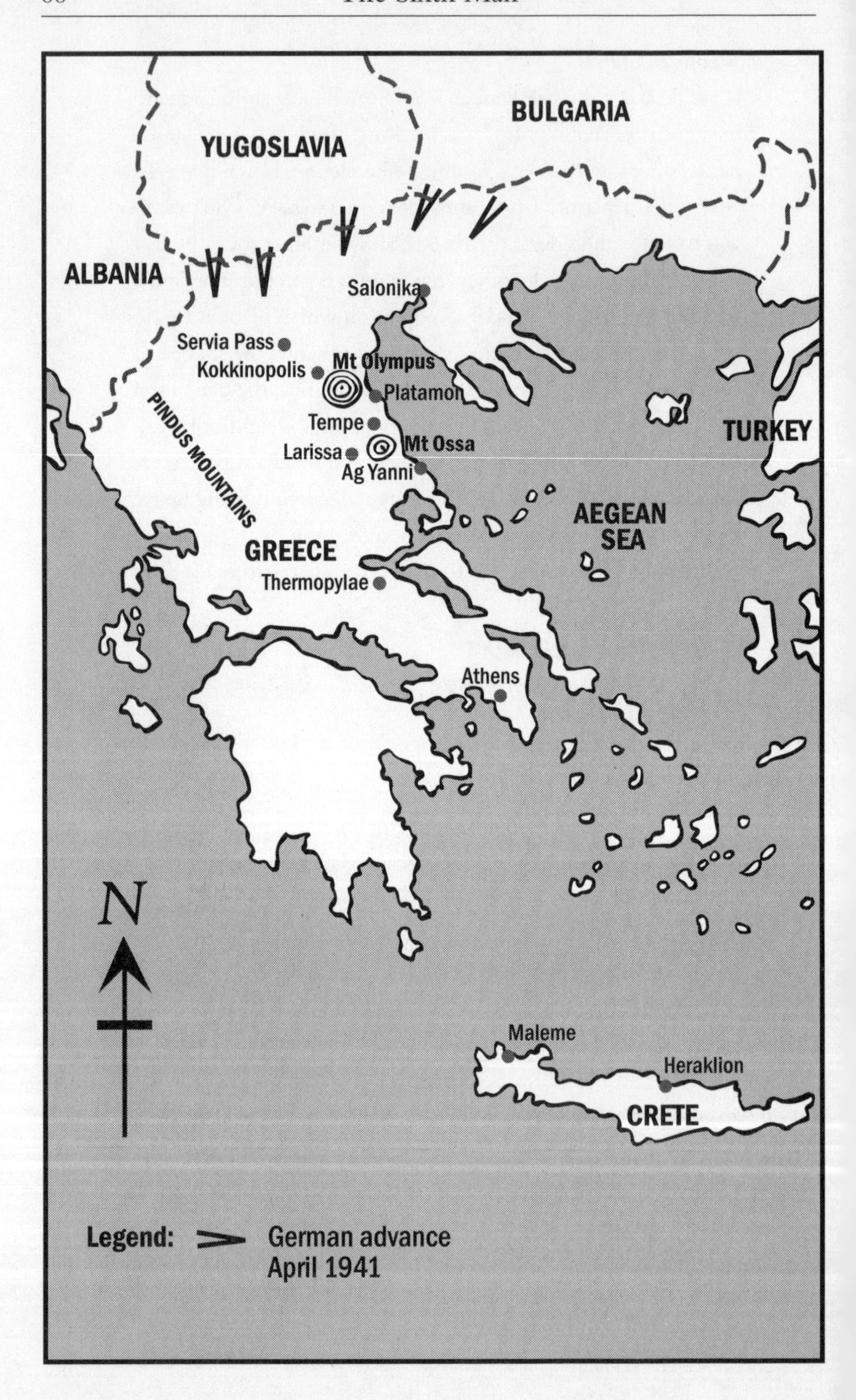

YUGOSLAVIA
BULGARIA
ALBANIA
Salonika
Servia Pass
Kokkinopolis
Mt Olympus
Platamon
Tempe
Larissa
Mt Ossa
Ag Yanni
PINDUS MOUNTAINS
GREECE
Thermopylae
AEGEAN SEA
TURKEY
Athens
N
Maleme
Heraklion
CRETE
Legend:
German advance April 1941

Prelude to a Battle

Closing down. Getting out.
— *Last message from Platamon castle*

COSTELLO WOULD BE separated from Bil and the children for nearly four years. When she wrote to him asking why he wanted to be a soldier, he replied with that mixture of mischief and schoolboy frankness that exasperated her almost as much as it would higher authority, "Parce que je veux risquer ma peau (Because I want to risk my neck)." The risk had come sooner than anticipated. Costello and his battalion steamed up the Saronic Gulf towards Athens on the last Saturday in March 1941. The sea was like blue glass. They reached Greece shortly before Easter, and just in time for German air raids which blew up a shed packed with artillery shells and set alight an ammunition ship tied to the wharf at Piraeus where they were docked. Costello and the men of the 21st Battalion saved the ship. They ran round the decks scooping up the red hot embers with their steel helmets and threw them overboard.

Ten days later Costello pitched his tent beneath an old Crusader castle guarding the coastline at the entrance to Thessaly, 150 miles north of Athens. He wrote to Bil,

> It seems mad, but you are very near to me now, though in fact farther away than ever before. Because I am now in the front line.

The front line was a ridge amid broken highlands in sight of Mount Olympus; and, despite the cold and drizzling wet, the spring-time as Costello described it to Bil was intoxicating. Not just the sight of violets and hyacinths "and lovely mauve flowers which the peasants call kuchiparies" — it was the excitement of talking Greek again, the easy intimacy of engagement as he went among the peasants with gold coins haggling for mules to transport their guns. Hellas revisited! The whole gigantic spell of the past rose up before him.

He had written to Bil from Platamon castle on Easter Monday, 14 April 1941. On Tuesday the Germans launched a full-scale attack. On Wednesday, escaping from two German Panzer divisions, Costello and his battalion fled inland to Tempe.

Withdrawing from the castle, they left the scrub and wooded uplands behind and entered through a pass a valley of pink Judas trees and budding planes, a world of vineyards and cyclamens and anemones gathered round a collection of white houses with peach trees in the gardens and an old mosque in Tempe's village street beside an Orthodox church. Alongside the narrow road they followed up the pass, a river flowed beneath tall trees. Suddenly it all came back to him:

> *TEMPE, a narrow valley nearly five miles in length in northern Thessaly, through which the Pinios River flows between the massifs of Olympus and Ossa. Because it lay on the easiest route between Thessaly and Macedonia and was so narrow it could be closed by a very small force, its strategic importance was considerable. In 480 BC the Greeks sent troops to hold Tempe against Xerxes . . .*

The river Pinios, "clear as crystal glass over the gravelly stones", Costello had read about in Pliny in a Ponsonby library as a nine-year-old. The road cut from the mountainside under tall trees shading the ruins of old fortresses and chapels — this was the route taken by the Persian invader Xerxes, about whom he had published his first essay in the Auckland Grammar School journal.

Costello's diary from the castle, we remember, reads:

15 April first enemy shell at first light. Shelling all day.

16 April Withdrawal to Tempe

Or "Vale of Tempe", to give it the old name beloved of the gods. Costello calls it the pass of Tempe. A lovely spot, he wrote, "drenched in the blood of history". We remember from the Prologue that when the German tanks came up the ridge to the castle, Costello's battalion got out just in time. The German commander who ran up the flag at the castle was thwarted. Colonel Balck wrote that the New Zealanders "got clean away". We remember too that when the battalion reached Tempe it was ordered to stand and hold the pass, "if necessary to extinction". It was a cruel blow. They were expecting to be evacuated. Until then they had felt isolated and abandoned. Now they were being cast to the wolves.

When Costello awoke that morning at Tempe, on Thursday 17 April 1941, it was to the sound of rushing water.

Battle of Tempe

Contact with 21 Battalion had been lost. The tanks were in Tempe and nothing more was known of its fate.

— New Zealand War History *series*

COSTELLO AWOKE. HE was wet through. He could hear a nightingale singing. He was lying under a ground sheet beside a river, a man's head beside his groin. A second man's boot protruded beside his left ear. He lay a moment trying to remember.

Where was the battalion?

He remembered the Colonel's last message. "Closing down. Getting out." He had given it to the cipher clerk to send, the clerk had tapped it out en clair. There was no time to encode it. They had marched all afternoon. Towards evening they came to a ferry. Two of their guns were waiting to be loaded on to a ramp. The battalion had only six guns, four anti-tank guns and a couple of mortars in support. The ferry was a flat-bottomed barge, hauled by ropes. The river had scoured a thirty-foot path between high walls beside a railway — the railway was on one side of the river, a narrow road on the other. Further on was a tunnel. The engineers were preparing to drive a boxcar into the tunnel and blow it, then, when the guns were across the river, to sink the ferry. The Germans when their tanks got through the quagmire below Platamon castle would follow the same route.

While they were waiting to board the ferry, two women arrived with a flock of mixed goats and sheep and requested a passage. One of the platoons took time off from the war to haul them across. It was a scene out of Herodotus, or comic opera. Costello and the signallers crossed the river in swirling mist ahead of the guns but behind everyone else and came up the gorge in the dark, having walked the ten miles from Platamon heads down, disconsolately, like mules out in the rain. They had lost their only wireless set and there had been no time to collect the telephone lines.

Costello got up slowly. All about him figures with two and three days' growth on their chins were sprawled on the river flat in attitudes of sleep. He recognised young Watts from Captain Tongue's company, lolling on his trigger guard. Tongue's lot, he remembered, had had to fight their way out.

He must have lain down and bivouacked with a rifle platoon by mistake. Costello shouldered his kit and walked on.

The road followed the river. In places the granite walls rose sheer, in others the embankment shelved to the rushing waters. Patrols were already out on the spurs leading to the river as he approached Tempe village. A troop of guns lumbered past him heading up the gorge. Muffled explosions came from that direction. A makeshift sign beside a first-aid post directed him to Headquarters company, but before he got there he came upon the Colonel in the village street. The latter was in conference with a brigadier.

"How nice," he heard Macky say to the brigadier, "to find someone from higher up taking an interest in us."

Costello knew that tone. Colonel Macky, in private life a lawyer, had risen from the ranks and won the Military Cross on the Somme in the First World War. He was a compact man with a sardonic stare and a voice rich in sarcasm — Colonel Neil Lloyd Macky, known to all as "Polly". Polly Macky had a beak for a nose. He resembled a bird of prey.

Macky's sarcasm was lost on the brigadier. The brigadier had red tabs and had come from Corps HQ, or perhaps from Division. He had parked his car beside the Orthodox church. Above it, Costello noticed, a stork had built a nest on top of the bell-tower.

"How long?" he heard someone say. The Colonel had his gunnery officers with him, and the Intelligence officer, Wallace. Two other officers — Australians, Costello guessed — were also there.

"Six hours," the brigadier said.

They were talking tanks. Apparently the German panzers were not far behind.

An argument broke out.

Macky snorted.

Costello caught the word "imbecilic".

"Tanks can't swim," someone said.

Macky snorted again. He was seething.

Costello walked on. Later he knew the first sensations of fear. At Platamon he had been less frightened, because they were too busy repairing telephone lines; they had stopped the leading German tanks and got away. Now they were ordered to stop a whole armoured division from getting to Larissa. Larissa was the bottleneck.

Lieutenant Wallace, the Intelligence officer, took him up a zigzag path above the main road. Today the tourist traffic spins past from Larissa oblivious of the scene and its significance. But there it was at their feet — a road, a river, and the railway. And beyond, a small plain dotted with wheatfields running south to Larissa. The Vale of Tempe was spread out before them. If the enemy got into Tempe village, Wallace was saying, the Allied troops withdrawing through Larissa to Thermopylae would be trapped. Larissa was a fifteen-minute ride away.

They had climbed up to a vantage point with a party of Australian officers and the Greek mayor. Looking down, the mayor averted his eyes from the railway bridge spanning the river. The bridge was a mass of twisted steel with a gaping hole in the middle. The river was high. "At least we're tank-proof," one of the Australians said.

"How is that?" Costello said.

"Tanks can't swim."

The Australians were sending reinforcements. The reinforcements were due to arrive in the night.

Later Costello realised he had been looking down on a scene exactly as it must have appeared 2500 years earlier when the Greeks deployed to face the Persians, except that after a few days the Greek generals had thought better of it and withdrawn to Thermopylae. Perhaps it was then Wallace told him that all their transport had been taken away and he felt the first prickly sensation of sweat run down his arms. He wanted to run and hide.

> I claim no merit in having been in battle [he wrote to Bil later].

> But I do insist it is an absolutely ghastly experience and quite the most ghastly thing in the world.

Costello spent the rest of the day interpreting, relaying messages, gulping down his first hot meal in three days and sending out runners. It never ceased to surprise him how things got done. The rail tunnel blocked solid, the road blown and cratered in several places, weapon pits dug — wherever he went there was activity. Men were gathering cover on the rocky slopes, cursing each other. Only yesterday they had been knotting ties or totting up accounts in peacetime occupations in Auckland, infirm of purpose; now they belonged to the nation, 700 citizen-soldiers. They actually were the nation. But did they feel the same constriction in the diaphragm that he felt? Were they as frightened of death as he was?

In the afternoon it drizzled and O'Neill's platoon was heavily attacked in the gorge. Polly Macky was seen going round the defences, his cape billowing in the mist. Towards evening it cleared. Across the river the inhabitants of Gonnos could be seen trudging into the mountains with their possessions heaped on mules and donkeys. Costello lay down on a concrete floor in a basement to sleep. In the morning a big concentration of vehicles could be seen milling about the village of Gonnos. German Mark II Panzers were reported bumping down the coast road from Platamon on the railway track.

Accounts of the battle next day vary. For example, when the last of the battalion's field guns was silenced — "our four lonely guns", Costello wrote — we read that the mortars were still intact and that the mortar detail kept firing with great pluck. But Colonel Macky's diary says that when the mortars arrived from Platamon, the vital parts were missing and the detail had to make do with rifles.

Rifles against tanks?

Here the German account is most helpful. We read that when the panzers got to the gorge, they crossed the river and simply shouldered aside the demolitions blocking the road. How was this possible? The river was in spate. A New Zealand report says the advancing tanks "disappeared in sheets of flame and smoke" as artillery shells struck them. Yet the Germans insist that five tanks crossed the river. They "appeared to be swimming".

In a German war diary, 3rd Panzer Regiment, we read:

> A Mark II tank drove determinedly down the high steep embankment into the water. It struggled through the water like a walrus, with nothing showing except its turret, the driver sitting up to his middle in water. The waves completely prevented him from seeing anything. Finally the tank clambered out on the other side, amid cheers from the spectators.

It seems that Balck, the German tank commander, was in luck. He had found a ford. Unobserved, his tanks crossed and then with darkness coming on laagered for the night, screened by mountain troops. On Friday morning, where the river makes a sharp bend behind Gonnos, more tanks "forced a crossing" on pontoons on the front held by the Australians. It is difficult to know, once the German artillery opened up, how Costello or any of the runners, exposed to constant shelling, plunging machine-gun and mortar fire, managed to reach any of the defending platoons in the gorge. Communications had almost completely broken down. Macky's platoons were battered and driven back in a welter of dust and explosions. There were dead and dying on both sides of the river.

"Men killed in battle," Costello would write to his wife,

> are such shabby grey things. And maybe even worse than the aesthetic revulsion is the moral side; being afraid for a long time at a stretch; because shells *always* make people scared to death. You sweat and prickle all over.

At noon or thereabouts, shortly before the tanks broke out of the gorge, Macky held a conference. Costello was there. A gunner named Croft, 33rd Battery, remembers seeing them in the street. As the Colonel walked past his gun Don Croft heard him say, "There's five of the bastards up there [meaning tanks]". This must have been during a lull, because Costello stopped, he tells us, to listen to the silence. He looked up and heard the bell-tower clatter. There was a stork, perched rakishly on the tower, building its nest — and no doubt, from its perch, with a better appreciation of what was happening on the ground than anyone else taking part in the battle. (Three years later, in July 1944, forced to spend a day in the Moroccan town of Rabat on his way to Moscow, Costello noticed two storks on the towers of the walls of the kasbah. He wrote in his journal that night, "I heard the old storks clatter

Right: "Sincerely yours, Christopher and Mary Costello". Costello's parents on their wedding day in Melbourne.

Below: The Three Lamps, Ponsonby, as it was in Costello's day when he walked up the hill and crossed over on his way to Curran Street primary school. The Ley's Institute library, where he read about the Vale of Tempe in Lempriere's Classical Dictionary at the age of nine, is just out of the picture at right.

Bottom: Paddy Costello (back row centre) as a grammar school boy, aged 15, in 1927. His mother is in the front row. His brothers and sisters are, left to right: Phil, Len, Molly, Frank and Kathleen (Kath).

Top: Costello's mother and his favourite sister, Kath, with her children in Morrinsville. "It is handy to have well-wishers in a land like NZ where the cream need not be bootlegged," he wrote to her in 1942. He sent Kath matchbox lids; she sent him food parcels in the African desert, and whitebait and toheroa soup to his children when he was posted to Moscow.

Above: Hunger marchers from the north of England entering Cambridge on their way to London, 1933. Left-wing students such as Costello brought them into the colleges for a meal and found accommodation for them in the town. In Jarrow, Lancs., 80 per cent of the population was unemployed.

Above left: The Great Gate at the entrance to Trinity College, Cambridge.

Above right: All Saint's Passage, leading to Trinity College, where Maclaurin had his bookshop (today a barber's). After Maclaurin's death, the bookshop was run by his widow, then it moved to Rose Crescent.

Far left: Griff Maclaurin, the first New Zealander to enlist against Franco in the Spanish Civil War and at left, John Cornford, the first Englishman. Maclaurin died defending Madrid in November 1936, Cornford on the Cordoba front in December.

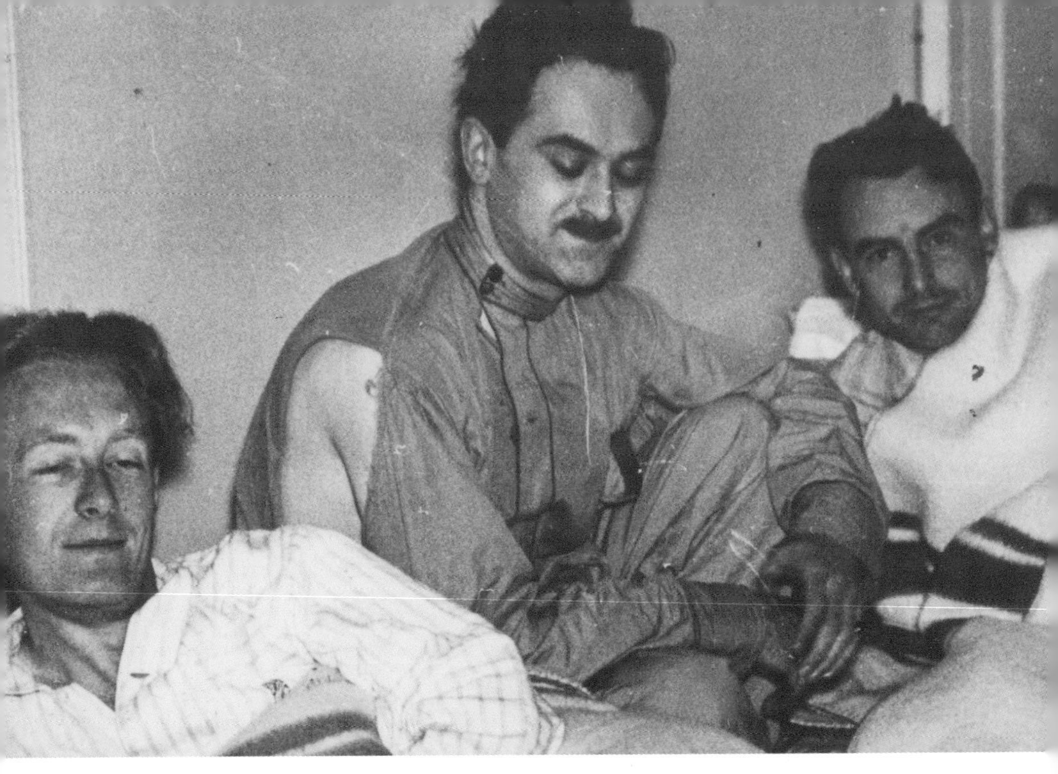

Top: Geoffrey Cox (third from left at rear) taking refuge with other journalists in the British Embassy, during the siege of Madrid in November 1936. When the Spanish government and the press corps fled to Valencia, Cox remained, one of only two Fleet Street journalists left in the capital.

Above: Costello and Bil, Exeter, 1937.

their bills, just as the one on the church-tower at Tempe did on that fateful Friday April 18th 1941.")

The outcome was never in doubt. Troops from the 6th German Mountain Division arrived at one end of the village, the 3rd Panzer Regiment burst through the mouth of the gorge at the other; once they joined forces, 21 Battalion was completely cut off. The point at issue is, what were Macky's orders? Colonel Macky said he received no orders. He wrote in his diary that it was decided at the conference that if the battalion was overwhelmed and cut off, those left should make their way in small parties to the coast at Volos.

"That was my understanding," he said. "I, myself, could see that no effort was going to be made to withdraw us." One of the Australian guns bravely continued firing late into the afternoon. None of this however seems to have impressed General Freyberg. The General's view of Macky's performance would be later defined not by the phrase "position held, ranks decimated" but by the ignominious "position vacated, ranks missing". Freyberg himself, commanding the New Zealand forces in Greece, appeared in Tempe that day. Freyberg dashed up from Larissa in a scout car, observed the battle and left again. He was desperate. The withdrawal of 55,000 men through Larissa had become a nightmare, with units held up by fog or fighting rearguard actions in the Olympus passes. The whole of the New Zealand Sixth Brigade had yet to arrive.

By an astonishing oversight, once the German panzers were in Tempe, they waited there until they had infantry in close support, although the road to Larissa was open. By then it was getting dark. Colonel Macky writes,

> The last of our brigades was due through Larissa at dusk. The tanks had taken much longer to get through our positions perhaps than they need have taken. However that was our luck. Thus darkness fell on the enemy on the Larissa road and he could get no further.

When the panzers reached Larissa on the morning of the 19th, Colonel Balck found himself again thwarted. He was too late. The last Allied convoy had passed through at midnight.

A few days later the Allied force was evacuated to Crete. Except for a remnant, Macky's men were not among them. At first it was feared the greater part of the 21st Battalion had been lost. But they were not all lost. In the words of the official historian of the Crete campaign, Dan Davin, thanks to "a tall lance-corporal in horn-rimmed glasses" they reappeared at Heraklion on the coast of Crete twelve days later. Amid mutterings that he had abandoned his position at Tempe prematurely, Colonel Macky would be relieved of command and invalided home to New Zealand in unofficial disgrace. It was unfair, outrageous. Though broken and dispersed, his tiny force had held up a full armoured division including 400 tanks and vehicles, a feat of arms recognised by the German commander Balck as unequalled by any other British unit in Greece. But the New Zealand General's censure of Macky, never publicised but nonetheless whispered through the Division, carried weight at the time.

Freyberg stopped short of accusing Macky of outright cowardice, but even today talking to survivors of that campaign you get a whiff of disgrace, of what used to be called "desertion under fire". Survivors say the 21st "didn't hold the ground they were supposed to". The blame fell on Macky.*

Macky later conceded that he had made a mistake — he had put the road block in the gorge in the wrong place. The Germans had been able to clear it, unobserved. But there it was. Every man, says Wendell Phillips, the American anti-slavery orator, meets his Waterloo. Colonel (later General) Balck's citation commending 21 Battalion would not become public for many years.

That leaves Costello. Costello's account of the battle is lost. He wrote a full account of the 21st's "pasting" but lost it in a fire. However notes from his letters and diaries and other fragments survive which support Macky's story and confirm what by now the reader has probably guessed. Namely, that when you are surrounded by Germans on three sides to a depth of half a mile, with ahead of you (to quote the *Illustrated London News*) "a river running with blood", you have little choice but to imitate the smart lover and depart. Or, in Costello's phrase, "leg it into the hills". This is what they did.

---

* Macky never forgave Freyberg. According to the legal historian R.C.J. Stone, after the war when Freyberg became Governor-General of New Zealand, he wrote inviting Macky to Government House in an attempt to bury the hatchet. Macky did not deign to reply.

Escape to Crete

Oh, I expect we shall meet again.
The evacuation season's just getting under way.
—*John Connell,* The House by Herod's Gate

IT IS TIME — once again — to introduce Dan Davin.* Dan Davin, the official historian of the Crete campaign, is the man who first brought Paddy Costello into view. Until then Costello had been hiding in the ranks in imitation of a good proletarian, unlike Davin who was an officer. The two had never met.

While Costello was escaping from Tempe on Friday 18 April 1941, Lieutenant Davin and his platoon were hooking it through Larissa. Davin had particular reason to be grateful to Costello's battalion; he and his men had been detained on Mount Olympus. Davin's platoon was further forward than anyone's, and the most exposed. Stalked by an unseen enemy in the rain and mist, Lieutenant Davin had got his platoon clear to the waiting trucks below Kokkinopolis, minus five men, after a fire fight; and so to Larissa, grey with fatigue and plastered from head to foot with mud, and on to Thermopylae and subsequent evacuation. Davin's battalion, the 23rd, was one of the last through Larissa which was, he wrote, badly smashed. "Dead

* See James McNeish, *Dance of the Peacocks*, page 161.

men on roadside, horses, trucks, Greek soldiers making their way back in little groups, disorganised, tails down. Little sleep. Much buggering about."

Dan Davin was another Irish-New Zealander. He had come to England in 1936 as a Rhodes Scholar and volunteered for the war, convinced he would be dead within twelve months. On Olympus he had believed his battalion was doomed. He had been twice wrong. Unlike Costello he was not prescient in this way, being gloomy by nature. But the two had much in common. They had the New Zealander's peculiar appetite for war and believed, at least Costello told his wife Bil he did, that military service was a metaphor for life itself. "War is to man," he wrote to her, "what motherhood is to woman." Costello would irritate and goad his wife — and vie with Davin later, amusing and provoking each other — with stagey remarks of this kind. Both men felt for Greece, however. They condemned Churchill and Wavell for committing the crime of letting the Greeks think they could save them and then abandoning them to their fate. As their service in the New Zealand Division lengthened and the horrors of war continued to mount, each man would take to the same drug, finding solace and refuge in the poets and historians of old. Davin, another classics man, would go through the battle of Alamein reading the *Aeneid* in Latin; Costello, reading Thucydides's history of the Peloponnesian war in the original Greek.

But so far, as indicated, the two had not met.

Virgil's *Aeneid* opens with the well-known words, "I sing of arms and the man", as Virgil announces his intention to sing of Aeneas, the man who led the refugees to safety out of the sacked city of Troy. It seems somehow appropriate that Davin should first learn and write about Costello after hearing stories of the man who led the refugees from the sacked village of Tempe.

They climbed out over the snows of Ossa. Polly Macky and his men departed Tempe on the afternoon of Friday 18 April 1941 and climbed up under fire towards dense beech forests. Costello wrote:

> I was clambering up the slopes of Mount Ossa from rock to rock, with a shower of Hun bullets all around my ears every time I emerged into view. I thought it very unlikely at the time that I'd ever get out of it. When night came we were still climbing.

Later Costello remembered an intense white light. While dozing beside a goat track, he looked down and saw far below Larissa burning. There was the road, and tanks lit by flares, with Very lights in the far distance, the tanks deployed over the small plain with the Larissa road running through the middle of it. Larissa had been bombed almost off the map.

Towards midnight everyone lay down and fell asleep. But it was so cold, Macky wrote, that "after an hour or so I decided we must go on". Unfortunately it was found later that four men had failed to wake up, and were left behind.

They marched all night.

With Macky were seven officers and thirty-five other ranks. Most were from Headquarters. (Versions saying "half the battalion escaped with Macky" are exaggerated.) Later Macky's party swelled to over fifty. Costello first persuaded a shepherd to guide them. The shepherd led them over a precipice into a valley and became lost. They had discarded everything but their arms and ammunition; they were in the heart of the mountains, just in the snowline. Before them across the valley rose Ossa, to a height of 6000 feet. Some idea of the journey can be gained today by driving up to the village of Spilia and on to Melivia; the road is third-class, blinded by woods of stunted oak and beech trees, barely signposted. It seems to lead nowhere. Couloirs of thick forest alternate with a grandeur of precipice and silence where no animals move and no birds sing.

They lived on raw potatoes and hard-boiled Easter eggs. One of their number, an inhabitant of the Coromandel Peninsula, cooked two tortoises in a ravine before being interrupted by a hailstorm. They slept in twos and threes, under pine branches broken from the trees in the snow; in churches; and once, after reaching the coast, in a henhouse. Costello found a tobacco smuggler who guided them out of the snow and down to the sea where they came upon the padre, Rev. Sheehy, lying up in an open boat. Other parties were arriving from up and down the coast. The coast was already in enemy hands. A fragment from Costello's diary reads:

> Bombers. Weeping women . . ? Bedded down in bracken while smuggler went on to see if OK. Up and on to Ag Yanni where slept in a church.

Thanks to the smuggler, and Costello's Greek, they found a boat. This was near the bay of Volos in the village of Ag Yanni where the mayor, Costello told Macky, wanted to turn them in. They arrested him. Faced with desperate men, "not one day hungry but constantly", a Tommy gun on either side of him, the mayor was induced to provide a caique, and at midnight they sailed for Skopelos. So began ten days of zigzagging among the islands of the Aegean — whenever they touched at one island, the inhabitants warned them the Germans were landing on the other side — which ended with them landing on Crete and rejoining General Freyberg's force a fortnight before the battle for Crete began. They were amazed to discover that the main body had not been evacuated to Egypt. Macky's party had been machine-gunned, bombed, starved; they had foundered at Sirtos, trans-shipped five times; they had sheltered "on half the islands in the Aegean Sea", and almost landed in Turkey but recoiled from it for fear of being interned; fevered and suffering from dysentery, they were almost as disoriented as the shepherd who had led them astray in the mountains above Spilia. The latter had greeted Costello with the words, "Who's winning? How are the Austrians doing?"* A remnant of the 21st Battalion — 132 from 700 — had already arrived on Crete. Most of Macky's party refused to be hospitalised in their eagerness to rejoin the battalion. Colonel Howard Kippenberger counted up to 190 of the 21st. Soon they would be nearly 250. More battalion parties yet would come. One man rowed across. A later group was more than sixty strong. But it was Macky's party landing on 2 May 1941 that captured the imagination.

"Colonel Macky, Captain Dutton, Padre Sheehy, all safe," Davin wrote in his diary as news of the landfall travelled along the coast to Maleme airfield where Davin's battalion was now digging in. "Glad about Macky. For a colonel, he is intelligent and courteous." Macky had been an accomplished sailor in peacetime, commodore of a yacht squadron and known to most yachtsmen on the Auckland harbour; undoubtedly it was his skill as a helmsman that had brought them through. But Macky was ill with dysentery and already relieved of his command; his place taken by a skinny lance-corporal who spoke Greek. Amplified by gossip and anecdote, embellished by newspaper articles comparing the episode to "one of the legends of ancient Greece":

* The shepherd had apparently never left the valley. Twenty years earlier he had heard there was fighting down below. Now there was fighting again.

"OUT OF THE BLUE:
Men Given Up for Lost"

ran a headline in the press — the story acquired momentum, reinventing itself and splitting into a hundred pieces, like amoebae. By the time the news reached Second Lieutenant Davin, the pieces had solidified, half-epic, half-miracle, and the name on everyone's lips was no longer that of the gallant Colonel Macky.

Costello would not be long on Crete. General Freyberg was now in charge of the entire Allied force on the island and would have to defend it against invasion from the air. His troops were lacking the most basic type of equipment. Morale was low. It is easy to see how an incident magnified by rumour was seized on by a defeated army.

Dan Davin was playing chess on a friend's improvised bamboo set when news of a "miraculous" landing reached him. It interrupted his game. Davin was a student of rumour, a connoisseur of gossip. Deployed with his men near Maleme aerodrome, peering up at the skies for the expected air invasion — a sitting target, it transpired, for the first wave of German paras and gliders would descend directly on top of them — Davin had time on his hands. He had had "excellent opportunities to study the genesis of rumour":

> A rumour [he told his diary] can traverse a deployed battalion in less than an hour.

The melancholic and normally sceptical Davin does not seem to have questioned this rumour, however. Costello, he wrote, was the saviour of the 21st — "the chief instrument of their escape". Davin noted it in his diary on that very day. It is even possible that Davin himself started the rumour. He had in fact heard of Costello before, on the grapevine, although they had still not met.

General Freyberg did not question the rumour either. The General was attempting to rally his troops' spirits by starting a Forces newspaper. He was told of Costello's conduct and he sent for him. Costello it seems did not at first relish his newfound fame; he would protest later to his son that his Greek was mainly classical Greek; the strangulated demotic that Georgios the tobacco smuggler had uttered he could barely understand. Costello played down the rumour, spurning the credit that he felt was not his but Macky's.

But what could he do? Macky was no longer there. He was on his way back to New Zealand.*

Dan Davin, at some point learning that Costello's battalion was reforming and bivouacking nearby, in and around the village of Kondomari, resolved to walk over from Maleme and introduce himself. He was too late. The General had already hauled Costello before a selection board and had him flown out to Cairo to be trained for a commission.

* It was Macky's second sacking in three years. In 1938 he was purged from the Territorial Force after leading a revolt of four colonels who publicly rebuked the New Zealand government for its lack of military preparedness for war. He was reinstated when war began in 1939. Macky was invalided back to New Zealand from Egypt, promoted Brigadier (home defence) and became after the war the senior partner in the law firm of Russell McVeagh. He died in 1981.

A Meeting in Cairo

Spending the days and nights drinking plonk and talking with Paddy. The best talk I have enjoyed since the old days in Oxford.

— *Dan Davin, Tripoli 1943*

WHEN THE TWO men did finally meet, it was in the bar of the National Hotel in Cairo. This was courtesy of Geoffrey Cox. Cox was another refugee driven from Greece to Crete and subsequently evacuated under fire to Egypt.

On Crete Davin had had the luck to be shot by a German parachutist on the first day of the air invasion and be evacuated. He suffered greatly and was unwell for a long time. He was lying in a hospital at Helwan near Cairo recovering from his wounds when he was visited by a neat smiling figure with dark hair parted off-centre, short back and sides. Geoffrey Cox had been a foreign correspondent for the *Daily Express*, operating out of Paris when the war began, and had joined up in England at the time of Dunkirk. They had met at university in New Zealand and had last seen each other in England, in camp near Aldershot. Cox had enlisted hoping to see action as an infantryman but on Crete Freyberg had ordered him to produce a newspaper for the troops instead. Cox had done this, writing and editing the last of four issues of *Crete News* in the heat of battle moments before a bomb fell on the printer's shop in Canea and destroyed the premises. Cox found Davin in hospital preparing an eye-witness account for the British of the aerial assault which had produced yet another Allied defeat and the loss of Crete. Davin was an early witness to the battle. Cox, one of the last to be evacuated from the island, added his testimony to what Davin had experienced.

Davin's report so impressed the British authorities that he was invited to join the Intelligence section of Eighth Army General Headquarters (GHQ). He began work at GHQ in the Garden City suburb of Cairo in August 1941. He was engaged on the Balkans desk and lodging at the National Hotel.

> I was living dismally in a grim little room, with the musical accompaniment of the adjacent lift and lavatory as solace for persistent illness, hepatic gloom, and guilt for not being with Battalion friends in the forthcoming desert actions.

It was here that Davin ran into Cox again. Cox had also booked in at the National. Each had checked in without knowing the other was there. Cox was now on a course at the Kasr el Nil barracks, like Costello — Costello being trained for officer rank, while Cox, already a junior officer, was being trained for Freyberg's Intelligence staff.

A few days later Cox brought Costello along to meet Davin.

They met in the hotel bar. According to Cox, and also Davin's biographer, Keith Ovenden, "they became friends instantly". But it was not quite like that. Costello's diary has Davin, still recovering from his wound and a subsequent attack of hepatitis, hunched over a glass at the counter in a wasteland of cigarette stubs, pistachios and peanuts. He had had several drinks already. Costello, acutely observant, instinctively drew himself in, stomach flattened. This was not the Dan Davin whom Cox had prepared him for. The Southlander whom Cox had represented to Costello was a Byronic figure, a poet, a woman-slayer and a warrior who had risked his life on Olympus to save his men — not this broken-nosed tramp in uniform with staring headlamp eyes. At the counter Davin steadied himself, leaning on a cane, and thrust out a hand. Costello took it, without enthusiasm. Davin ordered a Tom Collins, the Aucklander Stella beer, a local product tasting of onions he didn't particularly like. Costello wore instead of the regulation red pugaree round his hat, a white one, denoting his cadet status.

He remained erect, immaculate in a newly pressed tunic, unsmiling. Davin for his part was remembering another occasion. Five months earlier he had caught sight of Costello on the deck of a boat, the *Ionia*, a Greek tub transporting troops from Alexandria to Piraeus. He had noticed a tall lance-corporal in a lifejacket talking in apparently fluent Greek with a member of the crew, and knew at once it could only be the prodigy from Auckland about whom he had heard. He had been about to approach Costello when something stopped him.

> Some timorous instinct, something in his demeanour told me that if I, a one-pipper [Second Lieutenant] were to accost him, he would not be able to resist the chance of snubbing an officer.

Lifeboat drill was just ending. Overcome by a mixture of insecurity and awe, Davin had turned away.

Now — Cambridge Hellenist and Oxford Latinist, immaculate cadet and broken-down officer — they faced each other with what is commonly called a fish-eyed stare and feigned indifference, the desire for fraternal embrace held in check by adolescent mistrust and vanity. It took all of Cox's powers of social bridging to lubricate their inhibitions. Soon they were skirmishing in Latin and Greek and contradicting each other on the relative merits of Virgil and Homer. They parted noisily.

A few weeks later in September 1941 Costello was commissioned Second Lieutenant. Shortly afterwards, at the end of September, Davin visited him at the New Zealand base camp at Maadi south of Cairo. Davin's diary records in a howl of anguish:

> The best linguist in the Division, and he's put in the Long Range Desert Patrol.

Evidently a friendship had begun. Soon it would deepen and become lifelong.

Second Lieutenant Costello was not yet thirty. He took to his elevation in status like a pro. This is both odd and entirely natural. Odd, because until then Costello had sedulously declined to be promoted, on principle, saying he would rise from the ranks on merit or not at all; he had already been offered a commission in Greece, but had refused "because I deemed wires were being pulled". Natural, because the hedonist in him relished the privileges and pleasures available to the officer class in Cairo in wartime.

On patrol with the Long Range Desert Group, Costello was enjoying himself. Operating behind the lines in Libya, he began mugging up colloquial Arabic from a book Bil had sent him and interrogating Nazi and Italian prisoners brought in from raids on enemy supply convoys.

He caught malaria, declared Arabic to be "the hardest of Semitic languages" and discovered that roughing it in salt-pans and oases in a Hannibal country of sand, palms, camels and lions — did he mean leopards or gazelles? (He fired at a gazelle with a Tommy gun and missed) — had about it a special charm. It was like pretending the world was in its childhood again. He loved the blue weathered hills and spent hours yarning with villagers "whose problems are the same as those of father Abraham".

What happened? Nothing. The Long Range Desert Group was a small private army. They travelled in old Chevrolet trucks and undertook missions, co-operating with the Free French and British SAS, as far afield as Chad. Off duty, the protocol of the mess obtained. Either Costello kept his political views to himself, or more likely — as it seems in the case of Paul Freyberg — he did not. Paul Freyberg, son of the General, had been air-lifted out of Crete at the same time as Costello; they were on the same OCTU course in Cairo, and in the Long Range Desert Group together; what passed between them is not known but an initial warmth seems to have cooled, glacially. Years later in a biography of his father, Paul (now Colonel Lord Freyberg) would single out for special mention two of the General's three Intelligence officers, Cox and Davin. But of the third, he would not say a word.

Back in Cairo, Costello looked up Davin. He was fit and bronzed after three months behind the lines and clearly going forward. But in which direction?

A period of relative calm was beginning, after a combined operation named "Crusader". This was the tank offensive in which the New Zealand Division, though badly mauled with 4620 losses, broke through the Afrika Korps to lift the siege of Tobruk, helping to swing a lost battle in favour of the Allies.

The Division is refitting. Reinforcements are arriving. Davin is still on loan to the British, working with military Intelligence at Eighth Army GHQ. Early in 1942, we discover from Davin's diary, Costello is there too.

"New Zealand," Davin grumbles, "is creeping in on my racket."

In fact it is Davin himself who has engineered Costello's secondment to the British. Costello has been assigned the task of producing a new handbook on the Italian army. Davin is upstairs working on the Balkans desk. Geoffrey Cox is in action with the New Zealand Division in Libya. Then Cox arrives from the desert, shaken from the Crusader battles, and joins them — another job has been manufactured for Cox, a kind of survivor's leave, getting out the daily news summary at Eighth Army. So they are three, nesting together in the lee of British GHQ in Cairo's Garden City suburb.

Earlier, moping in hospital, Davin had lamented the lack of mental stimulation. He told his diary, "I wish Cox and Costello and I could get jobs together." Now, though it would not be for long, it had happened.

Cox and Davin shared a flat near GHQ. "When Geoff is in town," Davin wrote, "I have the feeling that I know a lot of people and that life is really more exciting than I thought." Cox seemed to know half the journalists and writers and poets in Cairo. Davin's relationship with Costello was something else. With Cox and his quick intelligence, Davin might be merry. With Costello he became intoxicated:

> Knife mind, fanatical honesty, Irish pugnacity, skill in mimicry,
> great raconteur, but always content precedes manner.

To which Davin might have added a beautiful tenor voice, a way with women, an urgent libido, and Costello's enjoyment when drunk of a good stoush. The two men borrowed money, shirts and books from each other, acquired mistresses at the same time — Davin's was a German woman masquerading as a Dane, Costello's a White Russian emigrée already involved with a Rumanian engineer — read and debated each other's manuscripts and indulged in the sort of scuffling and antic horseplay after dining out on the Continental and Badia Hotel roof gardens that frequently ended in violence and would continue later, in peacetime, into their middle age.

It has been said with only slight exaggeration that as the war progressed, senior officers on the eve of battle would sometimes find themselves being given Intelligence briefings by "a dazed Major Davin", with blackened eye and swollen lip, or "a tottering Captain Costello", evidence of a previous night's carousal. Davin describes an evening in the mess, "full of indescribable clamour — bawdy songs and Paddy. The men outshouting each other.

Everyone in various wrestles. I notice," he says, "that Paddy and I, the men of culture, are the most prone to violence in our cups. God knows what bloody jungles writhe in our subconscious."

Did such bouts have to do with the war itself? In part. Reading Davin's and Costello's diaries and letters is to learn something about the nature of friendship between men in wartime that no amount of dispute or disagreement or even betrayal can put asunder. But in Costello's case it has been suggested by some of his friends that behind the frenzied drinking lies something else, something hidden in the psyche, a private disquiet indicating a troubled man. Troubled by what? The friends cannot say, they are at a loss. Certainly the drink will have consequences for Costello, but otherwise speculation of this sort appears to be futile.

That summer of 1942 Rommel turned the tables. His Afrika Korps broke through to the outskirts of Alexandria at Alamein. The prospect of defeat loomed. Then came Alamein itself, the break-out and the pursuit across North Africa until Rommel was finally seen off in Tunisia. After the fall of Tunis in May 1943, the New Zealand Division was stood down and returned by convoy to Cairo — both with (and without) Costello and Davin. Davin missed the final North African battles. In February he had been sent to Sarafand in Palestine on a staff course. He arrived back across the top of Africa to rejoin the Division in May, arriving just in time to turn around again and retrace his steps with Costello and the returning convoy. At Enfidaville outside Tunis the two acquired a truck to themselves, and drove ahead of the convoy, peeling off independently whenever they could. They visited the classical sites and swam in the sea at Daba. They sang and declaimed poetry in the Roman amphitheatres and basked in the dry powdery white sand of the North African beaches, like truants out of school. Previously the pair had been together for brief periods only, moments stolen from work schedules or the perils of war, neither knowing if the other would be still alive on the day after. Now they had sixteen uninterrupted days. The episode is lovingly described in Keith Ovenden's *A Fighting Withdrawal*, and in *Dance of the Peacocks*, a full flush of friends dealt under the burning African sun. Enfidaville to Cairo. Sixteen days, 1960 miles. Never to be repeated.

So a friendship which thrived on mutual admiration, common experiences, an Irish Catholic heritage, fierce anti-clericalism, a hatred of fascism and their shared hopes for a postwar world — not to mention abuse and insult — matured and ripened.

Probably at this stage the friendship meant more to Davin than Costello — "My one worthwhile friend in Cairo," Davin noted. Costello had his own circle. This included an Italian bookseller, Mengozzi, the European wife of a prominent member of the Egyptian government, Armenian and Syro–Eyptian bankers, Sephardic Jews, a Cypriot called George Patsalidis who spoke a bastard demotic Greek called *katharevousa*, the journalists Richard Hughes and Alan Moorehead, and an electrifying Russian emigrée mistress whom Davin would put into his war novel, *For the Rest of Our Lives*, as "Paula". Costello went to the Russian Club, the Poetry Club, the Libreria Italiana, and spent hours off-duty eavesdropping on Greek and Jewish traders and studying their intonations as they argued ("hand on heart — 'Well, you know me. An honest man.'") and gesticulated in a pot-pourri of Yiddish and other tongues. "A feast for a connoisseur."

One of Costello's acquaintances in Cairo was Henri Curiel, a Marxist bookseller who directed him to out-of-the-way book and record shops. Curiel was a mysterious figure who would later be expelled from Egypt by Colonel Nasser. He was one of the founders of the Egyptian Communist Party, the son of a banker of Jewish descent. Costello told Bil that Henri Curiel's father would have been surprised to learn of his son's political activities, just as Costello himself would be surprised later to learn that the British double-agent and Russian spy George Blake (real name Behar) was Henri Curiel's cousin. Blake had come to Cairo as a teenager and received his English education growing up with Henri Curiel in the father's household in Zamalek.

At British GHQ, Costello's time was running out. He had been in Cairo for three months. He was beginning to know Cairo better than he knew London.

"You'd hardly know there was a war on out here," he wrote to Bil early in 1942. Native Kiwi, adoptive Brit, self-styled cosmopolitan *flâneur*, he was both at ease and uncomfortable amid the vapid pleasures and sporting clubs on offer in the city. Then the bubble burst.

Geoffrey Cox was the first to be recalled to the Division. Cox had spent only a couple of weeks resting up at Eighth Army Headquarters. He was recalled by Freyberg in March 1942. Costello's turn came in May.

He had been keeping his head down, like Davin, hoping that the New Zealand General had forgotten his existence. Both men dreaded a return to the base camp at Maadi where life, Costello wrote, was "barely twitching". His letters are full of references to the plots he and Davin were hatching so they could transfer to the British on a permanent basis (the pay was better). Davin advised caution. Davin claimed to be heartily sick of the Division and to prefer Englishmen to New Zealanders, "because I find it easier to dominate Englishmen." Costello was living with an Armenian family a mile from the Garden City; he was working at GHQ six days a week, haunting the secondhand bookshops and cutting a dash at night, alighting from a gharry at Groppi's or the Badia roof garden restaurant and creeping home to his cramped digs like one of the Whitechapel boys in a Roy Sandler novel. He was improving his Russian, taking lessons from an elderly professor at twenty akkas a time. At Eighth Army he was turning an outdated British handbook on the Italian forces into a model document. His work was appreciated and his camouflage holding, as he thought.

Then honesty — that schoolboy frankness once again — led him into error. He applied direct to General Freyberg for a transfer. Freyberg awoke, reasoning that if the British wanted his best linguist, New Zealand must want him even more. He hauled Costello back to the Division "by the scruff".

The New Zealand Division was then resting up in Syria.

"Costello's going," Davin wrote, "has removed a man who had the force to shoulder one into interest which seems to lie latent when there is no one strong enough to stir it." He added, "Paddy [departed], consoling himself with the thought that Eighth Army was sure to make a balls-up without the Div., that Auchinleck would have to recall it to the desert and there would be excitement and action to compensate."

In 1942–3 General Freyberg contrived to have Cox, Costello and finally Davin recalled to his divisional Headquarters. It was a deliberate stratagem. From this trio of scholars he would receive a flow of Intelligence summaries and reports which would be the envy of rival Allied commanders for the duration of the war. "The old scamp", as Costello dubbed the General, contrived to play them like fish, allowing each an illusion of freedom while having them trained at no expense by Auchinleck's Eighth Army academy, then reeling them in one by one when he needed them. Freyberg's strategy is revealing when set against the recent criticisms by the British, blaming him for the loss of Crete. British writers talk of Bernard Freyberg's "obtuseness" and "muddled thinking", implying he was a Bernard of little brain.

The General's Caravan

Ura!
— *Costello to Bil, on Russia's entry into the war*

THE "BALLS-UP" OCCURRED, as Davin had predicted. In Syria, the classical itch reasserting itself, Costello made time to visit the rose-red city of Petra in southern Jordan. But that was all. He had barely begun to learn the ropes of the Intelligence game, skivvying for Cox in Freyberg's Headquarters, when the Division was urgently recalled to Egypt by the Eighth Army commander, Auchinleck. The desert fighting was going badly.

Costello arrived at Davin's flat in Cairo in the night. They spent the evening drinking and dining, arguing politics and literature. Next day he was off to the desert. That night Davin heard part of the convoy passing through the streets, "and recognised it in the dark by the accents of the men in the trucks. And I realised that Paddy had recovered his NZ accent."

Two days later, on 21 June 1942, Tobruk fell. Costello, going forward with the Division in a Headquarters truck, in the van of a convoy 2800 vehicles-strong, met a rabble of men and vehicles pouring back from the Libyan frontier — the British Eighth Army in headlong retreat from Rommel. Freyberg was ordered to put his Division into the Mersa Matruh fortress, but, scenting annihilation, refused to be boxed in. Even so, amid the chronic confusion, the Division was pinned down and encircled by panzers at Minqar Qaim. Freyberg himself, struck in the neck by a shell splinter the size of an egg, was nearly decapitated. In Davin's words, "That same night the Division, with him on a stretcher, broke out in a ferocious night attack and went exulting back to help stabilise the hastily formed front at Alamein."

Costello's only wounds, he said, were "slit-trench knees". At Minqar Qaim, in a single onslaught to smash its way out, the Division took a thousand casualties. Pandemonium reigned, everyone, in the words of Howard Kippenberger, commanding the Fifth Brigade, "bolting like wild elephants":

> overtaking and being overtaken by other frantic vehicles, dodging slit trenches, passing or crashing into running men, amid an uproar of shouts and screams. I recognised the men as Germans, pulled out my revolver and was eagerly looking out for a target when suddenly there was silence and we were out running smoothly on level desert. We were through.

Bloodied, aged somewhat and still shaking, Costello told Davin he had survived by touching wood at frequent intervals. Of this celebrated incident, in which the Division escaped almost certain extinction, Costello wrote only — in a letter to Bil — "Minqar Qaim was the most dangerous day of my life".

By now Costello has become Freyberg's divisional Intelligence officer and acquired a driver and vehicle of his own. This was a bullet-scarred LCV or light truck with a canvas top bequeathed to him by Geoffrey Cox. (Cox, having been withdrawn for a special operation, will shortly be posted to Washington.) Henceforth Cox's vehicle, known as the "I" truck (I for Intelligence), will under Costello's and later Davin's stewardship be nicknamed the Café (also the Gin Palace), acquiring a reputation in the Eighth Army beyond its station.

After the break-out at Minqar Qaim (28 June 1942), Rommel stood at Alamein only fifty miles from Alexandria. There followed what became known as "the Flap". Costello seems to have amused himself at this period by inventing what became the New Zealand Division's slogan, "Hooray-fuck", and reminding a number of panicky staff officers of the might of their "new-found allies", the Russians, in the east. He was overheard singing Spanish songs and invoking the words of La Pasionaria, the woman who had rallied the inhabitants of Madrid against Franco's besieging army with the legendary cry, "*No pasarán* (They shall not pass)". Alexandria was bombed from the air. Italian shopkeepers put up signs of "Welcome" to the Germans. Hardened British nerves began to crack. The navy sailed out of the harbour in such a hurry it forgot to tell the army it was leaving. The civilian population gathered at the railway station and fled south to the Delta. In Cairo public buildings emptied and documents were burned in a holocaust of secret papers, including Costello's cherished handbook on the Italian army. Rommel, it was said, would bypass Alexandria and occupy the capital "within twenty-four hours".

Costello, according to Davin, stayed calm, immune to the general panic. Costello's conviction that the Afrika Korps would not be able to pierce the line commended itself to Davin so strongly that this melancholy man became almost cheerful. Davin had been left behind in Cairo in an almost-vacant GHQ, ordered to burn documents and files by the lorryload. Costello, he said, had converted him to

> a fervent and unreasonable nationalist. I just could not believe the Germans would get past our line at Alamein, past Paddy, past Freyberg, and those high New Zealand voices, full of confidence and courage, I had heard passing through the Cairo night.

Altogether it was an interesting moment for the son of a grocer to enter a General's caravan. For the Allies, the coming battle of Alamein would mark a turning-point of the war. For Costello who served right through the break-out and the pursuit across North Africa, rarely out of sound range of gunfire, sometimes actually under fire, it meant several things. One of them had to do with conquering fear. Costello was no hero. He was unlikely, he told Bil, to win a Victoria Cross. He was not one of those who could advance unconcerned over fire-swept ground and describe it afterwards as "a rather sticky show":

> No harm in that really, but I have to think harder, remember all sorts of quotations from Heinrich Heine to Georgi something or other, in order to do things that an ordinary brave man does without over-much blinking.

Costello says this lightly. In his diaries and letters to Bil he touches on his insecurities and fears so often, usually in a jokey self-deprecating way, that it is not until Bil accuses him of glorifying war that we begin to understand some of his true feelings. He writes:

> You still seem sore about some high and mighty stuff I had written representing myself as the warrior going forth to battle while you sit and spin.

Artillery fire terrified him, he said. Shelling filled him with dread:

> You don't feel very New Statesman-ish after a battle or two [he added], and you don't feel the repulsion expressed by some people against "methods of violence" as a means to an end.

Battle, whatever the rights and wrongs, was producing in him the seeds of both pacifism and political realism.

Something else we learn. Costello the frightened man is concerned not just about courage, but his good name. After Minqar Qaim he writes out a poem by C. Day Lewis at some length in his pay book. "It may help me some day, to say to myself" he tells Bil,

> *Though song, though breath be short,*
> *I'll share not the disgrace*
> *Of those that ran away*
> *Or never left the base.*

Characteristically it was Freyberg, the man reputed to know no fear, who helped Costello overcome his own. One incident stands out. It occurred on 28 October 1942 during a lull between the artillery barrage that began the second battle of Alamein and the break-out that found a gap in Rommel's lines. The General was being driven to Australian HQ by a young liaison officer named Currie who was teaching Costello the guitar, with Costello and another officer in the back, when their Jeep was dive-bombed by a Stuka. All departed the Jeep and scattered, flinging themselves to the ground. The bomb exploded a few feet away. Gingerly they picked themselves up, except for Colin Currie who lay motionless, a chunk of metal protruding from his chest. The General was silent for a moment. They drove on. Later, returning past the same spot, Freyberg turned to Costello and said: "Pity about Colin. He was a good officer."

"And a brave one too, sir," Costello said.

"Courage, my dear Costello, is something I take for granted in all my officers."

Recounting this to Davin next day, Costello said, "If only the old scamp knew how terrified I was when that Stuka came screaming down, he'd have taken away my commission." Costello would remember the rebuke. Years later when he became a professor in England Costello would quote it to one of his honours students to help her overcome a chronic anxiety about flunking her finals.

Alamein also produced in Costello a shift in his attitude towards his own country. Somewhere between his being commissioned an officer in the autumn of 1941 and the victory parade at Tripoli in February 1943, the cocksure Cambridge intellectual has been put on a shelf and Costello has become a New Zealander again. The early years of Costello's war journal are lost. But enough remains to recognise the effect of his immersion in the ranks of the New Zealand Division — a surge in self-confidence and self-worth brought about by "close living with ordinary and unselfconscious men". Davin would have the same experience of comradeship in Italy, both men rejoicing in the discovery of something outside themselves that was not intellectual. In the case of Costello — the Marxist in him taking pride in the quiet courage and drawling humour of the ordinary Kiwi soldier — it was exemplified by "Jonesie". Jones was Costello's batman. He was a fairgrounds rouseabout and occasional dodgems driver from the West Coast of the South Island, a dreadful bludger whom Costello taught to read and write:

> Jonesie continues to delight [he notes on 1 May 1943]. Some of his recent remarks — "He was a private, sir, but they've demoted him to a batman." — "Oh, the Yanks were LOB,* didn't you know?"

Something else was changing — Costello's relationship with Freyberg. There is a hint of it in his diary after the drive from Enfidaville. "A week of

* LOB, left out of battle.

almost no incident," he writes in August 1943:

> A few nights ago Julian and I went to call on Bernard. He was out but the native servant let us in and we started on the three bottles of wine that J. had brought. Glanced at B's books: Lao Tzô, "Texts and Pretexts", "What Must be Done?", from the last of which I read out long slabs . . .

Freyberg was then fifty-four. He had been made KBE the previous year and KCB after the review by Churchill at Tripoli. This was the occasion when Churchill, who earlier blamed Freyberg for losing Crete and had hardly spoken to him since, embraced the General before a 100,000 troops and in an emotional speech dubbed Freyberg "the Salamander of the British Empire". Freyberg, revered by his men, had several reputations as a commander. Chumminess was not one of them. There was a reserve and a formalism left over from his British training which meant a strict pecking order and a cordon surrounding his person that few of his staff penetrated unannounced. Costello's use of the General's first name "Bernard" does not mean they were on familiar terms. Still, it hints at a degree of access unusual for a junior staff officer, as it presages in the six months of Costello's remaining war service a relationship still to come. It was a relationship enjoyed by very few senior officers, one that not even Cox, Freyberg's longest serving Intelligence officer, to whom he would entrust the delivery of his son Paul from the Vatican where he had taken refuge, would be privileged to aspire to.

The reason for this, in a word, was Russia.

Costello had greeted the opening of a second front in Russia, as did almost everyone in the Eighth Army, with a hurrah of relief. Early in the war he had recognised, as had Cox, the might of the Soviet war machine. In 1939 Cox had witnessed Soviet troops in action against Finland and published a book, *The Red Army Moves*; while by 1941 Costello had worked out for himself a number of reasons to support Cox's thesis that in any future conflict with Germany the Red Army would prevail. There was a kind of rough symmetry between the battle of Stalingrad and the Alamein campaign.

When Russia entered the war against Germany in 1941, Costello was in Cairo. After he was promoted Captain in September 1942 and the German General Paulus was stopped outside Moscow, Stalingrad began to dominate the news, with reports of fighting in the sewers and cellars of the besieged town. Costello's interest quickened. During the pursuit of Rommel, when not interrogating German and Italian prisoners, he began keeping a daily note of the situation. Somewhere he acquired a map.

> I keep a map of Russia up to date here [he told Bil], for my own edification. Today I advanced the line from in front of Voronezh and pushed the Caucasus front line to the north of Kropotkin . . . Here we are lost in admiration.

Inspired by the defence of Stalingrad, Costello began giving lessons in Russian. "I am teaching a class of five men," he announced after the German surrender at Stalingrad on 31 January 1943. The course was known as "the Bible class". Recruits were given a catechism in Cyrillic in the lean-to or under the canopy of the tray of the Intelligence truck, sitting on jerricans and jacked-up bedsteads. The classes varied. Costello's wireless operators, to whom he taught German, were introduced to Marvell, Dryden and the Restoration dramatists. It was probably at this time that Costello taught his batman Jonesie to read and write. Two early students were his No. 2, Tony Cleghorn, and a field security officer, Lawrence Nathan. They enrolled for both Russian and Italian, their studies receiving a boost after Costello captured an Italian truck full of apricot jam and pumpernickel. In the driver's compartment he found, alongside *The Count of Monte Cristo*, a copy of Dante's *Divine Comedy*. "He made me learn and recite ten lines of Dante a day," Nathan recalled, "and read *Monte Cristo* right through."

Costello was a compulsive teacher and proselytiser. He was adept at detecting in an interlocutor the slightest twitch of curiosity and giving it a focus.

The artillery barrage of November 1942 which marked Montgomery's counter-attack at Alamein occurred in the same month and at roughly the same time as Zhukov's relieving counter-offensive at Stalingrad; Rommel's surrender marking the end of the North African campaign in January 1943 coincided with the defeat of Field Marshal Paulus's twenty-one German divisions scattered over the steppes of the besieged city on the edge of Asia, and the start of a new counter-push into the Soviet heartland. Likewise Costello's courses were entering a new phase.

Towards the end of the desert pursuit, with plans being made for the

Allied invasion of Sicily and the landings in southern Italy, the Bible class was superseded by impromptu mapboard lectures, with the latest Red Army moves picked out in coloured flags to engage the attention of visiting staff officers. It is not known how many profited from these courses of instruction, only that Second-Lieutenant Cleghorn, in private life an insurance clerk, did not proceed beyond the Cyrillic alphabet, and that by the time the Division got to Italy General Freyberg, ever anxious to learn "the broader picture", had become one of Costello's most devoted pupils.

From the Letters

1941, Cairo

1st July 1941
My darling Bil — What news? We are following the war in East Europe with attention. It seems that the Huns are going to break through near Minsk and that they may manage to get through to Leningrad. In which case, I fancy our newly acquired allies are foutus.

5 July 1941
Today's paper speaks of the "absurd heroism" of the Russian infantrymen, and somehow the vision of another 1812 is taking shape in my mind. You know, I always attached more weight to national traditions and characteristics than you did, and I think that the old Russian ability to take it on the chin and still carry on will save them now. I think it very fortunate that Russia is not populated with Italians . . . And so I can see the Russians first bogging the Nazi machine and then smashing it.

27th August 1941
Look, Bil, I wonder would you post me my Semonov's grammar and the little reader (not the key). I have a hunch that, after German, Russian is going to be the most useful language to know in this war.

Libyan Desert (Long Range Desert Group)

15th October 1941
My sweetest Bil
I reached here yesterday after a journey of several days. Just where I am I am not allowed to say. If you can recall "Légion d'Honneur" or any other French film of warfare in Morocco, you'll have an idea of the sort of house this is. A cool dwelling-place, very simple . . .

20 October
We've been in enemy territory now for several days. Tufts of dry camel-grass and thorny scrub. It is a country that grows on one: mal d'Africa, the Italians call this particular nostalgia.

24th 0945 hrs (ahem!)
You are obstinately convinced I am day dreaming when I talk of the war finishing soon. Well maybe but I do not think the Russians will ever be beaten. When we went out into Libya nearly a fortnight ago Moscow was "immediately threatened"; on our return, after hearing no news for quite a time, we find that Moscow is still threatened.

5 November 1941
You know, when we speak of destroying Fascism we tend to forget, or I have, that first and foremost of the victims of Fascism are the Italian and German people themselves. One of the four Italians, when captured this morning, put his finger on the red part of the Union Jack and said "*buono, buono*", and seemed by other things to indicate that his sympathy lay with the *communisti*. He was a lad of 21, just a child when Mussolini made his march

on Rome. He gave his profession as "landless peasant", and was also the wireless operator of the patrol. Extraordinary how the "red" infection can penetrate even through the blankets and bandages of Fascist propaganda continued for twenty years.

15th November
I have finished my little "Colloquial Arabic" and can now ask simple questions. Funny stuff this Semitic speech. Arabic is the hardest of the Semitic languages and if one mastered it, then the others — Hebrew, Phoenician Abysinnian and the rest — would be easy.

Cairo

12th December 1941
I arrived in Cairo the night before last. Flying was an interesting experience . . . But mark the sequel.

On the drome where I caught my second plane, who should turn up but Maj-Gen Freyberg, V.C. I bowled over to him and told him I was out of a job, and wot abaht it? He told me I could go to Divisional intelligence, where I would be a sort of coadjutor to Geoffrey Cox. And, girl, was I pleased! It pays to barge right in and damn the rules.

Monday 22nd December 1941
Some of our boys, casualties, are coming back from the Blue now [the Crusader offensive]. I met one officer in the mess today who had a bullet through the backside. Right through the *Sitzfleisch* without touching a bone. He was one of the chaps I came out of Greece with. He was in a casualty clearing station of ours where half the inmates were Jerries and the other half NZers. As the battle raged this way and that, the one half of the wounded would technically become the prisoners of the other. Thus the Jerry wounded twice captured Bill Roche and his companions without any of them getting out of bed. In the end it was the British tanks that shoved the Jerry ones back, and so all ended well. Bill Roche corroborates the evidence of all the other ex-captured I

have spoken to, that the Jerries treat their prisoners as well as they can. Not so the Eyetie rabble. There was an Eyetie guard put on during one of the periods when they were prisoners of the Jerries. This Eyetie went the tough way and shot one of our boys (I knew him) just for fun. But it was too bad for the Italian. When the British finally retook the place the Eyetie was recaptured too, and the NZ-ers lynched him: wouldn't shoot him, but knocked him over and kicked his face in till he died.

But what's the good of talking? C'est la guerre.

"A Fifth Wheel"

I have the marvellous prospect of seeing you again.
How long, O Lord?
— *Costello to his wife, February 1944*

OUTSIDE CASSINO THEY waited.

They were laagered in a wooded valley in southern Italy, between Naples and Rome. It was a beautiful spot in the Matese mountains, but the cold was relentless. Snow had come down from the hills, invading the camp and turning the ground to slush. The Division was in hiding — the New Zealanders still had their badges off and were observing wireless silence in a vain attempt to avoid identification by the enemy — awaiting its turn, after the Americans should they fail, to try and capture the town. Costello, chafing after his fourth Christmas separated from Bil, was waiting for Davin to return so he could begin his leave.

In Egypt each had earned three months' home leave, but Freyberg had insisted that only one could go. Costello had had less leave than Davin, but Davin had enlisted first. They drew straws. Davin won.

"Darlingest Bil," Costello wrote:

> The thought "so near and yet so far" was so painful that I decided not to tell you. Then I decided it would be better for you to see

> Dan when he arrived (his wife's in Bristol). He is a real Irish type. His nose is broken but he is distinctly good looking. He will call on you some time soon.

That was on 29 June 1943. It was now January '44. Where was he? Davin had been gone for over six months.

The Division had arrived in Italy — Bari on the Adriatic Coast — in November of the previous year. "Oh darling," he wrote on 27 November 1943, "Dan's leave will be up very soon and I am counting the days. We will have such a lot to talk about, when we have got beyond the stage of just sitting around and smiling at each other."

The next day General Freyberg's Division had gone into action on the Sangro River, with hopes of conquering Orsogna and opening up a path to Rome. Vain hope. The weather broke. Rain and mud turned to snow and ice. Stalemate set in. New Year brought a blizzard whose force bent the iron bars of the Intelligence truck holding up the canopy under which Costello slept. A bad-tempered Freyberg dragged his Division back across the bottom of Italy to where they were now.

Bil had sent him a photo of herself in a pullover. Costello carried it in his pay book. For some reason he preferred her in the mac. "I imagine you always in the long mac," he wrote. "Do you still wear it?"

He grew despondent, his temper as nasty as the weather, as the filthy little town of Alife outside whose ancient walls they were camped. His moods were broken by occasional ceremonial parades, training exercises and parties in the Intelligence truck. Much has been written about the revels in this vehicle where mud lay an inch thick on the floor of the steel tray. Howard Kippenberger was observed wiping his feet *before* he left the truck to step outside.

"We were very noisy in Intelligence," Tony Cleghorn recalls today. And Lieutenant-General Sir Leonard Thornton: "It was this little community set apart. I suppose one accepted that Intelligence people were a bit weird."

There was a singing chaplain, a left-handed staff officer who played the violin, and various strays from the Polish, French, Indian and American forces camped south of Cassino. Among the regulars were the exiled heir to the Greek throne, Prince Peter, who was living with the Division at the time, and Brigadier Kippenberger, both of whom came to yarn with Costello and play chess. Costello found the prince's chess unnerving, the latter barely pausing more than a few seconds between moves. Between games he and Prince Peter chatted in Greek. "Speaks quite good Greek, for a German," Costello remarked to Kippenberger.

"Everyone was roped in to sing," another habitué, Lawrence Nathan, recalled:

> We told stories and sang songs. Paddy was the centre of these gatherings. Men like wars and these nightly talk fests were some of the best things that happened in my war.

It had been going on since North Africa. But now at Cassino the monstrous cold persisted and the word *cafard* (depression) was on Costello's lips. Sometimes Tony Cleghorn would go for a leak and find Costello outside lying face down in a puddle of water, out cold.

Rome — he had told Bil they would be in Rome for Christmas — seemed as far off as ever.

And where on earth *was* Davin?

It was the morning of 23 January 1944. Costello had discarded his boots and was seated in the truck with his maps, his feet frozen and wrapped in a greatcoat, when Tony Cleghorn brought a message to say the Americans had landed at Anzio. Costello nodded and returned to the Sitrep he was writing.

"This place is like a morgue," he heard a voice say.

"There's no charcoal," Costello said. "I've got chilblains. Bloody brasier's given out." Then, "*Gesù Cristo,*" he said, recognising the face leering up at him and kicking over the brasier as he clambered out of the truck. He got down. They embraced. "What kept you?" he said.

"Did you see Bil?" Costello asked, as they walked across to the mess for morning tea. Yes. Davin had been to Exeter, taken presents for everyone as instructed. Met Bil, met her sisters, met the children, Mick, seven, and Josie, three. And the grandparents. Half the Lerner tribe seemed to be there. Bil was working in a munitions factory.

"But what kept you?" Costello kept saying.

It wasn't Davin's fault. Davin had underestimated the army's treachery, he said. Landing in Italy, he had been sent to the Adriatic coast, only to discover the Division wasn't there. He had recrossed the peninsula and spent a week looking for them. He arrived disorganised. He had crashed a military vehicle, forgotten his tent and bedding at Corps Headquarters and, not unnaturally, complained when Costello offered him a bed without blankets. The news that Davin had seen Bil in Exeter upset Costello.

"You take over tomorrow," he said.

He introduced Davin to Cleghorn, to the wireless operators. They reported in. Thornton, the G2 (Operations), said he was glad to welcome Davin back, in time to take over the reins from Costello's "nerveless fingers" — a facetious remark from a younger man which at the time Costello seemed to laugh off. But that night the recriminations began. In the mess he began to attack Davin for being late.

As Davin reports it, "There was nothing new in this, except the ferocity of the recrimination which one could forgive because of the long strain of work and battle he had been enduring." Recrimination turned to abuse. They quarrelled bitterly. The area was dry but Davin had acquired two bottles of cognac which went quickly to Costello's head. Costello in his cups "knew just what to say that would hurt you most". His Parthian shot just before he collapsed and had to be put to bed was to accuse Davin of being a false friend and of rigging the straw poll that had given him leave first.

Next day both men behaved as if nothing had happened. Davin, officially appointed G3 (Intelligence) took over. But, again according to Davin, the General's welcome was "a trifle perfunctory. Freyberg, a master of rearguard action, continued to work to Paddy as if I had not taken over." Davin found himself strangely frustrated.

In the truck the telephone would ring.

"Is that you, Paddy?"

"No, sir, it's Davin speaking."

"Oh, it's you Davin. Is Paddy there?"

"No, I'm afraid he's away somewhere, sir."

Costello meantime would be sitting opposite Davin, waving his pipe fiercely in an imitation of absence.

"Very well then, Davin."

And the General would ring off.

It was Davin's first inkling of Costello's new status. Davin was finding it hard to get on top of a deluge of malignant maps, reports and the daily Intelligence Summary — "How difficult to succeed such a man," he wrote, "and me out of the army these six months." He was feeling guilty. For the straw ballot *had* been rigged, he discovered. It was the General's doing.

On 30 January 1944 Costello wrote in his diary, "Dan got here on the

23rd and I have become more and more of a fifth wheel." Freyberg had been due to release Costello the following day. Instead he sent him to a conference at American Fifth Army Headquarters. Costello suspected he may have done his job in the past "too well" and was being kept on to break Davin in gently. The General's equivocation continued. Gradually it dawned on them both that a certain attachment had formed. Freyberg did not want to let Costello go.

When Davin rejoined the Division at Alife, the Americans, succeeding the French, were battling with absurd gallantry and losses to cross the Rapido River and storm the German defences at Cassino. In vain. "Yanks buggered," Davin recorded. The French having tried and failed, the Americans retired, fought out. It was the turn of New Zealand. Freyberg was now commanding a New Zealand Corps, comprising New Zealand, Indian and American troops. On 11 February the New Zealand Division went into the line under the command of Kippenberger. On 14 February 1944, three weeks after Davin's return, Costello was still there awaiting the order to begin his leave.

What followed no one foresaw. Not the loss of Major-General (as he was about to become) Kippenberger who stepped on a mine on Mount Trocchio and lost both feet. Not the repeated failure of the New Zealand Corps to dislodge the enemy from Cassino. Nor, to keep to the point, General Freyberg's obstinate refusal to part with Costello. He continued to hedge.

"Twisting and turning to avert letting him go," Davin wrote in his diary. "Simple as a child," he added, quoting Kippenberger, "and cunning as a Maori dog."

Davin suspected it was to do with Russia.

When he first entered Freyberg's caravan at Alife, Davin found himself confronted by three maps showing three fronts: "ours, the European front and the Russian front". The map of the Russian front filled an entire wall. Picked out in Russian script were the names of the towns taken or retaken by the Red Army. Davin was working until midnight, his truck "full of the things I should be reading and learning". Yet every morning he had to be up for the seven o'clock BBC bulletin, listening for news of the Red Army. To subdue the mountain stronghold of Cassino required every ounce of ingenuity and focus; the Germans had built concrete and reinforced steel dugouts and pillboxes all over Monastery Hill; Cassino was holding up the entire Allied advance, it "dominated one's whole horizon". Yet here he was scurrying to the General's caravan, with the General thirsting for news of the Russian front. "A hedgehog bristling with awkward questions."

It was largely because of Costello's influence. "No word of Paddy's departure," Davin wrote. "His stature dwarfs me into belittling myself and I become anaemic."

Freyberg's interest in the Russian front had quickened earlier that winter on the Adriatic front — on the Sangro River — according to Murray Sidey, the General's aide-de-camp. The General's interest had been growing since Costello's "Bible classes" in the desert, to the point of becoming during the Sangro campaign almost an obsession with him. It was a by-product of being hemmed in by weather and terrain; of frustration; of Freyberg's nostalgia for the desert and his envy of the scope and space the Soviet generals had for battle, able to deploy their tanks and manoeuvre freely in the open steppes. As Sidey said,

> The General was dependent on Paddy. Paddy used to go and chat to him about Russia.* He'd have his chinagraph pencil and go straight to the map on the wall. Everyone else had to wait outside. Paddy, a mere captain, would go straight in.

One morning, rising late, Costello missed the seven o'clock wireless bulletin. He was making his way towards C Mess when he encountered the General, driving out. "Oh Paddy — " Freyberg stopped the car and demanded a situation report. Costello fumbled. He invented a cock and bull story about the number of German divisions penned up by the Red Army in the Dnieper bend. The General listened intently. Then his mouth shut tight, the lips almost disappeared. He motioned to the driver to proceed.

"Thank you very much, Mr Costello," he said. "I shall keep you informed."

---

* Also about literature. The General's favourite author was Jane Austen. Freyberg had been denied permission to go up to Balliol to study as a young man and was, like Howard Kippenberger who envied Costello the chance he never had to go to university, a thwarted intellectual. Both men had a respect for scholarship and an appetite for intellectual debate. A few days before the Division's final engagement at Cassino, Kippenberger refought the Battle of Galighiano between the Spanish and the French (1504) with Costello in the "I" truck. Also see McNeish, *Dance of the Peacocks*, page 235, and Cox, *The Race for Trieste,* pp. 34-5.

Freyberg's Headquarters at the time were across the Sangro, at a place called Casoli in the Majella mountains. It was from here that Freyberg sent Costello one day to accompany a delegation of Soviet officers arriving to inspect the New Zealand sector during the offensive. Five Red Army generals and their aides arrived accompanied by Montgomery's chief of staff, General Sir Frederick de Guingand. Costello, speaking Russian, interpreted for de Guingand and conducted the visitors round the fighting. This was on 10 December 1943, two months before Cassino was bombed.

The aerial bombardment that reduced the Benedictine monastery of Monte Cassino to rubble occurred on the morning of 15 February 1944. There has been speculation that in taking the decision to destroy this ancient and picturesque monument to Christian culture, Freyberg was influenced by his two Intelligence officers, Davin and Costello, both militant atheists. The rumours were abetted perhaps by the coincidence of Costello's departure from the scene that very morning. But the speculation is false. Davin had his hands full, while Costello, mutinous and fuming at the General's "perfidy", was in no mood to advise anyone. For a day or two he had stayed around:

> 32 today, curse it! [he noted on 31 January 1944] I had hoped to be with Bil on my birthday . . . But Christ! Fancy having to clip the fetters on and start the treadmill again. Fuck 'em all!

Costello absented himself. He visited the Americans and the Poles and returned only to sleep, arriving out of the night blown by gusts of rain or head down tilted towards the cold, leaving Davin to cope on his own. One day he visited the French. He went from Corps HQ to Divisional HQ to Regimental HQ and eventually reached the front. Jonesie drove him in a Jeep. The route took them beyond Sant' Elia, round Mount Trocchio. They found the French dug in on a forward slope overlooking the Rapido valley. Several times, negotiating craters and dead horses, the Jeep almost left the road. As they approached the front, every half mile or so they passed a notice adorned with a death's head. "*L'ennemi vous voit. Ne stationnez pas.*" "The enemy can see you. No loitering," Costello translated for Jonesie. They were in full view of the German guns at Cassino. Costello stayed at the front, chatting and swapping slang with the French gunners — "*Ça cogne* (That was close)" — as shells whined overhead and crashed around them.

Once again he felt "the old sensation of constriction in the stomach and tautness of nerves". The batman, he noticed, said nothing. This surprised him. He considered Jonesie an amateur of horrors. In the desert the jaunty West Coaster had inspected burnt-out tanks at close range, "giving me vivid descriptions of the dead. The horror of mutilated men doesn't seem to affect him at all." Now in front of Cassino the batman turned pale.

Perhaps it was here (courtesy Jonesie) that the myth began. Of Costello's immunity. His disregard for danger. Those "nerveless fingers" that Leonard Thornton recalled. After months of conditioning on reconnaissance with Freyberg, having emerged from the battles of Minqar Qaim, Alamein, Medenine and the Mareth Line without so much as a scratch, perhaps something, some idea of Costello the Unkillable, had rubbed off. It was a fantasy. Naturally Costello did not deny it. Perhaps it was true. Perhaps he was immune. After all, Bernard Freyberg had been told by a soothsayer he would "never die in battle", nor had he. Freyberg "the happy warrior" had kept Costello at his side for so long that something was bound to rub off.

"Shelling never hurt anyone," he would say to Costello, despite the multiple wounds with which his body was decorated. "It's aimed fire you've got to watch out for."

Perhaps Costello had even come to believe it himself.

For all that, visiting the French in front of Cassino that February morning, he kept his eyes peeled and, like the Wazza-wazza bird, "watched where we were coming from".

"Christ!" he wrote to Bil on 8 February 1944 after a telegram he sent her had not been answered. "Here I am, still in the frightful land of not knowing when I shall get free. I am just wasting my time here." On 13 February Davin wrote in his diary, "1155. On wireless duty. P[addy] tight at lunch and asleep ever since in my bed. So I've got his."

Finally, on a Tuesday morning two days later, with snow falling on the ground and the first Flying Fortresses grumbling overhead on their way to bomb the monastery, Freyberg sent for Costello and told him he was free to go on leave. It would be another two years, inviting the pair to dine with him in London, before the General attempted to explain his apparent duplicity.

Davin went with Costello to the highway. They said goodbye. He describes their parting on Highway Six, the Roman Via Casalina:

> He looked along the road towards Cassino and said, like the first-

> rate Intelligence officer he was, "When I come back in three months' time, the Germans will still be in Cassino and the Gustav Line will still have to be broken."

A month later Costello was still in Italy, in the grip now of Army Movement Control. He was sitting on a Court of Inquiry at Caserta. He was just far enough forward to hear the guns at Cassino where two New Zealand brigades — six infantry battalions, supported by tanks — were engaged in a last-ditch but fruitless assault to dislodge the German paratroopers defending the town. General Freyberg's New Zealand Corps, at a cost of 343 New Zealand lives, was about to admit defeat and withdraw.

Costello was right, as Davin had said, to the month. It would take a new plan and a fresh onslaught by the Poles for the eventual break-through at Cassino in May. But Costello would not return. Although he did not know it, he was on his way to Moscow.

From the Letters

1942, Middle East

3 January 1942 [Cairo]
My sweetest Bil
Last week I bought a nice Italian edition of the Roman poet Lucretius. This gentleman has a terrific description of the "act" of love, the only realistic one I have ever found. I have copied it out inside the cover of my field message pad, to inspire me when I need inspiration!

3rd August 1942
Out here your hearing gets very acute. You learn to hold your head aslant in a way which deflects the full force of the wind from your ears and allows you to pick up sounds that otherwise you would miss. I am always conscious, or sub-conscious, of the presence of hot metal in the air, and realise that I am not armour-plated. (My batman ran away a fortnight ago and hasn't been seen since.)

You learn to distinguish the different types of explosion: the sustained bumping of bombs; the boost of a shell being fired, a sound reminiscent of a football being kicked; the cr-r-ump of shells bursting, very gruff, resonant like a door banging in an empty house; the difference between the chatter of a German machine gun and of a British. Needless to say, the German weapons have a sinister sound to our ears, while we are charmed by the kindly aspect of the Boston bomber or the Spitfire.

25th August 1942
Did I tell you I have a camera? Looted it off a German officer.

October 1942
Stalingrad has been a principal worry for six weeks now; but it looks as if my confidence (expressed to all doubters on this HQ) will be justified & the town will hold.

15th October 1942
I have just re-read a poem which throws some light on my July letters to you. The lines are:

The wind rises in the evening,
Reminds me that autumn is near.
I am afraid to lose you,
I am afraid of my fear.

On the last mile to Huesca,
The last fence for my pride . . .

Do you remember this poem of John's?* "I am afraid to lose you, I am afraid of my fear."

Still October:
I have been learning to use my camera. Last night, watching me

* "[To Margot Heinemann]" — *Poems from Spain, 1936* (John Cornford, *Collected Writings,* Carcanet Press 1986)

pawing the thing, Dan Davin remarked that the sight suggested to him a Goth in Rome curiously inspecting Greek temples.

12 December 1942 [Barce, Cyrenaica, after Alamein]
. . . a pleasant little town, if you don't look too closely. Before our conquest the price of tea was over 1000 lire per kilo. Tea & sugar will open most doors between Tobruk and Benghazi. I am told that one chap got into the museum at Cyrene for a half mugful of tea and then, for another half, persuaded the Arab overseer to turn his back while he abstracted the odd Parian marble. One might, in the language of economics, describe this phenomenon as "a flight into real values".

1943, North Africa

19th March 1943
What a lot of sand we've covered since we broke through the Hun lines on 4 Nov! When we came down from Syria in June last year, we had a good division; now we have a good army.

2nd July 1943
I don't remember the pullover you are wearing in this photo. In the photo your eyes are still humorous, your hair soft brown, your mouth wry. Darling Bil, do go on loving me; I'd die if I lost you.

1944, Italy

19th March 1944 [Caserta]

Still here. I am on a Court of Inquiry.

Yesterday I was at a Yank hospital and happened to catch sight of some of the survivors of the last battle for Cassino: chaps with stove-in foreheads, chaps that had lost an ear and chaps with stumps of hands. This afternoon I hope to visit the hospital where our own General Kippenberger is, minus both feet. I hate to hear people running down the Yank soldiers and I'd hate to hear civilians in England with no experience of war sneering.

As to my departure, don't despair. It is two months since Dan came back, but it wouldn't be the army if one were not buggered about. Nevertheless, one of these days I will be knocking at the door — "gardez-vous bien la nuit".

PART THREE
TO RUSSIA & BACK

1944–1950

The General's Telegram

Mr Fraser decided, while possessing the information*
. . . to appoint Costello to Moscow, stating that this
would probably be the means of disillusioning him.
— *New Zealand SIS file, 1950*

HE REACHED ENGLAND in April. Two-and-a-half months after Davin took over, Costello's leave became operational. He got away attaching himself as assistant to an American general who was flying from Italy, via Algiers and Casablanca, to England. Costello landed at Prestwich in Lancashire on 7 April 1944 and took the train next day to Exeter. From Waterloo he wired Bil that he was arriving by the 12.50 "from Wellington", an indication perhaps of his state of mind. Bil met him at Exeter Central.

She was wearing the long mac he remembered. She had come straight from the munitions factory, her face flushed from the furnaces still: her small figure with the wide lashes and high cheekbones, thick auburn hair, penetrating eyes and wry smile that he had pictured in thoughts and letters, and in the photograph of her he carried in his army pay book, still had the power to take his breath away.

He has lost weight, Bil thought. Fined down on legs thin as stilts. Crane-

* Unclear (reference blacked out), but probably refers to Costello's communist sympathies and his activities in 1936–7 in support of Republican Spain.

like, as he dropped his kit and bent down to hold and kiss her.

He had grown a silly little moustache. Changed somehow, she thought. It wasn't just the moustache, nor the face, tanned and lined from screwing up the eyes against sun and sand, but everything. Trained so lean and fine the uniform seemed an embarrassment on the body, on the razor-thin shoulders and hips. Just skin over bone, really. Yet somehow he was stronger.

He blinked a lot.

They wheeled her bicycle through the town, his kit balanced on the handlebars. He hardly recognised the place. Much of the city centre had been destroyed by incendiaries, the so-called Baedecker raids of 1942. The streets were bounded by piles of rubble and knee-high walls. No traffic. He counted one army lorry and two bicycles. Half the university including the registry appeared to have been burned out. At No. 9 Longbrook Terrace, the house they had rented, there was rejoicing. He had brought a couple of bottles of good Italian brandy for Momma and Totta, Bil's parents. Presents for everyone. Mick asked for a tommy gun and showed him the bomb shelter at the end of the street. Mick, four when he went away, was now an alert seven-year-old. He had something of Bil's amused look, wry and quizzical. Josie, three, was already chattering in Yiddish. This delighted him. He soon had Mick singing German and Italian folksongs with him. They were both musical, Bil said. Josie, he hardly knew — gap-toothed, a mass of golden curls. She was "a Dunkirk baby". Josie's birth in 1940 had coincided with the Dunkirk emergency and his dismissal from the university.

While he was away Bil had met up with some of his old university colleagues. He was still black-listed, she said.

This was one of the things they talked about, before the telegram came. What would he do when the war was over?

It was a difficult homecoming. He had planned a belated honeymoon. It wasn't possible. So much to talk about, yet so much he couldn't talk about. They started another baby. They had been married eight years and were as much in love as ever. But there were questions, "nerve storms". And not only to do with sexual relations. He had become attuned to listening. To the bumping of gunfire and the coming of shells — goers? or comers? The slightest noise distracted him and brought a reaction. He did daft things. Tried to get Totta drunk. Dangled Josie over a manhole and almost dropped her. Stepped in front of a lorry, daring it to hit him. Luckily there weren't many lorries about. What was troubling him?

"I have the marvellous prospect of seeing you again," he had written from Italy. Bil was the centre of his universe, he wrote. It was true. Everything he had written was true, all his emotional capital belonged to her despite the infidelities in Cairo and elsewhere — his "couchées", as he put it to himself. She had once, perhaps foolishly, raised the question of faithfulness in a letter, saying he could decide for himself the correct behaviour for grass widowers. But then, more foolishly still, she had asked for his views "on how grass widows should comport themselves". To which he had replied, "As they like." It was probably the most hurtful thing he could have said.

He continued to be jumpy and do silly things. She did not always know what he was thinking. Once in Italy, abandoned to introspection, he had shot up the room he was sleeping in. He had emptied his Smith and Wesson revolver at the electric light and shattered the wires. Six shots. "Not bad," he wrote in his diary, "for a drunken man, one boot on and the other boot off." He had told himself he would not get drunk but once started on the bottle, he had been unable to stop. It was after midnight. In the morning when the chap in the next room said a shutter had woken him banging in the night, "with a crack as sharp as a pistol-shot", he had to slap his face with cold water to hide his laughter. Crazy, he told her. Or, more likely, didn't tell her.

It was the sort of thing a psychopath might have done. But Costello had awoken the morning after feeling refreshed, pervaded by a sense of relief.

The trouble with Exeter was, they were not alone there. Besides Mick and Josie and Bil's parents, who had been living with her since they were bombed out in Hackney, there were Bil's sister Doris and Doris's three children, one a baby, and also a sister-in-law. The house in Longbrook Terrace was full. Also, because Bil's father acted as rabbi to the local Jewish community, there were frequent callers. Bil's job, renovating shells in a furnace factory, involved long hours. They were seldom alone in the house to talk.

"I keep waiting for something to happen to me," he had told himself in Egypt, "to make me suddenly start writing, some thunderbolt which will break the bonds that have held down until now such talents as I may have." But nothing happened. "Perhaps," he had day-dreamed, "if I were with Bil again?"

Now he was with Bil again, and the future seemed as uncertain as ever. He said, "I won't teach classics, unless I have to."

"What do you want to do?" she said to him.

Write, he said.

More than anything, he said, he wanted to write. Journalism, perhaps?

He had the example of Dan Davin before him, also Geoffrey Cox. Both were published authors. Costello was convinced he could do better than either of them. After all, he had the material to write. That's why he had been keeping a diary, wasn't it? Themes suggested themselves; they were spilling out of him; all he had to do was make them into art.

Like many academics capable of dissecting an argument and presenting a lucid exposition on paper, Costello assumed that writing — creative writing — would not be difficult.

"I wouldn't mind that job in Moscow," he said to her.

He had been reading a play in Russian — Chekhov's *Three Sisters* — one day when he saw in the *NZEF Times*, the troops' newspaper, that the New Zealand government was considering opening a diplomatic post in Moscow. He had written off to Geoff Cox in Washington, asking him to put in a word for him. "It is too good to count on," he confided to his diary. "But if one managed to get it . . . "

But that was August, the previous summer. Seven months had elapsed. He had heard nothing more.

"The war will soon be over. Something will turn up," he said to her. He gave it six months, a year at the outside. He would go back to the Division and stay till the war ended. Unless? He remembered Davin's Oxford friend in Cairo, Bill Williams. Williams was the one who'd got him into Eighth Army to do the Italian handbook. Williams was now back in England with Montgomery, helping to plan the Allied landings in France. "Wouldn't that be terrific?" he said to Bil. If he could wangle a transfer and get in on a second front? Williams was now a brigadier and Monty's top man in Intelligence. That would surely lead to something. He put it to her. She nodded, without conviction. They were in this state of indecision when, three weeks into his leave, on 27 April 1944, the telegram came.

It was from the General. Freyberg wired from Italy that the New Zealand government, learning of Captain Costello's linguistic ability, had written to inquire if he might be released from his army duties, to take up a diplomatic position in the Soviet Union. The government intended opening a legation there. Freyberg, after deliberating and with the approval of the Army Board, had granted the request. The telegram added that the New Zealand Prime

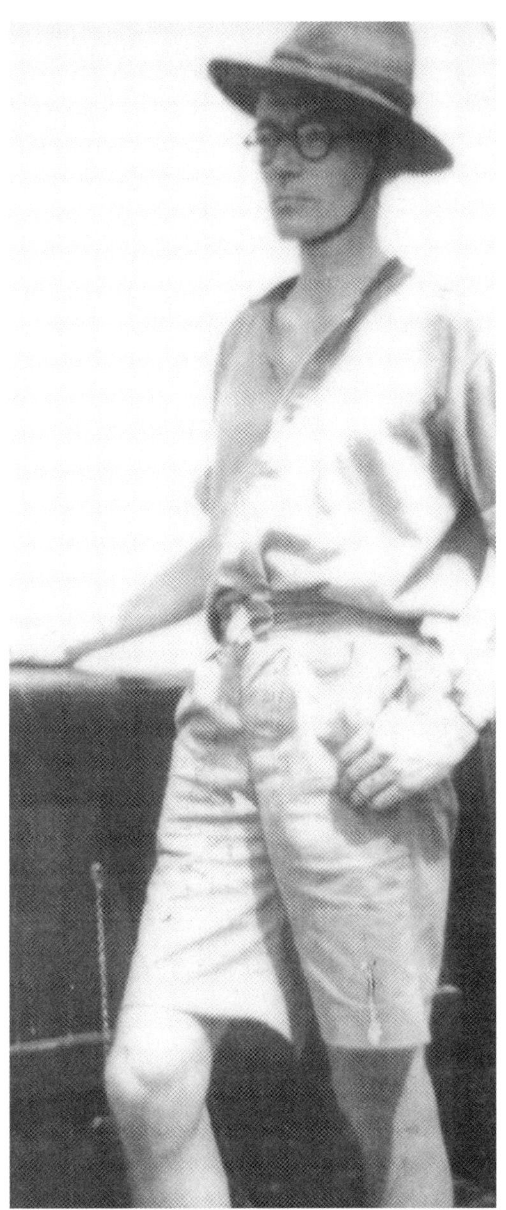

Previous page: German tanks fording the River Pinios at the start of the Battle of Tempe, prelude to the "pasting" taken by 21 Battalion and Costello's escape from Greece to Crete. The drivers of the two tanks ahead of the infantry assault gun in the foreground are under water.

Left: General Freyberg watching the assault on Canea from his headquarters dugout during the battle for Crete, May 1941.

Above left: Colonel N.L. (Polly) Macky, commander 21 Battalion — "the unluckiest battalion in the Division".

Above right: Lance-corporal Costello, sailing for the Middle East in 1941.

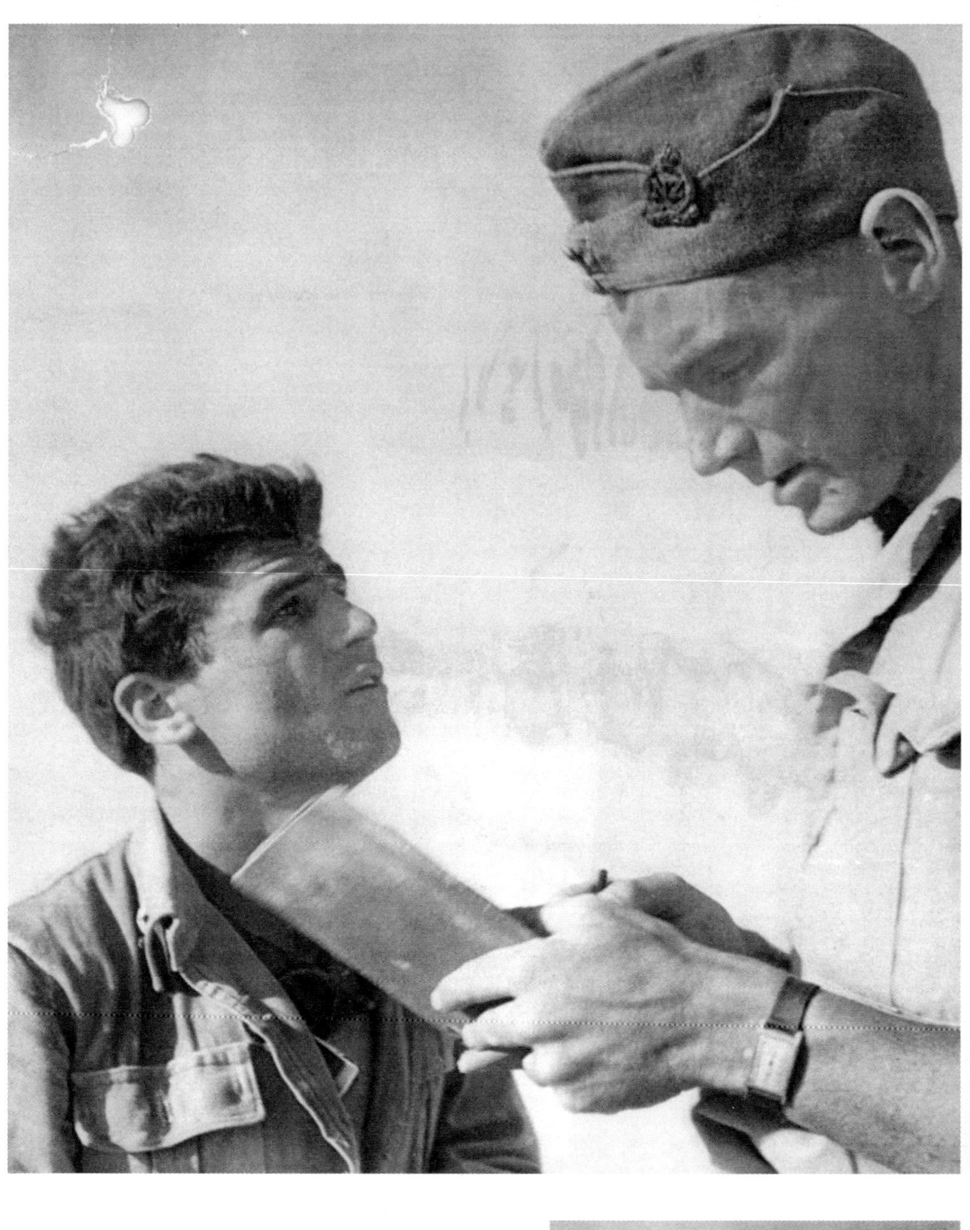

Top left: Middle East, summer of the Flap, before Alamein. Costello interrogating an Italian prisoner in 1942. Dan Davin observed, "how swiftly his technique adjusted itself to the different characters and how rapidly he got from them whatever information they might have to give".

Bottom left: Costello in 1943, Western Desert, after Alamein.

Above: Italy, summer 1944. Dan Davin (left) after he succeeded Costello in General Freyberg's HQ at Cassino. With Davin are Geoffrey Cox and the General. When the photograph was taken, Costello was arriving in Moscow to open New Zealand's "first hardship post".

2

LOT OF THESE (YOU MUST NEVER BE ONE OF

(DATES

THEM!), AND PLENTY OF DATE-PALMS AND

PYRAMIDS AS WELL AS A LOT OF

EYETIE PRISONERS AND MOSQUES

FULL STOP

I AM AN OFFICER NOW, INSTEA

OF A LANCE-CORPORAL, AS I WAS WHEN YOU

SAW ME LAST. THE DIFFERENCE BETWEEN AN

OFFICER AND A LANCE-CORPORAL IS THAT YOU

ALWAYS HAVE TO SAY SIR TO AN OFFICER AND

YOU MAKE HIM PAY MORE FOR EVERYTHING.

LAST WEEK I WAS ON A TRUCK

WHEN A BIG AIRPLANE

Page from a letter to Costello's six-year-old son, Mick, in England, sent from the Western Desert, 1942.

Above: Dan Davin, Costello's closest friend. Geoffrey Cox called them blood brothers.

Following page: The Vale of Tempe today. "A road, a river, and the railway" — with, in the middle left, the small plain veering south to Larissa. Behind are the foothills of Mount Olympus.

Minister, Peter Fraser, was due in England to attend a conference. Costello accordingly should hold himself ready to be interviewed in London and, if approved, to undergo a familiarisation tour with the Foreign Office before departing for Moscow.

He showed the telegram to Bil. "But — ?" she said. Her response was unexpected. She said nothing for a minute. Then: "But it means giving up your leave!" Costello's reaction was also equivocal. After the initial puff to his vanity had subsided, he was plunged into gloom and uncertainty.

How had it happened? So suddenly?

The received wisdom, as I wrote in *Dance of the Peacocks*, is that Costello already knew when he left Cassino that he was on his way to Moscow. But his journal makes it clear that Freyberg's telegram containing the government's proposal came as a surprise, catching him unawares. His despondency came from a fear of being compromised, his worry that the government should learn of his dismissal from Exeter and come to view him as a security risk. "Gloom" may be too strong. "Tension" is the word Costello uses in his diary — "the tension created in my mind by the ambiguous situation my appointment to the Moscow job puts me into."

Central to the appointment were two men, Alister McIntosh in Wellington, and Geoffrey Cox in Washington. Cox had been McIntosh's first choice for the Moscow legation.

In conservative New Zealand Russophobia was widespread; ten years of socialism under a Labour government had not dislodged the root of a nation's psyche. Just how this post, New Zealand's only diplomatic mission outside the English-speaking world, came about at a time when the national press and body politic were almost uniformly hostile to the Soviet Union, despite the heroic sacrifices of the Red Army in battle, is described in Malcolm Templeton's splendid little history, *Top Hats Are Not Being Taken*. Essentially the post was the creation of the Labour Prime Minister, Peter Fraser, who saw representation in Moscow as a step towards having New Zealand's voice heard among the major powers in any postwar European settlement. But Fraser's plan would almost certainly have been stillborn without his chief of staff, McIntosh. Embracing the idea, McIntosh first wrote to Geoffrey Cox in Washington and offered him the job of First Secretary. Cox with his Oxford education and journalistic skills was a natural choice. But Cox declined — he had been in the Washington legation for two years and hated it — saying he wanted to return to the army. Cox wanted his old job with Freyberg again. It was Costello, we remember, who had taken Cox's job in the desert, before Alamein; now Cox wanted it back.

It was the sort of problem that Alister McIntosh, with his funambulist gift for crossing the wire when everything around him had begun to blur and sway, was practised at solving. He was a historian by training but a subdued adventurer at heart. McIntosh had been sitting in his Wellington office one morning at the end of 1943 when his eye fell on a newspaper item datelined "December 10, Sangro River". It was headed:

RUSSIAN OFFICERS
Visit to NZ Sector
EIGHTH ARMY FRONT

The article described the visit by a party of Russian generals to the New Zealanders fighting on the Sangro. They had been shown around by a Russian-speaking New Zealand officer. The Russians "were amazed to find a New Zealander who could talk and joke with them in their own language". As McIntosh told Cox later, "It struck me that if a man could crack Russian jokes, he might participate effectively in the New Zealand–Russian joke No. 1 — namely the establishment of a New Zealand post in Moscow. Accordingly I sent a message off asking for identification of this humorous linguist."

At this stage McIntosh was attempting to fill the post with a team of stablehands lacking diplomatic experience, and hardly a linguist in sight. Costello was a gift from the gods.

As for positive vetting — the security matter that was making Costello nervous in Exeter — steps taken by McIntosh followed a predictable old-boy network. He had consulted first the army and then Cox. "A rather remarkable young man," the army reported back from the Middle East, after identifying Captain Costello. "He would be suitable for any appointment." Cox had some political reservations. He described Costello's "rigidity of mind [that] may mean he is another Sutch".★ But, he added, "Costello

★ William Ball Sutch (1907–1975), New Zealand economist and Marxist, author of *The Quest for Security in New Zealand* (1942) and one of the country's 20th-century "nation-builders". In 1932 Dr Sutch visited the Soviet Union. In 1975 in Wellington he would be tried on a charge of obtaining information helpful to an enemy, and acquitted.

would insist on his views openly." Cox had studied Marxism and spent hours in the desert arguing with Costello, often hotly. Today he recalls:

> Paddy and I got on but I was wary. He assumed I thought he was a traitor and on the same basis I assumed he thought I was a fascist hyena.
>
> Nothing about Paddy ever led me to believe he was an undercover man. What I was saying to McIntosh was watch out, he's a Marxist, a man of the extreme left. But he's open about it. Take this chap but read his despatches with a long spoon.

There was an irony here, for unknown to the New Zealand government Cox himself had almost joined the Communist Party (in 1937 over Spain). By 1944 however he had moved to the centre and was one of the few reliable weathervanes on the international scene the Dominion possessed; his word was trusted. Cox's recommendation clinched the matter. All that remained was for Costello to come to London and meet the New Zealand Prime Minister for his approval.

The meeting took place at the Savoy Hotel in May 1944. Buzz bombs were falling on London as the Prime Minister arrived to attend a Commonwealth heads of government meeting, with a delegation led by McIntosh. Cox, on his way back to military service in Italy, was also in London attending the conference. Costello was ushered into Peter Fraser's suite at the Savoy Hotel. Introduced by McIntosh, he said to the Prime Minister, "I'm afraid I'm a bit left-wing, sir." "That's all right," the Prime Minister is reported to have replied, "we can do with one or two communists in Moscow."

Costello began his tour with the Foreign Office, learning how to become a diplomat, the next day, while Bil who had travelled up with him from Devon prepared to return to Exeter and the children. She was distressed. Not only was his leave sabotaged but also a short holiday together they were planning — the delayed honeymoon he had promised her. Not even the few quiet days in London she had anticipated worked out. Costello had been asked to prepare for Mr Fraser, given three-and-a-half minutes' advance warning, a paper on the status of the various republics in the Russian Federation. He was still revising it when the train reached Paddington. In the streets the atmosphere was pervaded by V-1 flying bombs grumbling overhead and landing randomly in the city, causing widespread damage.

They had booked into a small B & B in Kensington. They spent the first nights sleeping under the hotel in the shelter, after the windows of their room blew in, sash and glass, the hotel clock having stopped at 2.31 in the morning. Then, on top of everything, Bil learned that a condition of her husband's acceptance of the post was that he go to Moscow alone. At this stage she — although McIntosh would not come clean about it until later — was considered the liability, not he.

Geoffrey Cox recalls:

> Paddy picked me up and we went to dinner at an Italian restaurant off Trafalgar Square. For some reason I was wearing a shirt a shade too big. Paddy met me in the lobby. "Good god, man," he said. "You're all collar!" Typical Paddy.
>
> I was staying at the Savoy with the New Zealand delegation. I was on my way to Italy hoping to rejoin the Div. — the job Paddy had just vacated. Paddy was already being briefed for Moscow by the Foreign Office. Bil was there too, a slightly strange figure in a raincoat. In the course of the meal she suddenly turned to me and said, "What's the snag about this job? Why have you landed Paddy in it?"

Bil's suspicions more properly should have been directed at Alister McIntosh whose elusive approach had kept them in the dark and who had told Costello, not understanding the strain it would put him under or realising Bil was pregnant with their third child, that she would not be welcome in Moscow. Later when the child was born McIntosh would waive his veto. For the moment however Bil was the least of his problems.

THE FIRST HARDSHIP POST

The establishment of a post in the Soviet Union
. . . was New Zealand's first "hardship" post.
— *Malcolm Templeton,* Top Hats Are Not Being Taken

A QUESTION OF CLOTHING

25 May 1944, London

Memorandum, McIntosh to Costello:

I have arranged with Foreign Office for you to be taken around in whatever section seems most suitable. Suggest you get in touch with Sir Cecil Day. Yr location allowance will be £500. NZ have advised this. Their opinion on the question of clothing is a little obscure.

24 May 1944, Wellington

Memorandum, External Affairs to McIntosh

SECRET

Clothing for Costello. Following is being adopted by Minister and Staff. Full dress evening suit, dinner suit, black coat (not morning) and vest and striped trousers, lounge suits and sports suit. Ordinary galoshes also boot galoshes covering ankles of rubber the latter to have tops fabric or leather lined which we have ordered in Washington for immediate despatch to New Zealand. Suggest Costello obtain his while there or in United Kingdom, also dress footwear.

We are having long lambskin coats made with outer surface of Gabardine. A good warm cloth overcoat is also recommended by Australian Legation which advises in addition, furlined coat. We have not examined cost of latter but have been informed by a local resident previously living in Russia that they are "de rigueur" for official classes, sheepskin coats being associated with peasantry. Furlined boots suggested for severe weather and we are investigating possibility of flying boots being made available.

Fur caps and furlined gloves are recommended. Top hats are not being taken.

A Question of Furniture

15 July 1944, Christchurch *Press*
Enquiries are now being made for furnishings for the New Zealand Legation in Moscow.

The lounge and salon of the Minister's residence will be furnished with 10 Chesterfields, 20 easy chairs and 12 fireside chairs, as well as three wireless sets, palm stands, cocktail and china cabinets, six standard lamps, firescreens, sparkguards and nine occasional tables.

The Minister's dining-room is to seat 12 persons, and will have only one sideboard, but it is to be large. Its efficiency will be added to by a waiter's cabinet, two dinner wagons and a clock.

Apart from a billiard table, two more settees and three smokers' companions are needed for the billiard room.

The instigator of the last item was the first secretary, a jovial tub-shaped bachelor named Patrick who emerges in a group photograph without benefit of Christian name. While Costello was being briefed at the Foreign Office in England, Patrick was instructed to draw up (courtesy, Public Works Department, Interior Decorating section) the above schedule in Wellington. The schedule also allowed for a quota of palm stands, smokers' companions and fireside chairs for each secretary, besides two wireless sets for each of the second secretaries, although the first secretary for some reason was allowed only one.

"I don't think there was a hall or passage or living room in the Legation or meanest secretary's apartment," McIntosh wrote, "that did not have its quota of palm stands and smokers' companions, whatever they may be; and what more natural than that they should include spark and fire guards to each room?"

In fairness it must be said that Patrick lacked any first-hand experience in setting up a diplomatic establishment and the Prime Minister, Peter Fraser, when McIntosh persuaded him to see the funny side, burst out laughing and cancelled the lot. But not before the news had travelled, inducing howls of derision from the parliamentary opposition. An augury of troubled times ahead.

"My Old Man of the Sea"

The Minister had arrived in Moscow as an
earnest Fabian socialist with an open mind . . .
— *Malcolm Templeton,* Top Hats Are Not Being Taken

ALISTER MCINTOSH WAS an elusive personality. In manner he was shy and deceptively self-effacing. Some thought him aloof. Very few colleagues addressed him as "Mac". Yet from his letters a different picture emerged, that of a man who was lively, witty and dangerously indiscreet — "a bit of a character". Almost everything about him was deceptive, like his professional pessimism which was encapsulated in a gift for deflation. "This idea will never work," he would admonish a bright young aspirant, then move mountains behind the scenes to ensure that it did.

The man who had founded New Zealand's foreign service was hard to place, the sources of power to which he appeared to have unlimited access ultimately mysterious.

It is humbling today to think that in 1944 when McIntosh opened the Moscow office, New Zealand's first hardship post, the country's diplomatic service was barely two years old. It was by any standard a quixotic thing to do. Costello's relief on receiving his credentials and the Prime Minister's approval at the Savoy Hotel was undoubtedly great. But McIntosh's relief at securing Costello may have been greater. Until then the Prime Minister's choice of a defeated politician to lead the mission had caused him only despair.

McIntosh's policy of recruiting university graduates as career diplomats instead of promoting regular civil servants had excited outrage and envy, and more than once put him on a collision course with the Public Service. He persevered. He wanted, he told his Prime Minister, *quality*. He wanted to extend New Zealand's reach to the world. "A man," McIntosh said, quoting the seventeenth-century diplomat, M. de Callières, "ought to have very quick parts, dexterity, cunning, wide knowledge and above all discernment." Qualities that Costello — though McIntosh was not sure about the discernment — seemed to him to possess in abundance. But McIntosh had to find and place his staff discreetly, at times almost invisibly. And with great — in hindsight one might say heroic — singleness of purpose.

In 1944 — it is worth repeating — New Zealand's diplomatic dealings did not include "a single foreign power". It was almost a boast. The mission to Moscow was controversial and unpopular at home. Much, as McIntosh knew, was riding on it.

The chief problem Costello identified at once. This was the Minister, Charles Boswell, who was elderly. They travelled on the plane together to Moscow. Mr Boswell had been recalled from obscurity by an indulgent Peter Fraser. He was a former teacher and a socialist who would become rapidly disillusioned with the Soviet Union. Probably the kindest thing that could be said of the Prime Minister's Envoy Extraordinary and Minister Plenipotentiary to the USSR was that he was a good man fallen among Fabians. Otherwise, as the New Zealand press reported with glee, Charles Boswell possessed no discernible qualifications for the job.

He embodied everything McIntosh was determined to do away with. Quite early on, when Boswell's despatches had settled to a stream of private letters, mostly grumbles, to the Prime Minister, unadorned by political thought or evaluation, a way was found to circumvent the problem. The flow was diverted. First it was diverted, then suppressed and finally reinvented. By 1946 Costello, a mere second secretary, would find himself sifting the winds that blew through the Kremlin and providing all the draft material covering the main political and economic trends for the Minister, besides writing separate papers of interest to New Zealand, effectively running the legation for him. It was one of the many devices McIntosh would employ, with Costello's connivance, to keep the legation afloat.

One cannot help suspecting that although Mr Boswell's duties would presently require him to receive from his subordinate an oath of loyalty and allegiance to the Crown, it was in reality the junior secretary who had been hired to keep an eye on the Minister.

The air journey to Moscow took nearly a month. Costello and the Minister left London on 17 July 1944 and travelled in crooked lines via Rabat, Gibraltar, Castel Benito and Cairo as far as Teheran where they were marooned for three weeks. They reached Moscow on 14 August. Costello's diary entries, seldom less than exotic when he is in travel mode, record his fascination with — (a) the gaffes of the Minister when visiting the archaeological museums of the Iranian capital, (b) the glances of the Persian women, "the slanting cutaway features, the beautiful reproachful eyes", and (c) the SAS hit man whom he met in the lobby of the British Embassy in Teheran, "on his way back to England from doing a job in western Persia".

Then comes, a portent of Charles Boswell's looming slide into Russophobia, "Moscow with the Minister":

> C.W. Boswell has found something he doesn't like about Moscow. The butter at supper last evening was white rather than yellow. "Good Lord, call this butter in New Zealand!", he remarked sourly. He does not like to see women working on the road-mending, and also remarked on the backwardness of the methods used compared with New Zealand.

In Leningrad old people and children who had survived the German blockade were still dying from malnutrition and starvation. Muscovites in the capital fared better — Moscow had suffered less than Berlin or London, and there were no destroyed buildings or signs of shelling that Costello could see. But there was little food and the Moscow joke that under Stalin you were granted "the freedom to queue" had yet to be born. There were no queues since there was nothing in the shops to queue for. (Not for another year would Costello observe to McIntosh, on 2 November 1945, six months after the European war had ended, "What a country, in which the occurrence of queues outside shops is a sign of improving conditions.")

As yet there was no legation staff or equipment. They worked and lodged at the Hotel National, overlooking the old Czarist Cavalry School. The hotel was reserved exclusively for foreigners and shut off by parks and radial boulevards from the real Moscow, a second city which the Costellos would shortly inhabit and come to enjoy with its distinctive smell compounded of sheepskins, fried potatoes, vodka, Speck, soiled clothing, cheap perfume and unwashed humanity on the trams once the trams began running again.

"We have nothing — except for this notepaper — and our greatest asset is Paddy Costello who speaks Russian," wrote Douglas Lake, the first of the staff to arrive. "No premises, no furniture and no staff."

Doug Lake had been extracted from the army by McIntosh on the advice of Geoffrey Cox. He had come straight from Italy where the Division was fighting. He joined the Minister and Costello at the Hotel National in September. Lake, a journalist hired as a clerk, was followed in no particular order by R.T.G. Patrick, first secretary, Ray Perry, second secretary and Costello's ranking equivalent, and Ruth Macky, archivist and the only other linguist. They ate, slept and worked from their hotel bedrooms, their ciphers locked in a safe at the British Embassy. Whenever a message came from New Zealand one of them had to get in the car and go there. It was difficult, Doug Lake wrote, to keep the ink out of the tomato soup. Ink, Ruth Macky discovered, was a rare commodity. She had the only typewriter, a Russian machine, and had to borrow ink from the Ethiopian Legation down the corridor. The National, Moscow's leading hotel, was decked with ferns and art nouveau panels and a motley of foreign envoys dependent upon one another, all hoping desperately, like the two tramps in *Waiting for Godot*, that conditions would one day improve. The hotel was situated a few doors from the Lenin Library — to Ruth Macky a comfortable, even sumptuous hotel, with "motherly maids in grey shawls and sisterly young ones in fresh white caps". It was said to boast the only elevator in Moscow, and provided from the upper floors occasional breathtaking views of the Kremlin. It would be their home for the next twenty-one months.

Staffless in Moscow, ignorant as he was of the furniture that had been cancelled for a legation and residence that did not yet exist, Mr Boswell, the Minister, was not idle. In that summer of 1944, two months after the D-Day landings, the Allies were across the Loire in France. In the south the American Seventh Army had entered the Rhine Valley. In the Soviet Union, Russian troops had retaken Odessa and Sebastopol. In Moscow the inherent unreality of the situation in which Costello found himself had become manifest. A week after arriving he was still finding his way, or rather Charles Boswell's way, about. They were making calls together.

> He is awkward in his movements, keeps failing to observe the kerb and either kicking it or nearly falling over it; trips over obstructions in the road; and seems to suffer from my animal magnetism — at least, walking by my side, he repeatedly lurches into me. What paralyses me is his helplessness and disinclination to part from me.

Some days later:

> I have done nothing in Moscow but accompany my Minister from place to place. It is hard to get away from him . . . So he remains my Old Man of the Sea.

For all his stumbling however, and before the war in Europe was out, Charles Boswell would succeed in doing his second secretary an unexpected good turn.

POLAND 1945

At present all entry into Poland is barred to our representatives . . . The American officers as well as the British who had already reached Lublin have been requested to clear out.
— *Winston Churchill to Franklin D. Roosevelt, March 1945*

THE PRIZE WAS Lublin.

Mr Boswell's part in it followed a private, semi-secret visit by Winston Churchill to Moscow in the autumn of 1944, ahead of the Yalta Conference in the Crimea. It came about this way. In the course of making ceremonial duty calls the New Zealand Minister, Boswell, was received by the British ambassador, Archibald Clark Kerr. The conversation reportedly went like this:

"I understand that one of your staff is something of a linguist, Mr Boswell."

"Yes. My second secretary, Mr Costello. His knowledge of languages is quite prodigious."

"Does he speak Polish?"

"I think so." The Minister thought hard. "He must do. He speaks just about everything else."

Polish as it happened was one of the few languages that Costello did not speak. In the event it hardly mattered. The Soviet armies had begun racing into Poland and the Balkans in the early summer. What mattered was to get a team of diplomatic observers across the border into Poland before the Russians imposed their own system. This was Churchill's worst nightmare.

The idea of the mission was twofold — first to contact British and Commonwealth prisoners liberated by the advancing Red Army and arrange for their repatriation; second, and uppermost in Churchill's mind, to report on the enigma of Soviet intentions in Poland in the hope of forestalling permanent Russian occupation. Churchill's visit to Moscow had produced from Stalin promises of "immediate access" to collection points where British subjects were said to be located. The battlelines of the future were already being drafted. Britain had gone to war for Poland; it was for Churchill a matter of honour, besides sentiment. More than Rumania or Yugoslavia, he regarded Poland as a test case, a barometer of future east-west relations.

Costello was summoned by the British, discussions held and preliminary plans drawn up. With his previous military experience and knowledge of Russian, he was a natural choice to lead the mission.

Then everything seemed to stall and wait on the Yalta summit.

"There is no doubt in my mind," Churchill would telegraph the American President in March 1945 after the Yalta Conference ended, "that the Soviets fear very much our seeing what is going on in Poland." It was Yalta which would shatter American illusions about Stalin's promises, and seal the fate of Poland. But four months earlier the mood in Moscow had been very different.

"Great excitement," Doug Lake wrote in the autumn of 1944, after Churchill and Stalin had appeared together in public:

> Both the Minister and Paddy Costello have been more or less hob-nobbing with Uncle Joe. They went to the Bolshoi Theatre last night where the diplomatic corps were guests and Joe with the British Prime Minister showed himself to an audience which was wildly enthusiastic. These are great days at the moment. The present confidence which Russia and Britain seem to have in each other stirs hope once more.

The British Prime Minister and his Foreign Minister, Anthony Eden, and accompanying chiefs of staff, had landed in Moscow on 9 October

1944. The same evening Churchill had his first meeting with Stalin in the Kremlin. This was the occasion on which an episode occurred which would significantly influence the political balance in Eastern Europe and the Balkans. Shortly after 9 p.m. Churchill said to his host, "How would it do for you to have 90% predominance in Rumania, for us to have 90% of the say in Greece, and go fifty-fifty about Yugoslavia?" While this was being translated, Churchill's biographer Martin Gilbert records, the British Prime Minister wrote the figures on a half-sheet of paper, added some extra percentages for Hungary and Bulgaria, and pushed it across the table to Stalin. Stalin, after a slight pause, took his blue pencil, made a large tick and passed the paper back again.

> There was a long silence. The pencilled paper lay in the centre of the table [Churchill recollected later]. At length I said, "Might it not be thought rather cynical if it seemed we had disposed of these issues, so fateful to millions of people, in such an offhand manner? Let us burn the paper." "No you keep it," said Stalin.

No mention was made in the document — the "naughty document", Churchill later described it — of Poland.* Nor, as Costello observed at the Bolshoi two nights later when a special performance was put on for the British Prime Minister, was there a hint of disagreement in the air between the two leaders. As the lights came up at the end of the first act of *Giselle,* a cheer was heard, "like a cloudburst on a tin roof". Costello was seeing something quite astonishing.

Churchill had arrived at the theatre late, with Stalin coming in some minutes afterwards. There had been no announcement. No one in the audience had realised they were there. The cheer that sounded was followed by sustained applause which in the words of the American ambassador's daughter, Kathleen Harriman,

> went on for many minutes. It came from below and above on all sides and the people down in the audience said they were thrilled at seeing the two men standing there. Perhaps this may sound odd to you but that night was the first time probably that most of the

* Germany and Czechoslovakia were also omitted from the document.

> audience had seen either man. Stalin hasn't been to the theatre since the war started and for him to go with a foreigner was even more amazing.

Churchill's visit was subsequently reported in Britain as a triumph. Before leaving Moscow, he had extracted from "Uncle Joe" verbal guarantees over Poland: Russia was "in favour of free and fair elections"; it had "no intention of interfering in Polish affairs". But amid the excitement of the almost daily military successes against Germany in the west, Churchill's behind-the-scenes comments reflected his gloom and growing fears of betrayal in the east. Four months later, at Yalta, the scene in the Bolshoi was repeated — this time with Churchill and the American President Roosevelt toasting Stalin in chorus in what was, Roosevelt said, the atmosphere of "a family".

"We really believed in our hearts," according to Roosevelt's special envoy, Harry Hopkins, "that this was the dawn of a new day we had all been praying for."

Yet all the time entry into Poland remained barred. The "Iron Curtain" that Churchill had yet to announce in his Fulton speech in America in 1946 had in effect already descended.

Then suddenly and unexpectedly on the last day of the Yalta Conference (11 February 1945), amid protestations of solidarity, a crack appeared in the curtain. The Soviets agreed to allow British representatives to cross the border into Poland.

The contact mission led by Costello left Moscow on 1 March. Costello was given a British army officer's uniform and promoted to temporary field rank. With Major Costello were Flying Officer David Floyd from the British Embassy and a British sergeant. They crossed the eastern border by train and entered Poland escorted by Red Army officers, but without the thirty tons of Red Cross supplies — food, clothing, cigarettes — and a Jeep which Costello had arranged to travel on the train with them. At the last moment he was informed their supplies were not coming. They had been impounded.

It was the first indication of the confidence trick about to be played upon them.

Five days later, on 6 March, Costello and Floyd reached Lublin in south-east Poland. They were put into a hotel. Permission to leave Lublin was denied. People were living hand to mouth, selling their possessions, as in Moscow. It was dangerous, they discovered, to be abroad at night — supporters of the London Poles, the anti-communist government in exile, Floyd wrote, "are still being sought out and arrested and shot". A Polish officer liberated from a German camp told Costello, speaking of the Russian occupation, that he had passed "from captivity to captivity".

They had no wireless, little money, and permission to communicate with Moscow was denied. The British and Commonwealth prisoners they had been expecting to meet in Lublin were not available. They had been moved out.

On the second day Costello drew up an aide-memoire of requests and interviewed the Soviet official in charge, Major Sigulya. He recorded the interview as follows:

SIGULYA	What need is there for any documents? You explained the contents to me on the 7th.
COSTELLO	We wish to have on record that we have acquainted you of our views.
SIGULYA	I know your views. There is no need to draw up documents.
COSTELLO	Well, Major Sigulya, we shall have to post the aide-memoire to you if you refuse to take it from our hands.
SIGULYA	How will you send it? Is the Polish post functioning?
COSTELLO	Yes. We have checked up on that.
SIGULYA	Well, I am probably going away — I shall not be here to receive it.
COSTELLO	We shall address it, "The Head of the Allied Escaped Prisoners of War Administration, Lublin."

SIGULYA It will not be delivered.

COSTELLO In that case we shall address it to Colonel Bogdanov, Military Commandant of the town.

SIGULYA Ah! I shall see if I may accept this letter.

The letter, demanding access to prisoners under the Yalta agreement of 11 February, was not delivered. Two days later Costello's party was put on a train and returned under escort to Russia, like so much damaged goods.

Back in Moscow, Costello and Floyd were sent for by the British Ambassador. They told him, as the ambassador subsequently cabled Whitehall, that most educated Poles were strongly anti-Russian and that the Russians, behaving clumsily, were squandering "a unique opportunity to effect a general Polish–Russian reconciliation". They had been prevented from seeing any of the hundreds, possibly thousands of Allied prisoners released from captivity and wandering the countryside; conditions, against a backdrop of conflicting reports of arrests, deportations and liquidations, were chaotic. Poland, David Floyd thought, was becoming a puppet state. Costello, less suspicious of Soviet intentions, described "a waif state".

Costello had been away from Moscow nineteen days, twelve of which had been spent travelling. Shunted into a siding, deprived of transport and kept virtually incommunicado, he and Floyd nonetheless had seen through some of the chaos being visited upon a dazed and liberated population. The two men often disagreed, but their reports, taken together, cannot but have helped to fuel Churchill's suspicions that the Western powers were being tricked, and that all effective power was passing to the Soviets who were efficiently clearing out all the foreigners they could find to the Black Sea port of Odessa, before their non-observance of Yalta led to a showdown.

On the surface the mission was a fiasco. And yet it was not. Costello may have failed to locate prisoners, the stated purpose of the mission, but in Lublin he had found something else. It was something no one had counted on.

He was standing in a complex of buildings enclosed by barbed wire. In front of him was a shower room containing seventy-two shower heads, spaced very close together. At the far end of the room was a short passage leading to the gas chamber. The gas chamber was in a small room with concrete walls and an iron door; in the middle of the low ceiling was a hole through which the arsenic poison ZYKLON was emptied from cylinders.

At first Costello could not comprehend what he was seeing. He was someone who did not normally set much store by his ability to solve problems. Whatever interested him he would learn, and learn quickly. He brushed aside his achievements, his brain having solved the problem of the moment and relegated it to a compartment marked "unimportant". His emotions were not involved.

In Lublin that changed.

He stood for a long time, unable to comprehend the magnitude of what he was seeing, the enormity of the crime that was in front of his face. In front of him — "I saw no reason to doubt the words of the guide," he said later — were 820,000 pairs of footwear. All the shoes were worn out. He was told that those which had been in good repair had been sent to Germany. Only the rubbish was left.

Costello knelt down and examined the shoes. They bore the marks of shopkeepers in almost every country in Europe. A big proportion were women's and children's shoes.

He felt numbed, as if afflicted by a cutting wind, although the air on the outskirts of Lublin that morning was quite still. He thought of Bil's parents, Momma and Totta, refugees from Jewish *shtetls* in the Pale of Settlement in eastern Russia. Of his children Mick and Josie, aged eight and four. And a third child, Katie, whom Bil had given birth to six weeks earlier and whom he had never seen. Costello heard the voice of the Polish guide accompanying him, but as he walked through the long silent barracked buildings made of planks and corrugated iron everything in the silence was jumbled and out of focus, as it had been in the desert during a sandstorm when he wore the celluloid eye-shields from his gas-mask case.

The informant who had directed Costello to the camp outside Lublin was the hotel chamber maid. The name of the camp was Maidanek.

The next day two more informants, a man and a woman, came to the hotel and begged Costello's help to get them out of the hands of the Russians. They were a woman doctor, Olga Lengyel, and a French saboteur working for the British, Maurice Lequeux. Captain Lequeux had been captured by the Germans in 1943; Madame Lengyel had been rounded up in one of the last selections in Hungary with her husband, her parents and her two small children and sent to a camp in Poland a hundred miles to the south-west of Lublin; she was the sole survivor of her family. The name of this camp was Oswiecim (Auschwitz).

In Costello's diary the two are not named. They appear only as "the two from Oswiecim".

Before returning to Moscow, Costello interrogated the pair closely. Back in Moscow, having completed his official report, he sat down and wrote a second, more personal account. He wrote quickly, his emotions on fire, his brain on ice. He was angry. "My only excuse for writing on the subject," he said, "is the fact that very few foreigners apart from the Press have been able to enter the country at all."

Costello signed and dated this second report and gave it to his Minister, Charles Boswell, who consigned it to the diplomatic bag. Mr Boswell addressed the bag to the New Zealand Prime Minister, then in London. He added a covering note:

> Mr Costello has brought me two reports dealing with his visit to Poland. They do not pretend to be more than opinions. However I trust they will be of some value.

In London Peter Fraser, accompanied by Alister McIntosh, was being briefed together with other Commonwealth leaders ahead of an Allied victory conference. The daily news was of mounting military successes across the Rhine, the Allied and Russian armies converging in their advance towards Berlin. At the Savoy Hotel, McIntosh opened the bag from Moscow. His eye fell on a report entitled "German Extermination Camps". He opened the report, and gaped. Unlike Mr Boswell, who appears not to have glanced at it, McIntosh began to read:

> It was the German practice to gas the prisoners before they burned them. Exceptions were made in favour of persons seriously ill or new-born babies; these were thrown alive into the ovens. The babies were thrown into the boxes as they were born; after a few days when the boxes were full (those in the bottom layers being presumably already dead), they were burned without any formalities.

Further on, he read:

> In many cases the victims were naked when they set out for the gas chamber. Captain —— saw one parade of 2,000 women, stark naked, marching "to the gas" with the German band at their head playing tangos and fox-trots. In cases where they were dressed, they were given numbered checks for their clothes in the shower room, and, passing to the gas chamber, filed past a notice which said, in several languages: "Keep hold of your check as otherwise you may not get your clothes back when you come out." The people were packed so tight in the gas chamber that Captain ——— believes 75 per cent of them died of simple asphyxiation; the rest were finished off, as at Maidanek, with ZYKLON.

Costello's report was dated 26 March 1945, six weeks before the end of the war in Europe. It anticipated the discovery of crimes at the Buchenwald and Bergen-Belsen camps, liberated by American and British troops in April, and is now recognised as perhaps the first draft of history in what would become known as "the Nazi Holocaust against the Jews". In his report Costello estimated that some "millions" of Jews and Poles had been murdered at Auschwitz, a figure later confirmed — though not by the Soviets. Russian troops had entered the Auschwitz–Birkenau complex as early as January 1945, but had then thrown a cordon round the camp to cover up their interrogation procedures and the dismantling and shipment to Russia of machinery from the Monowitz complex nearby and other industries that interested them. No Soviet report was made until May, when the war ended. The Soviet announcement was falsified to hide any mention of a mass extermination of Jews.

When Costello's report reached London at the end of March, the name Auschwitz, the most notorious of all the camps, was still unknown to the world.

"I thought I was hardened to reports of atrocities," J.V. Wilson, New Zealand's longest-serving diplomat, wrote to Costello, "until I read your report on Poland. I found it almost unbearably moving. The passages about the condemned children being taken to farewell their parents shows up the German mad streak better than anything I have read."

Peter Fraser, the Prime Minister, having received and settled 700 Polish refugees in New Zealand the previous year, had a soft spot for Poland. He discussed Costello's report with McIntosh and made sure that it reached the Dominions Office and the Foreign Office in Whitehall.

"The above sounds like the invention of an insane mind," Costello had written, as if he could not quite believe the contents of the report himself. But at the Cabinet Office in Whitehall he was believed. Cecil Day showed it to the Foreign Secretary, Anthony Eden, who passed it to Churchill and the King.

"Mr Eden read it," Day minuted to McIntosh, "and [agreed that] this grim story should be circulated confidentially and at least to the King and the Cabinet." Initially the report was circulated as a confidential Foreign Office white paper, then with Costello's permission given a wider circulation to embassies and the press to help counter allegations from Central and South America that stories of Nazi atrocities and the Holocaust were a hoax.

As for Olga Lengyel and Maurice Lequeux, Costello's two informants who had asked for his help to get out of Poland, all was well. Costello arranged for the pair to be repatriated by falsely declaring to the Soviets that they were brother and sister and fabricating papers which said they were "British citizens". Their names appear at the end of a list of twenty-one "British ex-prisoners-of-war", repatriated from Lublin in March 1945.

The nineteen other names on the list represented the only Allied prisoners Costello and Floyd were able to trace on their mission.

Of Maurice Lequeux little more is known. Madame Lengyel however — still alive in America in 1999 at the age of nearly a hundred but now dead — is remembered. After Costello's intervention, Olga Lengyel was shipped in a box car from Lublin to Odessa and eventually reached Paris. There in 1946 she published a book, translated from the Hungarian, entitled *Souvenirs de l'au-delà* (Memories of Another Land). The book described her experiences at Auschwitz and Birkenau and was an immediate best-seller, widely translated. It is one of the founding documents of Holocaust literature.

Meantime, while Whitehall hastened to circulate Costello's findings to other embassies, Wellington slept. In Moscow Costello was making arrangements to meet his wife and family. When the New Zealand government finally decided to seek his agreement to publish the report under its own imprint, in August 1945, the author at first could not be found. He was in Stockholm.

From the Letters

1945, Stockholm

15 August 1945 (to Dan Davin)
Dear Dan
I begin this with the salaams and apologies with which I usually open my letters. For hardly a moment of my Moscow life did I feel sufficiently ruminative and at ease to write to anyone but Bil. However for a week or two I am away from the Third Rome, and I hasten (he smirked) to write to you first of all.

It is a week since I left Moscow. Bil is due to arrive today. Stockholm after Moscow is really intolerable. Its shop windows are well stocked; the people are the best dressed I have seen; meals are magnificent. All the evidence of a well spent neutrality . . . I am particularly annoyed by the fact that the trolley buses today are decked with flags to celebrate victory [in the Pacific]. It is, I surmise, largely chance which has made the Swedes so repulsive. If they had been invaded in 1940 they might well have resisted and in resisting have lost some of their sleekness and gained a bit of the spirit which is empressed in the NZ Div. slogan: "Hooray — fuck". But they did remain in the margin of the whole thing, for whatever reason, and the result is I don't like them.

Today is the anniversary of my arrival in Moscow. My Russian is pretty good now. On the strength of a year in Russia one should, by current standards, have collected material for eight and two-thirds books. If I ever wrote one on Russia it would be so thickly studded with rathers, probablys, perhapses, tends and mights that it would be unusable. I can say however that I have lost a good deal of what an American called my starry-eyedness about the USSR. Theoretically the thing is perfect. In practice I am certain I couldn't live there as a citizen. Even if I survived the housing and the food, I'd undoubtedly be shot for temerarious remarks about the Holy Things. The censorship of literature is stricter than it was in fascist Italy.

All of this about the Soviet dictatorship was known for years to almost everyone outside Russia. I, however, did not know it. You'll gather that my eyes have lost their assurance of "certain certainties". And then on top of this highly delicate ideological condition comes the news of this atomic bomb . . . The upshot of all this is that I'm by no means sure what I think of the Soviet Union or the world as a whole.

Today is Sunday. The church bells are ringing and the air is charged with the same boredom that exhales from Sabbath England. Tomorrow my family arrives. From now on I'll be able to write to you fairly regularly.

"Moscow! Moscow! Moscow!"

— *Irina in Chekhov's* Three Sisters

COSTELLO WAS BACK in Moscow in September 1945 in time for the first snowfall, together with his family. They were Bil and Mick and Josie and the newly arrived daughter, Katie. He had told Bil they were privileged — an apartment was provided for them. But when they arrived, eight Yugoslavs were still living in it and the repairs promised by Protocol had not been started. They were absorbed into the foreign community at the Hotel National and Costello prepared for another winter writing reports in his room with blue fingers. Room 110 had a mullioned window facing out to a corner of the Kremlin; further south on the other side of the river the British Embassy, a former merchant's palace, enjoyed the most splendid view in Moscow directly opposite the Kremlin with thirty golden cupolas crowning the ancient hill. Costello's room had double glazing, but no heating except for a hot plate, a small surface heater plugged into the wall on which his samovar sat. The samovar, like the desk and bookshelves, had been scrounged from other embassies. Even the weatherproof Doug Lake, a tough rugby player who doubled as storeman, winced at the temperatures.

> Outside it is snowing [Lake wrote in February 1945], the chill comes in the window, my room half-bedroom, half-office, the rest a general store filled with books and boxes of rations.

But the Costellos were in luck. Their apartment was ready before the Minister's residence. By new year they were installed in a spacious flat in Khokhlovsky, an old winding quarter near the centre with burned yellow houses built by former merchants and pink Orthodox local churches. Round the corner was a former student accommodation block where Russian families lived in single rooms, cooking on primuses in the hall or courtyard. Smell of cabbages, kerosene and fried potatoes all round them. Lavatory at the end of a long corridor.

"Our flat was luxury by comparison," Mick recalls:

> We had running water and a maid. We had shops with special rations and white bread. Paddy's sister Kathy used to send us toheroa soup from New Zealand, and whitebait. Delicious. I've never tasted whitebait since.
>
> Round the corner the kids I played with were rough. Very very poor. They were very impressed with "Anglicky box" — boxing. And the name "Faraday". They knew the name of Michael Faraday who invented electricity.

It was here that one of Costello's theories about life as an accelerant to education was put into practice. Bil, ploughing through Segal's Russian grammar, floundering in an unfamiliar milieu with a baby and a five-year-old on her hands, seems not to have noticed. Probably only the five-year-old, Josie, too young to see anything strange in the queer way the neighbours' children spoke, was enjoying herself. According to Mick, within a few days of their arrival Costello had thrown him and Josie out on to the street:

> We stood miserably in the entrance to the block of flats for some days, except for food breaks. I remember thinking, an end's got to be put to this. Some kids were coming back from school, kicking a tin can. I joined in. A week later I was enrolled at a local school, learning Russian. This was deliberate on Paddy's part.

Today we would call it tough love. The first three Costello children, Mick, Josie and Katie — two more sons would arrive later — would become fluent in Russian and other languages, going on to become linguists, translators and interpreters in their adult life. Costello was an exemplary if occasionally brutal educator.

Near the flat in Khokhlovsky was a small tree-lined park. It surrounded a pond, Chistye Prudy. Once the New Zealand Legation was established in Metrostroevskaya with residence and chancery, Costello travelled to work by trolley bus or metro, but in summer he often walked, going first south then west along the river and past the Kremlin. In winter when the pond froze, and especially on weekends when Josie begged to be taken skating, he sometimes went north towards the boulevard flanking the park. The park surrounded the pond which was lozenge-shaped and froze early each year; it took its name from the place where in the eighteenth century the butchers had once dumped the innards and offal but, scoured and cleaned, had since been renamed Chistye Prude (Clean Pond).

This is the pond, today a popular summer rendezvous for young families, with a marquee built out over the water and a small band playing the latest pop and New Orleans jazz, where Levin encounters Kitty skating, in one of the opening scenes of Tolstoy's *Anna Karenina*. But it was not of Tolstoy that Costello was thinking when he first came to the park in 1946.

Rising over the entrance to the park was a giant statue of the nineteenth-century Russian playwright Griboyedov, who is famed for writing a single work which is still the most frequently quoted of all Russian plays. The pedestal at the base of the statue is decorated with reliefs of the characters in the play, entitled *Gore ot Uma*. *Gore ot Uma* is sometimes translated, "Woe from Wit", sometimes "Grief from Mind". In the Penguin Classics edition, entitled *Chatsky* after its main character, it appears in the subtitle as, "The Misery of Having a Mind". But given the fate of Chatsky, and that of the author Griboyedov, not to mention Costello, a better translation might be, "The Downfall of a Clever Man".

Alexander Sergeyevich Griboyedov was a linguistic prodigy, a scholar and a diplomat. He wrote the play in 1823 and was murdered three years later at the age of thirty-five.

Griboyedov first appears in Costello's journal in February 1946, coinciding with the move to Khokhlovsky. Costello probably saw the play performed first at the Maly Theatre. Over the next four years he went to see it increasingly, six or eight times a year. He saw the play so many times that in the end he knew all the roles by heart. Costello says in one of his notebooks that when he first became interested in Griboyedov he had to restrain himself while shaving else he become over-excited and cut himself with the razor. The play entered his soul. He found himself, he told a friend, ransacking the comedy when embarrassed or depressed, or "grazed by near-hysteria" if buttonholed by the Minister — "You know how it is taking your leave of Charles, like pulling your leg out of deep mud" — seeking an apt phrase or quotation. Quotations and lines from the play flooded his sub-conscious and restored his composure almost at will. Lines like:

Does a mind like that make for a happy home?

Or:

Fate's a practical joker, giving out presents
Each one gets what she thinks a suitable kind:
For fools — the bliss of being mindless,
For the wise — the misery of having a mind.

Griboyedov, as will be seen, was to have a profound influence on Costello's life.

He had missed out on Spain. In Spain there was colour and heat and danger. Things were significant, as in war. He had almost missed out on Moscow. At Cambridge he had felt the fascination with Marxism and the Soviet Union all round him, and dreamed of it with a mounting if spasmodic intensity, like the sisters in Chekhov's play. But now he had got there and was determined, like the perennial student he was, to make the most of it. He began by soaking himself in the theatre.

23 nov. Last night *Yevgeny Onegin* for the 5th time.
27 nov. Last Friday night *Pikovaya Dama* for the 5th time.
Yesterday evening "Paolo and Francesca" of Rachmaninov with Ruth.*

* Ruth Macky, and the only other linguist until Zohrab came in 1948. She married Doug Lake in 1946 and a daughter, Sarah, born in a Russian hospital "within the district of the British Embassy", arrived in 1948. The Lakes returned to New Zealand in 1949.

Travel was cheap. Theatre was cheap. There were, he told Davin, thirty-six theatres in Moscow, a whole art's world of plays, operas, ballet, puppet shows and concerts open to him: a night's ticket for the price of a dozen eggs or a tin of bully beef on the black market. He set about investigating and punishing the theatres with all the diligence of the ex-Intelligence officer. But first he had to master the language.

He wrote to Alister McIntosh:

> The Russian language is like a sack pulled over the head of the wretched foreigner. Those like Ruth Macky and me, who have cut an eyehole or two in the sack, have to lead by the hand those who are still living in the darkness. Curious, but the one who shows most promise of all the beginners is Mrs Boswell. For myself I reckon I'll know Russian well in ten years' time. It really is a monster of a tongue.

Costello's Russian was largely self-taught, bookish and, as he discovered when he arrived, quite inadequate except for reading the daily press. He did what he had done in Cairo when he wanted to learn Arabic, and would do again in Paris when he wanted to learn Persian — he hired a teacher. In Moscow his teacher was an enterprising teenager, a wide boy named Victor Louis. Victor Louis was thought to be the natural son of a Russianised French woman; he made money as an errand boy and fixer around the legations and embassies. He was assumed to be a KGB informer, but was later, according to Mick Costello, arrested by the KGB, accused of speculation and spying. Costello paid Victor for conversation lessons; Victor taught him the language of the streets and the Moscow race-track. This explains in part why Costello was drawn to Griboyedov: Griboyedov's play, *Gore ot Uma,* is peppered with colloquialisms which leap out with the force of proverbs.

Each day had its own singular flavour. Walking along the Sadovaya, the circular boulevard surrounding the inner town, one day after lunch to Griboyedov's house, Costello was overjoyed to learn from the barmaid that the playwright's nephew was living in the yard. But he was just as pleased to meet a cement worker and hear what the man thought of "the new order"; or strike up a conversation with an out-of-work droshky driver, an old Armenian "who told me that whenever he said anything he mentally translated it into eight languages (Armenian, Turkish, Persian, Georgian,

English, French, Italian and German)".

After Bil arrived, their diet improved — kerosene for cooking was once again "an available commodity" — and the sight of long queues waiting to buy *Pravda* and *Izvestiya* in front of news stands indicated, he told her, that newspapers had reappeared for public sale. There were no shops except the secondhand bookshops, the *antikvari*. Here he bought the French classics and editions of Greek drama and verse for a song, pleasant old volumes which had once belonged to aristocratic libraries. The Revolution had dispersed tens of thousands of books, and in the semi-starvation of the civil war and the siege of Leningrad those books that had not been sold or burned for firewood had trickled down into the secondhand bookshops. Costello haunted the *antikvari*, as he did the Lenin Library, the Maly and Bolshoi theatres and, stimulated by a commission from the Oxford University Press where Dan Davin was now employed as an editor, the homes and apartments of dissident writers and poets in and around the city. Chief among these was Boris Pasternak, then living precariously in semi-disgrace an hour's train ride out of Moscow at Peredelkino.

During his posting to Moscow, Costello visited Pasternak many times. On the first occasion he irritated the Russian poet, according to Isaiah Berlin, by criticising Pasternak's lack of enthusiasm for the Revolution and attempting "to convert him to communism". But it seems the irritation may have been more on the side of Berlin himself, perceiving in (as he put it) this "diplomat from a remote British 'territory'", a rival for the favours of the great Russian poet. Equally, sitting in the sunporch of Pasternak's dacha, sipping Russian tea, it would have been as natural for Costello to chide him for abandoning the Revolution as it would have been for a Jew to criticise the Russian poet, who was Jewish but pretended he wasn't, for denying his religious faith. Pasternak was after all, living in a sort of vacuum isolated from other writers, benefiting from a degree of immunity that has puzzled his biographers. Still, there seems no doubt that Costello's regard for Pasternak the poet was reciprocated. The two discussed Soviet nationalism, the enigma of Mandelstam's death, Costello ordered books in English for him, especially by Jane Austen, couriered poems and letters to family and friends in Oxford for him, enjoyed vodka and madeira in his company and took friends like the Lakes to see him in his Moscow apartment.

On his last visit in 1949, invited to bring his family for a children's Christmas party, Costello was present when his host was called away to the telephone. Costello related afterwards that Pasternak returned after some minutes white-faced, in a state of shock, saying: "That was Stalin. He says he is writing a poem. He wanted my advice."

Costello wandered for miles around Moscow. His office work done, he would put on his hat and slip out, with or without the Minister's knowledge — on foot, by rail, by trolley bus and — once the trams were running again — by tram, the last filled to overflowing, grotesque engines "crawling slowly like gigantic disabled wasps, covered with human barnacles". His enthusiasm for Russian life and culture communicated itself to other diplomats in Moscow like Marshall Crowe and Franco Venturi, at the Canadian and Italian offices, to whom he taught Russian, and his New Zealand colleagues, Ruth Macky and Doug Lake, who became his ardent pupils. Though not the Minister. Charles Boswell, a goose who would never become a swan, although at the end he did try to learn Russian, would never discover what it was that infected these young diplomats with enthusiasm for the Soviet capital.

The spirit of their enthusiasm is captured at a concert they attended in 1946, one of a number given by Russian artists and musicians returning home from exile or imprisonment, in this case a concert given by the pop-singer Vertinsky, "the Russian Bing Crosby". Vertinsky had left his homeland after the Revolution.

> Friends [he spoke to the audience before he began to sing]. Only recently have I returned after a long absence abroad.
>
> I doubt if even you know what it means to be here tonight. I cannot tell you how eager I was to be back in Mother Russia. When the train made its first stop across the frontier, the Customs inspected our baggage. Free of the examination, I went out into the open air. I put my bags on the ground and fell on my face and kissed the warm black earth and said, "O Mother Russia, here I am back at last." When I stood up and turned round, my bags were gone. Then I knew I was really home. Mother Russia, you haven't changed a bit.

The idea of an impressionable rosy-cheeked idealist (though Costello was rather gaunt), of a foolish and contented goat from a distant land grazing uncritically in the pastures of the world's first workers' state, is in marked contrast with the files of the British Security Service (MI5) and the New Zealand Security Intelligence Service (SIS). They present Costello as a traitor. Both views are fanciful. The New Zealand SIS refers to Costello's "links with the intelligence service of the USSR", an alleged relationship that is said to be "substantiated by other records held by the NZSIS which are unable to be released at this stage".*

"Life," says a line by Pasternak which Costello was fond of quoting, "is not a stroll across a field."

There is nothing new in these claims. Like the charges against the Canadian Herbert Norman, or for that matter George Orwell, accused of supplying the British Foreign Office with a black-list of British fellow travelling and crypto-communists, they have entered the realm of myth and passed beyond mere factual refutation.

Not only Costello's detractors but some of his colleagues, like the former Secretary of the New Zealand Foreign Ministry, Frank Corner, have voiced their suspicions. Claims like this cannot be dismissed lightly. Frank Corner was Costello's contemporary; he knew him, he worked with him at the Paris Peace Conference and he is in many ways an admirer. Frank Corner writes in an official publication (1993): "We received superbly written accounts of life in wartime Moscow from someone who could communicate easily with Russian people; we were told what life in a Moscow primary school was like by this parent whose child attended an ordinary Russian primary school instead of the one set up by Western diplomats; we (and other countries to whom we sent copies of his reports) accompanied him to buy tickets and travel to various parts of Russia, even on a boat down the Volga — experiences which other diplomats did not seem able to negotiate . . . Was it Costello's command of the Russian language and his known sympathy for its culture and travails that gave him a uniquely privileged position; or was there another explanation?"

Suspicions like this ignore the fact that in the Costello years — covering the life of the first New Zealand Legation in Moscow, 1944–1950 — areas like the Volga basin, the Urals, Odessa and the Black Sea, and the Caucasus — with the exception of the Georgian Military Highway — were not always off-limits, despite Russian reluctance to let foreigners travel about. The Australian head of mission, James Joseph Maloney, travelled about the

* The full SIS statement appears on page 367.

Urals in 1945 apparently without difficulty; the French first secretary, de Carbinnel, visited the Ukraine; the Canadian Dr McMorris went to the Caucasus with Costello. And so on. If Costello saw more and travelled further; if his reports contained information that escaped other diplomats it is not that he had inside connections or was secretly privileged, he was simply not as other diplomats were. He was not really a diplomat at all. He was a sport: an inspired and intensely curious sport (albeit a sport in a suit), an amateur, a radical and a renegade. Costello had a rather disturbing vitality. His children, involved in Russian life, whom he and Bil sent to summer camps in the Crimea and the Ukraine, may have had something to do with it. Like them Costello travelled with a purpose, as the following episode shows:

> I must tell you of one characteristically Russian episode [he wrote to a friend in 1949]. Katie is with her kindergarten in its summer pastures at Skhodnya, 32 kilometres from Moscow. Skhodnya is in a "forbidden zone". Yesterday (Sunday) was the one day in the month when parents are allowed to visit the camp, the parents' day, and in preparation for it I had written two days earlier to Protocol for permission to visit her. Permission was refused. "Skhodnya is in a forbidden zone and we have no authority to allow you to go there."
>
> We had no intention of letting Katie feel like an orphan on a day when all the other kids would have their parents visiting them and bringing them gifts of fruit and sweets; so we just went. Not by car, of course, but by bus. We first rang up the Moscow premises of the kindergarten and asked what time the parents could visit. Answer: "Not before 3 p.m." We took the 2.30 bus. Arrived at Skhodnya, at about 3.15 p.m., we found the kindergarten full of parents, many of them clearing up after picnic lunches on the grass, a few sleeping under trees. Katie's teacher said to us, "Why ever did you come so late? Poor Katie thought you weren't coming." With some sharpness I reminded her that the instructions were to come "not before 3". Oh yes, that was so, of course; but nobody paid any attention to the rules; come any time you like; also on the Sundays that are not earmarked.

Doesn't that give you a whiff of Russia? Costello added:

> I have not told Charles Boswell this story. If the news that Bil and I had made an unauthorised incursion into a "forbidden zone" were to find its way to the Protocol Department, the consequences could be serious. Imagine the paragraph in *Pravda* under the heading, "Morals of Anglo-Saxon Diplomats: The New Zealand First Secretary, who has long displayed a suspicious curiosity in Russian affairs, penetrates into a secret zone of the Soviet Union . . . etc".
>
> Needless to say, I intend to repeat this escapade on the next parents' day, if not earlier.

Incubus

Although there is no proof that Costello was implicated in the disclosure of military information, his close association with [Fyrth] raises a doubt whether he is a safe and suitable person . . .

— *Dominions Office, London, to High Commissioner Batterbee, Wellington, 25 October 1944*

IT WAS IN Moscow that the incubus that would shadow Costello's life and return after death to tarnish his name and reputation made its reappearance. It had begun as a bad dream at Exeter with the Fyrth affair, had haunted him in the army in the 1940s, it would oppress and drive him out of Paris in the 1950s, as it was about to catch up with him now in Moscow. This was an attempt by the British government to discredit him. The attempt, in the holier-than-thou colonial atmosphere of the times, took the form of a letter. The timing of the letter, coinciding with Costello's exemplary service to the British on his return from Poland, is interesting. The letter reflected Foreign Office disapproval of Costello and must have puzzled the British Ambassador in Moscow, Sir Archibald Clark Kerr. Only a short time before, Clark Kerr had been told by the Foreign Office that Costello had impressed them "in every way".

The letter cited the Exeter City Police but it was less a case of the law's long arm catching up with him than that of the security file, whose reach according to James Jesus Angleton could be even longer. "A file," in the words of the CIA's legendary head of Counter-Intelligence, "is not a perishable item."

It was at all events a form of hounding. Never made public in Costello's lifetime, it would follow him to his grave.

A less resilient temperament might have taken cover, or cracked, as did the innocent Herb Norman, who was hounded by Intelligence agencies literally to his death. In the case of the Canadian envoy, who served his country faithfully, innocence was not enough; the strain told and he took his life. In 1957 Herb Norman jumped to his death from an apartment building in Cairo where he had been posted as ambassador. Again Costello breaks the mould. He knew all along, according to his son, Mick, that he was being pursued, yet he made no attempt to alter his behaviour. Certainly the tone of his despatches to the New Zealand government, a blend of sympathetic yet critical reporting of Soviet affairs, did not alter. Nor did the tone of Costello's anti-Americanism soften. After McIntosh's letter reached him, he made no attempt to trim his views to more acceptable norms. He was by his own lights an imperfect diplomat. If anything, his lack of tact and his lapses in behaviour already noticeable in Cairo, usually as a result of drink, only increased.

This is all the more surprising given the atmosphere in Moscow when Costello arrived. A witness to this is Isaiah Berlin, who was in Moscow from September 1945 to January 1946. Berlin describes the paranoia and suspicion pervading every facet of Soviet life; how he was followed by the KGB; how, meeting at a party at the British Embassy the composer Prokofiev, the theatre director Tairov, the film director Eisenstein and other Soviet artists, he soon realised they were "gripped by fear". And how everything was "out of bounds". Costello ignored the restrictions, as did — both to his credit and sorrow — Isaiah Berlin. Berlin's famous encounter with Anna Akhmatova in Leningrad is well documented, as is his visit to Pasternak's dacha at Peredelkino. Berlin describes his own visit to Pasternak as "a courageous not to say foolhardy act". But Costello — making the first of several visits to Pasternak — was there months before Berlin. This is not to belittle Isaiah Berlin in any way, merely to indicate that if he broke the rules openly without fear of consequences, so did Costello.

It was not just Soviet life that was in the grip of paranoia and suspicion, the diplomatic colony as a whole was also cowed. Diplomats lived in a kind of zoo. They were regarded by the Soviet authorities and particularly

Stalin himself as spies. The heresy hunts and show trials of the 1930s, a decade of mass atrocities, might have ended; but a new period of repression culminating in the execution of fifteen Jewish doctors — the so-called Doctors' Plot — was about to begin. "If anything," says the New Zealander Douglas Zohrab, "when I arrived in 1948, things under Stalin had become not easier but worse."

But who could tell? Costello's behaviour, his reckless disregard of the rules, may have been a blind; he may, unlike Berlin, have been full of guile; not all swans are white, nor saints blameless; there is nothing like deceit to mask deception. One can argue all ways. There is the man and the mask, the fascination of peeling off skin to lay bare the poison that is within. The fact is that wherever one burrows in the Costello fabric, the arsenic of treachery is not there.

Spies fascinate us as do actors, because the pretence of being other than we are seems to fulfil a deep human need. In Costello's private journal there is no pretence. His journal is full of the absence of pretence, although (correction) he does hint at one point of leading "a double life". Alas. On closer inspection it transpires this has to do with the Minister Charles Boswell and office politics, nothing more sinister than that. What does emerge from the private journal is a contradictory personality much more interested in the foibles and idiosyncrasies of individuals than in politics or advancing the cause of a political system. We use our private journals as a retreat, a place where we can be alone. Costello's journal is full of secrets, but in the main they are the sort of secrets a man keeps from his wife in wartime. They are sometimes encoded, usually in a foreign language, but this is easily solved (a dictionary or interpreter will do). What shows occasionally is a vain man and a clever or arrogant man but — rather more often — a shy, restless, inquiring, intensely curious and insecure one, a prey to private thoughts and troubles. None of this proves anything. But perhaps it serves to remind us that we all dissemble. That we are all vulnerable. Most of us live our lives amid hidden fears and weaknesses which we do not readily confess or admit to, even in our private journals. Paddy Costello did it all the time.

About a month after he returned to Moscow from Poland, some time in April 1945, Costello received a letter from McIntosh. McIntosh said the British were asking questions about what he was doing in Moscow.

McIntosh wrote: "The British Security Authorities have reported that you have a record of undesirable Communist activities in the past, and that your wife is apparently at present associated with the Communist Party."

McIntosh had been visited, he said, by the British High Commissioner, Sir Harry Fagg Batterbee. Batterbee had a file on Costello, marked "Secret"; he showed McIntosh a memorandum from Downing Street. The New Zealand Secretary of External Affairs and Permanent Head of the Prime Minister's Department was (evidently) embarrassed. The discussion was perfectly friendly, but McIntosh realised he was being put upon. He was on the defensive. He was being asked to justify to this urbane upper-crust Englishman his own vetting procedures.

The documents mentioned Costello's 1937 visit to India. They spoke of the "Official Secrets" case which had resulted in Costello's dismissal from Exeter in 1940. Batterbee said to him, "Did you know about the Exeter matter?"

"No," McIntosh said.

McIntosh wrote to Costello, "It is upon this incident more than any other that the British Authorities apparently conceive doubts as to your safety and suitability for your present position."

"Dear Mac," Costello replied on 29 April 1945, "On the question of Communist activities, I am not, and have not been since well before the War, a member of the Communist Party." He described the circumstances which led to his dismissal at Exeter, and added:

> I may say that the general setting of these happenings evokes ironical reflections. I, alone of the College staff, had wanted to join up in the first few weeks of the war, and had only refrained for the reason that the recruiting station was taking advantage of the current mood to sign people on for the Regular Army instead of for the duration of the war. Subsequently, my Head of Department persuaded me to wait until my calling-up time should come round. Even now I am the only member of the College staff who has served at the Front. I heard there was some movement among the staff to rehabilitate me, but I have not heard the upshot. Certainly John Murray, the Principal, can't stand me and would do anything he could to oppose such a move.

> As to my wife, she ceased to have any connection with the Communist Party from the time I arrived in England last April, and has had none since to the best of my knowledge.

And that, apparently, was that. At least for the time being.

McIntosh duly reported Batterbee's visit to the Prime Minister, Peter Fraser, when he returned from the San Francisco Conference. Costello heard no more.

Here one might pause a moment to consider the relationship between McIntosh and Costello. Both were vulnerable, McIntosh in some ways more than Costello, for on the shoulders of this retiring man, whose foreign ministry was still in its infancy, rested the greater responsibility. In 1945 the thirty-nine-year-old civil servant, although a considerable influence in government in his own right, was in some ways still walking on tiptoe, especially as regards staff. McIntosh had grown up with a regard for the old-fashioned rule of anonymity and under the burden of a Public Service department which instinctively deferred to the Colonial and Dominions Offices in Whitehall, of which Batterbee was a supreme product.

The British High Commissioner had told McIntosh in effect that his choice of Costello was a mistake. In the view of His Majesty's Government, the man was unreliable. Better remove him.

What did McIntosh do?

McIntosh had a pastoral attitude towards his staff. As a lapsed Catholic, he had an instinctive sympathy for Costello; as a historian, a respect for the scholar's intellectual integrity; in sum he recognised a man of remarkable powers on whom he could rely to carry New Zealand's voice into wider counsels on the other side of the world. McIntosh was no liberal romantic. He had a strict code of loyalty to New Zealand but no axiomatic reverence for Britain or knee-jerk hostility towards the Soviet Union. He had few qualms about Costello, only about his hard-line wife, Bil. He had tried to prevent her joining Costello in Moscow, then relented. However he seems to have told Batterbee that Costello, communist sympathies notwithstanding, was in Moscow to stay, with the full blessing of his government.

What this little confrontation tells us is that, having succeeded in prising Costello from General Freyberg's grip, McIntosh was not about to relinquish him on the basis of British innuendo and suspicions.

Coming at a time when McIntosh was still battling to create an identity for New Zealand's foreign service, the incident, though small, is not trifling. It reveals in this mysterious public servant an anarchic streak, the stamp of the emergent New Zealander who is no longer a little Englander willing to be patronised or pushed around. Of course, McIntosh had a vested interest in protecting Costello; the probity of his department was at stake. Nevertheless he emerges in character, himself a reflection of the independence he is trying to mould for his country on the other side of the globe.

What McIntosh feared, he told Costello, was that the British ambassador in Moscow would be advised of London's misgivings and as a result New Zealand would be frozen out of their fortnightly briefings. The British Embassy community in Moscow numbered about a hundred; it was by far the largest of the Commonwealth missions. But McIntosh need not have worried. The ambassador, Clark Kerr, the future Lord Inverchapel, was a Scot. He was witty, worldly and in his way as unconventional a personality as Costello. There were no repercussions and, after McIntosh had informed Costello of Batterbee's misgivings, the flow of information from the British Embassy in Moscow, such as it was, continued unimpeded.

A bit later when Clark Kerr was succeeded as ambassador by Sir Maurice Peterson, this would change. The new man spoke not a word of Russian and was, by Commonwealth consensus, "thoroughly bored by it all". Accounts vary, but in Peterson's term of office Costello appears to have been struck from the invitation list. Still, this was no hardship. According to Marshall Crowe at the Canadian mission, the fortnightly briefings given by the British were largely a waste of time — "an embarrassment all round, with the Brits rather relishing the semi-colonial context".

The Paris Peace Conference

Quack, quack, quack, hour after hour . . .
— *Bill Jordan, August 1946*

IN MARCH 1946 during a short visit to England Costello was commissioned by the Delegates of the Oxford University Press to produce an anthology of contemporary Russian poetry which would revise and enlarge the out-of-date *Oxford Book of Russian Verse* (1925) edited by Maurice Baring. Dan Davin, who had joined the Press the previous year as an editor, had suggested the project.

In proposing the book, Costello told the Delegates that his compilation, beginning with Alexander Blok, would reflect "a flowering" of Russian verse that included three poets, a man and two women, whose lives reflected the dignity of the human spirit. This was coded language for three dissidents who bore witness to the fate awaiting those who resisted Soviet repression: Anna Akhmatova, destitute in Leningrad, Osip Mandelstam who had died in a labour camp, and Marina Tsvetaeva who had committed suicide. The edition would also contain a number of poems by Boris Pasternak.

Not long before this Costello had told Davin that he suspected he was turning into a liberal "or perhaps an anarchist". He certainly preferred the

New Statesman to the Comintern organ, *New Times*. Davin was delighted. Moscow appeared to be sobering him.

Back in Moscow, Costello drenched himself in Russian verse, rising at five-thirty in the morning and working at the Lenin Library in the evening. He oversaw the installation of £4000 worth of furniture ($NZ240,000 on today's values) bought in Sweden for the new legation, saw the Minister and his wife installed at Metrostroevskaya 21 in May, and in July, with the anthology taking shape, left Moscow with Bil for their first holiday together since 1937.

They left by riverboat from Khimki fort just outside Moscow, sailed north along the Moscow–Volga canal to the main Volga, then east through Uglich, Yaroslav, Gorky, Kazan (Chaliapin's home town), Ulyanovsky, Kuibyshev (Samara), Saratov, Stalingrad and finally to that peculiar Russian–Kalmuck–Armenian–Persian town of Astrakhan.

"We travelled the whole Volga from above Rybinsk down to Astrakhan," he wrote to Davin. "The trip lasted eleven days and gave me the quietest holiday I have ever had: changing shores day after day; a broad, quiet river; nothing to do but natter with one's fellow passengers, read or lie in the sun. It was more like our drive from Enfidaville to Cairo than any other trip I have made."

From Astrakhan he sent his mother a postcard:

> The heat and lush green remind me of Egypt, the markets are full of apricots, melons, cherries, tomatoes and lemons, but we are told that we are about a month ahead of the real fruit season; if that is so, Astrakhan must have some pleasant eating in August.

Costello returned to Moscow on 22 July 1946. Four days later, as he was resuming work on the poetry anthology, he was summoned to Paris. The 1946 Paris Peace Conference was about to begin.

The Conference of Paris was designed by the Allies to draw up peace treaties with Italy, Bulgaria, Hungary, Finland and Rumania, the so-called "lesser belligerents". It was held at the Luxembourg Palace. Among the hundreds attending, Costello was one of the few able to communicate with the other delegates in all four official languages, English, French, Russian and Italian. "As I sit in the Salle de Brosse in the Luxembourg," he wrote to Geoffrey Cox,

> with the delegates of twenty other countries sitting at the same table — inscrutable Russians, the English shopkeepers, moral and faintly bewildered Americans, esurient Greeklings — I reflect ironically that this is *IT*, this is the goal towards which, in our scuffles in Greece, our exercises at Forgloss, our goings and comings in the Western Desert, we were all the time striving . . .

In Paris he and another of McIntosh's rising stars, Frank Corner, sat on virtually every territorial and political commission. One of these, the Hungary Commission, would earn Costello notoriety, but in the early stages the limelight descended on an older delegate. This was the New Zealand High Commissioner to England, Bill Jordan, a former London policeman who sat on the Rumanian Commission and who told the Russian delegate, Andrei Vyshinsky, he was talking "blasted rot". Mr Jordan made headlines everywhere after his photograph decorated a French newspaper showing him listening to the Soviet delegate with his feet up, fast asleep.

> Here we sit [Jordan lamented], listening to "Quack, quack, quack", day after day, hour after hour. We are sick of it.

The conference lasted twelve weeks. There was still meat rationing, the markets half empty. Parisians were living on their past, like camels. But the French government and the city of Paris, anxious to restore their pride after the war, put on a series of brilliant entertainments. Versailles came to life again. At a state reception guests mounted a stepped carpet laid the length of two football fields. The way was lined with flunkeys in perouques and Spahis on horseback, French–Moroccan cavalry troops in helmets, bright red uniforms and white cloaks. Orchestras played and from the side gardens figures materialised in the dusk, from behind the box hedges — as Douglas Zohrab noted, "just as in the final act of *The Marriage of Figaro*".

Doug Zohrab arrived late, after his plane was hit by lightning and forced to land in Iraq. He was private secretary to the head of the delegation, the New Zealand Attorney-General, the Hon. H.G.R. Mason, known as Rex. Zohrab found his compatriots installed in a small but agreeable hotel, the Château Frontenac, in a street off the Champs Elysées, and at first his spirits rose when he was told they had been assigned to Claridge's in the Elysées for their meals.

> The food was superb [Frank Corner recalls]. We ate and drank very well. Claridge's had unblocked their cellars, and every night we had bottles of Château Haut-Brion.
>
> McIntosh and a dozen of us would meet for dinner at one table, though sometimes Costello was absent (Paddy liked opera, and girls). Nearby at a smaller table were Bill Jordan and the Hon. Rex Mason, and also Mason's secretary, Doug Zohrab. Mason was a theosophist and a vegetarian and neither he nor Jordan drank. Jordan was parsimonious, he always liked to go home with a credit balance. So their table was quite spartan, and no wine. Poor old Doug had to watch us enjoying ourselves and suffer in silence.

Nothing illustrates the gap separating the man of the world in McIntosh, the gulf between old and new, better than a scene glimpsed by a young Commonwealth delegate staying at the Frontenac. It was a night in September, lovely as only Paris can be on an autumn evening: the Arc de Triomphe and other buildings floodlit; the boulevards and cafés thronged, crowds strolling along the quais. On his way to the opera house, the delegate knocks at a door to deliver a message. Waits. Peers in. Beholds the New Zealand Attorney-General and the High Commissioner, reluctant inhabitants of a foreign shore, "crouched down together over a gas jet, sipping cups of cocoa in their hotel room".

The New Zealand delegation was provided with three cars. "I don't remember seeing a lot of Paddy in the evenings," Frank Corner's wife, Lyn, says. "This was thought to be because he enjoyed the opera, or the company of the British driver assigned to him. She resembled a sofa and was known as Turkish Delight."

Costello had told Bil he thought the conference would last two or three weeks, but it dragged on and on. After about a month Bil, left behind in Moscow, decided she had had enough and flew to Paris to join him. Very wisely.

In Wellington Peter Fraser received a telegram. It outlined a resolution his delegation intended supporting concerning Hungary over a border dispute with Czechoslovakia. The resolution involved 200,000 Hungarian peasants and an exchange of populations around the Slovakian capital, Bratislava — at least, that is what Mr Fraser understood, not realising that the Magyars were to be forcibly displaced. From Paris McIntosh had been keeping his Prime Minister regularly informed. But telegrams were expensive, the complexities of "the Bratislava Bridgehead", as it would become known, could not easily be conveyed in telegrams at a shilling a word. The New Zealand Prime Minister can be forgiven if, on misreading the Czech demands, he was persuaded to agree to them.

This was late in September. Committees had been in session through the night and two interpreters and a translator had collapsed in the small hours. Tempers over Hungary had begun to fray when the chief American delegate, General Bedell Smith, announced that the United States would not agree to a transfer of populations. The Czechs countered by reminding the Americans of Hungary's pro-Nazi war record. The Hungarians, pleading economic hardship, claimed "the London-Istanbul highway" ran through the disputed area (it was an unpaved country road). General Smuts for South Africa weighed in, accusing New Zealand of moving people around "like a bunch of Kaffirs". At which point Costello proposed an on-the-spot investigation — it wouldn't take long, he said, the area was no bigger than "a pretty good sheep farm in New Zealand".

The official minutes record:

> [10th meeting]
> 11 Sept. 1946 — A sub-Commission to deal with the Bratislava Bridgehead was constituted. Held its first meeting. Costello's view prevails.

Appointed rapporteur to the special committee, Costello set about subverting the American position. Frank Corner remembers a stream of delegations coming to the Frontenac to talk to Costello. The Soviets, New Zealanders and Canadians supported the Czechs; the Americans, British, Australians and South Africans backed the Hungarians.

The American delegation was led by Walter Bedell Smith, Eisenhower's chief of staff in the war, now the American Ambassador in Moscow.

"In the last two elections," Bedell Smith reportedly told the Assembly, "the Czech communists won nearly half the vote, but in Hungary the communists got only 18%. Therefore this piece of frontier goes to Hungary." Costello's view was equally blunt. The Czechs were on our side in the war, the Hungarians were not. Therefore the land "goes to the Czechs".

He continued to lobby hard. Corner says,

> He out-manoeuvred the Americans completely. McIntosh supported him. Paddy was brilliant in argument. He swept the floor with Bedell Smith over Bratislava which the Americans wanted removed from Soviet influence. Bedell Smith, quite a small man but conscious of his own importance. He was very angry. He was livid.

In Wellington, New Zealand's Prime Minister was receiving some strange advice. It included the notion that the 200,000 Hungarians to be deported were "Presbyterians". (Among the 200,000 were 20,000 Calvinist protestants known as Hussites. Someone had added an extra nought.) Peter Fraser was himself a Presbyterian. National elections were due in New Zealand. The Prime Minister remembered that his Otago constituents in the South Island were solidly Presbyterian. On 1 October, forty-eight hours before the Paris deadline, he cabled McIntosh instructing him to withdraw New Zealand's support for the Czech proposal.

"It is very odd," McIntosh said later, "that we should have to go to Paris to learn that Hungary is a hotbed of Presbyterianism."

Costello — and the Czechs — had been upstaged.

The Prime Minister's telegram arrived on the eve of the penultimate meeting of the Hungary Commission when according to the minutes General Bedell Smith lost his temper and threatened to walk out. Everyone was exhausted.

In the end New Zealand covered its retreat. The differences were papered over and a compromise reached to everyone's satisfaction except that of the Czechs. This was prefigured in an extraordinary scene witnessed by Costello and McIntosh.

The night Peter Fraser's telegram came they dined with the leaders of the Czech delegation, Masaryk and Clementis, and explained that the Czech proposals could not proceed in their present form. Jan Masaryk, the foreign minister, was the son of the founder of the Czech republic, Thomas Garrigue

Masaryk. Jan Masaryk is variously described as urbane, charming, outspoken, funny, and a manic-depressive. He was, like his father, a democrat. Vladimir Clementis was his deputy. During the dinner Masaryk became agitated and began to shout. "It's always like this," he said, in tears. "It's always like this for the smaller nations." Clementis, a hard-line communist, silenced him. At this stage, October 1946, Masaryk had eighteen months to live. It was a foretaste of what lay ahead.

It was Frank Corner who noticed in Paris how, as the conference proceeded, the nature of the Czech delegation was changing. "Masaryk stayed," Corner recalls. "Clementis stayed. But Masaryk was being edged out. These thugs arrived from Prague and began taking over. Clementis was less thuggish than the others. Somewhere we have a photograph of him dancing with my Lyn at a ball. But things were already starting to go sour in Prague. As the delegation changed, you could 'feel' the communists taking over there."

Eighteen months later in March 1948, two weeks after the communist coup in Czechoslovakia, the body of Jan Masaryk was found in the courtyard beneath his window in the foreign ministry in Prague; he had apparently committed suicide at the Stalinisation of his homeland. President Truman, like many others, thought he had been murdered. In his memoir, *Years of Decision*, Truman claimed that already in Paris Masaryk knew he was a marked man, telling an old friend that the Czech communists had been given orders "to liquidate their political opponents" — a view not shared by Costello or McIntosh at the time. They accepted the official line that Masaryk came to pieces under pressure. As McIntosh wrote on 18 March 1948:

> Dear Paddy,
> We are all distressed about poor old Masaryk, but is it not on all fours with that extraordinary exhibition he gave the night you and I dined with Clementis and himself? The thing that amazes me is that his nerve lasted as long as it did.*

Although watered down, the Czech proposals were far from demolished — Costello's lobbying, for example, had gained for the Czechs an additional

* The circumstances surrounding Masaryk's death — suicide or defenestration? — remain obscure. Clementis, one of the organisers of the 1948 communist *putsch*, was himself put on trial and hanged in 1952.

eighteen kilometres of frontier space on the Danube around Bratislava, a minor coup in the face of opposition by two of the three big powers, America and Britain. Costello's umpiring of "the Battle for Bratislava" earned him, according to his son, Mick, vilification in the Hungarian press, but it made him a hero in Czech eyes. The following year Costello and Bil were invited to Czechoslovakia as guests of the republic.

In Slovakia he was fêted and presented with a medal "for the Liberation of Bratislava".

As for General Bedell Smith, a future Under-Secretary of State in Washington, he would become in 1950 director of the Central Intelligence Agency, the CIA. Walter Bedell Smith had a precision-tool mind; he would not forget his humiliation in Paris.

Shortly after Costello returned to Moscow, he received a letter from McIntosh:

> Dear Paddy
> The Americans, while I was away, instituted an inquiry through their Legation here, as to your antecedents. No doubt they have a little biography of you potted in the State Department for future reference.

COSTELLO
ujzélandi kiküldött. a pozsonyi
hídfő és a kitelepítés ügyének

From the Letters

1945–1947, Moscow

2 Nov, 1945 [to McIntosh]
Dear Mac
What a country, in which the occurrence of queues is a sign of improving conditions . . .

I must say I haven't any idea of what happens next. Up to the atomic bomb, it all seemed fairly clear; now God knows. It seems there are 3 possibilities. Either the Americans can be logical and use the bomb to knock Russia out. Or the Americans can accept a situation in which Russia has a sphere of interest in Eastern Europe. Or they can let things drift. I have no means of guessing what will happen . . . but I say, with Lake, that if they're going to atomise Moscow, I hope they give us a day's notice.

13 November 1945 [to Davin in Oxford]
The trouble with letters from Moscow is that one feels under

some obligation to define in them one's attitude to the whole gigantic datum: RUSSIA. That is, two hundred millions of people, a thousand years of history, an unfamiliar culture, a difficult language and, worst of all, a peculiar social structure . . . I have resolved never in future letters to whoever it may be to announce my judgment of Russia, but to talk of Russian things and people as one would of any other country.

31 October 1946 [to McIntosh on return from the Paris conference]
I got my atlas in Berlin: 150 Eighteenth Century maps covering the whole world for £2 6s 6d (in cigarettes). One of the best buys I have ever made.

26 November 1946 [to Davin]
The book of Russian verse is practically finished.

4 March 1947
I mentioned to you that I am writing a little myself. I find that I am making progress.

28 March 1947 [Davin to Costello]
You don't tell me what it is you are writing, what genre. Don't have a revulsion against it and burn it. (I suspect that is the kind of thing you, as an arrogant perfectionist, might do: forget that we live by our standards but not on them.)

7 May 1947 [Cox to Costello]
I hear rumours that you are, or are to be, First Secretary.

30 May 1947 [to McIntosh]
My wife and I returned from Prague three days ago after nearly three weeks in Czechoslovakia. The invitation was nominally personal [but] in effect, our host was the Czechoslovak Foreign Office. The good feeling towards New Zealand . . . and more particularly to recognition of the sympathetic attitude we took in Paris, was astonishing. It was most noticeable in Slovakia, as

Slovakia was the beneficiary under the clause of the Hungarian Treaty extending the Bratislava bridgehead.

The Slovaks could not do enough for us. We were received by the Lord Mayor of Bratislava who presented us with the medal for the Liberation of Bratislava (fact!).

19 August 1947 [McIntosh to Costello]
Dear Paddy
You appear to have had a good time [in Czechoslovakia]. I am not at all certain as to the propriety of your taking that medal and I suggest you make discreet inquiries as to British practice and then say nothing more about it.

Tilting at Windmills

We like to think this is the vanguard of the working class, the citadel of the world revolution and all the rest of it, but, after all, how can you be sure?

— *Costello, journal 1946*

COSTELLO ARRIVED BACK in Moscow from Paris at the end of October 1946. The novelty of good food, truite-aux-amandes, turbot and mushrooms, even the superb clarets and burgundies, had failed to drain his nostalgia for Moscow. He missed the flat and the warm stink of the Khokhlovsky quarter and was glad, he told Davin, to be "home". He worked at the interrupted verse anthology — interrupting himself only to call on Boris Pasternak whom he regarded as "unquestionably the greatest living Russian poet".

He wrote to Davin on 26 November:

> I am seeing Pasternak again this week. Pasternak is in a peculiar position in this country. He will not write what or as the Party desires and makes it quite clear that he regards "socialist realism" as a phony doctrine (it is).
>
> All the other writers are either good Communists or pretend to be. He is therefore a most useful fellow to know, quite apart from the pleasure one feels in the company of

> a great man. He knew all the literary people since 1910 and can give me information on writers whose names are never mentioned at all in orthodox circles — Tsvetaeva and Mandelstam for instance — because they died outside the Church.

By the new year the completed text of his *Oxford Book of Russian Verse* was on its way to Davin in England.

The year 1947 was a productive one. Costello was made first secretary of the New Zealand mission and in September, when Charles Boswell went on leave, he became Chargé d'Affaires. It was a three-secretary mission, with additionally an archivist, a chauffeur, a Russian woman interpreter, a doorman and a boilerman-caretaker. When Costello became Chargé, the Minister's absence was barely noticed: the nuts and bolts of routine administration apart, he had effectively been running the post for three years. Trade deals did not take up much time. There was almost no trade. For the first time he found he had some leisure to devote to his family. That winter he took the children skiing in the Sparrow Hills outside Moscow.

Mick was now ten, attending a local Russian school every day and, once a week, learning the violin in another music school. He and Josie, aged six, were bilingual. And Katie, "aged two, monolingual Russian".

Later, as adults, Mick and Josie would comment on the quality of the education they received in Russian schools in Moscow. Paddy Costello's eyes had been opened not by the system directly but by ordinary Russians he met who were a product of it. A waiter at the hotel restaurant, "who expressed a preference for Chekhov's short stories rather than his plays". A chauffeur, a former private soldier, "who is an authority on Pushkin and can quote chapter and verse after verse". And the legation doorman, Pavel Pavlovich, who began borrowing numbers of the periodical, *Voprosy Istorii* (Questions of History), which were stacked upon Costello's table:

> He reads them steadily down there at his little table by the door. The other day he came in to replace one and take another. I asked him what he had been reading. He said, *"Zamechatelneishaya statya!* [A most marvellous article!] I had always wondered what lay behind the defection of the Constable of Bourbon to Charles

> the Fifth. A curious business. And now it is all perfectly clear to me. An excellent article!"
>
> What a people!

Costello admired Russian education for its rigour and attention to literature and music ("Like the French education system," Mick Costello recalls, "multiplied by ten.") Already Costello was beginning to watch over his offspring like a jealous hawk.

"Mick (aged 10) is now learning the violin," he told Davin in January 1947. "Josie (aged 6) and my wife are both taking piano lessons. Music is one thing that Russia does offer and my family are taking it."

He had the unfortunate habit, Josie recalls, of setting standards:

> He encouraged us all the time but he was also strict. I felt it wasn't decent if I didn't study hard. He read to us from Homer, the Iliad and the Odyssey. It was a habit. This, the puritanical streak in him perhaps, came from a Catholic upbringing. It was a black and white morality from his Roman Catholic background. And his mother, Mary. He was steeped in it. He referred to the Politburo in the Kremlin as the Central Committee of the Vatican.
>
> Mick and I used to play a game with him. Paddy would sing operatic arias and we'd have to guess which operas they were from. Tosca, Aida. Figaro, Boris Goudunov. When we went to the opera, we didn't just go and sit, we were thoroughly prepared. We knew the story backwards. The arias, he'd sung for us, so we knew what to expect.
>
> Later after the allegations came out, all the tricks he's supposed to have got up to, I remember thinking, when would he have had the time? The time, he gave to us.
>
> I could ask him anything. He never refused, no matter how busy he was. I realise now how unusual this was. When I wasn't well — I had a touch of TB — he had to give me special injections. Afterwards he'd play a game of chess with me. He just spent time with us.

In 1947 travel restrictions were introduced in Moscow, limiting foreign diplomats to a ten- or twelve-mile radius round the city. Mick recalls going on Sunday picnics in the legation car, sitting in front with his two sisters, Paddy and Bil in the back singing duets — "And Paddy urging the driver to go faster and race the old Packard and see how far we could get. We never got further than the towns around Moscow. At every checkpoint we were turned back."

One day, after a week in bed with quinsy, Costello sat down in the flat and wrote:

> The events I am about to relate took place upon our planet; but in a world so unlike the one we know that I am obliged first to devote some space to a brief description of it.

He wrote rapidly in a clear flowing hand. He was using the fountain pen his Russian lover had bought for him in Cairo. He paused to doodle on a sheet of paper, making a drawing like the sketch of a child. The drawing showed "the Dividing Sea". The sea separated a land called "Imro" on which the sun shone and another land, called "Timro", which appeared barren. He continued:

> The continent of Imro was a fertile land, in which men raised the grain and other crops on which they lived . . .

He had begun to write a novel. It was entitled *Imro*, and devised as an antidote to Orwell's fable about the animals who take over Jones's farm and run it as a socialist collective. George Orwell's famous attack on Russian communism, *Animal Farm*, had appeared in England in 1945. Costello read it in December 1946 during a bout of influenza and felt it his "moral duty" to answer Orwell.

"If nobody else was going to do it," he told Davin, "I had better try." "Try" was the operative word.

Costello worked on the manuscript for nearly a year and sent Davin the completed text without delay. He used as a nom-de-plume the name of a distant cousin, "Patrick Quilty", and was encouraged, he told Davin in a separate letter, by the news from a friend in Prague that *Imro* was to be translated into Czech. He asked for Davin's help to place the work with a publisher in England.

For a long time he heard nothing. (The covering letter had gone astray.) Then a letter came from Davin. "A MS arrived here with no covering note or indication of source," Davin wrote. He had glanced at the first paragraph, decided that the author was not illiterate, "even if crazy", and put it away unread. Davin's letter continued,

> A few nights ago I took it down again. As I did so W[innie] said: "You know, I bet that comes from Paddy." I read the first page and was sure of it. I have now read four chapters and am so convinced that I shall be very angry with you if you aren't.

Imro was a satirical fantasy about "the rabble and the Company" — but a polemic. It was devoid of human interest or character development. Costello himself called it "a scurrilous pamphlet". Davin praised the style — "a perfect rhythm and gravity where the irony is below the surface and working like a muscle" — but confessed that after reading four chapters the general plot eluded him. He failed to find a publisher for it in England.

"Burn him. Put him in the fire and there's an end of him," Costello wrote in May 1948. Then, having finished the eighth volume of Casanova's memoirs which he had begun to read earlier in the year, he began on Machiavelli — without, it seems, a twinge of regret. Still, to devote a year of one's life to a doomed enterprise is hardly a source of comfort. Again and again Costello expresses in diaries and letters his craving to become a writer. The rejection must have hurt, the more so as Davin's reputation — two novels and a collection of stories published in London since the war* — continued to rise. Geoffrey Cox too, with a profile in Fleet Street and three books to his credit, was making a name as an author.

"I have three things to do," Costello had written to Davin. "To earn a living, to read, and to write. The last is the most important." He was a jealous practitioner. One can *feel* the pain when he reports that the Minister's wife in Moscow, Jean Boswell, has earned twenty guineas for a short story accepted for an English women's magazine, compared with only seven guineas he has been paid for an article in the *New Statesman and Nation*.

Costello would go on trying; he would write another novel, unpublished, and begin and abandon a third work. He would never become an author

* *Cliffs of Fall* (1945), *For the Rest of Our Lives* (1947) and *The Gorse Blooms Pale* (stories, 1947).

in his own right. Davin and Cox had always thought it slightly indecent for one man to be possessed of so many talents, so they must have been relieved to learn that "writer" would not be added to the Costello portfolio.

The *Imro* failure helps us define in Costello a marked characteristic, his penchant for tilting at windmills.

Had he gone to Oxford one might speculate that he had inherited the Oxonian's gift for backing lost causes. It is not that. It seems to be the case of a man of intellectual integrity who is unwilling to compromise; a man whose allegiance is primarily to himself. The case of a man who travels alone: the single rider.

In context Davin was right to call the author of *Imro* "crazy". As well tilt at *Snow White* or *Alice in Wonderland*. Who else in his right mind would have considered trying to discredit the author of a fable containing the universal truth, "All animals are equal, but some animals are more equal than others"?

Costello's riposte to *Animal Farm* is useful nonetheless. It begs a central question: was he a communist?

The short answer is, no. A communist, to be pedantic, was both a paid-up Party member and one who bowed to Party discipline.* Costello was far too Irish and subversive, too indiscreet and irreverent for that. Mick Costello claims that until Khrushchev's denunciation of Stalin in 1956 his father never voiced other than "total admiration for Stalin". But this is a subjective view. It needs to be set against a climate of coercion and fear in which even Pasternak and Akhmatova abased themselves and wrote poems of adulation to Stalin. It does not square with Costello's letters to Davin, McIntosh and others; and is belied by his exasperation with the practitioners of Stalinist dogma. In a commentary on Russian propaganda dated 10 May 1949 Costello describes one such essay as,

> a declaration which only communists can read and which none would willingly read. In it two mighty traditions of turgid verbosity, the Bolshevik and the Latin, meet. The result is a tirade which contains few facts, no reasoning, and a super-abundance of violent accusations stated in tired reach-me-down phrases:

* As Bil did, although she was sacked from the Party in Exeter for "deviationism", and later reinstated. Bil remained a dedicated and unrepentant communist all her life.

Yugoslav renegades
Criminal clique
Mortal enemy
Octopus of Wall Street
Judas
Agent of Anglo-American imperialism . . .

Not even Churchill was immune to the teddy-bear magnetism of "Uncle Joe". Costello's selection of Russian verse, omitting the toadies of the literary scene and published while he was living in Moscow, makes it clear that he was not currying favour. His selection for *The Oxford Book of Russian Verse* included Mandelstam, Gumilyov, Tsvetaeva, Byely and Akhmatova, besides Pasternak, and would not have pleased the Soviet authorities.

Nor did Costello consider himself a communist. Marxist? Fellow traveller? Communist sympathiser? All of that. But a discrete Marxist. A critical traveller. He criticised Russian policy and interests almost as often as he sought to justify them. Costello is hard to categorise. He eludes definition. He is a gift to Intelligence agencies who predicate guilt "by association" (with alleged agents, communists, radicals) and, lacking any real evidence, use the ploy to discredit him.

Costello was ambivalent in his Marxism, according to two diplomats who knew him in Moscow: the Canadian Marshall Crowe and the Englishman Alfred Dobbs. Dobbs had four tours at the British Embassy in Moscow between 1947 and 1975, ending up as Minister. He says, "Paddy was steeped in Russian culture, as he was in Marxism. But I wouldn't call him doctrinaire. He was too intelligent to swallow Marxism whole, though he swallowed a good deal of it." Marshall Crowe says, "Paddy could see as well as anyone else that Stalin's USSR was a secretive and brutal dictatorship, and that Marxism or any other doctrine was quite irrelevant. That keeping the gang in power was the only ideology there."

Costello saw through the fog of propaganda surrounding the personality cult of Stalin — "He [Stalin] has already become more than a man," he told McIntosh in 1945. "Although the dogma of his virgin birth has not yet been proclaimed, one feels that it might well be." Yet he supported the communist takeover in Prague in 1948, just as three years earlier in Poland he had given the puppet government the Soviets were in the process of installing in Lublin the benefit of the doubt, believing in his romantic way that the end justified the means and choosing to overlook the fact that Soviet policy, no less than British and American policy, was causing the world to split into two hostile camps.

Occasionally Davin took him on. Over *Imro* he lost patience, calling it at one point a caricature. He wrote:

> Your account of the western campaigns, with the Russians drawing off the opposition, is a caricature to me. Moreover, it is unfair to all the people who fought on the western front.

But Davin also wrote, in the same letter:

> I could scarcely have believed the tide of public opinion would set so strongly so soon against our late allies.

Costello replied:

> . . . the real reason for the trouble between Russia and the rest, is the old old trouble: Russia is the land of the Revolution. They talk about "democracy" and "dictatorship": instead of enquiring what a government is doing, they ask how it is doing it, and they answer even that question with lies. Except for a brief period between 1940 and 1945, Russia has had virtually the whole world against her. The alliance with Britain and the USA was temporary and uneasy; now things are back to normal again. The Russians call this normal state of affairs "capitalist encirclement". An over-simplification?

He is as hard to define on communism as Graham Greene on the Roman Catholic Church or Boris Pasternak on the Revolution. Costello admits to being a romantic, thus naive. How naive was he?

Again Orwell gives us a measuring stick.

George Orwell did not go to Russia. But he fought in the Spanish Civil War where he witnessed the manhunts of innocent people carried out by Soviet commissars. "These manhunts in Spain," he wrote in a preface to the Ukrainian edition of *Animal Farm*, "went on at the same time as the great purges in the USSR, and were a sort of supplement to them." Orwell's fable, whose point Costello seems to have missed completely, as T.S. Eliot had missed it before him, was not simply an attack on Russian communism. It was an attack on what Orwell called "the gramophone mind", on the gullibility of middle-class intellectuals hoodwinked into believing that everything they read about the communist revolution, a beacon of hope amid the social and economic distress of the thirties, was true. Like the starving animals, hoodwinked by Squealer, told they had more oats, more hay, more turnips, and worked shorter hours and lived longer than in Jones's day, they "believed every word of it". They seemed incapable of recognising the brutality of a regime under which fifteen million people had died from collectivisation in purges and labour camps.

Costello was aware of the repression, up to a point. According to his son, Mick, who was twelve or thirteen at the time,

> The only time I can remember him touching on the subject [of labour camps] was when he asked me one day about what I'd heard, playing in the courtyard with the other Russian kids. "You ever hear anything about anyone being picked up in the middle of the night?" he said. And he laughed, to keep it light. I didn't know what he meant. I said, no, why? He said, "Just a joke," and let it go. I know he started writing a novel about a journalist who comes to Russia to investigate stories of people picked up in the night and deported, and of course in the novel that's all phony. This was a time when Akhmatova and others were being denounced. At home, they were talked about. But that was the basis for Paddy's attitude — "None of my friends have been carted off." A case of self-deception. He was in denial.

It was a form of moral blindness.

Today we are astonished at the "gullibility", to use Orwell's word, of the converts of the 1930s. We quite forget the climate of the times and the human difficulty of abandoning a faith, even when the Pope and his cardinals are exposed as rotten. As the Marxist historian Eric Hobsbawm puts it, beliefs formed by left-wingers at Cambridge "tended to be lifelong".

All this would change in 1956 when Stalin was denounced by Khrushchev at the Twentieth Congress as a monster, his secret policemen subsequently likened to the Borgia pontiffs and revealed to the world as assassins and virtuosos of murder. The scales would drop from Costello's eyes. But not yet.

Извлечение из „Положения о дипломатических и консульских представительствах иностранных государств на территории СССР“ от 14/I—27 г.

„Ст. 2, п. [illegible] Дипломатические представители пользуются личной неприкосновенностью, в силу которой они не могут быть подвергнуты аресту или задержанию в административном или судебном порядке.

Ст. 4. Помещения, занимаемые дипломатическими представительствами, а равно помещения, в которых проживают лица, упомянутые в ст. 2, и их семьи, являются неприкосновенными. Доступ в них может иметь место не иначе как с согласия дипломатического представителя.

Ст. 5. Принадлежность к числу лиц, упомянутых в ст. 2, удостоверяется соответствующими, выдаваемыми Министерством Иностранных Дел, документами“.

(Выдана на основании ст. 5 По
о дипломатических и консульских пр
тельствах от 14 января 1927 г., С.

Дипломатическая карто

№ 29.

Настоящим удостоверяется, что пр
тель сего Первый Секрета
Миссии Новой Зеланд
г. Д.П. КОСТЕЛ
пользуется всеми правами и преи
вами, присвоенными в СССР дипломат
представителям иностранных государст

Действительна по 27. I.

Министр
Иностранных Дел СССР
Заведующий Протокольным
Отделом МИД СССР

Москва 27. I.

Costello's diplomatic pass.

Doppelgänger

He's dangerous to know! He doesn't recognise Authority!
— *Famusov on Chatsky, in* Gore ot Uma

SOME TIME LATER, in 1955, after Costello was purged from government service, Douglas Zohrab who had been with Costello at the New Zealand legation in Moscow and was now first secretary in Paris, was invited to lunch by the British Minister. "He spoke in the highest terms of my knowledge of Russian," Zohrab recalls, "which made it quite clear to me that he thought I was Costello. Paddy's reputation as a scholar of distinction had obviously travelled."

Costello's reputation then rested on two publications, *The Oxford Book of Russian Verse* (1948) and, in particular, his edition of Griboyedov's comedy of manners, *Gore ot Uma*, or *The Misfortune of Being Clever* (1951), both published by Oxford University Press. They were undertaken as part-time jobs in the intervals of managing a legation by a man without formal training in the Russian language; they enjoyed a vogue, as they do still, among Slavonic scholars, although Costello's edition of *Russian Verse* initially drew fire, attracting criticism from both the right and the left for an alleged politicised preface.

To one "disgusted" critic Davin, who saw the book through the press, replied, "Our editor has taken as we should have expected a properly central position." To Costello Davin wrote, "I see how sensitive these Communists are."

Typically when the book was commissioned Davin forgot to arrange for Costello to be paid a fee; equally typically, Costello did not bother to ask for one. He took out his remuneration in the end in books.

Gore ot Uma is one of the masterpieces of Russian literature and Griboyedov's one major work. A hundred years before John Osborne's *Look Back in Anger*, it introduced the idea of the outsider — the angry young dissident and protagonist Chatsky — into Russian literature. The play initially had been banned; it was read first in samizdat editions — it is estimated that some 40,000 handwritten copies were in circulation — earning its author great réclame. Costello's Oxford edition included a seventy-page commentary on the Russian text. Forty years later when a younger scholar, Richard Peace, brought out a new edition of the play, published in Bristol in 1995, he left the commentary untouched, describing it as "a model of its kind, and so thorough that any later commentator can only tread ploddingly in his footsteps". Costello's annotations to the text still stand, unsurpassed.

Costello's fascination with the precocious Griboyedov is easy to see. Alexander Griboyedov, the scholar-soldier who became a diplomat and died murdered by a Teheran mob, is his doppelgänger — the murder of this ghostly double as enigmatic in its way as Costello's own death would be. It is generally recognised that Griboyedov the man and the play are one. The man *is* the play. But at first Costello seems hardly to have noticed the man.

> I played truant last Friday [he wrote to a friend on 8 February 1949] and went to a matinee at the Maly — *Gore ot Uma*, for the umpteenth time. I know a great deal of it off by heart now.

Again in October 1949 he wrote:

> The performance last night was the best I have ever seen. I felt as I listened to the sculptured lines, from the first word светает! ["It's getting light!"] to the very end, that this is *the* monument of the Russian speech, the poem which besides being great art is closest to the spoken language of Russia. I so nearly have it by heart now that I needed to make no effort to follow, but relaxed

> and listened in perfect contentment. Every act went too quickly. The play ended at 10 to 12, and it was too short.

Griboyedov wrote the play when he was twenty-nine years old. "Half the lines," Pushkin said, "are bound to become proverbs." As indeed they have. *Gore ot Uma* is as much quoted in everyday Russian speech, consciously or unconsciously, as Shakespeare's *Hamlet* is in English speech. It is a tour de force of wit and racy idiom, but, as with the title — literally "Grief from Mind" — the flavour is lost in translation. One might think that in bringing him before an English public, Costello had done Griboyedov a service. He had, but at an academic level only (the play is seldom performed on the English stage). Biographically, however, it is another matter.

"He was a first-class representative of his country in times of crisis, but in quiet times he was unhappy and wanted to quit. 'I'm of no use in ordinary times, and it's not my fault. People are petty; their affairs are stupid; one's heart grows hard, one's mind becomes fogged and one's moral sense is destroyed without any benefit to others. I was born for a different career.'" This is Costello writing about Griboyedov, but except for the hundred-year gap it might pass for Griboyedov writing about Costello.

Did Costello see himself as Chatsky in the play? Or as Griboyedov in life?

The story is told that after the first performance of *Gore ot Uma* in St Petersburg (1833), the Czar Nicholas I who was in the audience sent for the author and complimented him, saying he had enjoyed the play. He had found it, he said, "very amusing". Griboyedov replied with some temerity, "It wasn't meant to amuse, sire."

Sharp-tongued, idealistic, courageous, attractive to women, Griboyedov was a classical scholar and linguistic prodigy who had thrown up a university career to enter the army and had then become a diplomat. At one point a scandal — one recalls Costello's own dismissal from Exeter — obliged Griboyedov to go abroad. At another he was accused of treason and, although cleared of the charge, suspicion remained. In essence the career of the Russian diplomat, "brilliant, tragic and short", is the story of Costello's life; wherever one looks there are parallels; whether he knew it or not, Costello could not have chosen to write about anyone the shape of whose life more closely resembled his own.

Chistye Prude Park (Clean Pond) in central Moscow and the statue of Griboyedov at the entrance to the park (see "Doppelgänger").

Top: Boris Pasternak's dacha at Peredelkino, an hour's train ride from Moscow. Although there was no announcement of the poet's death, hundreds arrived for his funeral and turned it into a demonstration against the regime that had tried to silence him. Pasternak is buried half a mile from the house.

Above: The author (right) with Pasternak's son and literary executor, Yvgeny Pasternak, in Moscow, 2005.

Above: Alister McIntosh.

Top right: Ruth Macky and Douglas Lake at a reception in Moscow in 1948.

Above right: Jean McKenzie and Costello (at rear) at a reception in Paris for the New Zealand Prime Minister, Sidney Holland, in 1951.

Top left: Carl Berendsen.

Top right: Douglas Zohrab.

Above: New Zealand Legation staff, Moscow, 1946. Front row: R.T.G. Patrick, Charles Boswell, Paddy Costello; at back: Ray Perry (with pipe), Ruth Macky, Douglas Lake.

Above: Bear Mountain, circa 1950. From left, Frank Corner, Tom Davin and Richard Gray Collins, taking time off from UN sessions in New York. Tom Davin was posted in Canada; Collins and Corner, a future head of External Affairs, were in Wellington. Frank Corner attended three UN sessions in the McCarthy era with Carl Berendsen, posted in Washington. In 1954 Dick Collins, the victim of McCarthy-type persecution in Wellington, would resign.

Right: Kekushev's Mansion in Moscow, home to the New Zealand Legation in Costello's time. The building is now occupied by the Egyptian Defence Ministry.

Pension Waldruhe
Semmering, Austria
April 16, 1954

The New Zealand Consul
9 Rue Leonard de Vinci
Paris, France

Dear Sir:

While applying to the British Consul for an extension of my British family passport, I was informed that under the legislation now in force I should make application to you for the issue of separate, individual New Zealand passports for myself and my wife.

I wish to note that I was born in New Zealand and married my wife, who is Canadian born, in 1936, thereby making of her, according to what I understand, a New Zealand citizen too.

Left: The first page of the letter written by Peter Kroger which arrived at the New Zealand Legation in Paris in 1954 and led to Jean McKenzie, Charge d'Affaires, unwittingly issuing passports to two Russian atomic spies. Release of the letter and other Intelligence material in 2007 has removed blame from Costello and helped end 40 years of speculation.

Above: Lona and Morris Cohen, alias Helen and Peter Kroger, whose penetration of British security using New Zealand passports produced a scandal which helped bring down the Macmillan government of the 1960s. In his memoirs the Russian who master-minded the Krogers' operation in west London, Gordon Lonsdale, described them as "a charming couple who said they were New Zealand subjects" when he first met them by accident in Paris in 1955.

Following page: Photocopies of the Krogers' passports, on display at Scotland Yard's Black Museum in London. The originals are held by the London Police, Special Branch.

1

DESCRIPTION
SIGNALEMENT

Profession / Profession: Broker and Merchant

Place and date of birth / Lieu et date de naissance: Gisborne, New Zealand 10 July 1910

Residence / Résidence: United States of America

Height / Taille: 5 ft. 9 ins.

Colour of eyes / Couleur des yeux: Brown

Colour of hair / Couleur des cheveux: Grey

Special peculiarities / Signes particuliers:

CHILDREN-ENFANTS

Name / Nom	Date of birth / Date de naissance	Sex / Sexe

PHOTOGRAPH OF BEARER
PHOTOGRAPHIE DU TITULAIRE

Peter J. Kro

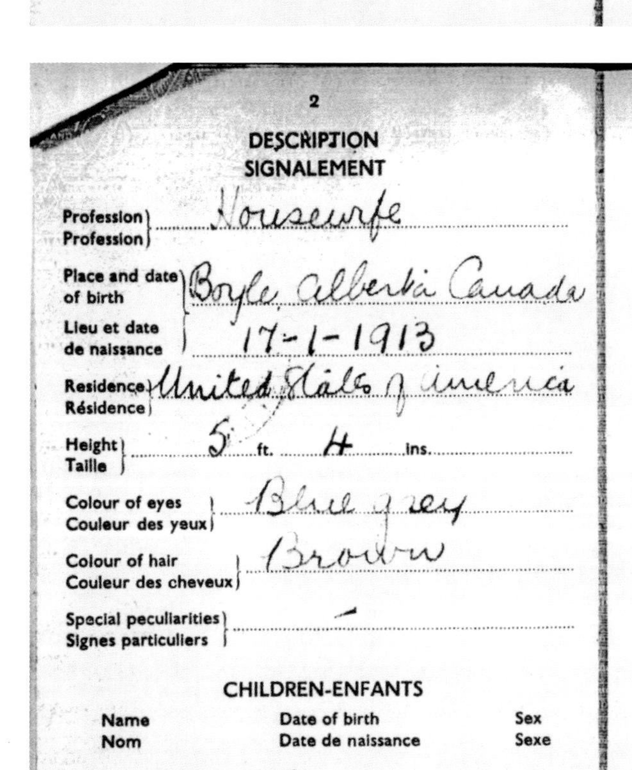

2

DESCRIPTION
SIGNALEMENT

Profession / Profession: Housewife

Place and date of birth / Lieu et date de naissance: Boyle, Alberta Canada 17-1-1913

Residence / Résidence: United States of America

Height / Taille: 5 ft. 4 ins.

Colour of eyes / Couleur des yeux: Blue grey

Colour of hair / Couleur des cheveux: Brown

Special peculiarities / Signes particuliers: –

CHILDREN-ENFANTS

Name / Nom	Date of birth / Date de naissance	Sex / Sexe
–		

3

PHOTOGRAPH OF BEARER
PHOTOGRAPHIE DU TITULAIR

Signature of bearer
Signature du titulaire

Helen J. Krog

He worked on the play for six months in 1949. He was again Chargé. Boswell having returned to Moscow from leave the previous year was being recalled to New Zealand, this time for good. It was probably Costello's happiest time. His letters to Doug and Ruth Lake reflect his mood:

> It is the most wonderful springtime, the tenderest green on the trees. As always in Moscow, the spring is so fresh, it seems to be happening for the first time.

In August he went with the Boswells to Leningrad to see them off and, predictably, seized the chance to see yet another staging of *Gore ot Uma* (also *Traviata, Pikovaya Dama*, and the Pushkin plays, *Skupoi Rytsar* and *Kamenny Gost*).*

> Not bad [he writes] when you consider I was there only three nights.
>
> The white nights were still on. When I went for a midnight walk along the Winter Palace after Pikovaya it was still light enough to read, if one had wanted to read and not look across the river towards Peter and Paul or to wander across the Palace Square, empty and vast at that hour.
>
> What a lordly city it is!
>
> I went with the Boswells to Peterhof, where Charles (in sports jacket, grey bags and sandshoes) nearly got run in for striking ballerina poses alongside the statuary and for walking on the grass despite notices and warnings. I think the attendant, one of those harassed little women with a red dezhurny band on her arm, suspected he had a tile loose.
>
> I resumed work on *Gore ot Uma* two days ago.

A change occurred. Early in September Costello announced to Davin that his work on the play was finished. All that remained was for his notes on two of the four acts to be typed up. Costello did not type, as he did not drive. Nor did he dictate. He wrote his commentary in the same clear unblemished hand that marked his political despatches — to have legible handwriting, he

* *Skupoi Rytsar* (The Miserly Knight) and *Kamenny Gost* (The Stone Guest, of *Don Giovanni* fame). The two plays are known as the "Little Tragedies".

used to say, "is the first mark of politeness" — then, turning to the next task, was at once absorbed in it. At least, going on past form, that was normally what would have happened. Not this time.

On 7 September we learn that, having "finished" Griboyedov's play, he is now reading all the memoirs and letters contemporary with Griboyedov "that I can lay my hands on". First he devours the memoirs of Yakushkin, Annenkova, Zhikharev, Vigel (the two-volume set — he couldn't find the seven-volume edition), and the letters of Pushkin and Turgenev. Then he turns to Gretsch ("an awful bastard but a valuable authority on the period") before going off to the Lenin Library to read plays by Shakhovskoi, Kuzazhnin and Ilyin, contemporaries of Griboyedov, which he has been unable to find in the bookshops.

Why?

Or rather, why now? Pushkin gives us a clue.

In June 1829, in one of those bizarre coincidences which seem to typify Russian life and literature, Pushkin — Griboyedov's contemporary and friend — was travelling in the Caucasus mountains when he met a party of Georgians accompanying an ox-wagon. "Where are you from?" he said to them. "From Teheran." "What's in the wagon?" "Griboyed."

Two years earlier, in 1827, war had broken out between Persia and Russia. Sent to the front with diplomatic status, the young Griboyedov had distinguished himself by negotiating a peace treaty with the Persians. Entrusted to carry the treaty back for ratification, he was received in Petersburg by the Czar. He wanted to retire, he told the Czar, and devote himself to literature, but instead was appointed Russian Minister to Persia and sent back to Teheran to supervise the terms of the treaty. He returned unwillingly, telling Pushkin no good would come of it. It was the old story. Three Armenians appeared at the Russian legation in Teheran and asked Griboyedov for asylum (under the treaty Griboyedov had negotiated they now qualified as Russian citizens). One was the chief eunuch of the Shah's imperial harem, the other two Armenian girls who had escaped from the harem of the Shah's son-in-law. Griboyedov took them in and granted them refuge, knowing that his action was bound to anger the Shah and infuriate the Moslem community. A few days later, on 30 January 1829, a mob of fanatics broke into the legation palace, killing Griboyedov and all but one of his staff. Griboyedov died fighting. His mutilated body, dragged through the streets and recovered three days later, was identified only by an old duelling scar on the little finger. He was just thirty-four years old.

That September in Moscow, having done the accounts and his quarterly report, Costello interrupted his reading at the Lenin Library and flew to Tiflis (Tbilisi) in the Caucasus where Griboyedov was buried. The foothills of the Caucasus begin just after Rostov. Costello describes the journey with some excitement. Putting down at an intermediate stop, he recognises palm trees and two New Zealand cabbage trees growing at the airport ("I am sure of it.").

He reached the Georgian capital at dusk, dined on shashlyk and Tsinandali, and the next morning straight after breakfast climbed a hill-side to the little monastery of St David. Griboyedov's tomb was on a terrace, inside a vault set into the foundations of the monastery; ivy surrounded the vault; through the iron bars was a sarcophagus surmounted by a statue of a kneeling woman embracing the cross; beside it an inscription composed by Griboyedov's young wife:

> *Your thoughts and actions live for ever in Russian memory*
> *But to what purpose does my love for you live on?*

Costello recounted:

> I sat on a bench by the tomb and smoked my pipe. While I was there, Georgian women on their way to the monastery, stopped by the tomb, knelt, blessed themselves and kissed the bars of the vault.

He did a lot of thinking, Costello tells us, sitting there that morning smoking his pipe, under the reproachful eye of Yelena, his Intourist guide. He told himself (modestly) that he knew a great deal more about Alexander Sergeyevich Griboyedov than he had six months before, more even perhaps than some of the Soviet authorities on the period. Yet he remained puzzled.

Who was responsible for the murder?

Who had incited the mob?

Was it the Shah? The religious clerics, the mullahs? Or were the British behind it? Was the crime organised, as some scholars suggested, by the English who hoped by organising disturbances to counteract Russian influence in

Persia?

There was an elementary mystery to which neither he, nor any of the Soviet authorities he had consulted, had an answer. The proof was still missing.

Presently he got up and walked to the edge of the terrace. The monastery overlooked a wooded hill-side of cedars, cypresses and chinars. Below was Tbilisi. He could see the tiled roofs and balconies of the "Turkish-style" old houses winding through the alleys of the old town. Lizards came out of the crevices and darted about his feet. He walked up some steps to a higher level, discovering as he wandered among the graves that Stalin's mother was buried there; then he returned to the bench by Griboyedov's tomb, the mystery preying on his mind.

He came again the next day, climbing the hill-side this time accompanied by a friend, a Canadian doctor named McMorris who had arrived from Moscow. They had lunch together at a small hotel. Afterwards they strolled round the town and attended Mass in the cathedral. Costello found a book about a Russian explorer who had visited Queen Charlotte Sound in New Zealand in 1820. He remembered that McIntosh had once written a history of Marlborough province. He bought the book for him. In the evening he and McMorris discussed over dinner whether or not they had been followed by the secret police. They thought not. They drank five bottles of good Georgian wine between them and went to bed "in a pickle".

Costello returned to Moscow none the wiser about Griboyedov's murder. But an idea had begun to form in his brain, another enthusiasm. He wrote in his diary, quoting John Aubrey: "*Then, thought Mr Hobbes, 'tis time for me to shift for myself, and so withdraw into France.*"

It would mean learning Persian. He could manage that.

He already had some Sanskrit. (His 1935 visit to Uday Shankar at Dartington Hall would come in handy, after all.) It would mean going to Teheran. He could manage that too. Teheran, from Moscow, was at his back door. He would for the moment keep the idea to himself, he decided. He was quietly elated, as in a dream. It was like finding a new tense in Russian, or discovering Housman, or seeing Ireland for the first time. It was like acquiring a second self. A month earlier, Costello had announced that his work on Griboyedov was finished. But really it was only just beginning.

He arrived back in Moscow by plane on 4 October 1949. Costello had hoped to return via the Georgian Military Highway but was refused permission. There had been a certain amount of world news in his absence, none of it entirely unexpected to him, except that word had come from McIntosh that the legation was to close.

The Retreat from Moscow

We will probably end up by walking out on the
whole show and leaving everything as a present to the
Russians who will, no doubt, charge us storage.

— Alister McIntosh, May 1950

"SO THEY'RE GOING to close us down," Costello wrote to the Lakes on 8 December 1949. "I am thinking of withdrawing into academic life and am going to ask Cambridge University what about it. Please don't mention this to anybody yet."

Alister McIntosh's telegram had not come as a complete surprise to him. In New Zealand the government had changed. Labour was out of office; for the first time a modern conservative National Party was in power. McIntosh had already warned Costello that if Labour lost the election, the legation might go. National's leader, Sidney Holland, was a fervent Empire loyalist. Holland believed that New Zealand's interests could be adequately served filtered through the British, and he wanted the Moscow legation abolished. Indeed, opening his election campaign, as McIntosh reported to Costello, "the only references Mr Holland made to External Affairs were this one and, with a break in his voice, he expressed the desire of the National Party to help 'dear old Britain'".

Costello replied, "We are keeping our fingers crossed."

Costello was philosophical about it. The legation, he knew, was costly.

Hadn't he already said it was an albatross? In 1948, meeting with the Prime Minister, Peter Fraser, and McIntosh in London, he had said that the cost of maintaining the post exceeded the value of the information New Zealand received. (But they had overruled him.) More colourfully, as Costello would put it to his son later, "All we achieved in Moscow in five-and-a-half years was to sell the Russians half a dozen crates of apples and receive two New Zealanders on motor-bikes." Certainly the amount of trade the legation generated was negligible.

On the other hand, in 1949 an event occurred which threw everything into a new light. It was that Russia possessed an atomic device. The news, coming four years after America dropped the first atomic bomb on Japan, broke the American nuclear monopoly and took the West by surprise. Costello was given the news when he returned to Moscow from Tbilisi. He immediately drafted and despatched a policy statement to McIntosh.

This statement in a sense was superfluous, for Costello had informed his government in 1947 that the Soviet Union had the bomb. As McIntosh said later, "Paddy told us the Russians had the atomic bomb long before the Americans realised. He showed us this conclusively, and so accurately you'd have thought he had inside information. He hadn't, he'd worked it out using methods built up from his Intelligence training."

What Costello had done in 1947, after listening to a speech by the Russian foreign minister, Molotov, was to sit down and analyse what Molotov said. First he analysed Molotov's speech, then he compared it with earlier rumours of a bomb reported in the Soviet press; then, after comparing notes with Doug Lake and studying the whole question, he alerted McIntosh and the New Zealand government. He demonstrated that the Soviet claim to have a bomb was to be taken seriously. By contrast, the British and American embassies in Moscow, with their apparatus of experts and attachés, had analysed the same speech and decided that Molotov was bluffing. They were wrong.*

Costello's warning was in vain. In 1947 nobody believed him.

He would continue to make predictions — about Tito's relationship with Russia, about the progress of Sino–Soviet relations — which would be proved accurate by the course of events. These too would go unheeded.

* As early as January 1946 Costello had begun to take seriously rumours that Russia had the capability to produce atomic weapons. He spelled out "the fallacy" of American foreign policy, its continued under-estimation of Soviet capability, in a despatch to McIntosh in 1949. See Notes.

Costello was not infallible. But he had prescience, a Cassandra-like gift for foretelling the future, based on an ability to put together casual bits of information, evaluate them and shuffle them into constructs, where others saw only unrelated patterns. It is tempting to speculate what he might have become, had he been born under a different flag or been the representative of a bigger and bolder nation.

The year 1949, the year Sidney George Holland succeeding in removing Labour after fourteen years in office, was a tumultuous one. It was the year Mao Tse-tung's communists came to power in China, the year of George Kennan's "long telegram", advocating the US policy of "containment" towards the Soviet Union. It was also the year when ambassador David Kelly invited 300 Soviet guests to the Queen's Birthday Party at the British Embassy in Moscow, and only seven came. It was a year marking one of the lowest points of the Cold War. Sidney Holland's 1949 election pledge to abolish the Moscow office was not made in a vacuum; arguably it made sense in financial terms. But coming on top of recent events in China and the Russian bomb on 27 September 1949, it was folly. At a stroke the bomb and all that that implied for East–West relations had transformed the situation. The New Zealand legation was just getting into its stride. It had become a valuable listening post.

Costello's reaction to the threat of closure had initially been one of dismay (he had once speculated that having staked so much in "the famous furniture", future New Zealand governments would think twice before breaking off relations with the Soviet Union). Now he became philosophical, accepting that "our days are numbered". Yet for a giddy moment — it was Christmas 1949 — it seemed that help was on the way. A telegram came from McIntosh:

> PERSONAL & CONFIDENTIAL FOR COSTELLO
> Have not given up hope some formula for reprieve may be found. You do same.

But this was followed the next day by another telegram:

> After further conversation with Minister I reluctantly conclude that there is little or no possibility of decision being altered.

On the night of 25 December Costello celebrated Christmas by reading the Lesson (1st Epistle of St John, verses 7 to end) at the British Embassy service in Moscow.

> I don't like C. of E. services [he told McIntosh] which seem to me always to be inspired equally by the Bible and Rudyard Kipling, but for things of this sort I don't regard myself as a private individual. The Christmas services here (conducted by the chaplain of the UK Legation in Helsinki) are a sort of manifestation of Commonwealth unity, and one must play.

It was their first and last Christmas in the legation building — Kekushev's Mansion, as it was known to Muscovites. The Costellos had moved in in July 1949, after Charles Boswell's recall.

"After the flat," Josie says, "there seemed to be rooms everywhere." The building at 21 Metrostroevskaya (Street of the Metro), built by the architect Lev Kekushev at the turn of the century, was a jewel of art nouveau. With its pointed tower, huge sculpted lion and ornamental reliefs on the facade, it resembled a medieval fortress. It stood out like a folly, as it does still.

> I lived in it with my dolls [Josie again]. At the top we played games. We had Russian maids and chauffeurs and doormen. It was magical.

It was almost as beguiling as the matinees to which Costello began to take Josie and Katie in a final all-out assault on the Moscow theatre. "We are giving the theatre a thrashing," he reported to the Lakes, adding that at a performance of Glinka's *Ruslan & Ludmila* his children went wild like the rest of the audience, clapping the hero and hissing the villain. Nowhere else in the world, he observed, would one find an audience of such goodwill:

> The Soviet spectator is the least blasé of men. The theatre is for him an enchanted world and he is determined to undergo the enchantment if at all possible, and to give the theatre the benefit of any doubt that is going.

Katie, not yet five, "will do anything [Bil reported], in order to go to the theatre".

In winter the snows came and the snows receded. The heaps of rotting snow inside the iron railings of the courtyards melted and turned to lakes; the ground dried between the boles of the lime and elm trees in the streets; the twigs turned with the coming of spring. On a Sunday walk with Katie along the boulevard leading from Dvorets Sovyetov towards Pushkin Square, Costello watched children skipping in the open spaces. People were out, capless, not wearing even demi-sezonny overcoats. Packs of children were running about so furiously he was "in constant danger of being knocked over" and had to hoist Katie in the air to avoid becoming a hazard in their game. He reflected wistfully that not again would he take his family on the drive to Yasnaya Polyana, "through the autumn birch forests"; nor again write to friends that

> A month from now we'll have the first snow. And then — Teatralnaya Ploshchad [Theatre Square] at midnight, the snow drifting down and *Pikovaya* still in one's ears.

With the closure looming, Costello told McIntosh that he had decided to quit. "I really am more interested in books than in diplomacy," he wrote. He said he wanted to resign from the service and return to academic life, preferably at Cambridge. McIntosh replied, "I cannot say how sorry I am . . . All that maddens me is the thought that this ridiculous move will have the possible result of our losing your services."

But Alister McIntosh did not give up, even yet. He had received written instructions to close the legation, but Cabinet had yet to ratify them. He was in no position to force the issue — McIntosh never made the mistake of confusing influence with power. But he continued nonetheless to lobby, "hoping against hope". It was futile. On 24 March 1950 he cabled Costello finally:

> CABINET HAS DECIDED TO CLOSE THE LEGATION ON GROUNDS OF FINANCIAL STRINGENCY.

Costello had until the summer to decide his future.

He was in two minds. The persona of diplomat no longer fitted him. He was not bred for straight lines and was too restless and independent for the placid round of duties and functions that he saw stretching away in front of him — "I really don't want to go and drink cocktails in Tokyo or Delhi." He saw his interest in the job unravelling from boredom and with it his usefulness to New Zealand. He told McIntosh he wanted a quiet academic job where he could work on questions that interested him. He wanted, he repeated, back to books.

The question was, did "the books" want him back?

He feared he had lost touch. On the other hand, his edition of *Gore ot Uma* though not yet published was circulating in galley form and exciting attention, Davin wrote, among Slavonic scholars in England.

Costello had written to Cambridge in December. He had a reply in February. It was not encouraging. The number of lectureships in Russian studies was fixed, he was told, and all were filled. He was not wanted. That left Oxford. Davin, we now learn, had passed on to Costello a request from the Russian professor, Konovalov, to visit him in Oxford. But Costello had declined the invitation.

What was wrong?

In some ways Costello was his own worst enemy. Brilliant, assertive, contemptuous of fools, with all the arrogance of the *Wunderkind*, he was also quite timid. Sitting on his shoulder was a Hamlet which would not let him make up his mind. It was either a Hamlet or the curse of the New Zealander, caution.

He wrote to Doug and Ruth Lake:

> The Oxford Press showed my edition of *Gore ot Uma* to Konovalov, the professor there, who said he was "full of admiration" for my work, and wrote: "I wish we could persuade Mr Costello to come to England. I shd. be glad to establish cooperation with him in the Russian field." Which is all very fine. But I am shy of pressing the matter. I feel like a young prostitute out on her first expedition: hoping to be accosted, but afraid to accost.

"I wish we could meet and talk about these matters," Davin had written. But it was now spring. Weightier matters intervened. Costello had £20,000 worth of furniture and other possessions to shed and, as March became

April, and May beckoned, there were no takers. He had less than three weeks, and no staff. The Lakes had gone. The first secretary had left and not been replaced; the second secretary, Douglas Zohrab, had been flown to hospital in Berlin with rheumatic fever. That left the typist, Miss Healy, who had married an Australian and been removed, also to Berlin, with gall-bladder trouble. Costello was doing the whole thing single-handed.

"Dear Dan," he wrote on 28 April 1950. "The business of closing a Legation in peacetime is complex":

> If we had gone to war with Russia my job would have been easy: I should have gone to the Soviet Foreign Office with my chin in the air and stiffly demanded my passport. Then I should have handed all the NZ assets — cars, furniture — to the Swiss or the Swedes and so have buggered off at the high porte.
>
> However, we haven't even broken off relations. And we own up to £20,000 worth of tables, chairs, curtains, motor cars and so forth which I can't just walk away from. In a word, I am now in the second-hand furniture business, and business is slack. So I sit here, "waiting for a wind", as the Russians say.

Having been kept at a distance by the Soviets for five-and-a-half years, Costello now found himself suddenly in demand. Doug Zohrab recalls, "I remember Paddy saying that the only substantive discussions he ever had, aside from Protocol, were when he went to tell them we were closing down."

The legation finally closed on 13 June 1950. Four days later, on 17 June, the Costellos sailed for England — Costello planning to fly on to New Zealand, he wrote, "to talk to my bosses". McIntosh had telegraphed inviting him to come to Wellington for talks. "What then," Costello told Davin, "I do not know."

From the Letters

1949–1950, Moscow

September 1949 (to Doug & Ruth Lake)
In a week's time I am going on a pilgrimage to a literary shrine in Tiflis — where A.S. Griboyedov is buried. He is the culmination of a long development in Russian drama. But what a culmination! He shoots up like a Matterhorn from a mass of foothills.

28th September 7 p.m.
At the Tbilisi airport I was met by my Intourist guide, Yelena Nikolaevna. I might as well admit that at Sukhúmi [an intermediate stop] I bought 7 large peaches for 4 rubles, 6 of them still bulging in my jacket pockets as I walked with Yelena across the field. I was carrying in my right hand a shiny aluminium suitcase bought in Paris last year and in my other hand a fearful great bundle of grapes wrapped up in a table napkin which like a lunatic I had bought on the airport at Sukhúmi — 5 rubles the kilo (22 in Moscow). After eating a few I began to fear the

possible effects of Tiflis tummy . . .

5th October 1949
Returned to Moscow by plane yesterday.
There has been a certain amount of world news — Soviet atomic bomb, Soviet recognition of Red China — but none of it unexpected to you or to me.

(to Alister McIntosh)
A few reflections on Russia's atomic bomb.

First, we were right in the Legation, and the UK and US embassies were wrong. I was convinced when I heard Molotov make his speech in 1947 that he was not bluffing; and Doug Lake reached the same conclusion as I: in November 1947 Russia either had or was about to have atomic bombs in her possession.

20 February 1950 (to Doug & Ruth Lake)
Everybody outside this Legation seems to have been surprised at the concessions made to China in the treaty agreements published the other day. We, on the other hand, were at first surprised that Russia conceded so little.

28 April 1950 (to Davin)
Before setting forth for New Zealand I shall run up to Oxford to see you. I confess to faint surprise that Winnie has a hankering for New Zealand. To live in, you mean? I'd rather, far rather, face English austerity than New Zealand plenty.

12 May 1950 (from McIntosh)
Dear Paddy
I am sending you a note from your sister, Mollie. She asked me to let her know when I have anything definite "as to the exact time when Des (Paddy is an affectation since the war and sounds queer to us) will actually arrive." Madie and I like that particular touch.

7 June 1950 (to Davin)

The Legation is hastening to its close. Today is Wednesday. This day week we'll be in Leningrad on our way home.

PART FOUR
A DIPLOMAT IN PARIS

1950–1954

McIntosh's Folly

He said, "Sir, we have all these francs.
We must do something with them"

— *Sir George Laking*

ALISTER McINTOSH WAS in a quandary. "God knows what's going to happen," he wrote to Jean McKenzie in Paris, when the decision to close Moscow had become irreversible. "That means much more than they imagine. I don't know what to do with Paddy." A little later in the same letter he wrote: "Paddy, as the most brilliant diplomatic officer we have, represents somewhat of a problem. I just don't know what to do."

McIntosh wrote this in December 1949. It was now September 1950. Costello had arrived back in New Zealand and McIntosh's predicament was unchanged. "No good sending him to New York or Washington," he wrote to a colleague, "and he would be wasted in London."

McIntosh had brought Costello home intending to send him to Paris where a new legation had been opened. Paris was the logical choice. Happily, after some discussion, Costello had fallen in with the plan. Back in New Zealand, the reality that he had probably left it too late to return to academic life had begun to sink in.

"Hold everything, kid," he wrote to Bil in England. "We're going to Paris."

McIntosh wrote to Jean McKenzie, the Chargé in Paris:

> He has not got another job, and he wants to stay with us and I want him to. What I propose is that Davin* should go to New York to the General Assembly, and Paddy should temporarily take his place. It is perfectly absurd to have our best linguist in the shape of Costello, without a job.

So far so good. What this letter obscures is the fact that the Paris Legation which on the surface appeared up and running, a done thing, was nothing of the sort. In concept it was as quixotic a notion as Moscow had been and, as McIntosh was about to learn, its future was just as uncertain.

Paris had appeared first as a glint in McIntosh's eye in the last days of Fraser's Labour government, when Moscow came under threat. McIntosh had detached Jean McKenzie from the New Zealand Secretariat in Canberra and sent her to Paris to open a post there, acting as Counsellor. In Paris, operating from the Hotel Bristol, this amiable woman had scurried about for premises and eventually found a handsome residence in the 16th arrondissement near the Etoile, in the rue Léonard de Vinci.

It was owned by an impoverished princess. With McIntosh's assurance that the purchase money was already earmarked, Jean McKenzie opened negotiations and began importing Wedgwood and Worcester china and other furnishings from England. She reported:

> There is a magnificent suite of 4 rooms, plus 2 bathrooms. Four rooms which are distinct from the main stairway with complete privacy. Then above a nice flat of 2 rooms and bathroom for guests. The garden is excellent, garage houses 4 cars and an apartment above it for staff etc.

Disaster had almost struck when Charles Boswell, after being recalled from Moscow, had suggested to the Prime Minister that he be appointed Minister to Paris. Confiding this to Jean, McIntosh said: "Fortunately, I have succeeded in blocking it." Then, when the National government was elected and it began to jib at paying for running costs and hiring staff,

* Dan Davin's elder brother, Tom Davin.

McIntosh fretted that the legation would succumb to the fate of Moscow "and be closed down before it is opened".

Early in 1950 Jean McKenzie clinched the deal, securing the Résidence from the owner, the Princesse de Béarn, for £35,000 ($NZ2.1 million on today's values). "So many grand possibilities!" she wrote.

Jean McKenzie's first despatches arrived in Wellington. She moved in with a couple of secretaries, a French-speaking typist, and established her style with a sparkling reception for 400 guests. All seemed well. She began scouting an apartment for the arrival of the Costellos and found the time, she told McIntosh, to run some personal errands for his wife.

> Doris wants a little shopping done [he had written]. I enclose a list of vegetable seeds. The address of the shop is given. She also wanted a kitchen utensil for sieving vegetables. It is described in a catalogue as a Moulin Légume.

Costello arrived back in New Zealand from Moscow at the end of July 1950. After family reunions with his mother and married sisters in Auckland and the Waikato, he travelled south to Wellington for talks. He had never been to the capital before. After Moscow, it was a shock.

> A shabby town [he told his diary]. The streets a jumble of buildings and styles and sizes. The main street, although narrow, carries tramlines, & the trams are old & noisy. On Saturday the town is dead.

Still, it was redeemed by the vibrancy of the small ministry McIntosh had created on the roof of Parliament Buildings, a family atmosphere not unlike that of a university common-room. Although forbidden by his Prime Minister Peter Fraser to advertise for the staff he wanted, McIntosh had succeeded in attracting nonetheless a band of enterprising young professionals, lawyers and servicemen with university backgrounds, from outside the ranks of the Civil Service. They were spread through a warren of rooms and cubbyholes including the cipher and communications room where the War Cabinet secretariat had once been installed. The ministry, a step away from the eyrie that was the Prime Minister's office, took up most of the top floor. After work on Friday the choicer spirits repaired to the Vegetable Club, in the offices of a law firm on the Quay. There were cheap vegetables for sale at one end of the chambers and a bar at the other; the talk was political, irreverent and went on late; it was hard to tell, Costello wrote, who was in the ascendant, "lapsed Catholics or left-wingers". He was in his element, despite the watery beer.

The days passed. He met the new Foreign Affairs Minister Frederick Doidge, travelled north to see old friends and made plans to leave for Paris at the end of September. In September came the bombshell.

McIntosh called Costello into his office and told him that Paris had been put on notice. The whole arrangement was under review by the government. He, McIntosh, was leaving to accompany Mr Doidge to a conference in London. And after that? McIntosh shook his head. The matter was out of his hands, he said. Costello, out of a job for three months since Moscow had closed, was high and dry.

If McIntosh was stunned, Costello said later, he did not show it. On 19 September 1950, writing from London to alert Jean McKenzie, McIntosh told her that the government had instructed Doidge to cross the Channel and report, "before any decision can be given about the disposal of Paris":

> And he, Paddy, is browned off, not knowing what the hell is going to happen. I am not in a position to force a decision.

It was a curious state of affairs. If one had not known the level of McIntosh's commitment, how much he had invested personally and how determined he was not to lose his ablest diplomat, one might be forgiven for thinking him craven, or heartless. His pet project is in jeopardy, the Minister preparing to descend on Paris. Yet here he is writing chattily to thank Jean McKenzie for the seeds which have arrived in the diplomatic bag — and adding a supplementary request "for some tiny tins of truffles, and some saffron" — the consummately phlegmatic servant of the state, moving with apparent unconcern through the turmoil as if nothing untoward is happening.

Had he seen it coming?

Certainly McIntosh knew that in serving Sidney Holland after Peter Fraser, he was dealing with a new breed of politician. The new Prime Minister was New Zealand-born. He was clever but culturally abject. He had no insight into developments in Europe. When Holland assumed office, McIntosh had tried without success to persuade him to take the foreign affairs portfolio himself, as Peter Fraser had done. Instead he had been given Fred Doidge. Doidge had worked in London as a newspaperman. He had grown up with the Beaverbrook doctrine, roughly translated as "the Wogs begin across the Channel". Doidge was another isolationist. As McIntosh would later inform Jean McKenzie, when New Zealand was invited to attend the founding session of the Council of Europe in Strasbourg,

> Mr Doidge is not keen on New Zealand becoming involved in European affairs, nor did he want any Members of Parliament to go, because he felt that they might be carried away with enthusiasm and might be favourable towards continued association by New Zealand with these effete Europeans.

This attitude, astonishing as it may seem today, was less so when the Holland government sought to stifle Paris. Holland and his Cabinet considered the Paris post an unnecessary luxury. They were right. There was no need for it. As Sir George Laking says:

> Paris was an accident. The real need was for a post in Germany. But Mac had all these blocked francs. He said to Peter Fraser, "Sir, we have all these francs. We must do something with them." That's what they did. They bought an embassy.

Like Costello en route to Tbilisi, unable to say no to a bunch of cheap grapes, McIntosh could never resist an opportunity. *Blocked* francs? It was a war debt.

After France fell in May 1940, New Zealand received a distress call. It came from Tahiti. Cut off from captive France, where a pro-German government had been installed at Vichy, the French possession of Tahiti was holding a plebiscite to decide whether to support Vichy or the Free French under General de Gaulle. According to George Laking,

> We sent a shipload of food and essentials and sent Berendsen with it. They anchored offshore and sent a message saying, here we are, we have food to which you're welcome, provided you vote for de Gaulle. Result, the island rallied to de Gaulle.

That is the short version. It omits to mention that there had been a coup.

It was a grey September morning in 1940 when the warship carrying New Zealand's top civil servant, Carl Berendsen, steamed into Tahiti. As HMS *Achilles* nosed into Papeete waters, the palm trees above the tide-mark shivered in the cool current blowing from the sea. The vessel approached "gingerly". The captain, Commodore Parry, feared mines and artillery fire from the shore. A hostile gunship, the *Dumont d'Urville*, was reported to be in the vicinity. The pair were surprised by a crowd of 2000 people, all ships in port decked and natives waving flags to greet them. When Berendsen went ashore, he found himself transported to a scene reminiscent of Thackeray's nineteenth-century burlesque. Carl August Berendsen, although as a young man he had volunteered for the Dominion force which captured German Samoa in 1914, was not a military man. The man who would become in the McCarthy era New Zealand's coldest warrior — "Old Carl" as McIntosh would dub him — had found ways since 1914 of avoiding active service. His training had not prepared him for what he described as "a peculiar and difficult situation".

All was confusion. The French governor had been deposed in a coup and the British consul, to whom Berendsen hoped to turn for advice, had gone bush. On the door of the British Consulate was a notice, "Closed by Order of Vichy". At the cenotaph the French flag lay on the ground in tatters. Truculent Madagascan seamen who had mutinied roamed the streets, the Tahitians who had voted in the plebiscite to support de Gaulle chanted and sang, while the French residents, mostly pro-Vichy and numbering about a hundred, appeared sullen and starving. Cargo boats were laid up. The Australian Union Steamship Company had cut off supplies. There was no flour, cooking oil or garlic. The British residents had no salt for their porridge. There was no telephone, no post, and the pro-Vichy gunship *Dumont d'Urville* might return at any moment and stage a counter-coup. Once the *Achilles* left, the island was virtually defenceless.

"New Zealand is asked to meet a shortage of eleven million francs," Berendsen reported.

In the end all was well. The British consul reappeared, the French governor deposed in the coup and his pro-Vichy henchmen were put on a ship and deported, and an administration loyal to de Gaulle was installed. Foodstuffs were unloaded for the population. On his last evening in Tahiti

Carl Berendsen gave a dinner, after which he and the commodore adjourned to the Cabaret Royal and "danced with the ladies of the administration". In a 31-page report to the New Zealand government dated 20 September 1940, Berendsen announced, "my mission completed".

So it was that some years later when McIntosh discovered that the New Zealand government had continued to feed, victual and arm Tahiti for the duration of the war, he found himself sitting on a windfall of French francs that had built up in Europe. They could not be spent outside France because of currency restrictions and they amounted to some 40 million francs ($NZ5 million at today's values).

Just for a moment McIntosh hesitated to put in a claim. France's finances by 1949 were shaky and Australia, he was told, had written off a similar war debt. Then on learning that the money owing to New Zealand far exceeded the Australian debt and that the economy of French Oceania was flourishing from a lucrative phosphate trade, he hesitated no longer.

> We would be foolish in forgiving them the whole of the advances we made to them,

McIntosh told Jean McKenzie in October 1949, instructing her to secure from the French government if not the lot, then a little — "or at any rate enough to buy, furnish and stock up a legation". She was as good as his word.

But what of the threatened closure? What of the anti-European envoy from Wellington, the Hon. Frederick Doidge, charged with casting a weevil eye over McIntosh's Folly and, if necessary, disposing of it?

The disposal of Paris, the reader may have guessed by now, was averted. Fred Doidge crossed the Channel to inspect Paris on or about 15 October 1950. He was received by Jean McKenzie who showed him over the legation with its walled garden and spreading magnolia tree and, having moved herself into the linen room, put the Minister to bed in her private apartment over the ballroom. Next day she accompanied him to the Quai d'Orsay and in the evening presided over a dinner at which he found himself seated next to General Vanier, the Dean of the Corps of Commonwealth Representatives. The Minister of External Affairs was an inordinately vain man. He was not averse to a small drink, or an after-dinner flutter at cards. Nor was his hostess. Jean McKenzie it turned out was a *very* good poker player. There was a great deal the elderly and infirm Mr Doidge did not know about this remarkable woman. Jean McKenzie wore long-sleeved full-skirted dresses and paua-shell earrings; her hair was blonde and wavy; her smile was like spun sugar ("comme sucre gelé", to quote General Vanier). Jean may have lacked formal learning — she had not been to high school — but she had made a name for herself as a hostess and served her country so well in so many postings, Toronto, London, Geneva, Washington, Canberra, her life encapsulating the entire history of New Zealand's early diplomatic years, that her translation to Paris in the twilight of her career was both a reward and a natural event, like sunshine after rain. Frederick Doidge, needless to say, was won over.

The Minister returned to Wellington and made a speech in the House acknowledging her brilliance and declaring her, "in the words of the Dean of the Corps of Commonwealth Representatives, 'the only woman in Paris to hold such a high position in diplomatic circles'". Paris was saved.

Fortuitously, New Zealand had just concluded a lucrative butter deal with the French government — "quite the best thing since the legation was established," McIntosh chirruped. One other incident, less fortuitous, occurred at this time. It concerned Costello, last heard of in Wellington kicking his heels in a state of uncertainty. He had been arrested.

"A Very Unfortunate Incident"

A journalist rang up and said "What is Costello doing in London and is he going to Paris?" I said if he printed anything he could cook your chances and for Christ's sake to shut up.

— *McIntosh to Costello*

McINTOSH WAS IN London at a conference with Frederick Doidge, the Minister, the future of Paris still up in the air, when on 1 October 1950 he was handed a telegram:

> HAVE ASKED COSTELLO TO GIVE YOU DETAILS OF A CERTAIN INCIDENT ON WHICH SUGGEST YOU LET HIM TAKE THE INITIATIVE STOP FAMILY WELL
> EXTERNAL

The telegram was from his deputy at External Affairs, Foss Shanahan, in Wellington. McIntosh gathered that Costello had now left New Zealand and was on his way to London. But he was puzzled. A few days later he received a letter from Shanahan, handwritten. It was dated 29 September 1950:

> Dear Mac
> A very unfortunate incident I have to relate to you. On Monday morning Bruce Young, Commissioner of Police, phoned to

> ask me if we had a D.P. Costello on our staff; he had been arrested in Auckland early that morning for drunkenness and was being charged before the Magistrate at 10 a.m. I confirmed our ownership of Paddy and asked him to ring Auckland immediately to make sure that the prosecutor would say no more than the name and the charge. He did this.
>
> Young was very irate. He said Paddy was suspected by the Police there of being Communist and that he had called all and sundry "f — Irish bastards". I suggested to Young that this was unfair as so few of them these days were Irish!

Costello had been arrested in the early hours of the morning, after a constable found him in Auckland's main street attempting to smash the glass in a lantern over some road works with a pocket knife. He was abusive and was taken to the police station. Crossing the park, he attempted to bribe the constable who arrested him. Shanahan continued:

> This failing he threatened to cut his [own] throat; arrived at the police station he refused to disclose his identity and insulted the Sergeant; the Police had to throw him and manacle him to discover who he was; because he had a diplomatic passport they thought he was also a thief; because he was so violent they put him in the padded cell; at 7 a.m. he was released on bail and on failing to appear in Court was fined the amount of his bail.

Even more unfortunate, Foss Shanahan went on, was the sequel. The Commissioner had told a Member of Parliament. The MP told the PM. At 2 p.m. the Prime Minister told the Cabinet — "some of whom were for sacking him".

Costello was then summoned down from Auckland by the overnight express.

> On Tuesday [Shanahan said] we saw the Prime Minister together. Paddy explained that he had been drinking and could remember nothing. The PM said he liked him and had confidence in his ability; he had however to consider the position of the Govt. He reprimanded Paddy severely. Webb* suggested he was the type

> of person who should not drink. It was left that PM and Webb would consider position and let me know.
>
> On Wednesday I saw PM [again]. He had not decided anything. I suggested that he let it ride, that in Paris Paddy would be under Jean McKenzie, that we would regard him as on probation. He said he would write to Mr Doidge but thought no cables. And I have written this in my dreadful hand to keep it all quiet — only Wilson** here knows.

Costello left New Zealand for the second and last time on a chilly morning at the end of September 1950. He departed Auckland by Solent flying-boat for Sydney and crept into London seventy-two hours later. A small tribe of Costellos had gathered in a corrugated iron shed at Mechanics Wharf to see him off. Among them was an admiring eight-year-old nephew, Terry Bishop, who had grown up imagining his "Uncle Des" as the double for the bespectacled Clark Kent character in *Superman*. Terry Bishop recalls clasping an armful of paper streamers and his uncle, muffled in an overcoat, suddenly picked up his nana, Costello's mother, and whirled her around in a jig; then when Terry's baby sister, Mary Rose, began snivelling, produced a box of chocolates, saying to his nana, "Here, give her these, and when you get home give her the boot!" Evidently Costello departed New Zealand with mixed emotions.

In London McIntosh advised Costello to lie low away from journalists. News of the incident had already reached the press in London. Fred Doidge had been telephoned by a New Zealand journalist demanding to know if Costello was going to Paris. The Minister was "completely demoralised". Costello accordingly went to ground, at Kew.

> Today I clocked in at the Public Records Office [he reported to McIntosh]. I have some research to do. I envisage eight full days, using every moment.

* Clifton Webb, Attorney-General. He would succeed Doidge as Minister of External Affairs in 1951.

** J.V. Wilson, scholar, classicist and senior diplomat, External Affairs, Wellington. Wilson came to New Zealand after a career at the League of Nations Secretariat in Geneva (1923–40).

The research was into Anglo–Russian–Persian diplomatic relations in the years 1819–1829 — he was back to the mystery of the murder of his hero, Griboyedov. The breather suited him nicely. After his stint at the Public Records Office, Costello awarded himself a sabbatical and disappeared to Ireland for a round of family visits. He turned up in Paris early in October about the time of Mr Doidge's speech to the New Zealand Parliament, and together with Bil, son Mick, aged fourteen, and daughters Josie and Katie, ten and five, settled into an apartment in the 7th arrondissement which Jean McKenzie had found and furnished for them.

Costello had been five years old when Jean McKenzie entered government service in New Zealand as a typist-secretary. She had left school at thirteen and joined the government at seventeen, an orphan, having lost both parents the previous year. She had come to Paris bearing tins of toheroa soup and Southern Alps whitebait in her kit and, encouraged by McIntosh and Sir Joseph Heenan, the former Under-Secretary of Internal Affairs, established her "New Zealandishness" as of right. She would put her stamp on the place and before long, appointed Minister, become New Zealand's first woman ambassador.

"Atta girl," Heenan wrote to encourage her in 1949. "I have heard all about your parties and your own cooking for them, so get to it kid and show these French people what you can do."

Jean McKenzie came from the town of Edendale in the deep south of New Zealand, a part of the country that was as foreign to Costello as Alabama to a New Englander. It took him a week or two to discover that his new boss who tinted her hair blue and wore flesh-coloured earrings was a woman of parts. Not only was Jean McKenzie an extremely capable woman — in acquiring the Paris property she had insisted that the Princesse de Béarn's cook, a Corsican with a reputation as the second-best chef in Paris, be included in the deal — but an extremely warm one, round and comfortable like her handwriting. She liked a drink which made her even warmer. After receptions and dinner parties, she would repair to a small parlour off the salon and invite Costello to join her. Cognac and liqueurs would appear and she would become, Mick Costello recalls, "not staggeringly blotto, but nearly", although compared with her first secretary she was quite a gentle drunk. McIntosh's deputy in Wellington, Foss Shanahan, had been right when he assured the Prime Minister that Costello would be in good hands consigned to Jean McKenzie. They got on famously.

The Unforgiving Mind

Mr Holland is not keen on burdening himself
with official engagements
— *McIntosh to Jean McKenzie in Paris*

COSTELLO WAS STILL first secretary. He and Jean McKenzie made a team — he the son of a grocer, she the daughter of a blacksmith. "Paddy is a grand person," she reported. "By far the most intelligent person I have ever met." At first there was a problem. The second secretary, an Englishman called Mason, didn't fit in. She told McIntosh. McIntosh promptly transferred Wyn Mason and from London Zohrab arrived. Douglas Zohrab had been with Costello in Moscow and at the Paris Peace Conference. At the return of Zohrab, there was rejoicing — "the rout," according to Costello, "broke up late." Doug Zohrab was a New Zealander of Armenian extraction, a musician, a linguist and a former cipher clerk who had served with Freyberg's Division in the early years of the war. He was yet another refugee from the Greek campaign.

> We have wonderful teamwork [Jean McKenzie wrote]. Paddy does the political reporting and commercial work, Douglas and I do the Consular work, and Douglas attends to the UNESCO and the Cultural side.

Using money left over from the war debt, she had set up bursaries enabling New Zealand students to study in Paris. One of the first graduates to arrive was an architect, Peter Bartlett.* "I had a full year at the Cité Universitaire studying French works and their architects," he says:

> The legation became our second home. Six or seven times a year Jean put on a function for the students studying in Paris. My wife and I were living hand to mouth, recently married. We soon had a small child. She always sent us away with a paper bag full of food.
>
> Paddy and Doug arranged introductions to, among others, Le Corbusier. I stayed on after my scholarship year, designing "Corbusier" housing and community projects among Algerian and Tunisian immigrants in the north-east of Paris. Paddy wanted progress reports. He and Bil were marvellous. They lent us a cot with a high chair that had belonged to Kit, their fourth child. They invited us to Viroflay for meals. Paddy was a father figure to us.

This is the period when Costello was under surveillance by the British and allegedly active, according to a book published in 1999, *The Mitrokhin Archive*, as a Soviet agent. The author of the book, Christopher Andrew, cites a KGB file for 1953 listing Costello, codenamed LONG, as "a valuable agent" of the Paris residency. The Paris *rezident* is not named. Professor Andrew has no further details, he says.

Jean McKenzie remained vulnerable. Members of Parliament in New Zealand sniped at her largesse and sought to close the post on financial grounds, while official delegations and guests poured through the legation in an unending stream. McIntosh, suspecting her of not always claiming expenses, retaliated by stealth. He raised her allowance and ordered her to spend every penny.

"Mr Holland didn't mention the future of the legation," she reported in 1953, "but I gather he thinks the whole setup a waste of time." In the margin she wrote, "Have since learned he had a talk with Doug [Zohrab], and told him this was the least important post abroad."

* Now Emeritus Professor of Architecture, University of Auckland.

She had furnished the residence with imitation Louis Quinze furniture, French and Chinese glassware, yards of marquisette and champagne brocade hangings. She practised economies. The chef doubled as gardener and relieved the concierge on her day off. Simon, the chef, kept Normandy hens in a part of the walled garden, screened by creepers, and from his vast underground kitchen, fortified by Pernod which he reportedly drank almost neat, produced culinary splendours and a flow of good wines and liqueurs that led senior French diplomats, according to Frank Corner, "to petition to be invited to one of Jean's dinners".

Guests stepping in from the street, admiring the white and gold furnishings and the sweeping wrought-iron staircase, did not realise it led to a warren of dingy offices where the staff laboured upstairs. One of the secretaries worked in a converted bathroom.

A whiff of atmosphere was caught by a visiting New Zealand sinologist, James Bertram:

> I remember a lunch at the New Zealand embassy in Paris, when there was nothing to drink but brandy, and I passed out on Jean McKenzie's bed. To be roused by P[addy] some hours later with all his medals up, preparing for a dinner party with French veterans of the Resistance in some apache hideout.

The security arrangements were a little lax. Jean's letters record her anger when McIntosh tried to persuade her to accept another clerk. There was no handyman or security officer; everyone took turns attending to locks, lights, electricity. She had no personal secretary, clerk-accountant or overall administrator. She did the financial work herself and "on occasion," she wrote, "the cables and typing, filing etc." She also helped out with consular duties, approving the issuing and renewal of passports.

The year 1953 was the year of the Queen's Coronation. Sidney Holland attended. The Prime Minister was popular in England and continued to maintain himself a Britisher through-and-through. He was "thrilled to bits", McIntosh wrote, "at all the wonders he sees". Holland's attitude to European affairs however had not altered. This had become manifest the previous year when, visiting the legation in Paris, he cancelled without warning a luncheon Jean McKenzie was arranging for fourteen officials from the Quai d'Orsay. The year 1953 was also the year when Costello was sacked.

Early in 1953 Jean McKenzie learned that the Prime Minister, after attending the Coronation, intended to travel to North America "in a leisurely manner", visiting Ireland, Paris, the south of France, Switzerland, Italy and the Indian sub-continent on the way. "He expects to be away from New Zealand about three months," McIntosh advised. Costello was invited to accompany Holland around Europe.

Costello was attending the Council of Europe at Strasbourg. He left Strasbourg and on 1 July met the Prime Minister and his wife in the Hague and escorted them through the Lowlands to Germany, then drove south and on to Italy. It was not their first encounter — a couple of years earlier Costello had taken the Prime Minister around Belgium and Holland. On that occasion Costello had hoped to see the Breughels in Brussels and the Rembrandts in Amsterdam, but was kept "too busy arranging wreaths for unknown soldiers". In 1953 Sidney Holland, who had been an artillery officer in the First World War, again expressed a desire to visit battlefields. The wish was fulfilled, except in Italy where Costello diverted the itinerary so that he could see the mosaics at Ravenna. In Rome the Prime Minister had climbed to the dome of St Peter's and been exposed to the Sistine Chapel. In Florence he beheld the Duomo and Giotto's Campanile. As the legation car entered Ravenna and drew up outside the octagonal San Vitale, home to the 1400-year-old mosaics symbolising the birth of Western Christian art, Sid Holland exclaimed, "O my God, Costello, not another bloody church!"

The anecdote is timely. It illustrates the gap between philistine and scholar, a reminder of the New Zealand to which Costello could not have returned even had he wanted to. Mr Holland was a shrewd Prime Minister but essentially a party politician who, having been to high school, "gave the impression that he felt he had had enough learning". He was resilient, domineering and cheerfully vulgar. Costello has described him as "the pinnacle of Protestant civilisation". But in 1953 Holland was riding a wave of public support built on his handling of the 1951 waterfront strike. In 1951 he had declared a state of national emergency, put the country on a near-war footing and after 151 days successfully crushed both strikers' and seamen's unions. The strike coincided with the rise of red-baiting during the McCarthy era in America, enabling the Prime Minister to portray a purely industrial dispute as a Cold War conspiracy "engineered by communists".

For all that, the 1953 journey through six European countries seems to have passed off well, even amicably. They parted on 28 July 1953, Costello waving the Prime Minister off at Rome airport. Costello kept his thoughts to himself. Likewise Mr Holland concealed from Costello the fact that before leaving New Zealand he had instructed McIntosh to remove him.

McIntosh would later put this down to prime ministerial pique, saying that Holland had neither forgotten, nor forgiven, Costello's drunken jag in Auckland in 1950. But other factors, it transpired, were at work.

Costello returned to Paris from Rome. The drive was more of a picnic, the route carefully staggered. "Allowing for engine trouble at Tarquinia," he wrote to Davin (he had never seen the Etruscan tombs), "and possibly Lucca" (he had never seen the amphitheatre or the famous garden walls), he calculated it would take him three days in the legation car to reach Paris. It did.

Costello returned at the beginning of August and took charge while Jean McKenzie went on holiday. At the end of August he wrote to McIntosh and explained his situation. He was replying to two letters he had received in June. In them McIntosh advised that the British authorities had made it known to the New Zealand government that they were not prepared to have any more dealings with Costello in his Paris post. No specific charges were made. But, reluctantly, McIntosh said he was obliged to put him on notice. Costello's career was finished.

In 1952, the previous year, Costello had moved his growing family from an apartment to a house at Viroflay, near Versailles. It was a rambling affair, with a big garden and a studio-attic upstairs. On Sundays they would walk through the woods to Versailles or go to the village market. He bought *L'Humanité*, the communist organ — his interest thriving, though the commitment was waning — and worked at home. He took them to the theatre — "Me, Josie, Bil, Papa," Katie recalls, "a very important group we were, striding out to catch the train from Viroflay to Paris. We were like a posse." Josie says:

> He took me to cafés and explained how the women walked and dressed. He was elegant too, *coquet*, bien habillé, smart. Well turned out. The hat. The suits. The top coat. We went to the zoo

> at Vincennes. He loved animals but Bil wouldn't let him have any, so he compensated by taking us to the zoo.

A visitor to Viroflay, Judge Alessandro Galante Garrone, invited to dinner, describes "a prodigious Spanish dish, a lobster *paella*", prepared and served by Costello. They sang songs and played recordings of *Boris Godunov* in Russian. "I met the eldest, Josie, twelve years old," Sandro Garrone wrote to his wife, "very pretty and clever (a little ill)."

Josie had contracted tuberculosis. Costello drove south to the Pyrenees and brought her back from the Spanish frontier where she had spent seven months at a sanatorium recovering. He administered daily injections of a new serum, streptomycin. "As a reward he played chess with me," Josie says. "We had a game every evening after the nasty injection! Mum told me much later that the whole thing worried him and made him nervous. He never showed it to me."

Sessions of the United Nations General Assembly and UNESCO were taking place in Paris, the Council of Europe was meeting in Strasbourg. Costello was much involved. He was hardly under-employed. At home he was tutoring the younger daughter Katie in French and English. He had become a father again. The latest arrival, a son and Bil's fourth child, was born in February 1952 almost in the back of the legation car in a rush to the hospital. At the same time he was translating a Russian grammar for the Oxford Press and was teaching himself Persian. He read a little-known Iranian novel called *The Blind Owl*. It terrified him. He began to translate it into English.

He worked on the two books, in Russian and Persian, simultaneously. Yet he had told Davin when he came to Viroflay that he was wasting his time in Paris. Now he wrote to him, seemingly unperturbed:

> I learned today you have gone into hospital for your gall bladder operation. You are unlucky with your juices. When I first met you your natural pallor was enhanced by a suffusion of bile, I seem to remember.
>
> We have not much in the way of news. Josie is not, contrary to expectation, completely recovered from her TB and may have to have a nodule excised from her lung.
>
> I am reading nothing but Persian . . .

This was in January 1954, four months after being put on notice. Davin knew none of the background. He was ignorant of the political intrigue behind the scenes, as was Costello. He knew only that Costello was unhappy — it comes out again and again in the correspondence, a discontent of years rather than months — and was determined to quit when an opportunity came.

"Paddy told me he was fed up with working in diplomacy," Davin told a friend, "because it was like working for a General in the Army who refused to believe your Intelligence summaries. As an example he gave his prediction about the Russian possession of the atom bomb, and nobody would believe him."

Costello wrote to McIntosh begging for time. He discussed the sacking with Jean McKenzie. "We both know and understand your position," she wrote to McIntosh, "and that there is no alternative." McIntosh had told her that there was no basis for the charges against Costello, but he was unable to resist the pressure which came "from the Prime Minister himself".

Costello was run down, she thought — "extremely thin, not well".

He told McIntosh that he was chasing a lectureship at one of three British universities: Oxford, Cambridge or Birmingham. He had been to Oxford (and been warmly welcomed by the Russian professor); he had approached Cambridge (and been cold-shouldered). Birmingham, like Oxford, was on hold. He begged for indulgence.

In Wellington Costello's despatches, "full of alarming penetration", continued to enliven diplomatic dinner tables. McIntosh had been circulating them among foreign diplomats for some time. He pacified the Prime Minister, telling Sid Holland that Costello had agreed to resign. His letter of resignation was "expected". At the same time McIntosh began a campaign of passive resistance, inventing schemes to keep Costello on the payroll as long as possible. He guessed that once he was out of government service, Costello's chances of further employment were practically nil.

A job at Oxford or a fellowship at his old university, Cambridge, ought to have been easy. In fact a vacancy had already occurred at Oxford, in 1953. Quite suddenly. Konovalov, the Russian professor, had urged him to apply but Costello dithered. The financial sacrifice involved was considerable. At the last minute he applied but was then obliged to choose between going to Oxford for an interview or cancelling a dinner arranged with Barbara

Freyberg, wife of the General. Costello kept the dinner date and the opportunity to teach at Oxford was lost.

As for Cambridge, he had blown his chances there, he suspected, long before. The professor, Elizabeth (later Dame Elizabeth) Hill, had once written to him in Moscow inquiring "about something or other" and he had confessed maladroitly that he had never heard of her. "Heaven hath no rage," he confided to Davin,

> *. . . like love to hatred turn'd*
> *Nor hell a fury like a tutor scorn'd*

So Cambridge, the most prestigious centre for the study of Slavonic languages, was out. Only half a dozen institutions in Britain taught Russian. There remained Birmingham. A vacancy at Birmingham University was expected, he told McIntosh, but had yet to be advertised.

He was now under two pressures, enforced removal by his government and surveillance by British security agents. It did not seem to worry Costello that he was being watched; or that he was observed, as espionage writers would later claim, meeting a Soviet agent "or agents". "Agents" is one of those unsubstantiated catch-alls beloved of spooks which can neither be proved nor disproved. In this case it probably refers to Costello's friend Henri Curiel who came to the house at Viroflay more than once.

> Paddy knew he was being watched [Mick Costello says]. It didn't make any difference. He would be up at five or six in the morning, studying, doing his research. He'd go to the legation, go to receptions with Mum, come home, stay home. He knew the British were after him. But he didn't change his behaviour. But then [Mick laughs], that might be bloody good cover!
>
> Paddy didn't to my knowledge have a life outside the family. At night we sat and listened to music or we read our books. He'd work or read. Never out of an evening on his own.

Henri Curiel, a communist and alleged KGB agent, came to the house at Viroflay quite openly, as did former British agents and Intelligence officers Costello had known in the war. Curiel was the antiquarian bookseller he had known in Cairo. Other visitors included the Australian journalist Dick Hughes, Japanese professors, American liberals, left-wingers, diplomats and UNESCO people who lived nearby, ferocious talkers and right-wingers like Richard Cobb, the historian of the French Revolution, the New Zealand Roman historian and former SOE operative, Ronald Syme, Resistance heroines, Irish cousins, and ex-partisans like Alessandro Galante Garrone and Franco Venturi.

In all this Bil was a background figure, reticent, a visitor says, "mature in reaction". Bil was there and not there. She is mentioned only in passing. This is true of almost every account, recollection, reminiscence or anecdote recalling her life with Costello, with the notable exception of police and security reports where she is singled out as a malign presence, like Barbara Allen in the folksong, to the detriment of the male. (A New Zealand Security Intelligence Service statement quotes a "summation" by a New Zealander who describes Costello as "a dedicated and ruthless communist, determined to out-do his Ukrainian Jewish wife in her intellectual toughness as a communist". The quotation is unattributed.)*

In the spring of 1954 a New Zealander, Shirley Tunnicliffe, was living with the Costellos at Viroflay. She says:

> Paddy cast a spell when he came home for dinner. In the attic he kept a gramophone and a stack of the latest long-playing records. In the evening the whole family would repair upstairs. I'd known Paddy before in Moscow. Bil was in awe of him. Years later I visited their home in Manchester. He had been dead some years, but "Professor D.P. Costello" was still on the letter-box.

The days passed. There was no word of a job. The position at Birmingham had still not been advertised.

Costello went to the legation, came home, took his children to the opera, and rediscovered in the latest child, two-year-old Christopher, known as Kit, the joy of being a father again. Life continued, as he put it, "son petit train-train".

---

* The full SIS statement appears on page 367.

The Passport Affair

Paddy Costello used his consular position in Paris to authorise the New Zealand passports. [His] incriminating signature appeared on the resulting consular paperwork.
— *Nigel West,* Seven Spies who Changed the World (1991)

IN APRIL 1954 a letter, postmarked Vienna, arrived at the New Zealand Legation in Paris inquiring about the formalities needed to obtain a New Zealand passport. The writer was a born New Zealander, he said, "and married my wife, who is Canadian-born, in 1936, thereby making her, according to what I understand, a New Zealand citizen too."

The writer explained that he held a British family passport but on applying to the British Consul in Vienna for an extension had been told that, "under the legislation now in force", he should apply to Paris for separate individual New Zealand passports for himself and his wife.

He added that a heart condition prevented him from coming to the legation in person. The letter was handwritten, addressed from a pension in the Austrian resort town of Semmering, south of Vienna, where the writer said he had been "residing for several months" while undergoing treatment.

The handwriting was large and looping, half child, half artist, as if copied from a book for an exercise in calligraphy. The tone was eighteenth century, reminiscent of Jane Austen, and the phrasing unusual —"making it compulsory that I apply to you by mail", rather than "because I cannot come myself". The letter ended on a note of urgency — "to ease my situation, please be so kind as to also let me know how long this entire procedure shall take."

It was addressed to "the New Zealand Consul, 9 rue Léonard de Vinci, Paris, France" and signed "Peter J. Kroger".

Peter John Kroger did not sound like, any more than his letter appeared to represent, an antipodean from New Zealand. In itself this was not unusual. In the same month of April 1954, a Mrs Dezera Audrey Nina Storper applied for and was issued with a New Zealand passport at the legation. The consular Register for 1954 reveals a string of applicants with foreign names — Winifred Vidaud de Plaud, Joseph Bartholdus Barnao — who applied for and were granted or who renewed New Zealand passports at the Paris office.

The legation duly despatched a routine application form to Mr Kroger in Austria, with a covering letter dated 20 April 1954 requesting certificates of identification for himself and his wife and a fee of 979 francs (one pound sterling) each, also the presentation of his British passport. The office copy of the covering letter — together with copies of the consular papers which became available in 2007, as this book was going to press — bears no signature.

Mr Kroger's application forms duly came back from Vienna and were signed off by the New Zealand Chargé, Jean McKenzie. Jean McKenzie was standing in for the regular consular officer, Douglas Zohrab, who was away. Paddy Costello may also have been away, attending a conference in Rome. There is some confusion about this.* The only certainty appears to be that the application forms on being returned to Paris were completed by Jean McKenzie herself in her upstairs office amid the warren of rooms where Sue

* In July 2003 I was given a briefing by an official at NZSIS Headquarters, Wellington, regarding the passports. There was no paper trail in the files, he said, nothing discovered to link Costello to the issuing of the passports. The regular consular officer [Douglas Zohrab], he thought, was on leave.

Douglas Zohrab today cannot remember if he was on leave or at a conference in Geneva. Costello, in the memory of Sir George Laking, may have been at an FAO conference in Rome. Understandably, after more than fifty years, neither Zohrab nor Laking, who are both alive at the time of writing, can be certain.

Copies of the consular papers and the two passports, 41 sheets in total, were made available to me by the NZSIS in April 2007.

Lawrence, the administrative secretary, and the rest of the staff worked.

Peter John Kroger, his application said, was a "broker and merchant", normally resident in New York City. He was born on 10 July 1910 in "Gisborne, New Zealand"; his wife, "Helen Joyce Kroger (née Hale)", was born on 17 January 1913, in "Boyle, Alberta, Canada". The certificates of identification on page four of the application form, requiring the signature of "someone to whom the applicant is known personally", had been stamped and signed by a lawyer in Vienna. The latter certified that he had known the applicants "for six years".

Helen Kroger's marriage certificate, predating the 1948 Act, made her automatically a New Zealand citizen.

Everything appeared in order, but the certificates, which looked genuine, were forgeries.

On Monday 3 May 1954, Jean McKenzie issued the passports. A few months later, armed with these documents, the Krogers, whose real name was Cohen, entered England.They set up shop, he operating undercover as a dealer in rare books, initially from a room in the Strand, London; presently they bought a bungalow in Ruislip, west London. Here, as the nerve centre of what would become known as the Portland naval spy ring, they hid a high-powered radio transmitter and began relaying sonar and other naval secrets to Moscow. They did this undetected for six years, until arrested and brought to trial in 1961.

At the Old Bailey the pair made a vivid impression, waving to the gallery and blowing kisses. Graham Greene would later put Peter Kroger into his novel, *The Human Factor*, as the antiquarian bookseller. The author and critic, Rebecca West, who attended the trial, wrote of Helen Kroger as a handsome Rubens figure who addressed the court "in a clear and beautiful voice"; of her husband as dignified, silver-haired, "his hair winding round his head like a gleaming bandage"; and she described the Ruislip bungalow where the two were arrested and the passports found as so crammed with the tools of espionage, "it was one of the most interestingly congested buildings in all history since the Ark".

The Krogers, it was revealed, had vanished from New York when the Rosenberg ring was broken up in 1950, and were rather more important to the KGB than Ethel and Julius Rosenberg themselves (executed despite protests across the world in 1953). It was Helen Kroger who brought the plans for the first atomic bomb out of Los Alamos to New York in 1945, wrapped in a newspaper, for onward despatch to Moscow — perhaps the most important secret document destined for a foreign power to escape detection in the history of the USA. She and her husband were seasoned Russian agents of more than twenty years and at the Old Bailey were given long prison sentences.

It seems unfair to single out Jean McKenzie as the instrument of their treason. She had simply followed the rules, acting in innocence. The documents which had deceived her and her staff, as an official investigation would later state, "could have been used with success at any passport office within or outside New Zealand". Unwittingly, she had helped trigger what would become the first in a series of spy scandals which would rock and eventually bring down the Macmillan government in England. The case itself and the role of the passports which enabled the Krogers to penetrate British security is a celebrated one, recalled today in Scotland Yard's Black Museum, commemorated for forty years in books and films, a play, and countless exhibits, lectures and television programmes. What has never been made public before is Jean McKenzie's part.

"It was obvious from the handwriting on the papers," Ian Stewart, the Counsellor at the New Zealand Embassy in Paris, would later report,

> that Jean McKenzie handled the application. She issued the two New Zealand passports, cancelled the British passport and returned it, and returned the birth and marriage certificates. The entry in the Passport Register appears partly in Doug Zohrab's handwriting but was completed by Jean. *

Two official investigations, one British and one New Zealand, have been held. Such material as has been made available to me by the New Zealand Security Intelligence Service does not mention Jean McKenzie. But in a public statement after he retired, the man who had conducted the New Zealand investigation, the first head of the Service, Brigadier Sir William Gilbert, said that "Costello had no direct part in that affair". Writing this in a national newspaper in 1981, Brigadier Gilbert sounded — and perhaps sincerely was — baffled by the affair.

* Report from Paris dated 8 February 1961. Ministry of Foreign Affairs & Trade archives, Wellington, NZ: PM's Dept., file 32/2/3/11, Mr & Mrs Peter John Kroger.

The blame for twenty-five years has continued to fall on Costello.

The finger-pointing began in 1981 in a book published by the British journalist Chapman Pincher, *Their Trade Is Treachery*. In the book Pincher said that Costello "might have been recruited as a spy", claiming in support of the allegation that "he had signed New Zealand passports for Peter and Helen Kroger". The smear stuck. It could not be refuted. Costello and Jean McKenzie were both dead. The allegation acted as a green light. It was repeated and amplified by Chapman Pincher three years later in another book and, although unsupported by evidence of any kind, has since been parroted and embellished by a generation of British writers. As a result Costello has entered the world literature of espionage as a spy. Today the charge that he "issued the passports" is accepted by intelligence and espionage writers, as it is now accepted uncritically by historians that he was a Soviet agent.

The charge is false. Papers dating from an inquiry by the New Zealand Department of External Affairs in 1961, released by the Ministry of Foreign Affairs and Trade in 2005, substantiate Jean McKenzie's unwitting role and demonstrate that Costello had no hand in the passport affair.

Sicilian Vespers

The letter of resignation was written for him

— *Michael King to Dan Davin, 1982*

COSTELLO WAS BACK in Paris early in May and a few days later took his annual three weeks' holiday with Bil. They travelled south by train, through France, Switzerland and almost the length of Italy to Naples, where they boarded the overnight steamer for Sicily. They landed in Palermo and criss-crossed the island from west to east — they followed in the steps of Goethe — Segesta, Agrigento, Selinunte, Syracuse — visiting the classical sites.

From Alcamo in the west of Sicily, waiting for a train back to Palermo, Costello sent Dan Davin a postcard depicting the Greek temple at Segesta:

> Roasting hot. I can't get the classical virus out of my system, and a fine landscape is made ten times finer for me when, as here, it has a bloody great Doric temple sitting in the middle of it.
> Love to you all from Bil and Paddy

When the Costellos returned to Paris in the early summer of 1954, the Birmingham Chair in Russian had still not been advertised. Four weeks later Costello wrote to McIntosh and enclosed his resignation.

2 July 1954

Dear Alister

Herewith my letter of resignation, as promised.

I am thinking of having a shot at a job with one of the international organisations. Could I refer to you? Before you reply "no", I would ask you to consider carefully whether, whatever it is that the Government has against me, it would affect my value as an official of UNESCO or Technical Aid. If it would, your course is clear. If it would not then please hesitate before you wreck my chances.

From the Letters

1950–1955, Paris

21 February 1951
Costello to Davin

I have been teaching myself Persian and have lately finished *Omar Khayyám*. I have found it amusing to see just how far FitzGerald [the authorised translator] got from his original. The comedy of the drunken old man and the drunken poet, both Moslems and both bandying the name of God, is beyond Fitz.

18 September 1951
In October I accompany Mr Doidge to Strasbourg for the "Council of Europe". Then in November the Nations dites Unies, as the French papers call them, start their brawling here in Paris, which promises me little respite until next spring.

30 October 1951

I have been inquiring about vacancies at English universities for teaching jobs.

2 December 1951

Bil is pregnant, and should be delivered in February. That makes four, which puts me even with you and Geoffrey, but puts Bil ahead of Winnie (having written that, I decide to address the letter to you at the Press rather than to Southmoor Road. But you will probably have recognised by this that the energy that drives my hand to answer you so promptly derives from the good wine of Alsace, and you will pardon the indiscretion which stems from the same bottle.)

5 May 1952

Have you ever read through *The Gallic War*? After reading [it] I am convinced that Caesar was not interested in people, except as instruments or opponents of his policy. Curious that as a boy I admired him more than anyone: my confirmation name is Julius.

22 April 1953

Did I tell you that I have discovered the hitherto unsuspected existence of a Russian perfect tense? True, it is only a perfect passive, but even that is something these days.

18 June 1953

Syme was here last week. The booze flowed freely. Incidentally I have lashings of the stuff, sufficient to slake any thirst, even yours. You'll be able to coast along nicely on whisky-and-soda or wine from the time you arrive until you go. I'll pace you.

22 April 1954

I don't know who of us is the more fortunate. At times I feel I have more luck than you, in that I am living in a great and agreeable capital and am permitted to observe something of events. At present I wish I lived in a University town and had erected, like the Caliph of Omar, a rampart of books between me and the wickedness of the world. The things I have to see and describe are so distasteful as to be now nearly intolerable.

What is on my mind is this cursed business of Indochina. For seven years the wretched Vietnamese have fought the French. They have the French licked. And now, having beaten France, they are going to be forced to take on the USA.

I have been studying all the information I have been able to scratch together. I do think that the danger is real . . . Probably the greatest hope lies in the uncertainty about Russia's strength: has Russia got the hydrogen bomb in quantity? Will she use them if China is attacked by the Americans?

Sorry to talk politics — had to get it off my chest.

I took Konovalov [Russian professor at Oxford] to lunch last week. I fear the opposition to him is very strong. The trouble with Russian studies in England is that they are considered (save at Oxford) as ancillary to Intelligence, political and military. The institutions run by Miss Hill and Mr Bolsover* evoke Scotland Yard in my mind.

27 December 1954
First I shall explain to you the state of my affairs.

I had known for some time that the NZ Govt. were nervous about keeping me. The cause was not so much anything I had done since I joined External as my pre-war affiliations, and less for their own sake than for the unfavourable prejudice they created in the mind of the Foreign Office. I understand that the heaviest pressure against me was exercised not by the State Department but by the boys in Whitehall.

Something like a purge of the External Affairs Department took

* George Bolsover, Director, School of Slavonic & East European Studies, London.

place this year. Three or four people were induced to resign. They included Doug Lake, whom you will remember.

My resignation takes place next month.

When I said the objection to me was not based on things I had said or done, I am probably exaggerating. The things I said in my reports, both from Moscow and from Paris, would probably not have been said by someone with a proper Atlantic viewpoint. For example: The Russians are well on the way to producing the atomic bomb (1947); there is no prospect of "Titoism" in China (1950); France cannot win the Indo-China war (1951–1954); France will not ratify E.D.C. (1952–1954). These statements of mine were no more acceptable for being correct. When all the major assumptions underlying a country's foreign policy are mistaken, it is folly on the part of an official to draw attention to the fact. I find myself in the same situation as the American diplomats in China who reached the conclusion that Chiang Kai-shek was not going to win the civil war.

However, New Zealand is not America, and I think that if my only offence had been a correct analysis of the main international problems, I should not have been forced to resign.

11 January 1955
You mention Jean McKenzie. She has an embarrassing habit, when she has a sup taken, of gazing at me with the tears running down her cheeks, and of lapsing from time to time into a kind of keening. She — and Doug Zohrab for that matter — is more intensely affected by this business than I am. I suppose it is normal for the corpse to be less concerned than the mourners at the wake.

"It Was All Very British"

They had no notion of how to handle these issues

— *Sir George Laking*

HOW HAD IT happened? Why did he have to resign?

No charges were brought against Costello. No allegations by the security authorities were ever made public. He was never interrogated or questioned. The only blot on his record that had any basis in fact was the red and apparently still lively herring of what MI5, the British Security Service, called his "pre-war affiliations". This referred, one is left to assume, to his accidental and innocuous association with the student Fyrth at Exeter.

Costello was once again high and dry. The gravity of the offence he was supposed to have committed, he could only guess at from a "rumpus" that had erupted in New Zealand, taking its toll, he learned later, on McIntosh. The latter's health had deteriorated. McIntosh, a prey to mysterious bouts of debilitating illness, was "near the end of his tether". The only constant was the Kafkaesque one of McIntosh's repeated statements to Jean McKenzie that the charges against Costello were baseless, coupled with the refusal of anyone in authority to say what the charges actually were.

"*Whatever it is the government has against me*," Costello had written to Davin. He sounded bewildered. He was.

In the wilderness of revolving mirrors that is the world of Counter-Intelligence, nothing is sure. Everything is distorted. The accuser is never named. Costello's downfall, McIntosh believed, was engineered by the British. Although later in an interview shortly before his death McIntosh cited Costello's mad drinking bout in 1950, saying, "The P.M. lost all confidence in him." This sounds simplistic. It was, as it turned out, a portent. According to the historian Michael King, the trouble began in 1945 when McCarthyism was stirring in America. Anonymous letters to members of Peter Fraser's Labour government denounced Costello as a communist and threatened to pass the information to the US Senate. The letters coincided with British misgivings about Costello's posting to Moscow and High Commissioner Batterbee's abortive attempt to have him removed. The crunch came in the 1950s after the government changed: the American Ambassador to New Zealand, Robert Scotten, called on the Prime Minister, Holland, and demanded Costello's dismissal. Sid Holland, under the combined British and American pressure, buckled.

> You never knew how it came about, where it originated [Sir George Laking says]. The British have their own way of operating. They would not make a direct accusation but in some way get the United States to raise the objection. It suited them not to have to accuse someone directly but rather to say, "The Americans have told us this."

In the climate of the times, under "the basilisk glare" of Joseph McCarthy during the televised Senate hearings in Washington, communist suspicions were easily fanned. In 1954 New Zealand had no Intelligence service; security was entirely in the hands of the police. The situation was primitive and the police, according to George Laking, out of their depth. "They had no notion of how to handle these issues."

One of the peculiarities of the Cold War in New Zealand was its hidden character. When McCarthyism called, it knocked with a gloved hand. The knock was so light that historians barely noticed. Not until Michael King's *Penguin History of New Zealand* and my own book *Dance of the Peacocks: New Zealanders in Exile in the Time of Hitler and Mao Tse-tung*, both published in 2003, appeared, would the public learn of a whispering campaign which deprived McIntosh of some of his best men and at a certain point threatened to undermine his entire department. This is the hidden purge Costello identified when writing to Davin in December 1954. It took the form of denunciations by police and anonymous agents, questioning the loyalty of state servants, sometimes without their knowledge and frequently on the basis of what amounted to mere tittle-tattle. Some reports uncovered grounds for legitimate concern but most were so inaccurate and naive that McIntosh launched an initiative to get security out of the hands of the police.*

About a dozen of McIntosh's staff had their loyalty questioned in this way. Four resigned.

One was Richard Gray Collins. As a student Dick Collins had joined his university college socialist club. He was a Wellington law graduate, recruited by McIntosh after the war, with an uncommon grasp of international affairs. He made an incautious remark overheard at the Vegetable Club by a police informer and was denounced to the Prime Minister. McIntosh was obliged to tell Collins that his chances of promotion were over. Collins resigned.

New Zealand's purge of state servants cannot compare with America's, where in the 1950s some 9500 civil servants were sacked and 15,000 resigned, but the effect on McIntosh's department was devastating nonetheless. The difference lies in the secrecy — in New Zealand the hysteria was covered up. McIntosh's men had their resignations written for them and were induced to go quietly. It was all very British. Ten years later in 1965 McIntosh himself would become a victim; on the eve of being elected to high office, an international position for which he was the front-runner, he would be secretly denounced by the moguls of British Counter-Intelligence and obliged to withdraw his nomination. He too would step aside quietly.

McIntosh's biography, another untold story, has yet to be written. His denunciation, although he would be made an ambassador on his retirement in 1966 and given a knighthood, was a private humiliation, the result of a peccadillo on his way back to New Zealand from a conference in Colombo. It is covered in the Notes, as is the case of Douglas Lake, another casualty whom McIntosh sought in vain to protect.

---

* He succeeded. In 1956 the Security Intelligence Service (NZSIS) was established. McIntosh's subsequent regret was that, as in Australia, the Service was headed by a career army officer, staffed largely by British imports and run on MI5 lines. In an effort, inter alia, to clear Dick Collins's name, McIntosh on his retirement in 1965 left a set of papers with his successor, George Laking, saying, "I do not want them to get into the hands of Security because I do not trust them."

In much of this the perceived villain was Costello. The fallout from Costello's posting to Moscow, his alleged political indoctrination of others like Ruth Macky and Doug Lake, was considered seditious. Costello's downfall was summed up by Davin. He wrote,

> I think Alister [McIntosh] was right when he said that Paddy's gifts as an Intelligence officer helped to make him a first-class diplomat. But the British appeared to have interpreted his liking for the Russians and his friendly relations with many of them, and his power to make inferences from casual bits of information, as a kind of proof that he was a Russian agent or at least a tool of theirs for disinformation.

In October 1954 McIntosh wrote to Jean McKenzie, "Needless to say, the awkward character in all this has been the Prime Minister himself." Clifton Webb, the External Affairs Minister, was thoroughly sympathetic:

> And is quite clear, as I am, that there is nothing against Paddy at all but he is not prepared to go against the P.M. It was only through Webb that I was able to arrive at the unsatisfactory compromise of the three months' leave. I can't say how ashamed and embarrassed I am about all this but, believe me, I have done the best I could.

By various subterfuges McIntosh had managed to get for Costello three months' salary in lieu of leave. It would tide him over to Christmas.

It was now the following March, 1955. Costello was still at Viroflay, "with my enormous family". *Zonam perditit*, he had lost his money belt. But he refused a loan from Davin when it was offered. "These months of unemployment have been one of the pleasantest periods of my life," he said. He covered up well. Paul Foote, a young Russianist who came from Oxford about this time to discuss the publication of a joint folklore reader, a project dear to Costello's heart, received a friendly but perfunctory reception.

"He was not relaxed," Foote recalls. "There was a tautness in him."

With Oxford, Cambridge and Birmingham universities out (the vacancy at Birmingham had still not been advertised), and the world of international agencies apparently closed to him, there remained a last possibility. Costello learned that a chair of Russian at Manchester, frozen for some years, was being revived. By now icicles of reality had begun to grow in Costello's mind. Two years earlier he had discovered "how little I know of the general laws of Russian grammar and phonetics". He was out of practice; a tilt at a professorship seemed presumptuous. But some time in March, urged on by Ronald Syme, he applied for the chair.

While he waited, Costello continued "to help Bil with the dishes & waste time with the kids". He found time to help friends, taking his teenage son Mick

> all the way to our flat in the 13th Arrondissement [Margaret Lawlor-Bartlett recalls], ostensibly so that I could coach Mick for his English language exams — but really because he knew that I needed the money. I had lost my teaching job.

But mainly he retreated and found solace — the habit of a lifetime — in his books.

He had always loved books. He bought books. He gave away books and he lent books. He lost books. He pursued books for others. In Moscow where books sold out as soon as they were printed he scoured the secondhand bookshops for a copy of Katherine Mansfield's collected stories in Russian for an enthusiast in New Zealand who had written to him. Like Graham Greene's character, Castle, in *The Human Factor*, he could not resist a call of distress, however it was encoded.

He grew out of books, dismissing English novels as written largely by adolescents concerned with the psychological growing pains of students. He returned to books. He filled folder after bound folder with notes and quotations from books. He sent for books. "In that little book of essays with a green cover I used at Grammar," he wrote to his mother from Cambridge on 15 August 1933, "and which is now on the second shelf of the bookcase on the right as you enter my room, there is an essay on Venice by John Addington Symonds . . . " He seems to have had an appetite for books as others do for cornflakes or lamingtons. The strange thing is that the more he read and the earlier to read he got up, usually at 5.30 a.m., the more he lamented the lack of time there was for reading; and the more he lamented, the more hours he seemed to discover to add to those whose absence he complained of, thus providing himself with enough time to read all the books he had acquired or re-acquired as replacements for the ones he had given away or lost during the war.

After the battle for Greece, Dan Davin lamented losing the manuscript of a novel he had begun to write about Paris. Howard Kippenberger, after being ambushed in the Servia Pass, wept over the loss of Palgrave's *Golden Treasury* which had been lent to him by a friend. Costello's catalogue of loss was more comprehensive. It included "my Viceroy razor, my complete Housman, my modern Greek grammar", abandoned on Mount Ossa, his revised handbook on the Italian army, destroyed in the flap before Alamein, his diaries for 1941 and 1942 which Davin (he said) packed by mistake and took to Sarafand; and, most grievous of all, "my 26,000-word epic on the escape from Tempe" which the sweepers burned while he was on a course in the Middle East.

Once after crossing into Cyrenaica he came upon a vast library in a house abandoned by an Italian settler — "but no more room in the Jeep for more than two". He wrote:

> If this campaign goes on, I'll have a chance to read Dante from beginning to end [besides] Don Quixote, War & Peace, Faust, Rabelais and Shakespeare,

a feat he seems to have accomplished (not Shakespeare), when not diverted by a variety of Latin and classical texts acquired in the pursuit of Rommel across north Africa and a long unfinished novel by Stendhal, *Lucien Leuwen*, "in that lovely Pleiade edition with fine paper, fine printing and soft leather binding" which he picked up browsing in the shop of his communist friend, Henri Curiel, in Cairo.

He read standing or walking, in whatever light was available. Booksellers were surprised at the breadth of interest recorded in the titles he ordered from a general catalogue, books on mycology and gardening and some arcane material on computer theory, everything from hard-core communism to Pascal's tenets on irresistible grace to a treatise on the caryatids in the Erechtheum in Athens. "If ever I were able," he wrote to Davin once, "I should like to take a year off in order to read the Classics for eight hours a day."

No one ever discovered who his preferred authors were, Michael Waller says. "He'd read so widely, he seemed to know them all."

In the spring of 1955 he was rereading *Anna Karenina*, one of the books he had read while recovering from malaria in Alexandria in the war, marvelling once again at passages from Vronsky and Levin he had quoted to Bil in his letters at the time, when he was interrupted by a motor-cyclist arriving with an express letter. The letter was from England, postmarked "The University, Manchester". It informed him that his application for the Sir William Mather Chair of Russian Studies, supported by General Freyberg, Professor Konovalov and Clifton Webb, his three referees, had come before the general faculty board and the Senate. The application had been received with interest. Would he care to come for an interview?

He went. Costello arrived in London on 28 April 1955, spent the night in Bloomsbury and the following day presented himself at The University, Manchester, to the faculty board. A few days of anxious waiting followed. At the interview, according to Davin, Costello tried to tell them of his communist sympathies "but was interrupted by the chairman, Prof. Stopford, who said they were interested in his qualifications not his politics".

Costello's reaction when he learned that he had been appointed to Manchester is best gauged from an entry in the diary of the educationalist Martha McCulloch, with whom he had stayed in Bloomsbury. A note in her visitors' diary, dated 6 May 1955, reads, "Paddy has the Russian chair at Manch. He stayed the night. A singing breakfast."

The appointment cannot have been a total surprise. "In those days," says Michael Waller, one of Costello's senior students who would later become a professor at Keele University, "there was almost nobody around who taught Russian." Behind the scenes Davin and Syme had been active, roping in people like Martha McCulloch, a former member of the Manchester Labour Party, to lobby on Costello's behalf. All the same, Costello was a realist. His Russian was self-taught. His energies as well as his horizons were contracting, he felt. "*Starost ne radost,*" he had begun to say, "Growing old isn't much fun." (But he had been saying that for years, according to Josie.) He was forty-two.

Life, Costello once said, was a series of battles with inertia. Occasionally something happened that was worthwhile — the Polish episode, the trip up the Volga with Bil, the meetings with Pasternak and other Russian writers, his discovery in Paris of a little-known classic he had translated from the Persian. But occasions like that were diminishing. The months of unemployment in Paris had led to a retreat into the mind, an acceptance of the law of diminishing returns, on the McIntosh principle that if you did nothing it couldn't happen and if you did something it probably wouldn't happen anyway. Though sometimes it did. And now it had.

By August he was hard at work preparing a course of lectures for the beginning of the academic year in October. He had given up smoking and was "very nearly teetotal". His cash — he had borrowed a substantial sum of money from Jean McKenzie — was holding. Jean put on a small farewell luncheon for him at the legation, an occasion without speeches. There were no speeches because at the end somebody, it might have been Doug Zohrab, got up and went to the piano. Costello stood up and inclined an ear, cupping it in the way he sometimes did when he would sing in his light tenor voice that made every song seem sad. Margaret Lawlor-Bartlett recalls, "About twenty of us attended. Paddy sang 'The Minstrel Boy':

> *The minstrel boy to the war is gone*
> *In the ranks of death you'll find him*
> *My song was made for the pure and free*
> *I shall never chaunt in slavery!*

"He didn't finish. He couldn't sing the last line. He choked and began to weep. We all did. Doug wept. I wept, Peter wept. Jean was sitting with her arms around our baby, Nicholas. Tears were pouring down her cheeks. But he was free, free at last."

Costello arrived in Manchester on 1 September 1955. He found a house in the leafy suburb of Withington and camped there while waiting for his family and furniture to come from Paris. He wrote to Davin on 8 September,

> I have been living in or near the house which henceforth is mine. No cooking apparatus can however be installed until next Saturday. In the meantime I make my tea and coffee, as befits a professor of Russian, with a samovar set up in the back yard.

PART FIVE
FULL CIRCLE IN MANCHESTER

1955–1964

"A Soviet Satellite Going By"

I gave a lecture the other evening on
"the end of the Stalin legend"

Costello to Davin, 1956

HE KNEW NO one in Manchester. Davin lent Costello money, sending two cheques which kept him going until his first pay day in November. His family arrived, preceded by a horse-box containing his gramophone and most of his books, which eventually filled a room beside the kitchen at the back of the house. This became his study (though he seemed to work equally well at the formica table in the kitchen). His study looked on to a chestnut tree in the garden and was the biggest room in the house.

A visitor found him here one day in October, surrounded by journals and dictionaries spilling from a refectory table in the middle of the room, all the wall spaces except the fireplace and a glass cabinet along the west wall lined with books. Costello was seated in slippers at a rolltop desk in the corner, poring over "the processes of academic life".

> Frightfully busy [he wrote to Davin]. Normally the man newly appointed to a chair has not to learn the processes of academic life. Not so I. All the time I have free from teaching is spent learning the rights and duties of a head of department.

Eleven-year-old Katie Costello came downstairs one day in the summer of 1956 to find him sitting at the formica-topped table in the kitchen reading *Gulliver's Travels* to himself, "and quoting passages to Mum". So evidently they had settled in. His teething troubles after a twenty-year absence from academia were over.

Costello had found a rambling semi-detached at the end of a row of semi-detached Victorian brick houses in Withington, south Manchester. Today the house is airy and light, the timber floors and walls gleaming after renovation. Withington was less posh than Didsbury, but the Costellos lived "at the posh end". The house was friendly rather than grand. Five bedrooms. Bicycles and a baby carriage in the hall, the walls two-toned as in an institution, the light in the passages filtered through stained-glass panels and the lino grey. "Mum left the lino," Katie remembers. The outside coated with a layer of soot, like the black drain that was the River Irwell dividing Manchester from Salford, like the cathedral, like the ink-black University in Lime Grove, a ten-minute bus ride away. Manchester, like Exeter where Costello first taught in England, was another red-brick university, a come-down after Moscow and Paris.

And yet, as Nick Costello remembers from 1957, it was an exciting time. Important things were happening.

The year 1957 was the year of the Wolfenden Report recommending an end to punitive laws against homosexuality in England; of the first heady days of the Macmillan era; the year of "A Great Leap Forward" in China under Mao Tse-tung; of the appearance in the West of Pasternak's *Doctor Zhivago*, a sensation, published first in Italian after the typescript was smuggled out of Moscow; and of the orbiting of the first man-made earth satellites, launched by the Soviet Union, Sputnik I and Sputnik II.

Nick Costello "remembers" being carried into the garden by his father one evening, "to catch a glimpse of a Soviet satellite going by". But as Nicholas was then only a baby — born in 1956 after they came from Paris and barely a year old — his older brother Mick's recollection deserves a hearing:

> When it was time for the satellite to fly over [Mick recalls], Paddy rushed upstairs, pulled Nick out of his cot and, with Mum and me, rushed into the garden. As the sputnik went over Nick was held up to see it, but as he had no understanding of what this was all about he was simply pointed skywards.

Above left: London 1943. Bil's brothers Jack (back left) and Arthur, with parents "Moishe" and Sophie Lerner. Arthur survived imprisonment and random executions in the Spanish Civil War. Another brother, Nat, was killed in France in 1944. In front, Mick Costello.

Above right: Summer 1938, in the south of France. "Remember our walk through the pine groves to that high cliff, the rust-coloured linen, the Bar de la Marine?", Costello wrote to Bil from Alexandria in 1942. "It was a stroke of genius on your part to send me that old photo of our holiday together at Sanary. Souvenir des beaux jours!"

Previous page: Moscow, 1945. The portrait is inscribed "love to Katinka" — intended for either Costello's second daughter Katie, born in Devon in that year, or his favourite sister Kath in New Zealand.

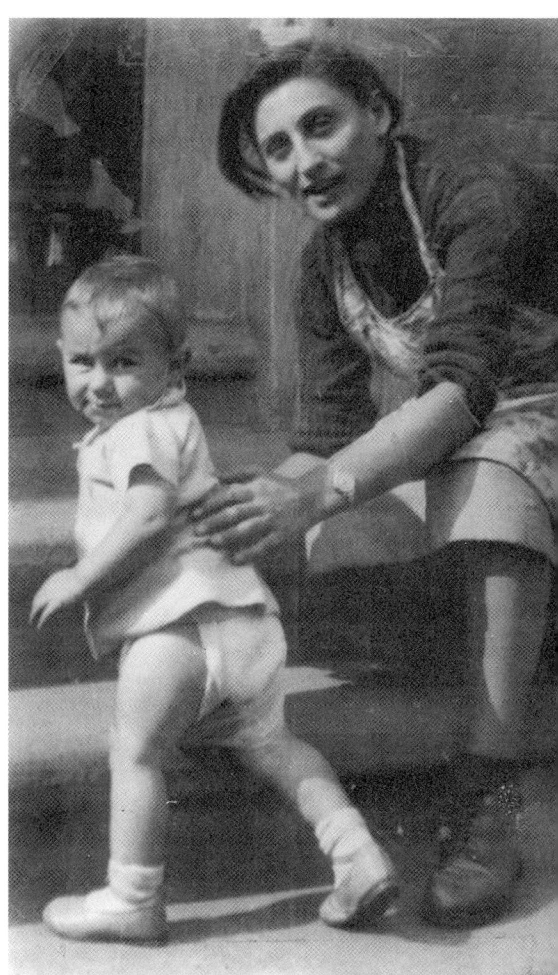

Above left, and right: Bil with Mick, Exeter.

Above: Bil with Mick and Josie, the two first-born, at Longbrook Terrace, Exeter, when Costello was teaching at the University College of Exeter (1936–40). After he went to war in 1941, she worked in a munitions factory.

Top right: The family in Moscow, 1948: Mick, 12; Josie, eight; and at right, Katie, aged three. In 1948 Costello was made Chargé. Two more children would be born in the 1950s.

Below right: Josie and Katie in Paris, 1953, the year Costello was sacked from government service.

Above: Outside the house in Rathen Road, Withington, Manchester, in 1958. From left, Mick, Nicholas (in his father's arms, born 1956), Bil, Josie and Katie. In front Christopher (Kit), born in Paris in 1952.

Right: Josie leaving the TB sanatorium in the French Pyrenees in 1954. She writes, "They gave me a cocktail party for a send-off. Paddy came. When he was given the bill, he complimented me on my taste in wine."

Above: Abba Lerner, the journeyman economist who went to America and failed to convert Trotsky to Keynes's theory of surplus value. Abba, born in Russia, was Bil's eldest brother.

Right: Anna Davin, the Davins' eldest daughter (left), and Bil's surviving sister, Doris Bornstein, outside the house in Bethnal Green where Bil was born. London, 2005.

Below: Mick Costello at home in Maidstone, Kent, 1999.

It was probably the second of these spacecraft that Nick, today living in Beijing as a member of the European Commission's permanent delegation to China, "remembers". For it was Sputnik II, fired in November 1957, which carried a live dog into space. It was the dog that caused most of the excitement. The dog, Laika, did not survive the journey but she captured the imagination of the world.

> You had people coming out of the Services School for Russian [says Michael Nicholson, one of Costello's students at Manchester]. I was at a state grammar school. There was an upsurge of interest in Russian studies in England. Then came the whole Sputnik boom. "Six million American housewives" were said to be learning Russian. And so on.

The teaching of Russian in the English state system had suddenly become respectable — even, to a Mancunian like Maureen Beresford, glamorous. "There were not many foreigners in Manchester in those days. If you heard of a Russian coming to town, great excitement."

There was an element of poetic justice in Costello's appointment, for he owed his position indirectly to his bête noire, the redoubtable Liza Hill, Head of Slavonic Studies and Director of the Russian course at Cambridge. He regarded Professor Hill as a tool of British Intelligence. In the years following the Berlin Blockade of 1948–9, she had master-minded a scheme launched under Prime Minister Attlee which saw the creation in England of a school for Russianists. The Cold War Joint Services School for Russian linguists, described in Elliott and Shukman's *Secret Classrooms*, had a practical military purpose; it was widely regarded as "a spy school" but was a remarkable venture nonetheless; in ten years Liza Hill's team of lecturers and instructors pushed 5000 of the country's brightest graduates doing their National Service training through an intensive course to provide translators and interpreters for British Intelligence.* The Cambridge professor who was said to coax Russian out of her language cadets "by the sheer brightness of her eyes" may have denied Costello a lectureship at his old university, but she had unwittingly helped guide him to a Chair. In response to her initiative the numbers applying

* Among the *kursanty* or language cadets who went on to a range of glittering careers as diplomats, academics, bankers, clerics and spies, were the future playwrights Alan Bennett, Dennis Potter and Michael Frayn.

to the Slavonic departments of British universities multiplied overnight. Manchester where the teaching of Russian had been frozen after years in decline reopened its doors. Costello was the beneficiary.

The north of England was hardly a fertile immersion centre for the teaching of an unpronounceable tongue with six cases in full working order (and fossil remains of a seventh). On the Services course, for instance, beginners, even those with a knowledge of Latin, were reduced to sobs by its system of verbal aspects — arcane, unpredictable and devilish. On arrival at Manchester Costello was informed that in the past, although the Russian Chair went back to 1919, few students had succeeded in graduating. This was because the man who first occupied the position and held it until about 1941, one Trofimov, was removed from office for refusing to teach.

Michael Waller says:

> Those students who registered to do Russian, he tried to put off. If they insisted on continuing, Trofimov failed them at the first exam and went off to his villa at Menton. This went on year after year until it became a scandal.

The story is that Trofimov was retired on full pay. Clearly Costello was not following upon an old and cloistered tradition, or even upon any tradition. Yet he seems quite quickly to have rebuilt a flagging department and won a following from his students. His lectures, according to Maureen Beresford, were "as good as it got":

> I never took any notes. He was so erudite, he had such a wide knowledge. You were aware of a great mind at work, analysing and giving you the benefit of his learning. I just sat and listened in astonishment. At the end I would find that I hadn't made a single note.

Michael Nicholson, today a fellow of University College, Oxford, recalls a lecture in the early 1960s:

> Do you know the Owens Campus? The lecture theatres are downstairs as you come in by the library, quite big. My memory is of a full house. These were weekly lectures by the

> Prof. on Tolstoy's novel, *Khadzhi Murat*, a blow-by-blow run through the text, commenting and digressing as he went. For me stimulating, although my Russian was hardly up to it. Very formal. Gowned. Intense magisterial stuff. The department turned out. An invitation to attend was like a command, as with Walter Lippmann in Washington. It was an exposition of the text, the linguistic peculiarities, the problems. It wasn't just a lecturer trotting through the course but a master-class performance. This was the boss doing his stuff. You paid heed. And you listened.

Costello was an oddity in the system. He had not climbed the normal academic ladder. He lacked the formal training to put a senior student through a doctorate. He possessed charisma but it was not by the brightness of his eyes as with Liza Hill at Cambridge that he won his students. Rather, the opposite — he maintained a distance. Standing erect, crisp and clipped and slightly nasal in speech, animated, yet conscious of his figure.

> The image of a man holding himself together [according to Michael Waller]. It's something I learned to do myself when I was under stress. Paddy was conscious of "the form", of holding the line: keeping the stomach flat and making himself as slim as possible.

Costello seldom smiled. It had something to do perhaps with the Russian language which requires a novel position of tongue and lips. When he said *"Da"* (Yes), his tongue kissed the roof of the mouth. Perhaps it was his teeth, the formation of his mouth? "It so happens [Michael Waller again] that a lot of Russians have their two rows of teeth set very close together. It seems to enable them to speak the language better. Paddy had teeth like that." In the war Costello's teeth had led him to adopt Lord Chesterfield's maxim, never to laugh. "A faint smile perhaps," he told his diary in 1943, "but no immoderate laughter. My teeth will just about manage a faint smile. For a good laugh, they are too gappy now."

Taking up a Chair, Costello was putting aside the rigidity of some of his beliefs. Nick Costello's recollection of a Sputnik glimpsed — or not glimpsed — from their garden at No. 21 Rathen Road, Withington, in

1957 coincided with a thaw in the USSR, as it did with a shift in Costello's attitude to Soviet communism. Already, while still in Paris, he had written in his journal: "The difference between the Socialists and the Communists is the following: the Socialists would like to secure a little more deck space and rather better meals for the third-class passengers; the Communists would like to turn it into a one-class ship."

But, although the years in Moscow had chastened him and the Utopia receded, it had not gone away. In Moscow he had told Davin repeatedly how conditions were improving — "They may not have Utopia. But they have got something." Costello's ambivalence was such that while on the one hand he had condemned a system that silenced freedom of expression, he also appeared to accept it and the need to restructure society, if necessary even condoning censorship. He cited Mayakovsky:

First of all we've got to remake life
When we've done that we can sing about it.

Too irregular and radical in his thinking to be a proper Red, he abhorred Fascism and Nazism yet had failed to draw the parallel with Stalinism, closing his eyes to a system that thrived on deception and fear and dehumanised its own people in Russia, just as Nazism had in Germany. Like many Soviet sympathisers Costello had no idea of the scale of repression in Russia; unwilling to abandon a faith and accept that the Marxist ideal was being betrayed, he repressed his misgivings for the good of the cause. Now, in 1957, Stalin was dead, denounced by Khrushchev at the XXth Congress the previous year. Somewhere between Moscow and Manchester, between the blinkered tunnel of diplomacy and the pure light of scholarship, Costello had come to see Stalinism and everything it represented for the monstrous fraud it was.

"I remember a discussion with Mum over breakfast," Josie says. "'Look,' he said to her. They were talking about collectivisation. Mum was sticking up for the party line. 'Doesn't work,' he said, 'it's a failure. Look, if you own your own cow and it's moaning in the night, you'd get up and go to it, wouldn't you? Under Stalin, it would probably die.' Mum of course stuck to the line, she didn't budge. She did not deviate at all."

He had accepted the show trials at face value, believing in the confessions of guilt extracted from the accused even though, as in the case of the Slovak

Vladimir Clementis whom he had known in Paris and Prague, he had enjoyed the company of some of them. Then the scales fell from his eyes.

What got to him, according to his son, Mick, was that he had been misled. Mick Costello recalls a row they had after the Khrushchev revelations of 1956:

> Paddy was quite negative about Stalin and the Soviet Union. He'd realised after the Congress that there were people who had been condemned at the trials as traitors, whom he himself had rejected, who were in fact loyal communists. He had been lied to. He felt betrayed. At this stage I myself was joining the Party. I wouldn't agree. But as far as he was concerned, the Russians had been proved to be liars. It was a short spat we had at table, not a profound discussion. But he was bitter, and savage in his condemnation.

In June 1956 Costello gave a lecture on "the end of the Stalin legend". He continued to believe with leading British Marxist intellectuals like Isaac Deutscher, the biographer of Trotsky, that for all Stalin's betrayal of the Marxist ideal, global socialism was more than a dream. So the *Daily Worker* as well as the *Manchester Guardian* continued to come to the house in Rathen Road.

Michael Waller remembers winning a British Council scholarship to visit the Soviet Union in his last year at Manchester and then, when his mother became ill, having second thoughts about going. He discussed the problem with the Prof., saying he didn't want to leave his mother. "'There's nothing worse than remorse, is there,' I said to him. 'S'right,' he said. Paddy talked like that. 'S'right,' he said. Then he said, 'Yes, there is. Regret.' And then he said, 'You want to get away from this Pornocracy anyway.'"

Costello may have seen through the false trappings of the Soviet state, yet he remained critical, as ever, of British society and the capitalist world.

He was forty-four. A deracinated, though not a denatured, New Zealander. A voluntary exile in Manchester. Eight years remained.

Richard Crossman, the British Labour politician, once told an acquaintance that his attitude to life was determined by his point of entry into politics. For Crossman it was Germany 1932. For the Anglo–Russian–Jewish philosopher, Isaiah Berlin, the turning-point was the Russian Revolution in 1917 which he witnessed as a child of eight in the streets of St Petersburg. For Costello it was his meeting with Bil in a Cambridge bookshop. Arguably she provided a compass for him to steer by; he saw the Revolution initially through her eyes. Yet he came to it in his own way, at a remove. For all his love of Marxist logic and class analysis, for all his political "certainty" and defence of the workers' state, Costello never allowed scholarship to become subordinated to ideology.

For him — for both Costello and Bil, who tutored for a time in the Russian department — Manchester was the completion of a circle. He had begun as a classicist in New Zealand, had risen to Cambridge, descended to Exeter, been sidetracked by the army, hijacked by the diplomatic service, and now found a perching place with Bil in the north of England, returning to what he loved best, research and teaching. After twenty years of married life Rathen Road was their first real home, a fulfilment in a way.

In the years that remained, with a son at university and four children aged one to fifteen still in the house, the routine tasks would be enlivened by visits to the theatre and opera and occasional trips to the west of Ireland. But what might have been for another man a contracting of horizons and a winding down, the years cushioned and rounded by a little security, would prove for a classicist-turned-Russianist a period of intense activity — the jobbing academic in full cry — dedicated to his ultimate hobby, the life of the mind. It was not Utopia, but it was something; he was content; he was doing, he told Josie, "what I want, and being paid for it".

A Black Eye in Oxford

People had a higher tolerance of alcohol then than they do now. We thought of heavy drinking as entirely natural.

— *Delia Davin*

ONE OF THE first things that Costello did after coming to England was to parcel up his translation of *The Blind Owl*, the Persian novel he had stumbled on in Paris, and send it to an agent Davin had recommended to him. After some weeks he learned, in June 1956, that the novel had been sold to a London publisher. *The Blind Owl* appeared under the John Calder imprint in 1957 and was a critical success. It has remained in print in Costello's English translation ever since.

Costello has been called a born translator. Also a born teacher, born linguist, born diplomat, Intelligence officer, and so on. This is debatable, akin to calling him a genius. Invariably he is described as brilliant. The word "brilliant" recurs in almost every contemporary description of him. What were his talents? Costello was an original and radical thinker; he had an exceptional power of concentration and an ear for music and languages (he spoke by my count nine or ten languages, with a working knowledge of several more); he brought flair and a touch of the actor to the pedantry of academia; he was a winning writer; he had in addition that special gift that most of us lack, gaiety. His songs, his letters, his spontaneity and irrepressible wit are as much a part of his oeuvre as his translation of *The Blind Owl*, his political commentaries and his editions of Griboyedov's play and *The Oxford Book of Russian Verse*.

But not everything came easily. If by genius one understands the capacity to take infinite pains, then he was perhaps an amateur of genius. It took him a year on average to learn a new language. He knew that because language was acquired, it could not be taken for granted. So with Persian.

Costello's interest in the Persian language had been kindled at Cambridge on a visit to Dartington Hall in 1935, and then reawakened in Russia. We remember that after visiting Griboyedov's tomb in the Caucasus, Costello resolved to learn Persian so he could go to Teheran to investigate the circumstances of the playwright's murder. The idea had not gone away. He had begun to learn Persian on his own in Paris in 1951, the year the author of *The Blind Owl*, Sadegh Hedayat, died. Then, having found a teacher, he began to translate Hedayat's novel, initially for his own pleasure. ("Why ever not?" one can hear him saying to himself. "I'm bored. What else is there to do?") Shortly before leaving Paris for Manchester, he attended a meeting in Paris on the fourth anniversary of Sadegh's suicide, and discovered to his surprise that the novelist was a sort of cult among the Teheran intelligentsia — "I got the impression he is to the Persians what Katherine Mansfield is to the New Zealanders or James Joyce to the Irish," he told Davin.

The Blind Owl describes a young man's despair after losing a lover, a nightmarish story which is considered the most important work in modern Iranian literature. "What made you do it?" Davin asked when he received Costello's translation. "Do you understand it?" No, he didn't think he did, Costello said. But the novel was a little masterpiece — "at any rate the original is":

> Why was I drawn to it? I've wondered myself. The main reason is probably that I received a considerable shock when I read it and thought that others might like to experience the same shock.

Mind you, he added, if it had been written in, say, French or German, "I suspect I shouldn't have bothered".

This tells us a good deal about Costello, about his working method, his approach to languages and by inference his approach to life. Linguistically he appears drawn to the unusual and the difficult. He had dabbled in

Yiddish, Sanskrit, Arabic and Church Slavonic before going on to master Russian and Persian. The study of Persian has been likened to the start of a journey into an algebraic equation ("it may or may not come out"). But languages were not an end in themselves. He wanted through languages to read the literatures they represented so that he might by reading the masters in the original understand something of the sweep of a people's history and of the people themselves. His sympathy for and identification with the lives of ordinary Russians, for example, was a logical consequence of his linguistic curiosity.

As a translator, Costello was lexically inventive. It is sometimes hard to separate the translator from the man. Hedayat, the writer, is said to have pioneered the plain style in Persian, concerned as he was to strip off false ornament. Costello's translation of *The Blind Owl* matches this simplicity, establishing a distinct voice, while making what is difficult in the original accessible to an English reader. This in turn gives a clue to Costello's real love, poetry. He is drawn to the spareness of Russian and Greek verse. Maurice Baring, who edited the first *Oxford Book of Russian Verse* that Costello revised and expanded, gives a wonderful example of the Russian language in the hands of a master like Pushkin — "evoking a whole picture in one line without ornament or epithet, such as we find only in Homer".

One can go on. The linguistic panache of Costello's master classes at Manchester and the intellectual tussles he indulged in with Davin in the army — in the Mess they liked to put Davin at one end of the table and Costello at the other, so that their conversation "would not be wasted" — suggest a bravura performer. But the flamboyance of Costello's personality masked an austerity, that of the scholar and monk within. Costello's love and knowledge of folksongs were part of this, a search for the simple truths that lie at the heart of complex human relations. One of Costello's last projects, in collaboration with Paul Foote, was an edition of Russian folk tales and folk songs.

The corsair in Costello needed the drama of the high seas but in the end the integrity of the scholar, returning to the calm of what Davin called "his monkish shelf", always prevailed.

This also helps explain Costello's Marxism. Marxist scholarship attracted him because it provided a "signpost", a formula to reason by. "A Marxist," he wrote in his journal in October 1946, "is a person who can apply Marxist methods of analysis to the problems which he has to solve, not any person who on the strength of a tuppenny pamphlet or of his own experience accepts the political leadership of a Marxist party."

In the autumn of 1957, about the time that Nick Costello was carried into the garden and pointed at a Soviet spacecraft in the sky, Costello travelled down to London at the invitation of the BBC and met Davin in a broadcasting studio. The two former Intelligence officers took part in a three-way radio discussion with the German general, Fridolin von Senger und Etterlin, about the battle for Monte Cassino. Von Senger, one of the senior German commanders who opposed the Allies in the battle, was, like Davin, a product of Oxford and a former Rhodes Scholar. It was a peculiar broadcast, the former enemies dancing a minuet in tones of almost hushed regard, like old boys at a Sunday School reunion. "They're so happy," as Mick Costello says, "to be sitting there together." Dan Davin's wife Winnie, who was present, refused to shake hands with von Senger afterwards.

The broadcast aside, it was for Davin and Costello a diversion. After the broadcast Costello stayed the night with the Davins in Oxford, returning on the train to Manchester — hung over, "with a bucket-and-a-half of beer on board" — the following day. The two had been close friends for fifteen years. The intensity of their friendship has been likened to an affair, but in the war their meetings were infrequent and meetings involving as they did a long train ride were no easier to manage now. Davin had become Academic Publisher to Oxford University Press and was swamped with extra-mural projects of his own, as was Costello. Meetings required planning and cunning. It usually took an excuse or an outside event — a thesis to be examined, a lecture to be delivered — to bring them together. Costello had few intimates outside his own family, Davin was probably the only one, and the relationship was such that as they got older it produced a reaction from the wives.

"I have an open invitation from Syme to stay at Brasenose," Costello would write to Davin, announcing his impending arrival:

> [But] I'd much rather impose myself on you. If I do stay with you, will I (a) irritate Winnie again ("the bloody man would save us a lot of trouble by accepting Syme's invitation") and (b) offend Syme? I don't know. I'd like to stay at your place if you will have me.

Invariably Davin would. And Costello did.

Winnie of course loved Paddy — the whole Davin household would rejoice when Costello came. His gaiety and human warmth were infectious. But when the two were together, drinking, Winnie became concerned. "He and Paddy drank whisky," the Davins' Brigid says. "That's what made my mother mad." Davin had made a full recovery from a gall-bladder operation in 1954 but, like Costello, was troubled with spinal problems. "I think Winnie resented the booze," Anna Davin says. "When they drank, they fought." Theirs was in some ways a friendship of boyish enthusiasms, marked by an Irish predilection for trials of strength and knockabout fisticuffs and wrestling at which each — though Costello usually seemed to come off worse — was practised. Costello had learned to box in New Zealand, fighting with an older brother; Davin had grown up with Cumberland wrestling in Southland.

As Delia Davin says, "We also loved arm-wrestling with my father."

Sometimes however, when male pride was aroused, the results were unpredictable.

A notable encounter had occurred in the summer of 1950 when the Moscow legation was shut down and Costello arrived in Oxford on his way to New Zealand. He was acting as courier for Boris Pasternak. Costello first visited Pasternak's sister, Lydia Pasternak Slater, living in north Oxford, and brought letters and presents to her from her brother in Moscow; then he came to the Davins in Southmoor Road and stayed the night. Anna Davin, the eldest daughter, tells the story:

> Winnie got clipped. I never knew whether Paddy gave her a black eye by mistake or my mother intervened in the fight and so invited it. Winnie could box. She told the story as a joke and she told it differently at different times.
>
> I know, because the next day Winnie came to our school sports wearing dark glasses to conceal the black eye. Lydia Pasternak Slater also came to the sports wearing dark glasses. I was about nine or ten. I remember the two women there together, and Paddy the messenger. He'd brought letters to Lydia and a copy of *War and Peace* in Russian. Lydia had stayed up all night reading it, she said, and ruined her eyes.

Delia says:

> My mother's version was that she had walked between them when they were arguing and come out on the other side with a black eye.

Of the two wives, Bil was the more exclusive. Although Davin did on occasion stay overnight in Manchester, made welcome at Rathen Road by Bil, he was left feeling an interloper. Anna again:

> Bil felt Dan came the closest to ensnaring Paddy into bourgeois deviation, including drink and having a good time. Being frivolous. Also, it wasn't family. For Bil what mattered was the Party and the Family. In a way it was a dysfunctional family. Bil didn't do "the Jewish momma" bit. Underneath I think it was deep jealousy. My sense is that the couple-relationship was what was most important, and even the children in some ways were threatening to her. Certainly close friends were.

Booze, Davin's health and conjugal complications notwithstanding, the relationship between the two men continued to prosper. They had always kept the friendship in good repair, their mutual admiration and respect proof against Costello's sometimes wounding jibes or Davin's sly mockery of Costello's ready-recipe political views. But the telephone was getting cheaper and there were fewer letters now. And the balance was shifting. Initially what had drawn Davin was Costello's gaiety — "Alone, and sober, I am subnormal," he wrote in 1944; "with Paddy I am wittier and entertain myself more." In Cairo and southern Italy where Costello had moved in many circles Davin was left wanting; now Davin was a powerful academic publisher, eminent in his field, and it was Costello, sidelined in the provinces, who was more often the one in need. In a subtle way their situations had been reversed.

The friendship can be measured today by its domino effect, reaching down in the next generation through the daughters, two Costellos and three Davins. In the 1950s Dan and Winnie Davin had three children at school in Oxford, Anna, Delia and Brigid. The Davins kept open house. Their home by the canal, a place of "glamorous raffishness" in Keith Ovenden's phrase, was often lit by BBC characters, bohemian spongers, out-of-work actors and poets, some of whom stayed for weeks, and — especially on the occasions when Costello came from Manchester — transformed by song.

> Paddy came sometimes when the poets came, Louis MacNeice and Bertie Rogers and Dylan Thomas [Brigid remembers]. We crept downstairs and hid behind the chairs and sofas in our pyjamas. We were allowed to stay because we were invisible, although everyone knew we were there. Sometimes, as the youngest, I was allowed to go and fetch some cheese from the kitchen. Paddy sang. Louis recited. Dylan Thomas told a story. Everyone took a turn.
>
> Paddy was handsome but he was most handsome (ooooh!) when he didn't smile. He wasn't a great smiler, even when he sang. But there was passion in it. It was moving. It was moving because you knew that he meant it. Sometimes he sang with a hand cupped behind his ear, in the Irish way.

They drank beer and whisky. Heavy drinking was normal. Delia says, "People were more tolerant then." If behaviour deteriorated, the girls were tidied away; next morning they might wake in a different bed to the one they had gone to sleep in.

Anna Davin remembers her father being up early next day singing in the shower, setting Costello off again.

Elsewhere I have written of the dynastic, almost tribal relationship among the daughters, explained in part by the fact that all were war babies. Once when Costello brought his family to stay — it was probably the trophy trip in 1950 when Winnie was awarded a black eye — Katie Costello aged five was put into Brigid and Delia's bedroom. The three girls shared the room, Katie sleeping in a cot. Katie was monolingual Russian.

"Brigid and I had a private nonsense language that we used," Delia says. "I was six and Brigid five, the same age as Katie. Katie used to wake in the morning quite agitated, shaking the bars of the cot and babbling away to herself in Russian. Some time later we had some Russians staying with us. One of them said to Winnie, 'I didn't know your children spoke Russian.' 'They don't,' Winnie said. What had happened, we'd incorporated Katie's babblings into our nonsense talk without realising. What we had been saying in Russian was, 'My God, my God, does no one understand me?'"

As the 1960s dawned, the Davins began to notice Costello's growing concern with the education of his children. In Paris he had been attentive to their needs but liberal. "Once he sent me back to boarding school with a bottle of port in my box," Mick says. "Paddy never censored what we read or did — only the use of bad English. Not using English properly was as bad as slouching. He took us to the theatre every week. He taught me to appreciate wine. He had a wonderful palate, he could identify years of good red wine." In France he had looked after the education of the senses. But in England for social and class reasons the problems of schooling increased. The question was more urgent. He became stricter, almost Victorian. Delia Davin, today a professor at Leeds University, noticed another side — how he took time to help and encourage others with their studies, in Delia's case her Gaelic studies, revealing an unsuspected kindliness behind the abrupt manner. She did not notice however (how should she?) the workload that he was creating for himself, the nervous energy he was expending; or that there was a drink problem, besides a back problem, and that he had begun to cough in the mornings when he woke up.

In 1962 when Katie gave her father a meerschaum pipe for his fiftieth birthday he had developed an impressive racking cough. Costello wrote to Davin about this time, "My days of playing squash are over, and very nice too."

Dinner with the Freybergs

Tomorrow I'm going away, brother. Perhaps we'll never see each other again. So this is what I advise. Put your hat on. Take a stick in your hand, walk away. Go without looking back. And the further you go, the better.

— *From Chekhov's* Three Sisters, *copied into the front of Costello's journal*

THERE HAS NEVER been a satisfactory explanation for Costello's death. His friends and colleagues were mystified. Even his detractors — a retired spook writes of his "deep misgivings about the timing and nature of Paddy Costello's death" — appear troubled. Some said that he wore himself out. Costello died eight years after he came to Manchester. He died in his prime. He died unobtrusively after a quiet day followed by some convivial drinking, brushing his teeth before going to bed, like the most ordinary citizen. He woke suddenly in the night, as one learned later, complaining of a pain in his arm. A few moments later he stopped breathing.

Doctors sometimes refer to a heart attack as the Silent Killer. They say that 50 per cent of those who "present" to them with coronary disease do so by dropping dead. And perhaps although there were no general symptoms or complaint of disease beforehand that *is* the explanation. That was the first sign. He simply "put his hand up and died".

Yet we remain dissatisfied. Costello was fit, well, active. He did not appear unduly stressed. The day before, a Saturday, he had been swimming in the university pool. Six months before that, after a number of abortive attempts, he had stopped smoking altogether. There was apparently no family history of coronary disease, although in the case of his father, who also died at an early age leaving a young family — the father died of a bleeding ulcer — "cardiac failure" is listed as a second cause. But did the father's heart give out first or did the heart stop because of the ulcer?

There was certainly a drink problem. Inherited? Paddy Costello's father, Christopher Costello, was born in or near a pub in Dublin where Christopher's father, Paddy's grandfather, was the publican. More than that we don't know. Costello's family and friends insist that he had the wrong profile for a heart attack. But the death certificate also insists. Under Cause of Death it says, "1(a) coronary thrombosis, (b) arterio sclerosis".

The drink is curious. Costello was at home drinking socially with some Irish cousins on the night he died. Apparently they drank well, and late. In his later years when he got drunk, Costello would put himself to bed. Friends would be invited for a meal. He would get up from the table in the middle of dinner, according to Katie, and leave. "Just go. He seemed to know when he'd had enough. Mum told me. She had to face the social consequences." Does this imply a severe alcoholic addiction?

Or was it simple tiredness?

Costello was not a habitual or addicted drinker. He drank in company. He was a binge drinker. He did not particularly like alcohol, he tells us. Bingeing strips off the veneer. It may lead to violence or the threat of violence, as when Costello threatened to cut his throat and had to be manacled when he was arrested in 1950. Those who study the problem tell us that this in itself is not abnormal. You don't have to be abnormal to behave abnormally when drunk. According to a British authority, the neurologist Dr Alwyn Lishman, "Binge drinkers tend to avoid the more florid complications of alcohol abuse, as if the brain were taking a breather, often preserving their memory and verbal fluency to an extent that hides any other deterioration."

Costello's diary and letters contain examples of aggressive behaviour, but normally these fall into the "bonkers sublime" category, perhaps involving acts of social disfigurement which he would afterwards in his diary attempt to analyse, pinning himself against the wall like a laboratory specimen.

A wartime entry in his journal reads:

> I remember nothing after 9 p.m., but I do remember making a complete fool of myself, bragging, attacking the qualities of the British and American soldiers (fool! fool! fool!). How cheap and easy for a NZer, and a NZer who hasn't been in the line for two and a half years, to run down the soldiers of other countries. Time and again I have resented this facile talk of mine and sworn not to repeat it — but I was sober when I swore.

When exhilarated he might tip the contents of whatever he was drinking from into the nearest receptacle, as he did at a diplomatic function in Paris one evening, emptying a bottle of brandy into Jean McKenzie's grand piano. An anecdote from Costello's inaugural Senate dinner at Manchester University has him ending up dancing a gopak on the table, with an upturned melon on his head.

In his cups he could be mischievous, maudlin, wounding, suave, aggressive, adolescent, operatic, lacrimose, comatose, jocose, or just plain malicious. A favourite ploy was to fasten on an unsuspecting victim and get him drunk deliberately. He did this to Bil's father, an Orthodox Jew who hated drink.* He did it to an abstemious headmaster, an old school friend in New Zealand, who vomited rum and raspberry afterwards for two days. It was both ploy and juvenile prank. Costello usually had an end in sight, as when the saintly and fellow-travelling historian Willis Airey came to Manchester and stayed the night. Professor Airey had taught Costello at university in Auckland. He arrived from behind the Iron Curtain, from Prague. According to his daughter, Dr Deirdre Airey, who was present, "Paddy spent the evening talking about Russia, drinking whisky and trying to make my father drunk enough to say Stalin was a bastard. Dad wouldn't. He justified Stalin. This was 1958. Time of *Zhivago*. Dad was still clinging to the remnants of his Marxist faith, he clung to the end. Paddy wouldn't give up. He said, 'Come on, Bill. You know he was a bastard.' It was past midnight. Everyone had gone to bed. 'Well, all right, Paddy,' Dad gave in finally. 'OK. Stalin was a bastard.' Dad didn't drink, he wasn't used to it. He was ill the next day. I went to bed. Paddy sat up for hours afterwards, playing Bach on his radiogram."

---

* Bil's sister Doris recalls her father saying that only goys got drunk. "So Paddy got him drunk. He sang to him songs in Yiddish. He had my father walking round the garden in Hackney singing, 'schicker ist ein Yid'."

Probably Costello's bingeing can be satisfactorily explained only in a psychological memoir of great insight. Neurologists point out that two-thirds of those who behave badly when drunk suffer from brain shrinkage. Some say that Costello was a deeply troubled man. It may, on the other hand, mean no more than that he was unfortunate in his genetic makeup. All is speculation. Certainly General Freyberg, who was aware of Costello's weakness, did not read anything strange into it.

Bernard Freyberg invited Costello to dinner two or three times after the war. The first time was in 1946 at his London flat, in company with Dan Davin and Geoffrey Cox. It was a decorous occasion since the wives were also present; but, as Costello wrote afterwards to McIntosh, not lacking in interest:

> It was a remarkable occasion. The three ex-Intelligence officers tackled the General in a way I had never dared before. It was like the baiting of a good-natured bear. If it was a new experience for him to have his tactics and strategy roughly handled by junior officers, it was interesting for us to observe how much he knew about things we had thought at the time to have got away with. The old man produced the best from his cellar, treated us and himself generously and kept us late. It was only afterwards that I realised the ladies may have felt a little out of it.

The next invitation came twelve years later, to Costello and Davin alone. This was an invitation to dine and spend the night at Windsor Castle, where Freyberg — having spent the years 1946–1952 as Governor-General of New Zealand — was now Deputy Constable and Lieutenant-Governor, residing in the Norman Tower. Arrangements had been held over for some months. They were confirmed at the end of January 1958 when Costello took the 8.10 train from Manchester on a Saturday morning, collected Davin in Oxford about midday and travelled on with him to Windsor in the afternoon.

Dinner was a lively occasion, with talk of Cairo in the war and Barbara Freyberg's account of trying to run a household in an antiquated Tower with no lift and disjointed passageways running off in all directions. Once again the General's hospitality was lavish. After dinner he bade the butler bring a flagon of the household's premier malt whisky, and everyone retired to bed about 9 p.m. As they were getting into bed, Costello said to Davin, "You know, there's a lot of whisky left in that decanter downstairs." Davin agreed. The temptation was great. They got out of bed and descended the central staircase in their pyjamas. What happened next is recorded — one among many versions — by Margot Ross, the wife of a mutual friend. They secured the whisky and returned to their room, as they thought, but in the dark opened a door off the wrong landing. Entering, they discovered Lord and Lady Freyberg sitting up in bed together, reading the *Windsor, Slough and Eton Gazette*. The intruders retreated on all fours, having put on (in Davin's version) "my cloak of invisibility". They reached their room and disposed of the whisky. In the morning the butler removed the empty decanter without comment, saying merely that breakfast would be in half an hour. Freyberg waited until the breakfast things were being cleared away, then looked them in the eye and said, "The car will be ready to take us to church parade in ten minutes."

From then on, whenever Davin or Costello came to Windsor, there was always a bottle of whisky by the bedside.

The story has travelled, regaled in university circles and judges' chambers — for a long time it was difficult to go near a judge's common room in New Zealand without tripping over a Freyberg staffer — with endless variation, one of the scores of anecdotes and stories in the annals of the New Zealand Division that reflect the humanity and considerateness of its grim and supposedly humourless Napoleonic commander. In 1958 General, now Lord Freyberg, was nearing the end of his life. Strangely anecdotes like the Windsor Castle one, helping to reveal the man behind the myth, have eluded Freyberg's biographers. Yet perhaps not so strange, since none of these writers campaigned with Freyberg in the war nor knew the unofficial man as intimately as Costello and Davin did.

As a mature writer Davin published a book of memoirs, *Closing Times*, about seven friends, all writers. Its success led him to conceive and plan a companion volume, to be entitled *Soldiers and Scholars*, in which Freyberg and Costello would both appear, with Costello possibly the centrepiece.

"I don't want to write a strict biographical kind of thing," Davin wrote to Bil after Costello died, "but rather a memoir portrait of the man I knew and liked best of all the friends I've ever had. I still miss him almost every day."

When Davin wrote this, in 1981, he had already begun to draft a portrait of Costello. He yearned to write about his friend, as he did about Freyberg — he had spent half a lifetime jotting down anecdotes about Costello and Freyberg's gnomic utterances and making notes on the two men. After Davin died in 1990 sketches of both men were found among his papers, left unfinished (Freyberg had died in the summer of 1963 and Costello a few months later in February 1964). Colleagues of Davin put this down to failing health and energies after he retired. Keith Ovenden, his biographer, however, is convinced that in the case of Costello it was Davin's inability to rebut the charges of spying and rescue his friend from his detractors which defeated him, robbing him of the will to complete the portrait.

In 1958, Costello went to Moscow to attend a world conference of Slavists. In Moscow he escaped the tedium of the congress in company with another ex-classicist turned Russianist from Birmingham University, Reginald Christian. Christian was a Tolstoy specialist and a former British diplomat in the Soviet Union. They spent the time revisiting old haunts and friends in Moscow, but Costello did not call on Boris Pasternak, who was out of town. Pasternak was in disgrace and fearing arrest, even as he was about to be catapulted to world fame by the award of the Nobel Prize for *Doctor Zhivago*. *Doctor Zhivago* had first appeared in Italy in November 1957, and in England in the summer of 1958 as Costello was about to leave for the conference. Pasternak's novel was a rejection of Marxism and the first completely unofficial account of the suffering inflicted by the 1917 Revolution on ordinary Russian families. But the sensation its publication caused in the West was as nothing compared to the furore when Pasternak, under pressure from the Soviet authorities, was forced to reject the Nobel award. That award (November 1958) was still a month away when Costello returned to Manchester from the conference and found waiting for him a request from Charles Brasch in New Zealand to review the novel. After reading the novel in translation, Costello declined. He told Brasch, the editor of *Landfall*, that *Doctor Zhivago* was, as he had long suspected, a bad book.

Costello's misgivings went back more than ten years, when he began to call on Pasternak in Moscow and became one of the first foreigners to learn that Pasternak had embarked on a new project about his own generation caught up in revolution and war, a novel which he saw as the culmination of his life's work. Pasternak had shown Costello the first part of *Doctor Zhivago* in typescript, suggesting that he might translate it. Costello, despite Davin's enthusiastic response — Davin wrote that any English publisher "would jump at your translation of his novel" — seems to have considered and then rejected the proposal. He had thought the novel bad in 1945, he told Brasch, and in 1958 he still thought so:

> Again and again I felt like bawling, "Stop showing how clever you are. Keep to the bloody story." And what is the story? The story of a man who contracts out of the history of his country. Solon, I seem to remember, ordained that those who stood aside from the broils of Athens should be punished. I don't advocate punishment for such; but I must say that my respect goes to those poets like Gumilyov (who was shot by the Reds) and to Mayakovsky (who wore himself out in the service of the revolution), rather than to the neutrals. This is a personal preference and I should not have mentioned it were it not for the complacency with which Pasternak describes himself. Indeed I found the vanity of the author disconcerting.

The 1958 English edition was translated by Max Hayward, long known to Costello from their Moscow days. Hayward's translation would earn him much kudos. But it was not pique on Costello's part that motivated his refusal to review Hayward's translation. He had never been interested in the rewards of fame. He told the editor of *Landfall* that he did not wish to criticise the book at length in public,

> (a) because I like Pasternak personally and love his poetry and (b) because the reason for my disapproval of the book could easily be misunderstood.

Having said that, Costello changed his mind. The following year he wrote an essay about *Doctor Zhivago*, tearing the novel to bits for its cardboard characters, contrived plot, religious longueurs and the self-indulgence of its author. He sent the piece first to the *Observer* newspaper, and subsequently to the editors of *Twentieth Century, Encounter*, the *London Magazine* and the *New Left Review*. All rejected it. Costello was swimming against the tide. By now, 1962, the chorus in praise of *Zhivago* was deafening. Pasternak himself had become an idol, the symbol of one of the greatest blows struck against Soviet prestige and a hero to the younger generation of Russians who had turned his funeral at Peredelkino into a protest demonstration against the regime that had tried to silence him.

The irony is that Costello's view of the novel as contrived and laboured is now the norm. Today no reputable critic, while praising Pasternak for his lyrical and descriptive passages (as did Costello), would say he had written a good novel. Once again Costello was guilty of being ahead of his time.

Finally he was rewarded. His friend Professor Christian invited him to present his view of the novel in a lecture to his students — "a demolition job", Professor Christian recalls today, "that was warmly applauded". The lecture, "Zhivago Reconsidered", would be published posthumously. It was delivered by Costello at Birmingham University in December 1963, a few weeks before he died.

Time's Thief

> I wish, how I wish, that I had more time. It is not that I wish life were longer — no point in living to a great old age — but that I wish it were broader. What could I not do if we had the 48-hour day!
>
> — *Costello's journal*

IN ONE OF his notebooks Costello writes, quoting Macaulay on Charles I, "His mind was as full of schemes as a rabbit warren full of holes." He was referring half-jokingly to himself. Costello's papers are filled with projects, some commissioned, some not, and burning ideas and enthusiasms abandoned for want of time, like his scheme to find the government papers that went missing in Teheran when the Russian legation was sacked in 1829. A major Russian dictionary to which he was contributing, besides two other books cut short by his death, would be published posthumously, as was his 5000-word essay on *Doctor Zhivago*. In the final Manchester years Costello's brain seems to have gone into overdrive.

In 1963 he turned fifty. Costello celebrated the occasion with his usual enthusiasm, managing to conceal a hangover the next day by "giving an impression of gravity and reserve" while supervising the oral examination of a B. Litt. candidate. He was examining a lot — in Manchester, Edinburgh, Oxford, Cambridge — besides travelling to Russia in successive years, and writing and reviewing for specialist journals in Canada and America and a variety of publications in England.

> Dear Paddy
> You are probably the only person in the world who could review these two books in a single article [the editor of *The Times Literary Supplement* wrote in 1961]. If so, could you do it fairly quickly?

Costello was a compulsive reviewer. He reviewed books on literature, linguistics, gardening, history and revolution with the same relish he applied to monitoring the university sweepstake for the Grand National Steeplechase, reading a story from Homer to his five-year-old son Nick or composing an article for the American *Slavic Review* entitled "The Meaning of the conjunction 'POKA'". In 1962 he was invited to contribute to the Oxford Russian-English dictionary. He seems to have worked on the manuscript draft of this up to his death, while at the same time making notes for a proposed new Russian grammar, completing his half of the Russian folk literature volume he was editing jointly with Paul Foote, and checking cognates for yet another dictionary — of etymology — all for the Clarendon Press, the learned arm of Oxford University Press. In his spare time he began to translate a rollicking pre-revolutionary novel by Ivan Kushchevsky, *Nikolay Negorev or The Successful Russian*. His knowledge both of Russian literature and the idiom of contemporary Russian speech made him sought after as a critic and contributor throughout Britain. He was invited by Penguin Books to oversee yet another Russian dictionary and in 1963 accepted a proposal by Oxford University Press to select and translate a new volume of Russian short stories for the World's Classics series, but seems not to have begun on either task. At some stage he picked up some notes he had been carrying around, either on paper or in his head, about his wartime escape from Greece, and began work on that too. It was a novel. The novel began,

> Good soldiers think of killing, bad soldiers think of being killed.

But the novel seems not to have got beyond the opening chapters in manuscript.

With so many projects on the go, it would not be surprising to learn that his university work suffered. It seems not. He became, if anything, over-conscientious. Costello enjoyed the teaching. Only the business of administration irked him. "His filing system," says Michael Beresford, a staff colleague, "was a model of economy, consisting of one shelf at the bottom of a bookcase."

At home he shut himself in the study and worked. But if he was driving himself, his children did not notice. In 1963 when the Lord Mayor of Manchester received a delegation of VIPs from Leningrad, Costello's daughter Josie was asked to interpret at the official reception. At the last minute she quailed, and asked her father to do it instead. Costello was preparing to leave for Stockport where he was due to give a lecture. "S'right," he said to her. "S'right. Too difficult for you." Then he cupped his hands, smiling slightly, and reassured his daughter, saying, "All you have to do, Josie, is stand up in front of these old farts and imagine them without any clothes on." Josie carried it off without a hitch and got her photograph in the papers.

In 1963 two of the children, Katie, seventeen, and Nick, seven, were living at home, the other three were away — Kit, eleven, at boarding school in Staffordshire, Josie, twenty-two, teaching in Paris, and Mick, twenty-seven, married and living in Manchester. Mick appears to have disappointed his father academically by abandoning his medical studies for a freelance career in journalism and politics. In the 1960s Mick Costello became an activist in the British Communist Party, subsequently industrial correspondent for the *Morning Star* and in 1977 the party's industrial organiser, one of the more powerful men in the Labour movement in Britain.*

Paddy Costello believed, although he didn't put it in these words, that education was so important that if he didn't provide it for his offspring, the best that could be obtained, he was no better than parents in primitive societies who put their children to work at the age of five. His reverence for learning led him to demand of them standards which first Mick, then Josie and Katie found difficult to attain.

"Those standards were inculcated in me from an early age," Katie recalls. "What I'm thinking today is, it's all very well for him to have these standards which he could live up to. But when it's translated into an inferior being like me, it might have a bad effect. It might explain why I'm always quibbling about things not being absolutely right." To this day she catches herself looking over her shoulder at an absent father, still trying to measure up.

---

* Mick Costello joined the Communist Party in 1957 and became, at Manchester, the only communist president of a university students' union in Britain. The *Morning Star* was the party organ, formerly the *Daily Worker*. It was renamed in 1966.

Josie, educated at schools in Russia, France and England, admits with a mixture of pride and pain to having had to cope with "three mother tongues" by the age of seventeen. Yet their home in Manchester, when the burden of a multi-lingual background began to show, was a happy one despite the standards Costello set and the discipline he imposed. What comes through, talking with them today about their father, has little to do with a controlling intelligence or with having to prove themselves in his eyes. Their talk is much more about the abundance of his company and about the side-effects, the invisible rewards which came from growing up alongside a walking encyclopedia radiating affection, and, in different ways, firing their imagination.

In the home Bil was always there, resilient, unsentimental, available on demand like strong army tea. Visitors to the house do not quote anything she said. They remark on her fierce loyalty, on her reserve and, paradoxically, her vividness. The vividness came from her stillness, the wry half-amused smile, and the eyes set in a perfectly oval face. She was less perturbed by life's accidents than he and less emotional — it was to Paddy the younger children ran for comfort if they hurt themselves — and, for better or worse, she kept from them the vicissitudes which had affected their married life. Of the children only Mick was told the reason they had to leave Paris.

Costello had written to Davin when he reached Manchester, "I remember your reproving me some years ago for sending Mick to the dim school he attended after our return from Russia":

> When I replied, feebly, that with his mixed-up past he couldn't have won admission to a decent school, you replied that by pulling strings I might have got him into one. Well, the question of strings now arises in connection with Kit, and I want to know if you're aware of any string-ends dangling within reach.

Costello pondered the mixed-up schooling fostered on the older three children and became passionately involved in the education of the youngest two, Christopher (Kit) and Nicholas, determined that in England they would not have to face the same hurdles.

There were not many letters now. Costello's mother had remarried and died in New Zealand in 1959. After 1960 his correspondence with Davin begins to dry up. Whether this was because he was more in Davin's company or travelling to Oxford more or because of administration or other pressures is not known. According to Richard Freeborn, who met Costello at conferences and took over the Manchester Chair when he died, Costello found the teaching and administration of a department stressful. "This undoubtedly contributed to his early death," Freeborn says. But his is a lone view, not shared by other colleagues.

He did not seem to tire. He swam and walked regularly. New Zealand visitors to the house in Rathen Road, renewing old acquaintanceships, said Costello was looking gaunt. But he had always been skinny. He was "so skinny", a Welsh farmer said to Bil, "two people couldn't look at him at the one time". That was in the summer of 1958, when they stayed at a farm in Caernarvonshire for three weeks. It wasn't as if he didn't take holidays, or shut himself up in a tower away from fresh air. On the contrary.

In 1960 or 1961 Costello discovered a wet slab of rock off the coast of Galway in the west of Ireland, called Inis Mor. Christopher (Kit) recalls their first holiday there. "We stayed at Kilmurvey House," he writes:

> My dearest memory of Paddy has us walking over the rocks at Inis Mor at four in the morning, towards the distant booming of the Atlantic on the western cliffs. We had been fed salt fish on Fridays and (to cut it short) came back with enough fresh pollack and mackerel to feed all the guests at Kilmurvey House. We didn't exchange many words over the crash of the surf, and didn't need to. He must have been around fifty, and I around ten.

What had drawn Costello to this barren place at the extreme edge of Europe? Possibly it was the folk-ballad tradition, a mode of reciting Gaelic ballads unchanged for centuries that reminded him of the desert. Or the chance it gave him to practise his Gaelic, for the drone of the Aran dialect mixed with gusts of wild laughter was all round him. Possibly Davin was the midwife, for having acquired a beautiful edition of *The Aran Islands*, by the playwright J.M. Synge, with the original Yeats illustrations, he sent or showed it to Costello.

Such was the impact of the place that after the first visit Costello returned to Inis Mor with his family every summer until he died.

The landscape of Aran is a kind of magical desolation amid shrieking gulls and near-vertical cliffs falling sheer to the Atlantic Ocean. It has few parallels. On Inis Mor, the biggest of the three Aran islands, Costello like Synge before him comes down to us as a solitary figure wandering by the shoreline after a storm, picking his way over the irregular blocks of limestone, hair stiff with salt, masses of spray flying up from the base of the cliff, and suddenly crouching down for an instant when one falls on him, "wrapped and blinded by a hail of foam".

He is absent from almost all the photographs. A rare snap shows him sitting with the Davins, Dan and Winnie, on a flat rock near a pagan fort. At Davin's back is the cliff and the sea, hundreds of feet below. They appear to be sitting on piles of seaweed. Winnie Davin, in a light blouse, is laughing. She looks like a young girl. Davin, in knee socks and brogues, stares at the camera. Costello is looking down. His hair waved, unruffled in the wind. He wears a collar and tie. His trousers appear ironed. One wonders if he ever changed out of them before going fishing or wading into the surf. He must have done, at least once, because his daughter Katie noticed the varicose veins on his legs. "I remember thinking to myself," she says, "that's what a real man has."

The snapshot with the Davins was taken in the summer of 1963, the only time the two couples were together on vacation. Probably the Davins stayed only a day or two — they visited cousins in County Galway and also went to Dublin; it is possible that Costello went alone without Bil, or taking just Kit and Nick. The holiday at all events lasted three weeks. The sun was low when they sailed for the mainland at the end of their holiday; they boarded the steamer at Kilronan on a clear evening, as it had been at the end of Synge's last visit to Aran sixty years earlier — "As we came out into the bay the sun stood like an aureole behind the cliffs of Inishmaan. A little later a brilliant glow came over the sky, throwing out the blue of the sea and of the hills of Connemara."

Early in 1964 a freshman reading classics at Manchester University, Martin Prior, was chatting to a friend outside one of the lecture halls when he heard the name Costello. As a thirteen-year-old schoolboy Martin had once met Costello on a train, introduced by his father who was the philosophy professor at Manchester. It was because of Costello that he was now studying classics. Hearing the name, Martin turned to the girl who had spoken and said, brightly, "Oh, do you know Paddy Costello?" She didn't reply. Martin's companion dug him in the ribs. The girl had turned away, tears in her eyes. Costello had died the previous day.

He died on a Sunday in February 1964. He had returned from Ireland at the end of the previous summer, exhilarated but tremulous — "I need a holiday to get over my holiday," he wrote to a friend — and plunged back into the Russian novel he was translating. He returned from the university at six or seven and worked into the night after supper. Bil was helping him. They worked together, sitting side by side at the formica-topped table in the kitchen, Costello pausing now and then to look something up or check a phrase with her. Bil's command of English, her idiom, was more direct and sometimes more illuminating than his. Neither the book he was translating, *Nikolai Negorev or The Successful Russian*, nor its author, Ivan Kushchevsky, were known outside Russia. In his devotion to this obscure pre-revolutionary writer Costello was being true to his daemon. Once again he had responded to someone who died young. First he had been drawn to the diplomat Griboyedov, hacked to pieces by a mob at thirty-four; then to the Persian writer, Sadegh Hedayat, who took his life on a visit to Paris at forty-eight; and now Kushchevsky, author of a sparkling tale of boyhood and youth, who died of privation and drunkenness at the age of twenty-nine. For all the gay humour and effervescence of Kushchevsky's novel, one cannot quite put aside the thought that Costello was preoccupied with early death.

That winter of 1963–4, December and January, seems to have been a hectic one. February was a little better. In the week of 17 February Costello gave a talk to a Celtic Studies group about the traditions and customs of the Aran islanders. A note in his university pocket diary for Wednesday 19 February 1964 reads, "BRING ARAN SLIDES"; and for Friday 21st, "closing date for Grand National sweepstake". That same Friday, 21 February, a first-year student who was attending Costello's weekly lectures on Tolstoy asked to see him. Michael Nicholson had a problem:

> I explained my dilemma to the Prof. — that I had a grant to spend a year in Germany. But that I wanted to deploy part of the year so I could have a semester in Russia, but the system wouldn't allow it. It wasn't possible. "It's impossible," he agreed. "I can see that." He chatted a bit. Until then I am not aware that I had in any sense *met* the Professor. Manchester was not especially formal but relationships were more hierarchical than they are

> now. We chatted for quite a long time, he seemed to warm to the subject. I was flattered. Then he said, "Let me see if I can think of something."
>
> Time collapses, notoriously, in one's memory, but my memory is that it was a Friday afternoon, and he died that same weekend.

Costello's university pocket diary for the second Sunday in Lent, 23 February 1964, has a note. It reads,

> "Write to Kharkov [University] about M.A. Nicholson."

He had spent part of Saturday morning at the university pool teaching Nick, his youngest, to swim. They had caught the bus. The rest of the day seems to have been given over to preparing draft questions for Cambridge examination papers, for which he was responsible, and — in the afternoon — going to the museum to hear a lecture entitled "Some Famous British Gardens". The history and corridors of influence on the architectural planning and planting of gardens were among his many interests. After supper some Irish cousins called. A convivial evening followed. But the revelry was over, the drinking ended and the cousins departed when Katie got home in the small hours of Sunday morning. She had been to a party. The house was quiet. Katie had been in bed for only a few hours when Bil woke her.

> My mother woke me at seven, she said she thought Papa was dead. Would I come and look. He was lying there in bed. I was still half-asleep. I felt his neck. I didn't know if it was his pulse I was feeling, or mine. My lips were pulsing.
>
> My mother said Papa had woken complaining of a pain in his left arm. It was bad. Could he have something to put him out? My mother gave him a paracetamol. Papa lay back and breathed out and was dead. That's what she told me.

The doctor came. He pronounced death from coronary thrombosis, a severe heart attack. The only other person in the house was Katie's small brother, Nicholas. Nick was then seven, going on eight. He was sleeping upstairs.

Nick Costello, who is today living in Beijing, writes: "I recall my father teaching me Latin — which must have been before I was seven-and-a-half, since that's when he died. When he did die, I said to my mother, 'I wish it had been you instead', and she replied 'So do I'."

He was fifty-two.

Postscript

BIL RETURNED TO teaching, while studying for a Master's degree, to earn the school fees that would be needed so that Kit and Nick, aged eleven and seven, could continue to have the education Costello would have wanted for them. Dan and Winnie Davin visited Bil in Manchester in May and in Oxford Davin solicited donations for a trust fund to help with the fees. Predictably perhaps, pushed by Bil to follow the example of their father, egged on by his own mother Mary in New Zealand a generation earlier, Kit and Nick sat for and got scholarships to top public schools, Kit to Shrewsbury and Nick to Winchester.

Bil reacted to the death as if mortally wounded. Her sorrow was internalised. Friends felt rejected. Bil's grief was such that for a long time she did not tell anyone outside the family that Paddy Costello had died. She kept his name in the telephone directory, and on club and faculty lists. Invitations to attend meetings were still arriving at 21 Rathen Road, Withington, addressed "Professor D.P. Costello" almost forty years later, as the twenty-first century dawned.

Christopher Costello (Kit) was away at a preparatory boarding school in

Staffordshire in February 1964, unaware that his father had died. He was not told, he says, until he came home for mid-term vacation a week later. "Bil met me at the station. We got a taxi back to the house, and after she told me I was in a state of shock. She asked me what I wanted for lunch and I didn't reply. (Couldn't.)"

The funeral was private. The Davins were not invited.

Costello's death had strange consequences, affecting institutions as well as people, many of whom did not know him, or barely. One of these was a New Zealand doctor, Edward McCullough. Teddy McCullough had met Costello in the war and disliked him. The dislike was probably mutual, but the relationship improved later. In 1984 when Dan Davin was soliciting recollections for his planned memoir of Costello, he wrote to McCullough who recalled visiting the Costellos in Manchester in the winter of 1963–4. "Paddy was fascinated boyishly by the electronically operated drophead of my Daimler," he wrote to Davin. McCullough added, "Martha telephoned one Sunday afternoon when Inez was staying with me. We three wept into the phone."

In Oxford Dan Davin was out playing squash on the afternoon of Sunday 23 February when *The Times* rang to ask if he would write the obituary notice. Winnie Davin answered the telephone. She got the news to Dan. "Dan came home," his biographer Keith Ovenden records, "went into his study, shut the door, and was alone and silent for three hours, when he phoned the obituary through to the paper."

The obituary notice is preserved among Costello's papers at his old college, Trinity, in Cambridge, though whether with pride or remorse is difficult to tell. "Papers" is a misnomer. There are no papers. Apart from *The Times* obituary, Costello is unremembered at Trinity College. Examination results apart, the record is bare.

Davin's obituary appeared in *The Times* on 25 February 1964. In Washington DC it is preserved in an Intelligence file, marked Secret, by the Federal Bureau of Investigation. The FBI's dossier on Costello is some 200 pages long. It was declassified in 1999 but the obituary notice, like almost everything else in the file, is blacked out. The obituary is still classified.

Costello's death, removing at a stroke the brightest star in his firmament, is said to have diminished Davin; is said to have turned him, "for all the conviviality of his later years", into a solitary, and ended by robbing him of the will and capacity to write and complete not only his planned memoir of Costello but a number of other projects he had dreamed of starting or fulfilling in retirement. These now stalled. Behind this, his biographer suggests, lay Anthony Blunt's reported allegation that Costello was a Soviet agent and, in Davin's own mind, the absurd yet ghosting possibility that he might have been betrayed by his best friend. Davin never believed Costello was a spy, and said so repeatedly; yet he was handicapped by the absence of proof; if Costello was not the victim of slander, how could he be sure he had not been deceived?

Davin's aim in writing about Costello was to celebrate his infinite gifts and the spontaneity that sprang from a warm and generous mind. But he also wanted to rescue him from his detractors, "to explain the unity of the man, how loyalty and integrity made treachery impossible".

Davin never got to the bottom of the slander attributed to Blunt. Anthony Blunt's alleged fingering of Costello dates from April 1964, two months after Costello died; it derives not from Blunt himself, nor from Chapman Pincher, who first aired it in his book, *Their Trade Is Treachery*, published in 1981; it derives at third-hand from a disgruntled former MI5 officer, Peter Wright, to whom Pincher spoke in Tasmania in 1980. Sixteen years earlier in London, when Blunt was confessing to his own spying as part of a secret deal to escape prosecution worked out with the British authorities, Peter Wright who was present at the interrogation "remembered" Blunt naming Costello — so he told Pincher. That is the extent and origin of the calumny.

Blunt's 1964 confession nowhere names Costello.

It is not uncommon for security agencies doing deals with defectors and confessors, like Blunt, to introduce the names of suspects for whom they have little evidence and may wish to incriminate and then add them to the list of names, if any, that the defector/confessor has produced. The literature of espionage contains many examples. So it may be doubted whether Blunt ever mentioned the name Costello at all. He hardly knew him. Blunt's self-serving "confession", smearing other innocents like the Canadian Herb Norman, is said to have ruined the careers of half a dozen senior British civil servants. As Phillip Knightley points out, "The reason MI5/MI6 'got' Blunt in the end was BECAUSE he wouldn't name names."

Peter Wright died in 1995. Both the book he published in 1987, *Spycatcher*, and Wright himself, who was a fantasist, are now discredited.

"A little story I have told all my children," says Mick Costello, Paddy Costello's son, "is an old Chinese story. It's about two friends who live next door to each other. One day one of them loses a purse. He suspects his friend. He watches him and thinks, by Christ, he's got shifty eyes. Never noticed it before. And he walks like a thief, the cur. And so on. Then he finds the purse which has slipped down the side of a sofa. He looks at his friend again and sees that his eyes are normal, they aren't shifty any more. And he no longer walks like a thief . . . "

Mick Costello became a businessman. After being, in his words, "hounded out" of the British Communist Party in the late 1980s before the collapse of communism in eastern Europe, he became a trade consultant. Following the dissolution of the USSR in 1991, he founded a company which established relations between Russian and Ukrainian factories, and firms in the United Kingdom and other Western countries, travelling from his home in Maidstone. He is now studying social anthropology at the University of Kent.

Josephine Proctor, née Costello, became a college lecturer in Manchester. She studied in Oxford and Paris and worked as a Russian interpreter in England and Russia. She lives with her husband in south Manchester, a stone's throw from the family home in Rathen Road. Katie Costello, following in her father's steps, studied classics at Cambridge and, later, after a varied career, music and linguistics. She lived in Moscow for two years, relearning the language, and is now an interpreter and translator specialising in police and court work, based in London. Both Christopher and Nicholas won scholarships to public schools. At Winchester Nicholas was the second top scholar of his day. He graduated from the London School of Economics and is now a diplomat in China for the European Commission.

Christopher began studying psychology, dropped out and later obtained an engineering degree. He was swept away by the software boom of the eighties and nineties, he says, "till the economic downturn and neurosurgery eventually washed him up in Munich".

Bil Costello lived until 1999. She remained protective of her late husband's papers. When Dan Davin asked to see them in the 1980s, to help with his planned memoir, Bil allowed him to glimpse some letters, that was all. After Davin died in 1990 Keith Ovenden arrived at Rathen Road in quest of letters and other material for his coming biography. He was made welcome. "Bil made me a nice lunch. But in four hours she did not discuss the papers."

Bil was, Costello wrote, "the most disturbing and consoling element in my life", while to her he remained "the tall Arts student with the naughty charisma" to whom she had been introduced by Griff Maclaurin in a Cambridge bookshop in the summer of 1935. For all Costello's philandering as a young man and her coolness towards some of his friends, the marriage was a rich and rewarding one. In the war he carried her letters until they disintegrated in his pockets. To him Bil was composed of elements that bore no relation to anything else in his experience. She remained the emotional equivalent of what Latin and the Ancients were to him intellectually, providing a ballast that kept him stable. Bil when he met her had not been to a university. He taught her Russian and French but often found himself, he said, when it came to translating from the Russian turning to her for advice. Her command of English idiom and imagery sometimes outdid his. He educated her in letters and she, him, in life. Who is to say that he was not in the end the richer?

After Costello died, Bil completed translating the Kushchevsky novel he had been working on and saw it published, then translated from the Russian in her own right a diary about the murder of Rasputin in the Yusupov Palace which was also published. She remained a communist and a Stalinist in her thought. Like Margot Heinemann, the lover of John Cornford, she was "in it for life".

As a young woman she looked Greek; as she aged people, remarking the head of thick silky grey hair, were reminded of Anna Magnani. Of all the wives conjoined to that exodus of expatriates in the 1930s, when New Zealand exported such a flowering of young thoroughbreds to war and revolution in Europe, Bil was the most secretive, the most vital, the most infuriating, the most reticent and the most attractive.

Costello is buried in Manchester. He lies in the immense Southern Cemetery, amid oaks and hawthorn, in non-conformist ground at the extreme western end. When Josie took me to see the grave in 2005, she explained that "this was as far as Mum could get him away from the Roman Catholic sector".

Among the notebooks and papers found in the house when Bil died was a scrap of paper containing some lines copied out from Housman's poem, "To an Athlete Dying Young":

Now you will not swell the rout
Of lads that wore their honours out,
Runners whom renown outran
And the name died before the man.

With Costello the opposite is true. The man died before the name. Unwittingly Costello's detractors have done him a service. Bent on disgrace, they have provided instead rank and progress, prolonging his life. They have given him both a life and an after-life.

In her only public comment on his death, in a London newspaper, Bil signed herself not as his widow but "his Relict", that which is left behind, using an archaism from the Latin he would have liked.

> Desmond Patrick Costello [she announced in *The Times* on 28 February 1964] was buried in Manchester without pomp. All who wish to pay homage to the memory of this man of integrity can try to emulate him. He carried out faithfully whatever he undertook. He was my University.

GERMAN EXTERMINATION CAMPS

REPORT FROM THE NEW ZEALAND LEGATION AT MOSCOW

WELLINGTON
DEPARTMENT OF EXTERNAL AFFAIRS
1945

PRICE 3d] [PUBLICATION NO. 12

Note

IN MARCH, 1945, a Contact Mission was sent to Poland to consider arrangements for the evacuation of British Commonwealth prisoners of war whom the advance of the Russian armies had liberated from German hands. The New Zealand Minister to the U.S.S.R arranged for Mr D. P. Costello (Second Secretary in the New Zealand Legation, Moscow, and a former officer in the Second New Zealand Division) to proceed with this mission in order to watch the interest of New Zealand prisoners of war, and as the senior officer — with the temporary rank of Major — he was placed in command of it. In the course of his mission in Poland Mr Costello visited the German concentration camp at Maidanek, and also received information from a French officer who had been imprisoned in the concentration camp at Oswiecim. His notes on what he saw of the one camp and what he heard from an inmate of the other are published for general information.

German Extermination Camps

(Vernichtungslager)

MAIDANEK

WHILE at Lublin I visited the German concentration camp at Maidanek, which has been declared a national museum and which is thereby to be preserved for the future.

Maidanek is laid out on lines reminiscent of our own military camps, and reminded me particularly of Maadi and Amiriya camps in Egypt. The whole complex of buildings is enclosed by barbed wire, and the camp is laid out in streets flanked by long barrack buildings of planks and corrugated iron. German notices are still in position on the doors and walls. In the company of a Polish guide, who spoke only German in addition to his own language, I made what is presumably the usual tour of the sights.

First of all one is shown the shower room and gas chamber. The shower room contains seventy-two shower heads, spaced very close together. At the far end of the room is a short passage leading to the gas chamber. This is a small room, about 25ft. x 25ft. with thick concrete walls and an iron door. In the middle of the low ceiling is a hole through which the arsenic poison

Zyklon was emptied from cylinders. There is a big pile of slack Zyklon near the gas chamber, and large stocks of the gas cylinders are preserved elsewhere in the camps. Apparently the effects of the arsenic are more immediate in the case of wet bodies, and it was for this reason that the victims were given a shower before they were gassed. Beside the door of the gas chamber is a window through which the German guards could watch the operation of the gas.

Near the shower room are sheds containing the personal effects of those who were murdered. In one there are piles of clothes, each jacket marked with a sign to indicate the nationality of the wearer: thus P stood for Polish, SU for Russian, F for French, etc. Jews wore, in addition, the six-pointed star. But more impressive than these heaps of rags is the mountain of shoes in the next hut. Here there are two parallel heaps of footwear, separated by an avenue down the middle; each pile is approximately 120ft. long, 12ft. broad and 7ft. high. The sight is overwhelming, and I saw no reason to doubt the word of the guide that there were 820,000 pairs of footwear there. All the shoes are worn out, and I was told that the shoes which had been in good repair had been despatched to Germany, only the rubbish being left. I examined some of the shoes; they bore the marks of shopkeepers in almost every country in Europe. A big proportion were women's and children's shoes.

About a thousand yards away is the furnace where the bodies were burnt. A high brick chimney communicates by an underground passage with the six ovens. There is an elaborate system of ventilation for the underground fires which heated the ovens; in the ovens there are still ashes and fragments of bone. Alongside is an autopsy table on which, according to the guide, the stomachs of those who were suspected of swallowing valuables at the last moment were opened and examined. Beyond the furnace area are acres of market garden which were fertilised with the ashes from the ovens. The area was covered with cabbage stumps, and on the ground between them I picked up several small fragments of bone.

Finally I visited the museum office, where are preserved albums of photographs of those who were murdered and burnt. These were ordinary family groups, holiday pictures, etc and, like the boots, had come from most of the countries of Europe. I also met the director of the museum, who told me that the total number of persons destroyed at Maidanek by the Germans was just under two million.

During my stay in Lublin I asked many Poles what they knew of Maidanek. They all confirmed what I had been told on the spot. One of those I spoke to had been imprisoned at Maidanek for a short period during the German occupation and had seen one drove of people being marched to the gas chamber. The circumstance which seemed most strongly to have impressed itself upon the memory of the people of Lublin was the presence, during two years, of a cloud of heavy smoke from Maidanek, which hung low over the town with a smell of burning flesh.

OSWIECIM

My official business in Lublin brought me into touch with a French officer, Captain ——— *, who had been captured by the Germans in 1943 while engaged upon sabotage work under the direction of London. I interrogated him closely, and was most impressed, as was my colleague Flying Officer Floyd, by his character and intelligence. What he told me about the concentration camp at Oswiecim, where he was imprisoned during 1944 and up to its evacuation by the Germans in January this year, was confirmed by another ex-inmate of the camp, Dr ——— *, whom I also met in Lublin. Both these people carry tattooed on their forearms their concentration camp number.

Oswiecim (on the Vistula, west of Krakov) was a much bigger camp than Maidanek, and far more people were murdered and burnt there. Instead of one furnace there were five, with five chimneys, as well as two ditches each 120ft. long, 25ft. wide and 12ft. deep, in which the bodies were burnt. There were always four furnaces working (the fifth being in reserve for boom periods) and the ditches, too, were used continuously except for the two or three occasions each month when the ashes were emptied. At Oswiecim the ashes from the ditches and the furnaces were transported in lorries and emptied into the Vistula.

Oswiecim seems to have resembled Maidanek except that it was on a bigger scale and the work there was more rationalised. The principle was similar and the sequence — shower, gas, oven — was the same. The Germans introduced some refinements into their treatment of the prisoners. The inmates of any particular shed in which a 'selection' (Auswahl) was to be held for that day's burning were always told some hours ahead, in order that they could think about what was coming to them. The 'selection' was

* Names supplied in report but withheld from publication.

completely arbitrary, the inmates of the shed parading past a seated German who jerked his thumb left or right to indicate whether the individual was to be burnt that day or not. Children who were 'selected' were always sent to take farewell of their parents.

In many cases the victims were naked when they set out for the gas chamber: Captain —— saw one parade of 2,000 women, stark naked, marching 'to the gas' with the German band at their head playing tangos and fox-trots. In cases where they were dressed, they were given numbered checks for their clothes in the shower room, and, passing to the gas chamber, filed past a notice which said, in several languages: 'Keep hold of your check as otherwise you may not get your own clothes back when you come out.' The people were packed so tight in the gas chamber that Captain —— believes 75 per cent of them died of simple asphyxiation; the rest were finished off, as at Maidanek, with Zyklon. They were so tightly jammed together that to pull the bodies out when the door was opened large iron hooks were used.

At Oswiecim the gas chamber was not, as at Maidanek, at some distance from the ovens. It was underground, and lifts carried the bodies up to the ground level in the furnace area. There the gold teeth of the dead were broken out of their mouths by a special team, autopsies were performed on a few, and they went into the fire. It took twenty minutes to burn the bodies, and Captain ——— said that the lifts with the next intake of corpses could be heard rising a minute or two before each lot of bodies had been consumed.

All those engaged in handling the dead were persons who were themselves condemned to be burnt. The prisoners' doctors likewise were appointed for periods of three months, at the end of which they passed to the gas chamber themselves. Captain ———, who worked around the camp as a mechanic, made the acquaintance of a Dr Pasch, who was burnt at the end of July last year and from whom he got the figures of the previous three months' burnings. These were:

May	360,000
June	512,000
1-26 July	442,000

On the day when they established their record of 25,000 executed in one day the Germans were issued with an extra ration of schnapps, and celebrated the occasion by a carousal. It may be pointed out here that, as from January, 1944, non-Jews were no longer burnt in the ovens, though they were massacred in droves. The main victims of the camp, apart from Jews, were socialists, communists, and members of the European resistance movements generally. A large number of Russian prisoners of war were also slaughtered. Captain ——— witnessed one occasion when a parade of the prisoners was held 'in honour' of five Russians who had been shot while attempting to escape. The prisoners, stripped naked for the occasion, and headed by the camp band, marched past the five bodies, which had been seated in a row on chairs, and gave the 'eyes left' as they filed past.

It was the German practice always to gas the prisoners before they burned them. Exceptions were made in favour of persons seriously ill and of new-born babies; these were thrown alive into the ovens. The babies were thrown into boxes as they were born; after a few days when the boxes were full (those in the bottom layers being presumably already dead), they were burnt without any formalities. Whenever contagious disease broke out in a shed all the inmates were gassed and burnt.

Among other pastimes of the Germans were vivisection and some gruesome kinds of plastic surgery. The women were sterilised by a peculiarly rigorous course of treatment.

After the publication by the Russians of the facts about Maidanek camp the Germans set about removing the traces of their activities at Oswiecim, and towards the end of November and beginning of December, 1944, the Oswiecim ovens were dismantled and destroyed. The surviving prisoners were shot, apart from a minority who lived to be liberated by the Russians on the 16th of January.

Captain —— puts the number of those murdered in Oswiecim at 6,000,000.

The above sounds like the invention of an insane mind. I am convinced that Captain —— was telling the truth, and Flying Officer Floyd agrees with me.

(*Signed*) D. P. Costello
Second Secretary

Moscow
26 March 1945

Obituary

PROFESSOR D. P. COSTELLO

BRILLIANT RUSSIAN SCHOLAR

Professor Paddy Costello, Professor of Russian at the University of Manchester, who died unexpectedly on Sunday at the age of 52, was a brilliant and highly individual scholar with a wide range of talents and experience.

Returning to university life in 1955, after 15 years in New Zealand army and government service, he was refreshingly unacademic and somewhat outside the familiar ring of sovietologists. His views were usually independent and always interesting; they were often pungently expressed in his slightly clipped and nasal voice. His friends here will remember him as unforgettably good company, an unscrupulous arguer, the subject of countless stories, a man who could make any occasion come alive.

Desmond Patrick Costello was born in Auckland on January 31, 1912, to parents of Irish origin, and was educated at Auckland Grammar School and University College. He then came on a travelling fellowship to Trinity College, Cambridge, where he got a first class in the classical tripos. While there he went to stay with his first cousins in Ireland, and learnt the Irish language; he was always very deeply attached to that country, sometimes seeming as much Irish as Antipodean. In 1936 he became an assistant lecturer in Classics at Exeter University College, where he stayed until the second year of the war.

He then joined Freyberg's Second N.Z.E.F. He was a lance-corporal in the 21st Battalion Signals when the battalion was overrun by German armour at the right end of the Olympus line in 1941, and battalion headquarters itself surrounded. Costello could speak modern Greek, and he helped lead its members down to the sea and negotiate for a caique. The islands proved to be enemy-held, and part of the crew were accordingly in favour of landing in Turkey and getting interned. They were voted down by the colonel, the adjutant, and Costello, who succeeded in bringing the boat safely to Crete.

On hearing this story Freyberg sent him to be trained as an officer, and so he missed the Cretan campaign. He became, briefly, a second-lieutenant with the Long Range Desert Group, then helped revise the official handbook on the Italian Army for G.H.Q. Middle East. Here he amused himself learning Russian. Freyberg soon pulled him out, however, and made him his Intelligence Officer at Divisional Headquarters, later his G.S.O.3 (I). As such he went with the division through the African and the early part of the Italian campaigns, briefing the General not only on the enemy opposite, but also on the Russian front, on which Freyberg always kept an impassive eye. He was generally respected by his colleagues in the British Army, where he himself would certainly have held a much higher rank.

DIPLOMAT IN MOSCOW

He left the Army in 1944 to go as Second Secretary to the New Zealand Legation in Moscow. It is said that Peter Fraser, the then Prime Minister, asked him what his politics were. "I'm afraid I'm a bit left wing, Sir," said Costello. The Prime Minister, jumping a bit ahead of the truth: "Oh well, it won't hurt us to have one or two Communists in Moscow." He was in Moscow for six years, where his elder children went to Russian schools (even fiercer crammers than the French, according to Costello) and he himself became a good friend of Pasternak. He moved thence in 1950 as First Secretary to the Legation in Paris, but found diplomatic life there a good deal less interesting. The ordinary social round of a diplomat bored him; his function as a glorified intelligence officer (once more), advising an uncompliant government on the course of events in France itself and the French Union, struck him as ineffective. He was not sorry when friends pressed him to put in for the newly created post of Professor of Russian at Manchester University, though he was conscious of the hard work which this would mean for one who had learnt his languages largely as an amateur.

His appointment in 1955 was a source of considerable strength to the university in general and the Faculty of Arts in particular. He rapidly won the admiration of his colleagues, and was instrumental in affording unique opportunities to students of science to study the Russian language in order to read original sources. He leaves the department revitalised by his energies.

In 1948 he had edited the second edition of Maurice Baring's *Oxford Book of Russian Verse*. The sheer need, however, to master every aspect of the subject for which he was now responsible left him little time for major writing, and his best work was certainly still to come when he died.

In his own field (and on the subject of traditional ballads in all languages, which he knew well both as scholar and as singer) he was a valued reviewer for *The Times Literary Supplement*, and he also contributed to other learned journals. He edited Gribodeyov's *Woe from Wit* (the Russian text) for the Oxford Press; he was preparing to translate a volume of Chekhov stories for the World's Classics; he was also helping to edit a new Russian-English dictionary for the same publisher.

Paddy Costello and Bil in their middle years, Manchester, late 1950s.

Above: On the Aran Islands in the west of Ireland: Costello and the Davins, Dan and Winnie, in the summer of 1963. This was the only time the two families were together on holiday, and is one of the last photographs taken of Costello before he died.

D.P.C. at
Dún Aengusa,
Aran.
July 1963

Costello on Inis Mor, Aran Islands. The last known photograph.

Outside this sphere he translated Sadegh Hedayat's novel *The Blind Owl* (John Calder, 1958) from the Persian — a language which he learnt while in Paris — and himself wrote a novel during his Moscow period; this, however, was unpublished. It is a very great pity that he was not able to do more.

He married Bella Lerner in 1935. They have three sons and two daughters.

[*The Times*, 25 Feb 1964]

NOTES & SOURCES

THE PRINCIPAL SOURCES are the Costello Papers, held privately by the family in England, and the Alexander Turnbull Library Collections in Wellington. They have been used extensively. In New Zealand the other archival sources are Archives New Zealand, the Ministry of Foreign Affairs & Trade Archives, the University of Auckland Library Special Collections, the Auckland Grammar School Archives and the Personnel Archives of the NZ Defence Force; and, in England, the British National Archives at Kew, Oxford University Press, Karl Marx House, London, and the University of Exeter Old Library, Special Collections. I am indebted to the Master, Fellows & Scholars of Trinity College, Cambridge, for hospitality and for access to material held in the Wren Library, and the Master, Fellows & Scholars of St John's College, Cambridge, for the use of their archives.

Besides photographs and offprints, the Costello Papers in England include official despatches and reports, a pocket diary, unpublished manuscripts, private papers and a cache of Costello's letters going back to his undergraduate days at Cambridge; also his *cahier,* Costello's private journal. The latter runs from May 1943 to November 1954 (the early war years and the entries from 23 July 1950 to 2 July 1954 are missing).

Costello's letters fall roughly into four groups: letters to his mother in New Zealand written from Cambridge and Exeter, 1932-1936, and letters to his wife in Exeter, in the war, 1940-1944 (Costello family archive); letters to Dan Davin in Oxford, 1945-1963, divided between the Alexander Turnbull Library (ATL) and the Costello archive; letters to Alister McIntosh in Wellington, 1944-1954 (McIntosh Papers, ATL); and letters to the Lakes in New Zealand, 1949-1950. The last are from the Douglas & Ruth Lake Papers, divided between the ATL and the Lake family. Those in the ATL include an unpublished manuscript by Doug Lake, "Goodbye Diplomacy".

Costello's political despatches to the New Zealand government, subsequently transferred to Archives New Zealand, could not at the time of writing be traced. An analysis of Costello's political reporting is contained in Templeton, *Top Hats Are Not Being Taken* (ch. 9, pp. 44-60).

Other unpublished sources are the Batterbee File, containing security reports of British origin dated 1944 (Michael King & James McNeish family archives), the Diary of Brigadier N.L. Macky (held privately by the family), the Sir Geoffrey Cox Papers, the Dan Davin Papers, the Sir Alister

McIntosh Papers, the Michael King Papers and the Bert Roth Papers, all held by the Alexander Turnbull Library. The McIntosh Papers include the Jean McKenzie correspondence; the Davin Papers contain an important file of Costello letters, also two unfinished memoirs, "Paddy Costello" and "Bernard Freyberg"; the Michael King Papers include King's 1978 interviews with McIntosh shortly before he died. Other letters by Costello written to friends are cited in the Notes.

A file of declassified FBI documents, courtesy Dr Aaron Fox, besides material made available by the NZ Security Intelligence Service, described in the Notes, have also been used.

I have followed an earlier practice and, except in a few cases, omitted the customary row of dots within quotations. My aim has been to help the reader and impede the narrative as little as possible.

Published works by D.P. Costello

The Oxford Book of Russian Verse (ed.), enlarged edition of 1924 publication, Oxford at the Clarendon Press, 1948

Gore ot Uma — "The Misfortune of Being Intelligent", Comedy in Four Acts in Verse, by A.S. Griboyedov (Introduction & Notes), Oxford 1951

The Blind Owl, by Sadegh Hedayat (translated from the Persian), London 1957

"Griboyedov in Persia 1820", *Oxford Slavonic Papers*, vol v 1954 (monograph)

Russian Grammar, by Boris Unbegaun (translated from the French), Oxford 1957

"The Murder of Griboyedov", *Oxford Slavonic Papers*, vol 8, 1958

"Griboyedov as a Diplomat", *Indiana Slavic Studies,* vol 4, 1967 (posthumous)

Russian Folk Literature, D.P. Costello & I.P. Foote, Oxford 1967 (posthumous)

Nikolai Negorev, or The Successful Russian (translated from the Russian, with Bella Costello), London 1967 (posthumous)

"Zhivago Reconsidered", *Forum for Modern Language Studies*, vol iv No 1, Jan 1968, University of St Andrews (posthumous)

NOTES

TITLE PAGE

"Loved your five 'Peacocks'": John Orman, Wellington, to author, 17 Dec 2003

"I think Costello": Sir George Laking interview, Wellington, 25 May 1999

AUTHOR'S FOREWORD

page 15

"a falsifier of passports": Chapman Pincher, *Their Trade is Treachery*, page 139; *Too Secret, Too Long,* page 255. Also Nigel West, *The Illegals,* page 168

"the ULTRA secret": *New Zealand Truth,* Jan 1989, citing John Costello (no relation) on publication *Mask of Treachery*

"Anthony Blunt": "Costello's recruitment at Cambridge had been confirmed by Blunt" (Nigel West, *Seven Spies Who Changed the World,* page 113)

page 16

"a valuable agent": Christopher Andrew & Vasili Mitrokhin, *The Mitrokhin Archive,* pp 534 & 864, note 73

"the man who transformed": "The man transformed by Paddy Costello into Kroger became the first [in the post-communist era] to be made a Hero of the Russian Federation by Boris Yeltsin."

(*Dominion,* 20 Sept 1999). Morris Cohen, alias Peter Kroger, died in 1995. Lona Cohen, his wife (alias Helen Kroger), had earlier been made a Hero of the Soviet Union for her deep cover work in America

"one of the KGB's top ten": *New Zealand Herald,* 21 Sept 1999, citing Christopher Andrew. "A rather important spy for the Soviet Union"; and, "according to the Paris station of the KGB, one of the top ten leading ones in the early part of the Cold War"

PROLOGUE

page 17

"A man called Walter Tongue": Account based on Polly Macky's diary, page 12 & passim; J.F. Cody, *21 Battalion*; Costello's letters to Bil, 1941 & 1942; and surviving fragments from his journal

page 18

"mildly astigmatic": "The oculist I went to told me I was myopic, slightly astigmatic and had a slight squint" (Costello to his mother, Cambridge, 1 Nov 1933)

"In the ravines": Costello to Bil, Easter Monday, 14 April 1941

page 19

"Shells are flying": ibid, ("Since I began this paragraph our artillery has opened up, firing overhead at the Germans who are quite near")

"most unpleasant": Polly Macky diary, page 12

page 20

"if necessary to extinction": Cody, *21 Battalion*, page 61; R.C.J. Stone, *The Making of Russell McVeagh,* page 146 (footnote)

"all his transport": Macky diary, page 22

PART ONE – HOME & AWAY

AUCKLAND

page 23

"His confirmation name": Costello would write to Davin from Paris in 1952, "Have you ever read through *The Gallic War?* I am convinced that Caesar was not interested in people, except as instruments or opponents of his policy. He was not a subtle or complex character, nor particularly interesting. Curious that as a boy I admired him more than anyone: my confirmation name is Julius"

page 24

"At fifteen Costello won": H.J.D. Mahon, Auckland Grammar School, Headmaster's Report for 1928, page 32

"He read Lycias": Costello journal, 29 Jan 1947

"His classics professor": Richardson & Crawley, *Classics in Auckland*, pp 43-47

"probably the most brilliant": ibid, page 98

page 25

"He was by far": obituary by A.H. McDonald, written for Auckland Grammar School *Chronicle*, sent to Dan Davin as typescript, Sept 1967

"moving about the half-empty corridors": Hector Monro, *Fortunate Catastrophes*, page 49

page 26

"Avoid cant": Jean Bartlett interview, Auckland, Nov 2004 (J.B. citing her diary for 1931)

"an arranged marriage": information from Phil Costello, Auckland, May 1999 & Nov 2004; also Sister Elizabeth Woods, Dublin, telephone conversation and various emails to author, Nov 2004

"What made all our family": Costello to Bil, 10 Oct 1941

page 27

"Paddy could ad lib": From Dan Davin's draft for his *Times* obituary of Costello, Feb 1964

"the Irish Nightingale": Dan Davin, "Paddy Costello" (unfinished memoir), page 40, citing Keith Scott-Watson

"he leap-frogged classes": information from Jack Leigh, Auckland, author *Ponsonby School Centennial History*, 1973. For Rawlings Scholarship see B. Gustafson, *His Way: a Biography of Robert Muldoon* (Auckland, 2000)

page 28

"The original shop": Jack Leigh to author, 9 April 1999

"sixty children to a class": Henry Shirley, *Just a Bloody Piano Player,* page 28 & passim

"The Woodses": Costello to his mother, 16 Jan 1933

page 29

"I told you how impressed": ibid, 18 Aug 1932

"Trevor O'Leary offers": Jean Bartlett (contemporary and mutual friend) interview, Nov 2004. "Politically, Trevor told me, he was 'gullible as a seagull'"

"Housman's *A Shropshire Lad*": A little book that most of the would-be poets and literary-minded of Auckland seem to have carried about with them in their pocket

page 30

"he sailed out of Auckland": Sailed 29 July 1932 (NZSIS file, report 1945)

CAMBRIDGE

page 31

"An asylum": Lisa Sargood, *Literary Cambridge* (Sutton Publishing, 2004)

page 32

"Uncle Mattie": Costello to his mother, 1 Oct 1932

"Did grandpa sing?": ibid, 25 Jan 1933

"They are all clever": ibid, 16 Jan 1933

"even in a semi-prosperous": ibid, 11 Feb 1933

page 33

"a splendid fellow": ibid, 19 Oct 1932

"who dominated him": Miranda Carter, *Anthony Blunt: His Lives*, page 157

"Then a cable arrived": Costello to his mother, 2 Nov 1932; and see Monro, *Fortunate Catastrophes*

"Now as soon as": Costello to his mother, 2 Nov 1932

page 34

"possibly the most objectionable": ibid, 25 Jan 1933

"Tell me James": Mick Costello interview, Kent, Sept 1999

"counted himself lucky": Penelope Fitzgerald, *The Knox Brothers*, page 83

"I heard Housman": Costello to his mother, 10 May 1933

page 35

"on the same staircase": Housman, according to a Trinity anecdote, had a lavatory on his landing which he kept locked. He would not allow Wittgenstein to use it

"the year Housman died": see Michael Straight, *After Long Silence*, page 65

"I have abandoned": Costello to his mother, 1 Nov 1933. Costello, according to Victor Kiernan, exaggerates: "Most of the rich youth were content with rugby and cricket, and I don't suppose Costello's classics were any worse than theirs" (note to author, March 2007)

page 36

"They marvelled": Sister Betty Woods, Sydney, telephone conversation Nov 2004

"getting on": "The New Zealand ideal is the man who has done well for himself, who has 'got on'. I cannot see why a successful man, in the sense of a man who has made money for himself, should receive respect or esteem" (Costello journal, 20 July 1950)

"Cambridge was still full": Miranda Carter, *Anthony Blunt*, page 148

"There was already": see Miranda Carter; also Andrew Boyle, *The Climate of Treason*; and Victor Kiernan's essay "Herbert Norman's Cambridge". This essay might equally be entitled, "Paddy Costello's Cambridge"

page 37

"Their faces had fallen in": Miranda Carter, page 110

"So many textile mills": Piers Brendon, *The Dark Valley*, page 167

"We are all Marxists": Miranda Carter, page 111

page 38

"a striking personality": Kiernan to author, 23 Oct 2004

"a bird called Brown": Costello to his mother, 27 Oct 1933

"he had still not read": ibid

page 39

"who admire Kim Philby": "I remember Paddy telling us that at a meeting of the Socialist Society, Philby said that 'the first task after the Revolution will be to build a prophylactorium for Guy Burgess'" (Mick Costello to author, 3 March 2007)

"There were three advantages": Costello to his mother, 15 June 1933

"to converting Indian undergraduates": "There were then about sixty Indians at Cambridge with a Society of their own, of which Jawarhal Nehru had been a member" (Victor Kiernan to author, March 2007)

"WALKING TO OLYMPIA"

page 43

"they appear to have sailed": 29 July 1932 from Auckland

page 44

"Richard Cockburn Maclaurin": see *Dictionary of NZ Biography,* vol 4

"his New Zealand references": These were from H.J.D. Mahon, his headmaster; H.W. Segar, professor of mathematics, K.E. Bullens, lecturer in mathematics, and J.P. Grossman, professor of history, all of University College Auckland

page 45

"He admired Maclaurin's rooms": These were in New Court (C2); they descended to the Backs and the river through Eagle Gate

"I was too slow": Maclaurin tutorial papers, 23 June 1933 (St John's College Archives)

"He has not much": James Wordie, tutorial papers, 1 May 1934

page 46

"recalled those pictures": Costello to his mother, 5 Oct 1933

"Lorie and Bob": Lorie Tarshis (Canadian), reading economics, Trinity; Bob Page (apparently English), reading economics

"I hope to do much better": Maclaurin to Wordie, tutorial papers, 23 June 1933

"the Wooden Spoon": A seven-foot-long trophy, traditionally awarded to the man who came lowest in the Third Class of the Mathematical Tripos

"covered himself in glory": Maclaurin to his parents, summer 1934

page 47

"We had not heard": Mrs Maclaurin to Mrs Costello, 6 Aug 1934

"And although": Costello to his mother, 27 Oct 1933

"John Pendelbury": see Dilys Powell, *The Villa Ariadne*; also Antony Beevor, *Crete: the Battle and the Resistance,* page 3 & passim

"work on Clazomenian pots": More likely refers to a study of terracotta sarcophagi peculiar to Clazomenae, an ancient Ionian Greek city near Smyrna in modern Turkey

"under the auspices": NZSIS file, reports Sept 1950 & Jan 1951

page 48

"I have one Athenian suit": Costello to his mother, 29 Jan 1935

"hammers and sickles": ibid, 17 Nov 1934

"going every day to a café": Police reports dated September 1950 and January 1951 in Costello's NZSIS file refer to him going daily to "a certain café" where "the waiter who was in the habit of bringing him the paper, stealthily showed him his Communist Party (Greece) badge, whereupon Costello related [in a letter to a friend] that he had produced his badge, showing him to be a member of the Communist Party of Great Britain." This however seems unlikely. Neither Eric Hobsbawm nor Victor Kiernan, Party members in Costello's day, can recall a membership badge of the CPGB. "Certainly there was none in my time," Professor Hobsbawm writes (7 September 2006), "but I remember unofficial hammer and sickle lapel badges were around. Possibly this is what the NZ security people are talking about"

page 49

"Invited . . . Costello declined": Unlike Geoffrey Cox, who in 1934 took up a challenge and spent three weeks working in a Nazi youth labour camp outside Hanover (see *Dance of the Peacocks*, pp 64-65)

"I loathe actual travelling": Costello to his mother, 21 March 1935

page 50

"I only came here": ibid, 19 April 1935

"all Sunday walking to Olympia": Some 30 miles. There was no road

page 51

"whom otherwise": Costello to his mother, 6 May 1935

"a land of oafs": ibid, 22 May 1935

"Early in June": Mick Costello & Josephine Proctor interviews, Maidstone & London, autumn 1999

"G.C. MACLAURIN BOOKSELLER": Today a barber's shop (see Illustrations)

LOVE IN A BOOKSHOP

page 53

"Maclaurin's Bookshop": letter to author, 5 Jan 2005. Maclaurin was one of the founding subscribers of the Left Book Club

"This is misleading": Bil was denied university. To matriculate, according to Bil's sister, Doris Bornstein, "you had to pass in one go. Bil had four gos. She got enough subjects to matriculate twice, but not in one go. She never matriculated"

"Bella's father Moishe": Moishe appears on the marriage certificate as Maurice Lerner (anglicised)

page 54

"Abba Lerner": Abba Ptachya Lerner (1903-1982) is said to have invented the term "stagflation". He left rabbinical studies in London at 19 and joined the Independent Labour Party. In America the footloose Lerner held many university posts and became a professor finally at 70 (according to his sister, Doris), at Tallahassee, Florida, where he died. His papers are in the Library of Congress

"Lerner's argument": information from Abba Lerner's daughter, Marion Lerner-Levine, USA, and the Internet

"after a tipsy frolic": Victor Kiernan in "Herbert Norman's Cambridge", page 44 (note 4). Maclaurin was recommended for a post at St Peter's School, York, by his tutor, James Wordie. The headmaster, S.M. Tongue, had written to Wordie saying, "I see he is a New Zealander and though we think imperially, the only other New Zealand man I have had here was by no means a success with the boys." Victor Kiernan writes (letter to author, 23 Nov 2004) that Maclaurin and a crony "were seen by the headmaster at an open window — on the ledge, pouring down the beverage [beer] and singing some improper song at the top of their voices. They were expelled on the spot." Jean Bartlett, an Auckland university college contemporary, visited Maclaurin in Cambridge in 1935. She found "a complete contrast to the Griff I'd known in Auckland" (telephone conversation, Oct 2004)

page 55

"surpassing sales of literature": Victor Kiernan, "Herbert Norman's Cambridge"

"They might have married": Account based on information from Mick Costello and other family members, 1999 & 2005

"And like a cat in winter": *Tales From Ovid*, translated by Ted Hughes (Faber, London, 1997)

page 56

"21 days London to London": Costello to his mother, 31 May 1935

page 57

"In Munich": ibid, 30 Oct 1934

page 58

"writes Emanuel Litvinoff": *Journey Through a Small Planet,* page 108

"There is a revealing glimpse": Poulsen, *Scenes from a Stepney Youth,* page 118

page 59

"YIDS OUT! and *P.J.*": Doris Bornstein interview, London, April 2005

"Doris Lerner . . . remembers": ibid

"Britain awake!": *The Dark Valley*, page 171 (citing Oswald Mosley, *The Rules of the Game*, page 231)

"Doris and her friend": interview, April 2005; email to author, March 2007

page 60

"My Mum's father": Mick Costello interview, 24 Sept 1999

"above a hidden synagogue": The synagogue in Princelet Street is still there

"Paddy had to stoop": Doris Bornstein interview, 21 April 2005

page 61

"the atmosphere . . . was saturated": *The God that Failed*, ed. Richard Crossman, page 21. Koestler converted in 1931

"Clear from the head": The lines occur at the end of a sonnet sequence "In Time of War", in *Journey to a War*, first published in 1939 after Auden and Isherwood's visit to China. Either Koestler is (mis)quoting from memory or Auden revised the verse, for the line "till they construct at last a human justice" no longer appears in Auden's collected verse (see *The Collected Poetry of W.H Auden*, Random House, New York, page 347)

SPAIN

page 66

"The only hope": Costello to his mother from Exeter, 2 Sept 1936

"Maclaurin left England": Griff Maclaurin was the first New Zealand university man to volunteer for Spain. The following account is pieced together from Costello's letters, family reminiscences and published sources. The best source for Maclaurin in England is Victor Kiernan, in his essay "Herbert Norman's Cambridge", and in Kiernan's letters and notes to the author written between 2004 & 2007. The main sources for Maclaurin's (and Cornford's) time in Spain are Galassi's *John Cornford: Selected Writings*, Stansky & Abrahams' *Journey to the Frontier*, Alexander's *British Volunteers for Liberty* and Fox's *A Writer in Arms*

page 67

"Cornford had already left": In Paris Maclaurin joined John Cornford and his seven English volunteers and then found that the hotel in Bellevue where they had been sent was the Paris organising centre for the First International Brigade. They were quickly co-opted, together with a polyglot bunch of "German exiles, many with the mark of the concentration camp on them, Polish miners and peasants, Italians, Frenchmen, Hungarians, Greeks, all kicking their heels in the café, waiting for word that would send them south". They went by night train to Marseilles, were hidden during the day, and were driven at dusk to the docks where they embarked for Spain. There they trained, absorbed as a self-contained unit inside a French battalion; and then, after the Spanish government fled the capital and it was being widely reported that Madrid had fallen, were rushed to Madrid by train. (Stansky & Abrahams, *Journey to the Frontier*, page 365)

page 68

"Sometimes he biked": Costello to his mother, 2 Sept 1936

"Bil's young brother": Jack Lerner interview, Hertford, April 2005

"Have you ever": Costello's army file, Recruiting Centre, Exeter, 19 Aug 1940

page 69

"when Arthur Lerner was captured": Doris Bornstein (Arthur's sister) interview, April 2005

"Maclaurin was reported killed": *Daily Mail*, 8 Dec 1936. James Bertram, a university contemporary in Auckland, dedicated his book *North China Front* (London, 1939) to Griff Maclaurin

"Maclaurin's bookshop still open": "The bookshop in All Saint's Passage was still thriving during my time and was being run by his widow" (Prof. Ralph Russell, London, to author, 27 Feb 2005)

"to look for working-class partners": Bowen, *Innocence is not Enough*, page 50 (note)

page 70

"thinking the Russians had come": Cox, *Defence of Madrid*, London,

1937; reprinted Otago University Press, 2006, page 75; see also *Dance of the Peacocks*, page 106 & passim

"dead at his gun": *John Cornford: Collected Writings*, ed. Galassi, pages 185-7; and see Ralph Fox, page 5

"the first Englishman": Galassi, page 11

page 71

"a martyr of mythic power": Denis Healey, *The Time of My Life* (1989), page 37

"He reached Bombay": police report UK, 25 Oct 1944, in Batterbee File

"a British police report": Batterbee File, Oct 1944

page 72

"Paddy did it for a lark": Mick Costello to author, Feb 2007; and interview UK, Sept 1999

"The British IB": The SIS and MI5 recruited regularly from the IB (see Knightley, *The Second Oldest Profession*, page 79)

"Groups like ours": Victor Kiernan, in "Herbert Norman's Cambridge", page 42

"According to the British": Batterbee File, Oct 1944

page 73

"But sometimes": Jack Lerner interview, Hertford, April 2005

EXETER AND THE FYRTH CASE

page 74

"He is a communist!": Hugh Stubbs to David Harvey, Exeter, 15 Sept 2004

"the Technical School": B.W. Clapp, *The University of Exeter: A History*. The university college was under the supervision of London University. Exeter did not have its own charter until 1955

page 75

"his advocacy of 'gentlemanliness'": ibid, page 80

"Costello tells us": Costello to McIntosh, 29 April 1945; and see "Incubus" chapter. We have only Costello's word that he decided to wait until he was called up; on the other hand his statement that no one else at the college volunteered appears unchallenged

"A vigorous and illuminating": 20 Sept 1939 (Principal's Papers,

University of Exeter)

"Britain must not attack Russia": Costello told McIntosh in 1945 that Murray "had spoken to me twice to no effect"

page 76

"DEEP ANXIETY": *Daily Worker*, 30 May 1940

"Costello's version": Costello to McIntosh, 29 April 1945

page 77

"feeling in the town": letter, 25 May 1940 (Principal's Papers, University of Exeter)

"Not by any stretch": *Daily Worker*, 30 May 1940

"Hubert Fyrth admitted": Both brothers pleaded guilty

page 78

"Paddy was congenitally": James Bertram interview, Wellington, 1991

"was duly ratified": The University College Senate unanimously approved Murray's action in suspending Costello. Letters of support for Costello by his colleagues were ignored. A staff member wrote, "I have found no more loyal and considerate associate . . . I have observed in Mr Costello a scrupulosity on the point of honour which would lead me to investigate with much care any charges affecting him"

"of being *vocatus*": Hugh Stubbs to David Harvey, 15 Sept 2004

"McCarthyism avant": ibid

page 79

"John Murray can't stand me": Costello to McIntosh, 29 April 1945

"They're a far better lot": Costello to Bil, 22 Aug 1940

PART TWO – GOING TO WAR

PRELUDE TO A BATTLE

page 89

"Closing down": Allan Borman, *Divisional Signals*, page 101

"Parce que je veux": Costello to Bil, 20 Oct 1941 (L.R.D.G.)

"saved the ship": Borman, *Divisional Signals*, page 127

page 90

"It seems mad": Costello to Bil, Easter Monday, 14 April 1941

"TEMPE, a narrow valley": *Oxford Classical Dictionary,* 2nd Edn.

"The river Pinios": W.G. McClymont, *To Greece*, page 316, citing Pliny (footnote)

"Costello's diary": Costello family archives

page 91

"got clean away": Kippenberger (ed.) *The Other Side of the Hill*, page 6

BATTLE OF TEMPE

page 92

"Contact with 21 Battalion": The Battle of Tempe and the curtain-raiser at Platamon are described in Cody's *21 Battalion*, McClymont's *To Greece*, Polly Macky's diary and, from a German perspective, "The Other Side of the Hill". These accounts are supplemented by references in Costello's correspondence and in his journal

page 93

"While they were waiting": Polly Macky diary, page 20

page 94

"Tanks can't swim": Cody, *21 Battalion*, page 62 ("The tanks would have to swim the river")

"I claim no merit": Costello to Bil, 9 March 1943

page 95

"Accounts of the battle": Amid the confusion, shortly before the tanks broke out of the gorge, a New Zealand soldier was observed in the hill village of Ambelakia where an observation detail had been sent. He was stripped to the waist in the plane- and mulberry-shaded square, below the Hotel of the Nine Muses. He was leaning over the fountain, his braces below the knees. He was shaving. (Eyewitness account given to author in Ambelakia, May 2005.) The witness added, "It might have been an Australian"

"disappeared in sheets of flame": McClymont, *To Greece*, page 33

page 96

"A Mark II tank": "Panzer attack in Greece", in *The Other Side of the Hill*, page 7

"Men killed in battle": Costello to Bil, 9 March 1943

"There's five of the bastards": Don Croft, Levin, telephone conversation Nov 2004

"noticed two storks": Costello journal, 19 July 1944

page 97

"That was my understanding": Macky diary, page 27. An order to withdraw later turned up in Egypt, he wrote. "I never got it"

"The last of our brigades": Macky diary, page 27

page 98

"a tall lance-corporal": Dan Davin, "Paddy Costello", page 1; also Davin's diary, 5 May 1941

"a feat of arms": *The Other Side of the Hill*, page 8. Balck was a hard, strong-willed man who later commanded an Army Group. Kippenberger noted that the 21st had an unhappy record and "was regarded as the unluckiest battalion in the Division" (*Infantry Brigadier*, page 113)

"didn't hold the ground": Maj-General W.B. Thomas, Queensland, telephone conversation 19 Sept 2004

"Macky later conceded": Macky admits in his diary to withdrawing a platoon guarding the roadblock at the wrong moment. The New Zealand military historian, Christopher Pugsley, writes: "A combination of armour and infantry unhinged 21 Battalion. One has to look at the problem Allen Force faced after Macky's battalion disintegrated and took to the hills." (email to author, 21 Feb 2007) For the defence of Tempe, Macky's battalion became part of 17 Australian Brigade, commanded by Brigadier Allen. Also see McClymont, *To Greece*, page 324 (& footnote)

"a river running with blood": *Illustrated London News*, 26 April 1941

ESCAPE TO CRETE

page 99

"detained on Mount Olympus": Ovenden, *A Fighting Withdrawal*, pp 139-141

"Dead men on roadside": Davin diary, 16 April 1941

page 100

"War is to man": Costello to Bil, 14 April 1942

"I was clambering": ibid, 18 April 1942

page 101

"Unfortunately it was found": Polly Macky diary, page 27. A fragment from Costello's diary begins, "18 — *First Day* battle, defeat, night in bracken overlooking road, to 3am"

"Costello found a tobacco smuggler": Macky diary, page 29

page 102

"ten days of zigzagging": Costello's diary reads, "21 Ag Yanni, 22 Skopelos, 23 German bomber — Chios, 24 Mykonos, 25 Sira, 26 Mykonos, 27 Andiporos, 28 Thira"

"Who's winning?": Mick Costello interview, 1999

"Kippenberger counted up to 190": *Infantry Brigadier*, page 47

"Colonel Macky, Captain Dutton": Davin diary, 5 May 1941

"But Macky was ill": "He was able to walk around on Crete but was hospitalised when he got back to Cairo" (Lloyd Macky email, 2007)

page 103

"OUT OF THE BLUE": *New Zealand Herald*, 26 May 1941

"Costello . . . was the saviour": Davin diary, 5 May 1941

page 104

"Macky's second sacking": R.C.J. Stone, page 132; *NZ Military History*, ed. McGibbon, page 179

A MEETING IN CAIRO

page 105

"Spending the days": Davin diary, 8 Feb 1943, after the victory parade in Tripoli

"On Crete . . . Davin": Ovenden, *A Fighting Withdrawal*, pp 147-150

"Geoffrey Cox had been": see Cox, *Eyewitness*; and McNeish, *Dance of the Peacocks*

page 106

"Davin's report": Ovenden, pp 150-1

"they became friends instantly": Ovenden, page 154. The meeting in the National Hotel is based on the account in Costello's journal, Davin's memoir "Paddy Costello" and interviews with Geoffrey Cox, 1999-2000

page 107

"Some timorous instinct": Davin, "Paddy Costello", page 2

"The best linguist": Davin diary, 26 Sept 1941

"because I deemed": Costello to Bil, 10 March 1941

page 108

"whose problems are the same": ibid, 20 Oct 1941

"an initial warmth": Paul Freyberg lent him Hemingway's *For Whom the Bell Tolls* (Costello to Bil, 7 Oct 1941)

page 109

"New Zealand is creeping in": Davin to his wife, Feb 1942

"I wish Cox and Costello and I": Davin diary, 5 May 1941

"Knife mind": ibid, 2 Jan 1943

"a White Russian emigrée": Costello journal, 12 Sept 1943 & passim

"It has been said": *Dance of the Peacocks*, page 200

"full of indescribable clamour": Davin diary, 14 May 1943

page 110

"he had been sent": *A Fighting Withdrawal*, page 166

"They sang and declaimed": Davin, "Paddy Costello"; Costello journal, May 1943; *Dance of the Peacocks*, page 228. Davin's diary for Sabrata, 17 May 1943, reads, "An animated female could not be convinced that Paddy was not a Sicilian." It continues 29 May 1943, "Daba. Delightful beach, clear water, sandy floor. We swam and made castles in the sand till four"

page 111

"My one worthwhile friend": Davin diary, 6 May 1942

"Curiel was a mysterious figure": *The Dictionary of Espionage*, page 35. Henri Curiel was murdered by unidentified gunmen in Paris in 1978

page 112

"because I find it easier": Costello journal, 25 May 1943

"by the scruff": Davin to Costello, 15 Oct 1947

"Costello's going": Davin, "Paddy Costello", pp 6–7

"British writers talk": see Antony Beevor, *Crete*, page 83 ("obstinacy, muddled thinking and an extreme reluctance to criticise subordinates")

THE GENERAL'S CARAVAN

page 113

"Ura!": Russian for "hurrah!" (rhymes with "caviar") – Costello to Bil, July 1942

"and recognised it": Davin, "Paddy Costello", page 7

page 114

"struck in the neck": after the war, a friend at dinner noticed Freyberg scratching his neck. "As he watched he saw a piece of shrapnel fall out on to his plate" (Denis McLean to author, Nov 2005)

"That same night": Davin, "Paddy Costello", page 8

"bolting like wild elephants": *Infantry Brigadier*, page 135

"At Minqar Qaim": "Did I tell you that a German officer who had fought on the Ostfront said that in the circumstances in which we found ourselves on June 27th at Minqar Qaim he did not think that a Russian div. could have fought its way out the way we did? I don't know if he's right. I do know that our fellows fought — and fight — with a ferocity that dumbfounded the Germans" (Costello to Bil, from hospital in Alexandria, 28 Aug 1942)

"slogan, 'Hooray — fuck'": Costello to Davin, from Stockholm, 15 Aug 1945

page 115

"Italian shopkeepers": Italians booked seats on balconies in Alexandria to be first to greet "i nostri" when the Germans entered the city (Michael Haag, *Alexandria: City of Memory,* Yale, 2004)

"a fervent and unreasonable": Davin, "Paddy Costello", page 8

"a rather sticky show": Costello to Bil, 15 Nov 1941

"No harm in that": ibid, 7 Nov 1942

page 116

"You still seem sore": ibid, from Tripoli, 9 March 1943

"You sweat and prickle": ibid

"Though song, though breath": from "Tempt me no more" in "The Magnetic Mountain", in *The Complete Poems* by C. Day Lewis (Sinclair-Stevenson)

page 117

"Courage, my dear Costello": Davin, "Paddy Costello", pp 17-18. Retold by Davin in *The War Lords*, page 594; and see *Dance of the Peacocks*, page 232. Costello quoted this back to Davin in 1959.

Writing about a mutual friend elected to a Chair in England, he said, "It is pleasant to see recognition accorded to a really nice man (I take his scholarship, like the bravery of a Kiwi officer, for granted)"

"Jonesie continues": Costello journal, 1 May 1943

page 118

"A few nights ago": ibid, 18 Aug 1943. Freyberg had gone on a painting trip to Helwan, to look at desert sunsets

page 119

"I keep a map of Russia": Costello to Bil, 30 Jan 1943

"I am teaching": ibid

"a field security officer, Lawrence Nathan": Laurie Nathan was a witty and wayward Aucklander who was captain of the épée team at Cambridge about 1932 when Costello arrived at Trinity. In January 1943 he lost a leg after he was blown up by a bomb under his bed in Tripoli, where he was working. The mattress saved his life. In his unfinished portrait, "Paddy Costello", Davin recalls Costello coming off duty "in a state of distress", after visiting Nathan in hospital. Costello described Nathan in a letter to his wife as "a sort of Peter Pan, trying to be light-hearted about losing his leg". Nathan was evacuated to Cairo and invalided back to New Zealand. He left Costello his Luger pistol as a keepsake

"He made me learn": Nathan to Davin, 19 Oct 1982

"A FIFTH WHEEL"

page 126

"I imagine you": Costello to Bil, July 1943

"and play chess": *Infantry Brigadier*, page 349

page 127

"Speaks quite good Greek": Davin, "Paddy Costello", page 44

"We told stories": Lawrence Nathan to Davin, 18 Oct 1982

"There's no charcoal": Costello journal, Jan/Feb 1944 & passim

page 128

"Costello's nerveless fingers": Davin, "Paddy Costello", page 41

"There was nothing new": ibid, page 42

"a trifle perfunctory": Davin, "Bernard Freyberg", pp 14-15

"How difficult": Davin diary, 24 Jan 1944; also "Bernard Freyberg", page 13

page 129

"Freyberg did not want": Costello journal, 30 Jan 1944

"When he first entered": account from Murray Sidey, correspondence with author, Feb 2001; Davin "Psychological Warfare at Cassino", in *Selected Stories*, page 213 and passim; Davin in Carver, *The War Lords*, page 595

page 130

"The General was dependent": Murray Sidey, telephone conversation Feb 2001

"refought the Battle": Costello in BBC broadcast, 31 Oct 1957

"Oh Paddy": Murray Sidey to author, Feb 2001

page 131

"Five Red Army generals": *Dominion*, 11 Dec 1943

"There has been speculation": Alister McIntosh to Michael King interview, Wellington, March 1978

"32 today, curse it!": Costello journal, 31 Jan 1944

"One day he visited": ibid, 4 Feb 1944

page 132

"told by a soothsayer": Alan Lomas (Freyberg's personal physician in Italy) interview, 1985. Freyberg, according to Dr Lomas, visited a fortune-teller in Alexandria

"Shelling never hurt": Davin in Carver, *The War Lords*

"He looked along the road": Davin, "Paddy Costello", page 46

page 133

"still in Italy": Costello to Bil, 19 March 1944

PART THREE – TO RUSSIA & BACK

THE GENERAL'S TELEGRAM

page 141

"Mr Fraser decided": Sub-Inspector P.J. Nalder to Commissioner of Police, 13 Nov 1950 (NZSIS file, declassified 11 Dec 2002). "[Mr McIntosh] informed me that neither he nor the Government considered there was a likelihood of Costello being a security risk"

"He got away": Costello journal, 2 April 1944

"from Wellington": ibid, 3 June 1944. Costello returned in April but did not write up his diary for two months. The following passage is based on his journal and on family interviews

page 142

"The streets were bounded": B.W. Clapp, *The University of Exeter: A History*, page 94

"nerve storms": Costello journal, 3 June 1944

page 143

"I have the marvellous": Costello to Bil, 16 Feb 1944

"As they like": ibid, 17 July 1941

"Not bad, he wrote": Costello journal, 3 March 1944

page 144

"It is too good": ibid, 18 Aug 1943

page 145

"the tension created": ibid

page 146

"a newspaper item": *Dominion*, 11 Dec 1943

"It struck me": McIntosh to Cox, 16 Feb 1944

"He would be suitable": Brigadier Stevens, Cairo, to McIntosh (*Top Hats Are Not Being Taken*, page 21)

"He described Costello's rigidity": Cox to McIntosh, 7 Jan 1944 (see *Top Hats*, page 21)

page 147

"had almost joined the Party": After he returned to London from Spain in December 1936, Geoffrey Cox says, he was asked by a New Zealand newspaper to interview Harry Pollitt, the general secretary of the British Communist Party. Cox discussed it with his wife. "I said to Cecily, if Pollitt asks me to join the Party, I will." Recounting this to the author in 2005, Cox said, "But he never asked me. Thank God he didn't!" (interview, Standish, Glos., May 2005)

"The meeting took place": *Top Hats Are Not Being Taken*, page 21; also *Dance of the Peacocks*, page 234

"Costello began his tour": began work with the Foreign Office 9 June 1944 (journal)

page 148

"the hotel clock": Costello journal, 25 June 1944

"Paddy picked me up": Cox interview, July 1999

THE FIRST HARDSHIP POST

page 149

"25 May 1944": Costello (Personal File, Prime Minister's Dept. PM 7/2/85). The file, made available by Foreign Affairs in 1999, appears since then to have been culled

"Clothing for Costello": *Top Hats Are Not Being Taken*, page iv

page 150

"*A Question of Furniture*": ibid, pp 25–26

"a jovial bachelor named Patrick": R.T.G. Patrick was a wartime recruit to External Affairs, ex-Customs, and for a time the Department's Pacific specialist. He was a career public servant (*Top Hats Are Not Being Taken*, page 17). "A sound and solid fellow who had been virtual Consul in Tahiti"

page 151

"I don't think": McIntosh to Berendsen, Washington (*Top Hats Are Not Being Taken,* page 27)

"burst out laughing": ibid, page 28

"MY OLD MAN OF THE SEA"

page 152

"The Minister had arrived": *Top Hats Are Not Being Taken*, page 45

page 153

"caused him only despair": McIntosh to Berendsen, *Top Hats Are Not Being Taken*, page 15

"A man, McIntosh said": Alister McIntosh in Templeton, *An Eye, An Ear, And a Voice*, page 20

"a single foreign power": In 1939 New Zealand's declaration of war had to be transmitted to Hitler via HM Government in the UK. Missions were exchanged with USA by 1942 and there were diplomatic dealings with the Free French in Noumea: "Does USA count as a foreign power?" (G. Hensley to author, 4 March 2007)

"unpopular at home": see *Top Hats Are Not Being Taken*, page 8 & passim

"no discernible qualifications": ibid, page 13

page 154

"Costello's diary entries": Costello journal, 19 July–15 Aug 1944

"C.W. Boswell has found": ibid, 15 Aug 1944

"there was little food": The only food readily obtainable to Muscovites, according to Douglas Zohrab, was beetroot and cabbages, small birds for sale in the streets resembling woodcock "and *kasha*, a kind of buckwheat, which we boiled and ate with butter for lunch at the legation" (interview, February 2004). Lady Kelly, wife of the British Ambassador, David Kelly, records that once, exploring the embassy attic and finding a locked door, she demanded a key and was astonished to see in the gloom row upon row of roosting chickens. The eggs and yolks were quite white from lack of light. The previous ambassador's butler had sold the eggs to other diplomats suffering from the chronic shortage of food in Moscow (Beeton, *The British Embassy Residence Moscow*, page 58)

"They worked and lodged": *Top Hats Are Not Being Taken*, page 28; also Costello and Lake correspondence

page 155

"We have nothing": Doug Lake to his mother, 3 Sept 1944

"Whenever a message came": Doug Lake to his family in New Zealand, 25 Feb 1945

"had to borrow ink": Ruth Macky to her family, 29 Jan 1945

page 156

"He is awkward": Costello journal, 15 Aug 1944

"I have done nothing": ibid, 19 Aug 1944

POLAND 1945

page 157

"At present all entry": Churchill to Roosevelt, 16 March 1945 (Gilbert, *Road to Victory*, page 1252)

"I understand": conversation based on reported speech. The appointment of Costello was apparently on Boswell's initiative (*Top Hats Are Not Being Taken*, page 30 and Note, page 102). Full accounts of the Costello Mission are held by Archives NZ (379 series, ABHS series 950) and National Archives, London (FO 371/47648–47651). They include Costello's and Floyd's reports on conditions in Poland, the Foreign Office and New Zealand External Affairs telegrams, and copies of Costello's report on the Death Camps

page 158

"There is no doubt": Gilbert, *Road to Victory*, page 1252

"Great excitement": Doug Lake to his mother, 14 Oct 1944

page 159

"How would it do . . .?": *Road to Victory*, page 992

"There was a long silence": ibid, page 993

"went on for many minutes": ibid, page 1016

page 160

"We really believed": Martin Walker, *The Cold War*, page 9

"The contact mission": Costello's journey is described in his journal, "Travel notes" (2–16 March 1945), and the Lublin episode in Appendices to his reports (Archives NZ, 379 series). See also *Top Hats Are Not Being Taken*, pp 30–33

page 161

"What need is there . . .?": Archives NZ, 379 series; also *Top Hats Are Not Being Taken*, page 32

page 162

"squandering a unique opportunity": telegram from Sir Archibald Clark Kerr, Moscow, to the Foreign Office, London, 23 March 1945

"The two men often disagreed": Flying Officer David Floyd was a right-winger. He was a member of the military mission attached to the British Embassy in Moscow and spoke good Russian. After the war he joined the Foreign Office; he later became, as the London *Daily Telegraph*'s communist affairs correspondent, a noted Kremlinologist and the contact man for Russian defectors. He translated many books by defectors and also Solzhenitsyn's novella *For the Good of the Cause.*

Floyd's report on conditions in Poland in 1945 was more objective than Costello's. Costello seems to have believed what he was told by a Polish officer he met on the train returning to Moscow, that Russian intentions were "strictly honourable". Costello, according to his son Mick, was at odds with Churchill's view of events. He cites as an example his father's belief that the second Front in Europe was delayed "in order to let the Germans and Russians bleed each other".

In Lublin Costello and Floyd met representatives of the underground forces loyal to the London-based Polish government-in-exile, the biggest of which, the A.K., still controlled large areas between Warsaw and the east Prussian frontier. The A.K. (Armia Krajowa) included some British ex-prisoners who had been fighting with the A.K. against the Soviets. When a British officer began to brag about killing Red Army soldiers, Costello, according to Mick, "wanted to turn him over to the Russians, and would have done but for the presence of Floyd"

"He was standing": see Costello's report on the Death Camps in Appendices

page 163

"the hotel chamber maid": it may have been the waitress, who had herself been imprisoned by the Germans. Floyd wrote in his report, "When we told her we must leave, she said: 'We have waited for you for five years, and now you go away so soon,' and at that she started to cry"

page 164

"the two from Oswiecim": Costello journal, 12 March 1945

"My only excuse": Costello to Boswell, memorandum 26 March 1945 (Archives NZ, ABHS series 950, accession W4627-379/4/3 part 1)

"Mr Costello has brought me": Archives NZ, ibid

"It was the German practice": Costello report, see Appendices

page 165

"It anticipated the discovery": Maidanek was liberated by the Russians on 23 July 1944; and Auschwitz/Birkenau on 27 Jan 1945; Buchenwald by the Americans in early April 1945, Bergen-Belsen by the British on 15 April 1945, and Dachau by the Americans on 29 April 1945

"thrown a cordon": Richard Overy, *Interrogations: The Nazi Elite in Allied Hands*, page 194; and email to author, 22 Feb 2005

"I thought I was hardened": Wilson to Costello, 9 May 1945

page 166

"The above sounds": Costello report, final paragraph

"Mr Eden read it": Sir Cecil Day, Cabinet Office, London, to McIntosh, Wellington, 29 May 1945

"by falsely declaring": According to his son, Mick, Costello facilitated the repatriation of other French ex-prisoners, "kidding the Russians that they were French-Canadians"

"Madame Lengyel however": Olga Lengyel's American editor at Academy Chicago Publishers, Jordan Miller, wrote to her in Dec 1999. "She was probably nearly 100, [but] is now dead. Alan Wieder, a young man in New York, telephoned me and identified himself as her nephew, and put me in touch with her. When I rang, a taped voice announced it was the 'Memorial Library'. It could well be one in her name but 'Memorial Library' was all it said" (Miller to author, 14 Jan 2005). Olga Lengyel's book, *Five Chimneys: A Woman Survivor's True Story of Auschwitz*, is still in print with Academy Chicago Publishers

"MOSCOW! MOSCOW! MOSCOW!"

page 170

"Outside it is snowing": Doug Lake to a cousin in NZ, 25 Feb 1945

"Our flat was luxury": Mick Costello interview, Kent, 9 April 2000

"We stood miserably": ibid, 24 Sept 1999

page 172

"taking your leave of Charles": to Doug & Ruth Lake in New Zealand, 12 May 1949

"Does a mind like that": *Chatsky*, Act Three, sc. 1, in *Four Russian Plays* (Penguin, 1972)

"Fate's a practical joker": *Chatsky*, title page

"23 nov. Last night *Yevgeny Onegin*": Costello journal, 1944

page 173

"The Russian language": Costello to McIntosh, 20 Jan 1945

"a wide boy named Victor": Victor Louis said he was a university student. It was "accepted that he reported to the Soviet authorities. He appeared to have the run of the hotel [National]" (Doug Lake to John Scott, 6 March 1991). After the war when Katie Costello returned to Moscow as an adult, she lived with Victor Louis and his wife. They had an ice rink, "a fancy place", Katie recalled in 2005

"an out-of-work droshky driver": Costello journal, undated

page 174

"diplomat from a remote British 'territory'": "Meetings with

Russian Writers" in *Personal Impressions* (1998 edn.), pp 225 & 229. For an account of Isaiah Berlin's 1945 meeting with Pasternak see Ignatieff, *Isaiah Berlin: A Life*, page 144, Vintage edn. "Berlin became the first foreigner to learn that Pasternak had a new project (*Zhivago*)." Possibly Costello, who had met Pasternak before this, already knew of the project

"he irritated the Russian poet": A counter theory, making it conceivable that the Russians had leaned on Costello to try to persuade Pasternak to heed the Party's teachings and conform, as a condition of continued access, would — some say — confirm Isaiah Berlin's story. Berlin's recollections date from a period towards the end of his life when his recall was becoming distorted by age and prolonged eminence

page 175

"Costello related afterwards": Peter Bartlett, telephone conversation June 2006

"crawling slowly": Isaiah Berlin, *Flourishing*, page 602

"a goose who would never": Costello's diary and letters are filled with anecdotes about C.W. Boswell, a man who seemingly — to quote the other Boswell — seldom allowed his occupation to degenerate into work. One might hesitate to criticise the unfortunate Charles Boswell, were it not for his parsimony.

The Minister left Moscow owing about thirty dinners, having banked most of his expense allowance. "I must say," McIntosh wrote to Costello on 20 October 1949, "that of all the poor fish I have ever struck he is by far the poorest, but not of course financially. No one on our payroll has ever saved so much in so short a time."

Among Costello's items of "Boswelliana" is Charles Boswell's attempt to learn Russian from a Linguaphone course. "Four years in Russia, Russians all round him — and Charles starts to learn Russian from gramophone records. These records are each divided into two parts. The first is questions. Then, after a blank strip over which the sound arm of the gramophone has to be lifted, come the answers. Boswell's machine is a complex one. If you lift the sound arm, you can't put it down again further on — it swings back to the start point and proceeds to play the record da capo. So there is Charles, trying to help the sound arm over on to the second half of the record, so that he can hear the answers. But no. Inexorable. It moves back and Charles hears the questions once again. He will never know the answers" (Costello to the Lakes, 17 Feb 1949)

"Friends . . . Only recently": Doug Lake to his mother, 1 April 1946

page 176

"Life is not a stroll": the last line of Pasternak's 1946 poem,

"a black-list": see Christopher Hitchens, *Orwell's Victory*, pp 111-121

"Frank Corner writes": Templeton, *An Eye, An Ear, And A Voice*, pp 98-99

"The Australian head of mission": Costello to McIntosh, 20 Jan 1945

page 177

"I must tell you": to Ruth & Doug Lake, 4 July 1949

INCUBUS

page 179

"Although there is no proof": Batterbee File; and Michael King correspondence, Aug 1998, Oct 2003

"haunted him in the army": An entry in Davin's diary for 28 Feb 1944, after Costello departed Cassino to go on leave, reads: "Jonesie's story about Paddy and the Secret service. /What?" A probable reference to Exeter and Hubert Fyrth's prosecution under the Official Secrets Act. Costello's dismissal obviously still rankled. He did not tell Davin about Exeter (see *Dance of the Peacocks*, page 238)

page 180

"is not a perishable item": Roger Bowen, *Innocence is Not Enough*

"In 1957 Herb Norman": ibid

"Costello's anti-Americanism": Costello believed, as did Davin, that the Americans made unreliable allies, his view conditioned in part by his wartime experiences. Costello did not visit America, did not read books by Americans and laid most of the blame for the Cold War on British and American shoulders. In March 1948 in a letter from Moscow he put the main responsibility for the conflict between Soviet and American policies "fairly and squarely on the present US (i.e. Truman's) administration". This elicited from New Zealands's Ambassador to the US in Washington, Carl Berendsen, a predictable response. "I have never heard a more perverted and wrong-headed interpretation of events," Berendsen told McIntosh, "or a stronger expression of naive and childish nonsense." Berendsen, the ultimate cold warrior, believed that the wisdom of American foreign policy was not to be questioned.

Costello's attitude to America however was not as myopic as it seemed. In 1943 he wrote to Bil from Cairo: "The war is moving on but all I do is watch it. This is a land in which it seems always afternoon; my only battles are on the squash court and the only advances I am concerned with are advances of pay . . .

"The news this morning — end of the Mussolini regime — has reminded me that the last phase of the war is now on. I can see that the Germans will try to hold their Russian front while not making any difficulty about admitting us in the West; the essential thing is to get us into Berlin before the Russians. Then Roosevelt's vision of a federated Europe under American influence becomes practical politics, as it never could were the Russians installed in the most important country in Europe, Germany" (26 July 1943)

"gripped by fear": Ignatieff, *Isaiah Berlin*, pp 135-6; also *Flourishing*, page 626

"Berlin's famous encounter": Ignatieff, ibid, page 148 & passim

"a courageous, not to say foolhardy": Berlin, "Meetings with Russian Writers", page 210

page 181

"the so-called Doctors' Plot": Ignatieff, pp 168-9

"If anything": "Nobody said anything, because nobody knew what was going on" (Zohrab interview, Wellington, 21 March 1999)

page 182

"The British Security Authorities": McIntosh to Costello, 22 March 1945

"Sir Harry Fagg Batterbee": High Commissioner for the UK in New Zealand, 1939-45. The information on Costello came to him from Sir Eric Machtig

"Dear Mac, On the question of Communist": More likely, as he told Davin, Costello left the Party in 1939 over the Nazi-Soviet Pact

page 183

"from the San Francisco Conference": Fraser had been in London, then to San Francisco for the drafting of the UN Charter

page 184

"Clark Kerr was succeeded": Peterson succeeded Clark Kerr in Jan 1946. Clark Kerr (Moscow 1942-6) was posted to Washington

"thoroughly bored . . . an embarrassment all round": Marshall Crowe to author, 21 Sept 1999

THE PARIS PEACE CONFERENCE

page 185

"Quack, quack, quack": New Zealand Press (probably *New Zealand Herald),* 17 Aug 1946

"or perhaps an anarchist": Costello to Davin, from Stockholm, 15 Aug 1945

page 186

"We travelled the whole Volga": ibid, from Paris, 26 Aug 1946

"The heat and lush green": Costello to his mother, 20 July 1946

page 187

"As I sit": Costello to Cox, 27 Aug 1946

"our exercises at Forgloss": Forgloss, Syria, where the New Zealand Division held exercises in May/June 1942

"Mr Jordan made headlines": According to Costello, the New Zealand High Commissioner spent the first eight days "plotting the route the knight would take to travel the whole chess board" (journal, 10 Dec 1946). Mr Jordan appears to have absented himself from the conference at a certain point and returned to London, taking the Hon. Mason with him

"Spahis on horseback": Spahis – first-class regular mounted troops, of Algerian, Tunisian or Moroccan origin, originally conscripted from the local populations as irregulars for the French Army of Africa

"hit by lightning": The plane, a retired Lancaster bomber, made five unscheduled stops on the journey which took more than two weeks. In Iraq, eight pounds of New Zealand butter, which Lyn Corner was taking to friends in Paris, melted on the runway

page 188

"The food was superb": Frank Corner interview, Wellington, 19 Oct 2004

"crouched down together": interview, 2005 (source privileged)

"I don't remember": Lyn Corner interview, Wellington, Feb 2005

page 189

"Bedell Smith, announced": Archives NZ, minutes of the Hungarian Commission, 102/8/11 pt 1 box 1963

"the London-Istanbul Highway": ibid

"like a bunch of Kaffirs": ibid

"10th meeting": ibid

"In the last two elections": Costello's account, reported to Mick Costello (interview, Sept 1999)

page 190

"He out-manoeuvred": Corner interview, Wellington, Oct 2000

"It included the notion": Foss Shanahan to McIntosh, 1 Oct 1946 (McIntosh Papers)

"The Prime Minister remembered": Tom Larkin in *Peter Fraser: Master Politician*, page 198; see also newspaper item New Zealand Press, 29 Jan 1947, re Presbyterian Clergy and Hungary; and Costello to McIntosh, 21 Feb 1947. On 29 Jan 1947 McIntosh told Costello that the Labour government was holding on to office "by a slender thread"

"It is very odd": McIntosh to Costello, 29 Jan 1947

page 191

"It's always like this": Account of the dinner from Tom Larkin, a former New Zealand Ambassador to Japan, who talked with Costello in London in 1948 and in Wellington in 1950 (interview and conversations, Wellington, 1999, 2005, 2006)

"Masaryk stayed": Corner interview, Oct 2000

"Although watered down": The final resolution omitted any mention of forced transfers of population. The expulsion of the Czech Hungarians from their lands began early in 1947, after the Conference ended. The Czech proposals appeared heartless but were the best, Costello had argued at the Conference, the Hungarians were going to get (full compensation and international inspection). If America and Britain did not support the Czech offer, he argued, "They will still deport their Magyars not to Hungary but to Bohemia, and minus the humanitarian trimmings." Reminding McIntosh of this on 22 January 1947, Costello wrote, "It appears that we were right. Nobody can interfere in what is now an internal problem of Czechoslovakia, and all that the Magyars will get from Alexander and Bedell Smith is . . . sympathy"

page 192

"Dear Paddy, The Americans": McIntosh to Costello, 20 Nov 1946

TILTING AT WINDMILLS

page 196

"We like to think": Costello journal, 1 May 1946

"unquestionably the greatest": Costello to Davin, 26 Nov 1946

page 197

"Trade deals": Trade was not entirely negligible. New Zealand exports to USSR jumped from half a million dollars in 1947 to nearly three million in 1948 and again in 1949, chiefly from the sale of wool. Previously the Russians had bought most of their wool from Persia

"He reads them steadily": Costello to Doug & Ruth Lake, 17 Feb 1949

page 198

"Mick (aged 10)": Costello to Davin, 22 Jan 1947

"He encouraged us": Josie interview, Manchester, April 2005

"Mick recalls Sunday picnics": interview, Sept 1999

page 199

"The events": unpublished typescript, Costello family archives

"The continent of Imro": ibid

"If nobody else": Costello to Davin, 19 Feb 1948

"He asked for Davin's help": Costello had earlier tried to find a publisher in Moscow for Davin's war novel, *For the Rest of Our Lives*, without success

page 200

"A few nights ago": Davin to Costello, 7 Feb 1948

"Burn him": Costello to Davin, 14 May 1948 (OUP archives)

"I have three things": Costello to Davin, 4 March 1947

"One can *feel* the pain": Costello to the Lakes, 21 Feb 1947

page 201

"total admiration for Stalin": Mick Costello, email to author, 3 March 2007. Mick writes, "I well remember Paddy waking us up late at night when he came home to the flat in Khokhlovsky Pereulok to tell us joyfully that at that evening's reception given by Stalin for representatives of Western or British missions in Moscow, Stalin had raised his glass to 'the best troops in the British Empire — to the New Zealand Division'. Paddy's joy was all the greater for seeing the discomfort of the British Ambassador"

"in a commentary": Costello's report, recalled and written out in full in Howard Kippenberger's *Commonplace Book* (courtesy Denis McLean)

page 202

"He eludes definition": The only label in the trade that seems to fit Costello is agent of influence, a proselytiser or apostle for the cause — as distinct from an active agent or asset, someone recruited and paid for his or her services. "Agent of influence" is not a derogatory term

"Paddy, was steeped": Dobbs, UK, telephone conversation 28 Aug 1999

"Paddy could see": Crowe to author, 21 Sept 1999

"He has already become": Costello to McIntosh, 1 July 1945

page 203

"Your account": Davin to Costello, 16 March 1948

"the real reason": Costello to Davin, 22 March 1948

"These manhunts in Spain": Orwell, *Collected Essays*, vol 3, Penguin edn, page 457

page 204

"as T.S. Eliot had missed it": Michael Shelden, *Orwell: The Authorised Biography*, 1991, page 403

"The only time": Mick Costello interview, Sept 1999

"he started writing a novel": The novel *Moscow Assignment* survives in typescript, as does *Imro,* in the Costello family archives. The novel is about a third-rate British journalist who is invited to lecture in America on the strength of a fourth-rate book about the Soviet Union

"beliefs formed by left-wingers": Hobsbawm interview, London, 24 May 2005

DOPPELGÄNGER

page 206

"He's dangerous": *Chatsky,* Act 2, translated by Joshua Cooper, in *Four Russian Plays* (Penguin Classics, 1972)

"He spoke in the highest": Zohrab interview, Wellington, March 1999

page 207

"I see how sensitive": Davin to Andrew Rothstein, 4 Sept 1953 (OUP archives)

"The idea of the outsider": Costello was drawn to outsider figures, what the Russians call *lishniy chelovek* — odd or superfluous people in their literature — and especially to the Byronic hero of Pushkin's novel, *Eugene Onegin*. Douglas Zohrab has suggested, after a reading of Costello's letters ("What an eighteenth-century writer he was!"), that there was something Byronic in Costello's own persona. Certainly the urge to display his talents and the impulse that drove him to conquer an attractive woman were the same

"a model of its kind": Bristol Classical Press/Duckworth, London 1995, ed. R.A. Peace. "Notes by D.P. Costello"

"I played truant": Costello to Doug & Ruth Lake

"The performance last night": ibid

page 208

"Half the lines": Puskin – cited in the introduction to *Four Russian Plays*, page 22

"He was a first-class representative": D.P. Costello, "Griboyedov as a Diplomat". See Bibliography

"The story is told": The same story is told of Gogol after the first performance of his play *Revizor* (The Government Inspector) in 1836

"At one point a scandal": In 1817 Griboyedov fought a duel, the result of an involvement with a ballerina. He was appointed, unpunished, to government service in Persia

"accused of treason": Arrested and interrogated for his alleged complicity in the Decembrist revolt against the Czar in 1825, Griboyedov was eventually vindicated and given promotion

page 209

"It is the most wonderful": Costello to Doug & Ruth Lake, 12 May 1949

"Not bad [he writes]": ibid, 3 Aug 1949. In his journal Costello wrote (17 July 1949), "At Peterhof Charles, in Panama, grey bags, checker sports jacket and tennis-shoes, performing a ballet pose on one toe beside a gilded statue on which he rested one hand. Blast of the attendant's whistle!"

"to have legible handwriting": "To have legible handwriting is the first mark of politeness (Klyuchevsky)" — one of the first entries in Costello's journal. Klyuchevsky was a 19th century Russian historian

page 210

"in one of those bizarre coincidences": Pushkin's memoirs "Journey to Erzerum", cited by Costello in his Introduction to *Gore ot Uma,* page xii

"Two years earlier": account taken from Costello's essay "Griboyedov as a Diplomat". See also Mirsky, *A History of Russian Literature*, pp 108-113

page 211

"two New Zealand cabbage trees": Costello to the Lakes, 28 Sept 1949. Costello describes the trip in a series of letters written between 28 Sept & 5 Oct 1949

"*Your thoughts and actions*": Griboyedov had married only months before a sixteen-year-old Georgian girl, Princess Nina Chavchavadze. They were said to be wildly happy

page 212

"He bought the book for him": "Dear Paddy", McIntosh wrote on 23 Nov 1945. "The little book on the voyages of the *Vostok* and the *Mirny* has been duly placed in the Turnbull Library. It is an extraordinarily good narrative and, as Tom Larkin says, must be the least publicised of all the voyages of the world"

"His 1935 visit": see Note, "Costello's interest in Persian", in "A Black Eye in Oxford", part 5

"but was refused permission": letter to the Lakes, 5 Oct 1949; also to Max Hayward in UK, same date

THE RETREAT FROM MOSCOW

page 214

"We will probably end up": McIntosh to Berendsen, 12 May 1950 (McIntosh Papers)

"the only references": McIntosh to Costello, telegram 3 Nov 1949

"keeping our fingers crossed": Costello to McIntosh, 4 Nov 1949

page 215

"In 1948": see *Top Hats Are Not Being Taken*, page 60; and *Undiplomatic Dialogue*, page 166, note 1. Fraser was attending the Commonwealth Prime Minister's Conference in London, Oct 1948

"All we achieved": Mick Costello interview, Sept 1999

"Paddy told us the Russians": McIntosh to Michael King, interview March 1978

"What Costello had done": recounted in a personal letter to McIntosh, 27 Sept 1949

"They were wrong": Costello wrote to McIntosh in September 1949 that American policy since 1945 had been based on two fallacies, 1) that the bomb was the *decisive* weapon of war and 2) that it was a US monopoly and likely to stay so for several years more. He believed that the most dangerous mistake in foreign policy was to underestimate Russia — "The British and the Americans are always doing it." On his return to New Zealand the following year Costello amplified the statement, telling a parliamentary select committee that, "the reason Moscow strikes the foreigner as drab is that a disproportionately large share of the Soviet national income is being diverted to heavy industry . . . such industries as steel, heavy engineering and now atomic energy production. The superficial observer, observing the shabbiness, tends to deduce from it that the Russians are backward in the decisive branches of industry. The exact reverse is the case." (*Top Hats Are Not Being Taken*, pp 49-50)

page 216

"But he had prescience": A witness is Doug Lake who first encountered Costello in the Western Desert in 1942 or '43. Lake wrote to the NZ Secretary of External Affairs, John Scott, in March 1991: "I heard Costello give a talk in the open air, an account of the war in Russia at a time when British generals including Freyberg wanted to know why the Red Army had not collapsed under the German onslaught in six weeks, as they had predicted.

"But I remember the talk mainly for Costello's prediction that China would emerge as a world power of even greater significance than Russia in the second half of the century" (Lake Papers)

"George Kennan's 'long telegram'": In the autumn of 1944 George Kennan, chief advisor to the American ambassador in Moscow, Averell

Harriman, drafted in a long telegram what was to be the basic principle of western policy towards the Soviet Union for a generation. He emphasised the need "to determine the line beyond which we cannot afford to permit the Russians to exercise unchallenged power" (Martin Walker, *The Cold War*, page 12)

"and only seven came": *The British Embassy Residence Moscow*, page 58

"it was folly": Costello to McIntosh, telegram 3 Dec 1949

"Have not given up": McIntosh to Costello, telegram 21 Dec 1949

"After further conversation": ibid, 22 Dec 1949

page 217

"I don't like C. of E. services": Costello to McIntosh, 24 Dec 1949

"After the flat": interview, Manchester, April 2005

"I lived in it": ibid

"We are giving the theatre": Costello to the Lakes, 10 April 1950

"The Soviet spectator": ibid. Costello is citing Franco Venturi of the Italian Embassy in Moscow. Venturi was an authority on Russian revolutionary history

page 218

"Katie will do anything": to the Lakes, 8 Dec 1949

"A month from now": ibid, 7 Sept 1949

"*Pikovaya*": *Pikovaya Dama,* opera by Tchaikovsky, based on Pushkin's story, "The Queen of Spades"

"I really am more interested": Costello to McIntosh, 24 Dec 1949

"I cannot say how sorry": McIntosh to Costello, 7 Feb 1950

"I really don't want": Costello to the Lakes, 28 April 1950

page 219

"The Oxford Press": to the Lakes, 7 Feb 1950

"I wish we could meet": Davin to Costello, 19 Oct 1949 & 22 Dec 1949

"in the secondhand furniture business": The furniture was either given away or abandoned. The legation mansion itself, today occupied by the Egyptian military attaché, was taken over in 1950 apparently by the Syrians

"Doug Zohrab recalls": interview, Wellington, 16 Feb 2005. "In Moscow (Zohrab adds) we were kept at a distance by the Soviets. No bilateral trade agreements existed, only a bit of trade in wool and butter.

As a French diplomat said to me later, 'We have very good relations with New Zealand, because we have no relations with New Zealand'"

"The legation finally closed": New Zealand would not be directly represented again in Moscow until 1973. The present embassy building, known as Mindovsky's Mansion, at Povarskaya St 44, is another art nouveau creation by the Moscow architect Kekushev

"McIntosh had telegraphed": to Costello, 24 March 1950

FROM THE LETTERS 1949-1950

page 222

12 May 1950

"Madie and I": Madie Browne, McIntosh's typist

PART FOUR – A DIPLOMAT IN PARIS

MCINTOSH'S FOLLY

page 227

"He said, 'Sir'": Laking interview, Wellington, May 1999

"God knows": to Jean McKenzie, 22 Dec 1949

page 228

"He has not got another job": ibid, Aug 1950

"There is a magnificent suite": to McIntosh, 13 April 1950

"I have succeeded": to Jean McKenzie, 19 Aug 1948

page 229

"So many grand possibilities!": to McIntosh, 3 April 1950

"Doris wants a little shopping": to Jean McKenzie, 23 Sept 1950

"A shabby town": journal (undated), winter 1950

"the Vegetable Club": The Vegetable and Political Club was on Lambton Quay, upstairs in the offices of Duncan, Matthews & Taylor, roughly where Parsons Bookshop is today

page 230

"some tiny tins of truffles": McIntosh to Jean McKenzie, 8 Oct 1950

page 231

"Mr Doidge is not keen": ibid, 10 Aug 1951

"Paris was an accident": Laking interview, Wellington, May 1999

page 232

"there had been a coup": A plebiscite was held on 2 Sept 1940; the coup occurred on 4 Sept; the *Achilles* arrived on 10 Sept

"a grey September morning": account based on Berendsen's 31-page report on his mission — Archives NZ, Defence of Tahiti, Prime Minister's Dept, EA series 1. 86/16/3 pt 1 (Political and Admin Intrigue)

"New Zealand's coldest warrior": A choleric man who found it difficult to delegate, Berendsen was from 1926 until the outbreak of war in 1939 virtually the only official in the New Zealand government charged with conducting foreign policy. He headed the Prime Minister's Department until 1943, when he was unexpectedly posted to Canberra by a Prime Minister, Peter Fraser, who favoured McIntosh and subsequently adopted the younger man almost as a grandson, or godson. McIntosh, the real founder of New Zealand's foreign service, took over from Berendsen in 1943. In 1948 Berendsen went to the USA as New Zealand Minister (subsequently Ambassador) where between Washington and New York, he became and remained through the McCarthy years a fervent pro-American. Berendsen imagined Reds under many beds, including the cracked leather couch on the roof of Parliament Buildings that symbolised McIntosh's own Department. His belligerence, real and imagined, gained him among junior officers an aura of mock infallibility from remarks such as, "If a thing is said to be 51% black and 49% white, then for Chrissakes, it's black!"

On the oft-enunciated maxim of democracy versus communism — "The choice between the secret ballot and the secret police" — Berendsen saw the Soviet Union as run by charlatans and gangsters. But in the end, according to Tom Larkin (interview 2004), "though we in the McIntosh camp often said Berendsen was mad, when we looked back after the collapse of the Soviet Union, he was more often right than wrong"

"the British consul": The consul, Ernest Edmonds, was a former Anglican curate who had taught in Christchurch, New Zealand. Commodore Parry reported that initially Edmonds had supported the weak and vacillating French governor

"the French governor deposed": The Governor, Chasteney de Géry, apparently had barely heard of De Gaulle; he considered him an upstart

page 233

"to feed, victual and arm Tahiti": Besides food, New Zealand supplied Tahiti with fertiliser, vaccines, vanilla, water bottles, trouser buttons, boots, rifles, machine guns, grenades and enough defence materials to equip a small colonial force — Archives NZ, Prime Minister's Dept, EA series 1 86/16/18 pt 1 (Civilian Supplies Tahiti)

page 234

"a very good poker player": Jim Weir interview, Wellington, 18 May 1999

"a speech in the House": 2 Nov 1950

"a lucrative butter deal": McIntosh, New York, to Jean McKenzie, 12 Oct 1950

"A VERY UNFORTUNATE INCIDENT"

page 235

"A journalist rang up": McIntosh to Costello, 8 Oct 1950

"HAVE ASKED COSTELLO": Shanahan to McIntosh (McIntosh Papers)

"Dear Mac, A very unfortunate": ibid

page 237

"Terry Bishop recalls": Terry Bishop, Hamilton, to author, 19 Nov 2004

"completely demoralised": McIntosh to Costello, 8 Oct 1950

"Today I clocked in": to McIntosh, 13 Oct 1950

page 238

"Sir Joseph Heenan": Joseph Heenan (1888-1951), an imaginative and energetic public servant, left Internal Affairs in Jan 1949 and was knighted the same year

"New Zealand's first woman ambassador": Made Minister in 1955, Jean McKenzie became known as "the NZ Pearl Mesta", the Washington hostess President Truman appointed minister to Luxembourg. Pearl Mesta was the model for the Irving Berlin musical, *Call Me Madam*

page 239

"Jean McKenzie came from": Jean McKenzie (1901-1964) – see *Dictionary NZ Biography* vol 4

"not staggeringly blotto, but nearly": Mick Costello interview, Sept 1999

THE UNFORGIVING MIND

page 240

"Mr Holland is not keen": McIntosh, London, to Jean McKenzie, 10 Jan 1951

"Paddy is a grand person": to McIntosh, 23 June 1953

"a New Zealander of Armenian extraction": Douglas Zohrab was a consummate diplomat. A reputation for restraint hid Zohrab's musical gifts and an ability to improvise and enliven a party in several languages.

Born in 1917, he volunteered for war service in 1939, serving in Greece and throughout the desert campaign. In the withdrawal and evacuation from Greece, after being dive-bombed by Stukas at Katerini, Zohrab was isolated from his unit, was picked up and driven all night to an unknown destination. He lay down to sleep, waking, as he described to a friend later, "to a ghostly dawn, hills, a bay and a wine-dark sea". He realised afterwards it was the bay of Volos — the Aulis of legend where the stag appears in place of Iphigenia, enabling the Greek expedition to sail for Troy (interview, 2004).

After the war Douglas Zohrab joined the Prime Minister's Department in Wellington; he served in Moscow, London, Paris, Tokyo, Geneva, Malaysia and finally, as New Zealand Ambassador, 1969-74, in the Federal Republic of Germany

"We have wonderful teamwork": to McIntosh, 23 June 1953

page 241

"I had a full year": Bartlett to author, 19 Feb 2007

"a valuable agent": In *The Mitrokhin Archive: The KGB in Europe & the West,* Christopher Andrew dutifully copies Chapman Pincher, John Costello (no relation) and Nigel West in falsely charging Paddy

Costello with providing passports. He writes:

"In May 1954 the Cohens were issued with passports in the name of Peter and Helen Kroger by a Soviet agent at the New Zealand consulate in Paris, Paddy Costello (codenamed LONG), who later became professor of Russian at Manchester University" (page 534). In a source note on page 864 Christopher Andrew adds, "A KGB file for 1953 describes LONG as a 'valuable agent' of the Paris residency."

The KGB *rezident* is anonymous. Professor Andrew has no further information about Costello, he says. Without this information, the statement must be taken with a large dose of salt. Just as journalists try to justify big expenses, so "agents" try to inflate the extent and importance of their "sources", and *rezidents* their networks. Had Costello been of any value to the Russians, it seems unlikely they would have given him a codename by which he could be easily identified. Costello was almost 6ft 4in tall

"Mr Holland didn't mention": Jean McKenzie to McIntosh, 10 July 1953

page 242

"according to Frank Corner": interview, Wellington, Oct 2000

"With all his medals up": James Bertram to Davin, 9 Nov 1981. Costello was always conscious of form and presentation. "Paddy Costello, I remember, always put up his medals," Bertram wrote to Denis Glover on another occasion, "when calling on the Russkies in Paris and other places. He said it was the only way he could hold his own with the Russian war correspondents." (27 May 1975). Dan Davin was saying something similar, when he wrote on 13 Aug 1982 to Michael King: "Evelyn Waugh used to do for my hangovers what a dark tie, clean shirt and best suit did for Paddy Costello's."

"She did the financial work": Jean McKenzie to McIntosh, 23 June 1953

page 243

"in a leisurely manner": McIntosh to Jean McKenzie, 2 Feb 1953

"too busy arranging wreaths": Costello to Davin, 7 Feb 1951

"O my God, Costello": Shirley Tunnicliffe, Wellington, telephone conversation April 1999

"the pinnacle of Protestant": Costello to Davin, 7 Feb 1951

page 244

"prime ministerial pique": McIntosh to Michael King, interview March 1978

"Allowing for engine trouble": Costello to Davin, 18 June 1953

"Me, Josie, Bil, Papa": Katie Costello interview, London, March 2005

"He took me to cafés": interview, Manchester, April 2005

page 245

"a prodigious Spanish dish": Galante Garrone to his wife in Italy, 20 Oct 1952 (courtesy Giovanna Galante Garrone, Turin, email to author, Dec 2005)

"Josie had contracted": interview, Manchester, April 2005; email to author, Feb 2007

"translating a Russian grammar": Translating from the French a grammar by Boris Unbegaun. Unbegaun's *Russian Grammar*, translated by Costello, was published by OUP in 1957. Unbegaun was a White Russian who served in the civil war, then emigrated to France. He became professor of Comparative Slavonic Philology at Oxford in 1953

"I learned today": to Davin, 26 Jan 1954

page 246

"Paddy told me": to Michael King, 19 Dec 1982

"We both know and understand": Jean McKenzie to McIntosh, 22 June 1953

"Costello's despatches": "His despatches I used to lend to other Commonwealth people, particularly Herbert Norman" (McIntosh to Michael King, March 1978)

page 247

"or cancelling a dinner": Costello to Davin, 24 April 1953

"about something or other": ibid

"Paddy knew": Mick Costello interview, Sept 1999

page 248

"Dick Hughes": Hughes was a larger-than-life Australian journalist stationed for many years in Hong Kong, whom Le Carré put into one of his novels, *The Honourable Schoolboy*, as Old Craw. He met Costello in the North African desert. In the 1950s Hughes would breeze in to Paris and turn up at Viroflay, the Costellos' house, wearing a mitre and impersonating a bishop

"Richard Cobb, the historian": in his autobiography, *A Classical Education*, Richard Cobb describes his sudden involvement with a school friend who became a notorious axe-murderer

"the New Zealand historian Ronald Syme": Sir Ronald Syme O.M. was part of the "Oxford New Zealand mafia" (see *Dance of the Peacocks*, pp 363-4)

"ex-partisans": In the war Garrone was exiled to Sardinia. He belonged to an anti-fascist group of liberal scholar-historians, as did Franco Venturi. Costello knew Venturi in Moscow

"Paddy cast a spell": Shirley Tunnicliffe, telephone conversation April 1999

"An NZSIS statement": The official New Zealand security position vis à vis Costello appears, at least in relation to the passport affair, curiously one-sided. This may be because much of the NZSIS material on the Krogers is of British origin and cannot, the Service says, be disclosed. In July 2003 the Director of Security, NZSIS, Richard Woods, kindly granted me a briefing with one of his staff to discuss the passport matter. The briefing followed a request of mine in 2001 to the Prime Minister, Helen Clark, for access to the Costello files held by the NZSIS; and subsequently, following the intervention of the Chief Ombudsman, Sir Brian Elwood, to the release by the Service in December 2002 of a quantity of press cuttings and 54 pages of declassified documents pre-1952 of New Zealand origin related to Costello. The documents were from NZ Police Special Branch files and the records of the wartime Security Intelligence Bureau (SIB) which was under police control in its latter years.

At the request of the Chief Ombudsman, the Service issued the following statement: "Some of the material released refers to links between Costello and the intelligence service of the USSR. That such a relationship existed is substantiated by other records held by the NZSIS which are unable to be released at this stage.

"After his death a summation was offered by a New Zealander who had known him well. Interviewed in 1968, in the context of Service enquiries into Costello, he described him as 'a dedicated and ruthless communist, determined to out-do his Ukrainian Jewish wife in her intellectual toughness as a communist'.

"In so far as the issue of passports to the Krogers is concerned, an investigation was conducted both in New Zealand and overseas; the result was inconclusive."

The investigation referred to was conducted by Brigadier Sir William Gilbert, a former head of the Service, in 1961. In a statement published in the *New Zealand Herald* in 1981, Brigadier Gilbert dismissed the journalist Chapman Pincher's allegations, saying, "Pincher's account that Costello was responsible for the issue of passports is incorrect, as Costello had no direct part in that affair. The real story of how these passports came to be issued has never been determined."

In February 2006 in an effort to resolve the impasse, I wrote to the Service asking about the fate of the original consular papers from the New Zealand Legation in Paris. These documents were sent in 1961 to British Special Branch in London for the Krogers' trial and subsequently, according to papers held by the NZ Ministry of Foreign Affairs and Trade, returned to New Zealand. They could not be found in the files of Ministry nor were they held by Archives NZ, I was told. Did the Service hold them? I asked. I received the following reply: "Among archives relating to the Kroger case held by the NZSIS is a file of documents identified as the 'original Internal Affairs Department file'. This file, classified secret, includes papers originated by the Department of External Affairs and the Prime Minister's Department, as well as the Department of Internal Affairs. This material was used in the Service's investigation into the Kroger case."

THE PASSPORT AFFAIR

page 249

"In April 1954 a letter": chapter based on documents released by Ministry of Foreign Affairs & Trade, Wellington, in 2003 & 2004, and on declassified NZSIS files. Forty-one pages of the latter relate to the passport affair and include Peter Kroger's letters to Paris, made available in April 2007

"the Austrian resort town of Semmering": Semmering, a mountain resort frequented by the aristocracy

page 250

"The consular Register": Archives NZ, ABHS series 950, W4627 32/2/26 pt 1, box 1092

"requesting certificates of identification": i.e., birth & marriage certificates. The New Zealand journalist Mervyn Cull says that in the 1960s he stumbled on "the owner of the genuine birth certificate bearing the number of the forgery which one of the Cohens [Krogers] carried. The SIS traced the original to the vault of an insurance company. It was attached to an insurance policy" (letter to author, 23 May 2006)

page 251

"in a clear and beautiful voice": Rebecca West, *The Meaning of Treason*, page 328

"his hair winding": ibid, page 327

"it was one of": ibid, page 322

"It was Helen Kroger who brought": Andrew & Mitrokhin, *The Mitrokhin Archive*, page 174

page 252

"given long prison sentences": The Krogers were given twenty years but were released after eight years in an exchange for Gerald Brooke, a British lecturer imprisoned by the Russians for allegedly distributing subversive literature in the USSR

"could have been used": Secretary Internal Affairs to McIntosh, 4 May 1961. Ministry Foreign Affairs & Trade, Prime Minister's Dept, File 32/2/3/11, Mr & Mrs P.J. Kroger

"It was obvious": Ian Stewart, Paris, to McIntosh, 8 February 1961. Stewart, acting-Chargé in Paris, examined the consular papers before sending them to London for the Krogers' trial in March 1961. In the event, the papers were not produced at the trial.

Journalists were buzzing about the Paris legation "like flies", Stewart reported, "dreaming of a scoop by unearthing the European end of a UK spy ring."

The New Zealand passports were discovered by British police when they raided the bungalow in Cranley Drive, Ruislip, where the Krogers were living. Two such high-profile Russian spies could not have wished for better cover. In the interim between 1954 and their arrest in 1961 they had used the passports travelling from Ruislip to Switzerland, Germany, Austria, Italy, Hong Kong, Bombay and Calcutta. The passports were found in their bungalow tucked behind hundreds of books and a family Bible containing extracts from transmitter signals.

The trial itself, following the confession of the British atomic spy, Klaus Fuchs, and the defection of Burgess and Maclean in the early 1950s, gave rise to a storm of indignation in Parliament and the press about failures in British security.

In America Morris and Lona Cohen (not yet become Kroger) had belonged to the Rosenberg ring, which passed details of the first atomic bomb to the Russians, saving Soviet scientists an estimated eighteen months in the nuclear arms race against the Americans. After the Cohens disappeared from New York in 1950, tipped off on the day that Ethel and Julius Rosenberg were arrested, the Cohens were not heard of again until they surfaced by letter under the Kroger alias in Paris in 1954.

It is a profound irony that Costello's reputation should have been destroyed by this couple — they, who helped the Soviets develop their own weapon, thus hastening the start of the Cold War; he, the diplomat who blew the whistle on the Russians, announcing Soviet possession of the bomb, in a vain effort to forestall it

"writing this in a national newspaper": *New Zealand Herald*, 29 Aug 1981, reviewing Pincher's book, *Their Trade is Treachery.* Brigadier Gilbert directed the NZSIS from 1957-1976

page 253

"might have been recruited": *Their Trade is Treachery*, page 139

"in another book": *Too Secret Too Long*

"The charge is false": Costello's accusers might have advanced, as motivation for his allegedly "providing passports", the potentially damaging argument that in helping the two atomic spies he was seeking to correct the American nuclear monopoly over Russia. Surprisingly, the balance-of-terror theory was never invoked. The theory in any case would have been false. In February 1950 Costello wrote to Doug and Ruth Lake, "I have an idea that the Russians, reluctantly, may be putting more of their resources into armaments, including atomic, than they were doing a year ago. Which, if true, is very sad"

"Papers dating from": Two files dealing with the issuing of New

Zealand passports to Morris and Lona Cohen in the names of Helen and Peter Kroger are held by the Ministry of Foreign Affairs and Trade in Wellington (Prime Minister's Dept., B23/498 and 32/2/3/11, Mr & Mrs P.J. Kroger). They are dated January to June 1961, embracing the period of the Krogers' trial at the Old Bailey (February-March 1961), and contain correspondence between the New Zealand Embassy in Paris and External Affairs, Wellington; between Paris and Special Branch, New Scotland Yard, London; and between the New Zealand High Commission in London and External Affairs, Wellington. Included is a report by the acting-Chargé in Paris, Ian Stewart, saying that he examined the consular papers before sending them to the security authorities in London for the trial. It is not clear from the Ministry files if these papers of Paris origin which included the original passport application forms were ever returned to New Zealand, as requested. The passports themselves are retained and zealously guarded by Scotland Yard's Black Museum in London.

Recommendations by the Ministry in 1961 to tighten the procedure for the issuing of New Zealand passports have since been adopted by the New Zealand government, though not, in the light of the Kroger case, as fully as one might expect. A loophole regarding identification by a witness, which helped the Krogers to escape detection in 1954, remains to this day.

SICILIAN VESPERS

page 254

"The letter of resignation": letter, 24 Sept 1982

"Roasting hot": postcard, 25 May 1954

FROM THE LETTERS 1950-1955

page 257

2 Dec 1951

"That puts me even": Davin had a fourth daughter, Patty, born to his wartime lover, Elisabeth Berndt, in Palestine in 1943. In 1946, after the war ended, mother and child were stranded in Palestine without money or papers. Winnie Davin paid for them to come to England and adopted them into her home in Oxford where Patty, recognisably Davinish, was brought up initially as one of the family (see *Dance of the Peacocks*, pp 338-9; and *A Fighting Withdrawal)*

"IT WAS ALL VERY BRITISH"

page 260

"They had no notion": Laking interview, April 2004

"*Whatever it is*": Costello to Davin, 27 Dec 1954

page 261

"the trouble began in 1945": Michael King to Davin, 24 Sept 1982

"The American Ambassador": Robert M. Scotten of Michigan, Ambassador to New Zealand from 1948-1955 in the Truman and Eisenhower administrations, "gave an unusual twist to his responsibility of keeping in close touch with the New Zealand government by having his residence at 'Fernside', in the Wairarapa" (Tom Larkin to author, 20 Oct 2004)

"You never knew": Laking interview, April 2004

"Not until": Michael King, page 428; McNeish, pp 390-1. In his biography of Walter Nash, Keith Sinclair refers (page 342) to secret condemnations from "tittle-tattle collected by anonymous agents", but the emphasis is more on events outside New Zealand. At the time, Sinclair possessed some telling information about what was happening in Wellington from an anonymous article which had appeared in the *New Zealand Listener* in 1974. The article was written by R.M. Campbell, former chairman of the Public Service Commission. Sinclair consigned the information to a note at the back

page 262

"About a dozen": Michael King to author, 19 Oct 2003

"an incautious remark": According to Tom Larkin (interview April 1999), Collins was harassed by SIS men ringing him up in the night, abusing him for his left-wing sympathies.

On resigning, Collins went back to his old law firm. Some years later in the Holyoake-Marshall era, when George Laking was deputy-Secretary of External Affairs, Laking says he received a call from John Marshall in the course of a Cabinet meeting. "Marshall sent me a message saying, 'Cabinet is considering Dick Collins for a judicial appointment. But wasn't there something in his background . . . ?' You see, this is ten or twenty years later. They had remembered. I had to look into it. Result, Dick Collins wasn't appointed. All because of an incautious remark. Dick would have made a High Court judge, not a doubt about it." (interview Wellington, April 2004)

Tom Larkin himself, an addict of the Vegetable Club, counts himself lucky. "McIntosh said to me one day, 'I hear you like cheap vegetables.' I said, yes. He said, 'Buy them somewhere else.' Mac, I concluded, was warning me that there was an informer in the club planted by SIS"

"the effect on McIntosh's department": "We are faced with an appalling staff situation," McIntosh wrote to Frank Corner on 27 July 1954 (*Unofficial Channels*, page 169)

"Ten years later": In 1965 at a meeting of Commonwealth Prime Ministers in London, a ballot was taken to elect the first Secretary-General of a renewed and modernised Commonwealth. The man tipped for the job, a post that would have crowned a lifetime of public service, was Alister McIntosh. McIntosh was the front-runner ahead of a gifted Canadian diplomat, Arnold Smith. In the run-up to the ballot the British had shown signs of sulking and, as described by Smith in his book, *Stitches in Time*, put up as their candidate a retired colonial governor no one had heard of. The day before the ballot, McIntosh went to Arnold Smith at his hotel and told him that on health grounds — McIntosh said he was becoming increasingly deaf — he had decided to withdraw his nomination. He had asked his supporters, McIntosh said, to go over to Smith.

Arnold Smith was elected Secretary-General by a handsome margin.

It is true that in 1965 McIntosh's hearing was declining, but this was an excuse. The reason for his withdrawal lay elsewhere. There were two possible causes. One was a raid by British police on a gay bar in Singapore 15 years earlier.

In January 1950, on his way back to New Zealand from a conference in Colombo, McIntosh had been seen in a compromising situation. According to Michael King (letter to author, 7 Jan 2002), shortly before the heads of government were due to vote at

Marlborough House in London in 1965, the New Zealand Prime Minister, Keith Holyoake, "was approached by MI5 and prevailed upon to withdraw McIntosh's nomination". Holyoake appears to have succumbed, accepting without protest that his own man was a security risk on the grounds of his homosexuality — "that glorious indiscretion", as McIntosh once called it.

(With breathtaking candour McIntosh himself referred to the incident, in a letter to Carl Berendsen on his return from the Colombo trip, saying "shame prevents me from describing what happened" — *Undiplomatic Dialogue*, page 204.)

The other possible cause had to do with the Suez crisis and the theory that in spiking McIntosh the British establishment, of long memory, was moved by a spirit of revenge. At the time of the Suez crisis in 1956, the NZ External Affairs Liaison Officer at the High Commission in London was a stormy petrel named Frank Corner. Corner — a future NZ Foreign Secretary — was McIntosh's man, one of his brightest and earliest recruits. He had been "in at the creation". In London Corner's status accredited him to the British Cabinet Offices, where he had a suite of rooms; he sent coded messages to New Zealand, telling McIntosh and the government ahead of the Middle East invasion what Anthony Eden, the British Prime Minister, and the French, were secretly planning.

"In the middle of the operation," Frank Corner says, "it became clear to me that the Foreign Office man advising Eden was intercepting and reading my messages. This man later went to the UN and there, when we met, he was aloof. He spread poison about me in New York."

Frank Corner was not forgiven by the British, nor it seems was the record of his independent-minded boss forgotten. Alister McIntosh's anti-Suez record had earned him a black mark. When it came to the Commonwealth Secretariat, the British, according to Corner, "used the pretext of Mac's homosexuality as a means of knocking him. They were determined not to have him at Marlborough House" (interview, Wellington, Oct 2000; telephone conversation, June 2007)

"the case of Douglas Lake": Lake lost his job with External Affairs on suspicion of being a communist and a security risk after his wife,

Ruth, published a 30-page pamphlet printed and distributed by the NZ Society for Closer Relations with the USSR. The pamphlet (1950) was a reply to a series of newspaper articles critical of the Soviet Union by Jean Boswell, the wife of the former NZ Minister in Moscow, Charles Boswell. In March 1950, in an attempt to save a promising officer's career, McIntosh wrote to Ruth begging her to desist — in vain. The Boswell articles were liverish and one-sided; equally in the current climate Ruth Lake's pro-Soviet pamphlet was a folly. Lake himself supported his wife's decision to publish, saying afterwards, "I had too much respect for her as an individual to attempt to over-rule her."

Doug Lake was first transferred to "the grocery trade", the section of foreign affairs dealing with aid to Third World countries, then he resigned; with McIntosh's help, he joined the Press Association as a journalist; finally in 1962 he took his wife and family to communist China, saying, "They got rid of me without any reason. Now I'll give them a reason." In Beijing Doug and Ruth Lake worked as language polishers. Lake's resignation in 1954 coincided with the Petrov affair in Australia, which added a spurious twist to the cloak-and-dagger atmosphere in McIntosh's department: the Russian defector claimed before a Royal Commission in Canberra that there was a spy in the Prime Minister's department in New Zealand. On return to Wellington from China, Lake found jobs in journalism and the government closed to him. He went to work as a storeman.

Doug Lake's resignation was an embarrassment for the Holland government in the 1950s — his brother, Harry, was a National MP. But it did not affect his career. Harry Lake became Minister of Finance (1960-7) in the Holyoake Ministry

page 263

"that he was a Russian agent": Apparently the view of the British and New Zealand security authorities today. The NZSIS statement cited on pages 367-8 alleges links between Costello and the Russian secret police, a relationship substantiated it says "by other records" it holds (i.e. British records). It seems that these records cannot amount to much or Costello would have been arrested and charged, or at the very least questioned. But Costello was never questioned or interrogated. British suspicions have to be put in the context of the times. Just as Isaiah Berlin, visiting Anna Akhmatova in Leningrad in

1945, was assumed to be a British spy by the Soviet authorities who then began to persecute Akhmatova and, tragically, Akhmatova's family, so Costello, who appeared to have special entrée to the homes of Russian writers and artists in Moscow, seems to have put the British authorities on red alert. In Moscow Costello, with his lack of instinct for self-preservation, *invited* British suspicions and surveillance. As a Russian-speaking diplomat with a lively interest in Soviet affairs, he would have been approached by Soviet Intelligence as a matter of course, because of his cultural contacts, and automatically given a codename. Certainly as a result of his occasional bingeing and diplomatic lapses he would have been viewed as interesting recruitment material (but more likely, on the same count, as a liability). Had Costello been recruited as an agent one might have expected him to benefit materially and his lifestyle to take a financial lift, or series of lifts. This did not happen.

In 1947 British security officers inspecting the NZ Legation premises in Moscow found that a needle-thin hole had been bored through the stem of the handle of the office safe containing the legation cipher book and its one-time cipher pads (Doug Lake to John Scott, 6 Mar 1991). The Russians, it was concluded, had taken away the pads and copied them. Had Costello been acting for the Russians, it seems strange that they would have needed to do this.

Costello's situation brings to mind Jeremy Wolfenden, the brilliant Russian-speaking Englishman who became entrapped by a combination of alcohol and political intrigue, and died in Washington in 1965 at the age of thirty-one. See Sebastian Faulks, *The Fatal Englishman* (1996)

"Needless to say": to Jean McKenzie, 11 Oct 1954

"And is quite clear": ibid, 20 Oct 1954

"These months of unemployment": Costello to Davin, 10 March 1955

"He was not relaxed": Foote interview, Oxford, 22 March 2005

page 264

"how little I know": Costello to Davin, 22 Oct 1952

"all the way to our flat": Margaret Bartlett to author, 19 Feb 2007

"an enthusiast in New Zealand": Guy Morris, who wrote to Costello from Auckland early in 1947. Costello sought *The Collected*

Mansfield Stories in vain; as consolation he sent to Morris a reader for Russian students containing four stories by Katherine Mansfield (Morris Papers, Turnbull Library)

page 265

"my Viceroy razor": Costello to Bil, 19 Jan 1942

"my 26,000-word epic": ibid, 9 March 1943

"If this campaign": ibid, 12 Dec 1942

"If ever I were able": Costello to Davin, from Manchester, 19 Aug 1958. Nick Costello writes, speaking of Manchester: "We didn't have a car. I remember asking my father why couldn't we have a Jaguar, his favourite car? And he replying that he had enough money in the bank to buy one but that we wouldn't be able to buy all the books we wanted, and books were more important" (to author, 28 April 2006)

page 266

"He'd read so widely": Waller interview, Cambridge, April 2005

"Paddy has the Russian chair": Davin Papers (McCulloch corres.)

"In those days": Waller interview, Cambridge, April 2005

"*Starost ne radost*": Josie to author, 12 April 2006

"a series of battles": Costello journal, 23 Jan 1947

page 267

"he had borrowed": Costello to Davin, 13 March 1956. The over-generous Jean McKenzie "has earned lots but squandered it on her friends," he wrote. "A cher collegue to whom she lent 500 quid has been booted out. She'll never see that money again"

"Margaret Lawlor recalls": to author, 19 Feb 2007

PART FIVE

"A SOVIET SATELLITE GOING BY"

page 271

"I gave a lecture": Costello to Davin, 9 June 1956

"Frightfully busy": ibid, 14 Oct 1955

page 272

"and quoting passages": Katie Costello to author, 26 Jan 2006

"Nick Costello 'remembers'": Nick to author, 28 April 2006

"When it was time": Mick Costello to author, 27 Feb 2007

page 273

"You had people coming out": Nicholson interview, Oxford, May 2005

"There were not many foreigners": telephone conversation, Manchester, Jan 2005

"by the sheer brightness": Michael Frayn, *Secret Classrooms*, page 141

page 274

"Those students who registered": Waller interview, April 2005

"The story is": memorandum from John Elsworth (prof. Russian, Manchester, 1987-2004), to Malcolm Jones, Nottingham, 17 Aug 2004. "Trofimov stayed until about 1941. The chair was refilled in 1947 by a man called Dobryn [and then lapsed until 1955 when Costello came]"

"I never took any notes": telephone conversation, Jan 2005

"Do you know the Owens Campus?": Nicholson interview, Oxford, May 2005

page 275

"*Khadzhi Murat*": Translated as *Hadji Murat: A Tale of the Caucasus* (London 1962). A novella, and one of Tolstoy's last works. Here once again (see "Postscript") one senses Costello's preoccupation with early and violent death. Hadji Murat, a famous Caucasian brigand, died fighting, hacked to death by Russian Cossacks

"an oddity in the system": Dr John Sullivan of St Andrews University, a Costello student from 1956-1960, writes: "I suppose that view was created from the very first day I set foot in the Department when we were all informed that Professor Costello would not be lecturing that week (it turned out that he had gone off to London to see the Bolshoi Ballet on what was perhaps their first visit to the UK)" (Sullivan to author, 18 April 2007)

"The image of a man": Waller interview, April 2005

"a faint smile perhaps": journal, 27 Aug 1943

page 276

"the difference between the socialists": journal, 28 July 1954

"They may not have Utopia": Costello to Davin, 2 Sept 1949

"I remember a discussion": Josie interview, London, April 2000

page 277

"Paddy was quite negative": Mick Costello interview, Kent, Sept 1999

"There's nothing worse": Waller interview, April 2005

"once told an acquaintance": Michael Straight – see *After Long Silence*, page 234

page 278

"never subordinated scholarship": Unlike the historian James Klugmann, one of the "heroic" figures of 1930s university communism. At Cambridge the genial Klugmann wielded a Socratic power over many undergraduates, and influenced Costello. It was possibly he who financed Costello's 1937 mission to India.

During the war Klugmann became one of the key figures in British relations with Tito's partisans in Yugoslavia; he returned to England singing the Serb hero's praises, Tito's enthusiastic supporter. After Stalin's break with Tito in 1948, Klugmann published an insincere book, *From Trotsky to Tito* (1951), almost certainly at the instigation of the Kremlin, lambasting the Yugoslav leader. According to Mick Costello, when Paddy Costello was appointed to Manchester, Klugmann came to see him but was rejected. "Paddy broke with Klugmann. He had proved himself to be intellectually dishonest"

"he told Josie, 'what I want'": Josie interview, April 2005

A BLACK EYE IN OXFORD

page 279

"People had a higher tolerance": telephone conversation, France, May 2005

"the word brilliant": "His intellectual brilliance has not been surpassed among his colleagues then or since" (Malcolm Templeton, *Top Hats Are Not Being Taken*, page 24); "Our most brilliant linguist and diplomatic officer" (McIntosh, *Unofficial Channels*, page 37); "Beyond all doubt, the most brilliant linguist New Zealand has produced" (Alex McDonald, obituary)

"he spoke nine or ten languages": Besides English, Costello spoke and/or wrote fluently (in) French, Italian, German, Latin, Greek, Hebrew, Russian, Irish and Persian. He derided his attempts to learn

Arabic and Sanskrit, but he probably had a working knowledge of Arabic as well as old Church Slavonic, old Russian and Yiddish

page 280

"It took him a year": Not everyone agrees. Lawrence Nathan wrote, "I had a French mother and spent a year in Germany after the war. Paddy had no background in languages, but he spoke the ones I knew far better than I and countless others, and a new one was child's play to him" (to Davin, 19 Oct 1982)

"Costello's interest in Persian": "I am a terrible person for getting enthusiasms which I cannot possibly find time to pursue to the end," he wrote to Bil on 20 February 1943. "Take my Sanskrit episode. Who else after a visit to Dartington Hall [1935, Michael Straight's home in Devon] to see Uday Shankar, would have bought a Sanskrit grammar and got as far as reading part of the Mahabharata? I know as little Sanskrit now as I know Hebrew, Irish or Arabic, all languages which a foolish interest in foreign cultures led me to undertake." However, Costello's helter-skelter enthusiasms were not as romantic or foolish as he thought. His 1935 foray into Sanskrit would help him unlock the mystery of Persian and lead to his translation and publication of *The Blind Owl*

"I got the impression": Costello to Davin, 25 April 1956

"Why was I drawn to it?": ibid

page 281

"It may or may not come out": Robert Byron, *The Road to Oxonia* (1937)

"evoking a whole picture": Introduction to *The Oxford Book of Russian Verse* (1948 edn). Baring quotes the line, "*And the sea where the ships were scudding*"; and compares the English poet Tennyson, praised for the line, "*And white ships flying on a yellow sea*". But, as Baring says, "In Tennyson's line there are two epithets"

"would not be wasted": Costello to Bil, 10 Oct 1942

"a signpost": What distinguished Marxist scholarship, Costello wrote in his journal in 1947, "is that it shows the facts in relation to one another, not in isolation. One fact explains another; and is a signpost to another, which in turn points to another, so that one gets a curve, which may be prolonged into the future. A Marxist study of any problem is a rounded thing, a complex like a syllogism: A = B; B = C; A = C"

page 282

"a three-way radio discussion": BBC Home Service, 31 Oct 1957. Davin called Cassino, "the hinge battle of the battle for Italy"

"likened to an affair": Ovenden, *A Fighting Withdrawal*, page 155. Geoffrey Cox noted that Costello and Davin shared similarities of background, strength of mind, relish in language, and alcohol. He likened them to blood brothers. "What did they argue about? Everything. Plato, sex, religion, God, though they were both lapsed Catholics, politics. This was part of the attraction for Dan, Paddy's complete conviction in a political faith at a time when political faith mattered. He knew exactly where he was going. He wasn't floundering around like the rest of us." (Coln St Dennis interviews, Glos, July & Oct 1999) Cox added, "This was what Bella [Bil] had given Paddy. She'd provided him with a kind of certainty"

"I have an open invitation": Costello to Davin, from Paris, 22 April 1955

"He always cheers": Delia Davin to author, 20 Feb 2007

page 283

"He and Paddy drank whisky": interview, London, 21 April 2005

"I think Winnie resented": interview, London, March 2005

"Costello seemed to come off worse": Tom Larkin recalls meeting Costello at a conference in London in 1948. "He came to dinner at the Savoy where Peter Fraser was staying, with a hefty bruise under his left eye. I said, 'How'd you get that, Paddy?' He said, 'Oh. A night out with Dan'"

"Winnie got clipped": Anna Davin interview, May 2005

page 284

"My mother's version": to author, 20 Feb 2007

"Bil felt Dan came the closest": interviews London, Aug 1999 and March 2005. Anna Davin, social historian and author of *Growing Up Poor*, says she got on with Bil better than the others. "Bil grew up in Spitalfields where I lived from 1970 to 1975 with Ralph Samuels, the historian. He was from a communist Jewish family. Bil lived in a street in Bethnal Green I knew very well. It was everyone's ambition to better themselves. Her parents' move to Hackney, moving north, was a betterment.

"Bil said that if she ever wrote an autobiography, she would call it, *Where have all the bugs gone?"* (The area was rebuilt in the post-war era of municipal socialism, the maze of streets Bil had grown up in and walked along to school now just names on a map)

"a dysfunctional family": A visitor to the Costello house in Manchester in 1969, the New Zealand ophthalmologist David Murdoch, was invited by Bil to "borscht and tea, served in handsome Russian glasses in silver holders". In letters home, Murdoch described a rambling house with Czech lodgers living in rented rooms and echoing with Slavonic tongues. He gave a series of lively vignettes: Bil, not so well off, tutoring in Russian at the university; Nick, 12 or 13, home from prep school and smart as paint ("Nicky is a Maoist with pictures of Mao all over his room"); Kit, 17, just finishing at Shrewsbury; Katie, back from Moscow where she had been re-learning Russian; and Katie's 14-year-old niece, Susie, who had earlier run off to London and been brought back by Bil, "whom we took to a pub in Manchester where she was attending an Anarchist meeting". David Murdoch, whose father was at Auckland Grammar School with Paddy Costello in the 1920s, was then a post-graduate student at the Manchester Royal Eye Hospital (correspondence with author, 2004-5)

"Alone, and sober": Davin diary, 26 Feb 1944

"glamorous raffishness": *A Fighting Withdrawal*, page 250

page 285

"Paddy came sometimes": Brigid Sandford Smith interview, April 2005

"People were more tolerant": telephone conversation, May 2005

"Elsewhere I have written": *Dance of the Peacocks*, page 351

"a private nonsense language": Delia Davin interview, Oct 1999

page 286

"Once he sent me back": Mick Costello interview, Cambridge, April 2005

"My days of playing squash": Costello to Davin, 21 Oct 1960

"He wasn't a great smiler": A late vignette from a student in Costello's honours classes in the early 1960s, Kate Clark, has "the Professor" striding along corridors, a distant academic figure, "his black gown billowing out behind him, his jaw jutting forward. He had steely eyes, which seemed to communicate that he didn't suffer fools gladly, yet when he *did* smile he radiated an immediate and surprising warmth.

"Lectures were never dry. The Professor would break off into asides on history, philosophy and the arts. Occasionally he would make some witty comment or relate an anecdote, and that amazing smile of his would light up the whole auditorium" (Kate Clark, London, to author, 10 May 2007)

DINNER WITH THE FREYBERGS

page 287

"deep misgivings": Christopher Bennetts (retired NZSIS officer) to author, 24 Oct 2006

page 288

"Binge drinkers tend": Lishman interview, Kent, May 2005

page 289

"I remember nothing": journal, 10 Oct 1943

"dancing a gopak": John Sullivan, St Andrews, to author, 18 April 2007. A gopak is a spirited Ukrainian dance

"According to his daughter": Deirdre Airey interview, Coromandel, Oct 1998

"So Paddy got him drunk": interview, London, March 2005

page 290

"It was a remarkable occasion": to McIntosh, 7 March 1946

page 297

"recorded by Margot Ross": Margot Ross in Wilson, *Intimate Stranger*, page 65

"to plan a companion volume": among other candidates for inclusion were Kenneth Sisam, Howard Kippenberger, Ronald Syme and Christopher Hill

"I don't want to write": Davin to Bil Costello, 6 Sept 1981

page 292

"Keith Ovenden is convinced": *A Fighting Withdrawal*, page 364 and passim

"revisiting old haunts": Christian to author, 29 April 2006

page 293

"would jump at your translation": Davin to Costello, 27 June 1947

"Again and again": letter, 18 Sept 1958, sent to James Bertram, for

Charles Brasch

"long known to Costello": Hayward was at the British Embassy when Costello came to the NZ Legation. They met and corresponded and, later in England, reviewed examination candidates together

page 294

"a demolition job": Christian to author, 14 March 2007

TIME'S THIEF

page 295

"I wish, how I wish": journal, 15 Feb 1947

"His mind was": letter from Cairo, 5 July 1941

"his essay on *Doctor Zhivago*": The essay, "Zhivago Reconsidered", appeared in the January 1968 edition of the journal, *Forum for Modern Language Studies,* published by the University of St Andrews. The edition, devoted to the Russian novel, was edited by Prof. Christian

page 296

"in 1962 he was invited": *The Oxford Russian-English Dictionary*, by Marcus Wheeler, "with the assistance of D.P. Costello & W.F. Ryan", appeared in 1972 (repub. 1984). Both Wheeler and the general editor, Boris Unbegaun, paid tribute to Costello's part, noting that the whole Dictionary benefited from his criticism and suggestions. Costello at the time of his death had worked through almost half the MS draft

"a proposed new Russian Grammar": According to his New Zealand friend, Alex McDonald, of Clare College, Cambridge, when he died Costello "had just begun work on what would have been the definitive Russian Grammar" (obituary, Davin Papers 5079-426). McDonald may have been referring to an expanded edition of the old Forbes's *Russian Grammar* of the 1920s which eventually appeared in 1980, revised by Prof. Dumbreck of Manchester whom Costello in 1958 recommended to OUP for the job (Martin Maw, archivist OUP, to author, 9 March 2007)

"another dictionary — of etymology": C.T. Onions, *The Oxford Dictionary of English Etymology*

"invited by Penguin Books": Richard Newnham, Penguin Books, to Costello, 30 July 1962

"Good soldiers think of killing": He probably began on the novel in

Paris in 1954. Some twenty hand-written pages survive

page 297

"S'right. Too difficult": Josie interview, Manchester, April 2005

"Those standards were inculcated": interview London, May 2005

page 298

"I remember your reproving me": Costello to Davin, 21 June 1958

page 299

"This undoubtedly contributed": Freeborn to author, 14 Sept 1999

"He was 'so skinny'": Costello to Davin, 19 Aug 1958

"We stayed at Kilmurvey House": Christopher Costello to author, 6 April 2005. Christopher thought it strange for people to live on an island surrounded by water and not eat fresh fish. He and his father were perhaps the only fishermen among the guests. In 1962 there were still turf fires on the island (the turf coming from the mainland on sailing boats), no running water at Kilmurvey House, nor electricity — "so candles to light our way to bed. A few cars on the island, but the main means of transport was the bicycle and the horse." The spirit of the place is captured in a classic documentary film by Robert Flaherty, *Man of Aran* (1934)

page 300

"wrapped and blinded": Synge, *The Aran Islands*

"piles of seaweed": In fact, they are piles of rough vegetation growing between the rocks

"I remember thinking": Katie Costello interview, May 2005

"As we came out into the bay": Synge, *The Aran Islands*

"Oh, do you know Paddy Costello?": Dr Martin Prior, London, telephone conversation 9 Nov 2005

page 301

"I need a holiday": to Reginald Christian, 22 Aug 1963

"I explained my dilemma": Nicholson to author, 26 Jan 2005

page 302

"*Write to Kharkov*": A number of people — Richard Peace of Bristol and John Sullivan of St Andrews are two — say that they received letters (in Sullivan's case a testimonial) from Costello, written on the day he died

"My mother woke me": Katie Costello interview, Aug 1999

page 303

"I recall my father teaching me": Nick Costello to author, 28 April 2006

POSTSCRIPT

page 305

"Bil's grief": Barbara Lerner, Bil's sister-in-law, says: "One of the things Bil talked to me about was the night Paddy died. He got up and walked around, she said. He must have been agitated. He had this pain. He must have thought it was indigestion. He got agitated, and walked about. Worst thing he could have done" (Hertford, conversation 22 April 2005)

"She kept his name in the directory": And revived it in other ways. Nick Costello relates: "One of her grandchildren — Josie's son, Patrick — once remarked to me that family Christmases were more like Easter as he grew up, since the purpose and theme was the resurrection of Paddy Costello" (Nick to author, 11 Mar 2007)

page 306

"Bil met me at the station": to author, 4 July 2005. "Nobody told me my father had died. I wasn't able to go to the funeral"

"Martha telephoned": McCullough to Davin, 9 Oct 1984. Martha McCulloch and Inez Hill were friends of the Davins. Inez Hill was the ex-wife of the Oxford socialist Christopher Hill, Fellow of All Souls and later Master of Balliol

"Dan came home": *A Fighting Withdrawal*, page 320. Davin told Michael King in 1982 that he wrote the obituary in an hour

"There are no papers": Trinity College has almost no tutorial records of its undergraduates until after the end of the Second World War, according to the Wren Library archivist, Jonathan Smith. Costello's tutor, Andrew Gow, was not noted for personal relationships or keeping notes about his students for the college records. As William Whewell, a nineteenth-century Master of Trinity famously said: "The relationship between the institution and the tutor is similar to that between the institution and its baker"

"for all the conviviality": Ovenden, *A Fighting Withdrawal*, pp 320-1, 364-6

page 307

"it derives at third-hand": Chapman Pincher, Berkshire, telephone conversations 24 April & 22 May 2005. "Everything I wrote about Costello came from Peter Wright. I remember what he told me was of no great significance to him at the time"

"The reason MI5/MI6 'got' Blunt": Knightley to author, 19 Feb 2007

page 308

"A little story": Mick Costello interview, Sept 1999

"till the economic downturn": to author, 10 April 2007

page 309

"Bil made me a nice lunch": interview Warsaw, Sept 1999

"the most disturbing and consoling element": Costello to Bil, 26 July 1943

"Her command of English idiom": "I find it useful when translating," he wrote to Paul Foote (19 July 1962) "to appeal to someone else, in my case my wife, for an opinion on whether a phrase or a sentence sounds like natural English. Someone who has not been drenched in Russian is often a better judge"

"completed translating the Kushchevsky novel": *Nikolai Negorev, or The Successful Russian*, translated by D.P. & B. Costello (Calder & Boyars, London 1967)

"the Murder of Rasputin": V.M. Purishkevich, *The Murder of Rasputin: A First-Hand Account from the Diary of One of Rasputin's Murderers*, translated by Bella Costello (Ardis, Ann Arbor, 1985). Bil had previously translated Gogol's *The Marriage*

Acknowledgements

I AM INDEBTED to many people.

I owe, first, years of thanks to Margaret Calder and Philip Rainer at the Alexander Turnbull Library in Wellington, besides David Colquhoun and his staff in the manuscripts room; together with Roger Swanson and his research staff in the National Library, they have answered queries and provided help and services in countless ways. Malcolm Templeton, James Kember and John Mills kindly provided access to files at the Ministry of Foreign Affairs and Trade.

I have benefited from the advice of former New Zealand senior diplomats and civil servants who have helped to revive the towering, enigmatic figure of Sir Alister McIntosh, in particular Sir George Laking, Frank Corner, Tom Larkin and Gerald Hensley. Their insights have been invaluable. I have troubled Frank Corner, his wife Lyn and Tom Larkin on several occasions. Without their recollections, the 1946 Conference of Paris would have remained a dull affair.

At an early stage Paul Foote in Oxford and Douglas Zohrab in New Zealand began to guide my Russian researches. I owe them a great deal, as I do a group of others, beginning with my daughter-in-law, Caroline McNeish — whose spontaneous aid led to the archivist at the University of Exeter, Charlotte Berry, finding the documents which solved the puzzle of Costello's dismissal in 1940 — David Harvey, Professor Janet Wilson and Professor Ron Tamplin.

Three contemporaries of Paddy Costello have answered innumerable queries: emeritus professors Victor Kiernan and Reginald Christian in Scotland and Eric Hobsbawm in London. I am truly grateful. A number of people have read draft sections of the typescript and made valuable suggestions, among them Reginald Christian, Frank and Lyn Corner, Victor Kiernan, Sir George Laking, Alwyn Lishman, Denis McLean, Harry Shukman and Malcolm Templeton.

I thank Professor Jim Miller for help with translations from the Russian and also Sarah Lake, the Moscow-born daughter of Doug and Ruth Lake (née Macky), who brought me letters and other unpublished material which have enlivened the text. I thank Sarah especially for the Ethiopian ink.

In New Zealand connections multiplied. A chance meeting led to the environmental counsel, Rebecca Macky. One day Rebecca sent me an unpublished diary which had belonged to her great-uncle, Polly Macky, Costello's wartime commander in Greece. I had forgotten that I had been to school with her cousin Lloyd. Lloyd Macky, Polly Macky's son, dug up more documents. It seemed only fitting that I should end up tracing Costello and Colonel Macky's wartime escape route over the mountains of Thessaly in company with Rebecca Macky and her husband, David McGregor.

I owe thanks to Jack Leigh, who guided me through the streets of working-class Ponsonby where Paddy Costello grew up; to Costello's brother, Phil, who is still alive, as are nephews and nieces, two of whom, Terry Bishop and MaryRose Lithgow have provided photographs and reminiscences. I thank Sister Elizabeth Woods in Belfast who sent a stream of information about the emigration of the Woods family from Ireland to Melbourne and Auckland.

On Intelligence matters Phillip Knightley in London and Aaron Fox in New Zealand have been sources of enlightenment. They have the gift of offering advice that is without prejudice. I thank the historians Ian McGibbon and Chris Pugsley for keeping my military facts (and tanks) in order.

I owe thanks to the late Dan and Winnie Davin for first bringing Paddy Costello to my notice; to Brigid Sandford Smith (née Davin), Dan Davin's literary executor, Anna Davin, Professor Delia Davin and also Keith Ovenden, for reading parts of the text and making suggestions, often quite stern ones. I apologise for my waywardness and thank them for their integrity and patience amid busy schedules.

In Cambridge Malcolm Underwood, the archivist at St John's College, unearthed a file on Griff Maclaurin who seems to have been the first New Zealander to enlist against Franco in 1936. In Oxford, Ann Pasternak-Slater provided a welcome introduction to Yvgeny Pasternak in Moscow, Boris Pasternak's son and literary executor. It was a great pleasure in Moscow to be welcomed by the New Zealand Ambassador, Stuart Prior. Stuart and his staff took a personal interest in the project and made my stay rewarding and memorable.

Finally my heartfelt thanks to Bernard Brown, the law teacher and poet; to Michael Gifkins my agent; to Trudy Beatson for last-minute aid with the Notes and, for the index, Elaine Hall. Once again I have gained from having two editors, John Bright-Holmes in London and Harriet Allan at Random House in New Zealand, and I thank them for putting up with my eccentricities. I am truly grateful for their patience and professionalism.

My warm thanks to the others who have aided my travels, written letters of encouragement, sent photographs and given of their time and hospitality: Brian Abbott, Prof. Christopher Andrew, the late Dr Deirdre Airey, Neil Atkinson, Jim Baltaxe, the late Jean Bartlett, Margaret Lawlor-Bartlett & Peter Bartlett, Herbert & Ulrike Beck, Alexandra Barratt, Antony Beevor, Maureen & the late Prof. Michael Beresford, Murray Bloxham, Bronwyn Bolt, Roger Bowen, George Brandak, Faye Bunbury, Justin Cargill, Carolyn Carr, Diana Cavendish, Ann & George Cawkwell, Dr Ann Cawley, Diana Chardin, Brian Clapp, Helen Clark in Athens, Kate Clark, Peter Clayworth, Tony Cleghorn, Martin Collett, Richard Collins, Hon. Justice Cooper, Christine Costello, Emilie & Phil Costello, Walter Cook, Sir Geoffrey Cox, Rachel Cox, John Crawford, Don Croft, Mervyn Cull, Antonia Davin, Bronwyn Dalley, Rev. Brian Davis, Mark Derby, Alfred Dobbs, Peter Doyle, Dr Deane Drew, Robin Edmonds, Dr Ron Easthope, Brian Easton, Ann Elder, Vera Eyal, Joyce Fairgray, Hamish Finlay, Tui Flower, Dr Paul Foote, Ian Fraser, Nicola Frean, Yvonne Gallop, Giovanna Galante Garrone, Jonathan Galassi, the late Robert Gilmore, Prof. Douglas Gray, Phillip Green, Walter Guttery, Hilary Hale, the late Bryce Harland, Rod Hancox, Paul Harrison, Gerald Hensley, Seddon Hill, Clem Hollies, Prof. Ronald Hingley, Dr John Hood, Susan Johnston, Sara Joynes, Graham Kerr, Stephen Innes, Peter Ireland, Tom and Sarah Larkin, Barbara & Jack Lerner, Marion Lerner-Levine, Nat Lerner, Frances Levy, Dr Alwyn Lishman, Cliff Lord, John McArthur, Douglas MacDiarmid, Jim McIntosh, Gordon McLauchlan, Dr Campbell Maclaurin, Marie Maher, Natalie Mahoney, Brian Martin, Bronwyn Matthews, Keith Matthews, Jacqui Matthews, Michael Morrissey, Kiri Manuera, Natalie Marshall, Russell Marshall, Martin Maw, Prof. Jim Miller, David Murdoch, Michael Nicholson, Warwick Nicoll, Mervyn & Françoise Norrish, Bryan Nicolson, Michael O'Shaughnessy, Prof. Richard Overy, Paul Paton, the late Ray Perry, Dr Ian Prior, Martin Prior, Mary Prior, Donna Prince, Baruch Rosen, Peter Rider, Anthony Richards, Derek Round, John Scott, Dr Harold Shukman, Murray Sidey, A.P. Simm, Ian Stewart, Susan Skudder, Sir Graham Speight, Lisa Stephenson, Ian Stewart, Ray Stone, Dr John Sullivan, Helen Sunderland, Dr Sue Sutton, Prof. Jeff Tallon, Maj-General W.B. ("Sandy") Thomas, Lieut-General Sir Leonard Thornton, Shirley Tunnicliffe, Christine Turner, Ann Thwaite, Prof. Vera Tolz, Prof. Robert Wade, Prof. Michael Waller, Alan Watt, Jim Weir, Angela Werren, Nigel West, Sir John White, John Willett, Prof. Janet Wilson,

Michael Wolfers, Elvina Yerofeeva, Douglas Zohrab.

Acknowledgement is due, for permission to quote from published works, to: Carcanet Press, Manchester, for John Cornford, pp 70 and 135 ("Poems from Spain, 1936" in *John Cornford Collected Writings*, 1986); Columbia University Press, New York, for Arthur Koestler, page 61 (*The God that Failed, 1949, 2001)*; and The Random House Group Ltd for C. Day Lewis, lines from "Tempt me no more" which appear in the poem, "The Magnetic Mountain", page 116 [from *The Complete Poems by C. Day Lewis* published by Sinclair-Stevenson (1992) Copyright © 1992 in this edition The Estate of C. Day Lewis]. Also the Alexander Turnbull Library, Wellington, for the cover of a Christmas card showing the NZ Legation in Paris in the 1950s on page 238, from the Alister McIntosh Papers; and the pages of a letter from Paddy Costello used on the inside covers, from the Dan Davin Collection.

Every effort has been made to trace copyright holders. Any omissions are regretted and will be rectified in future editions.

Select Bibliography

Alexander, Bill, *British Volunteers for Liberty*: Spain 1936-1939, London 1982

Andrew, Christopher and Mitrokhin, Vasili, *The Mitrokin Archive*, London 1999

Barrowman, Rachel, *Mason*: *The Life of R.A.K. Mason*, Wellington 2003

Bassett, Michael and King, Michael, *Tomorrow Comes the Song: A Life of Peter Fraser*, Auckland 2000

Berlin, Isaiah, "Meetings with Russian Writers" (essay) in *Personal Impressions*, London 1980, 1998

——— *Flourishing*: *Letters 1928-1946*, ed. Henry Hardy, London 2004

Berton, Kathleen, with John Freeman, *The British Embassy Residence Moscow*: *The Kharitonenko Mansion*, London 1991

Borman, Allan, *Divisional Signals*, Wellington 1954

Bowen, Roger, *Innocence is Not Enough*: *The Life & Death of Herbert Norman*, Vancouver, 1986

Boyle, Andrew, *The Climate of Treason: Five Who Spied for Russia*, London 1979

Brendon, Piers, *The Dark Valley*: *A Panorama of the 1930s*, London 2001

Bulloch, John, & Miller, Henry, *Spy Ring*: *The Portland Naval Spy Case*, London 1961

Carter, Miranda, *Anthony Blunt, His Lives*, London 2001

Carver, Michael (ed.) *The War Lords*, London 1976

Clapp, B.W., *The University of Exeter, a History*, Exeter 1982

Clark, Margaret (ed.), *Peter Fraser, Master Politician* (symposium), Palmerston North 1998

Clendinnen, Inga, *Reading the Holocaust* (ref. Olga Lengyel), Cambridge 1999

Cody, J.F., *21 Battalion*, Wellington 1953

Cornford, John, *Collected Writings*, ed. Jonathan Galassi, Manchester 1976, 1988

Costello, John, *Mask of Treachery*, London 1988

Cox, Geoffrey, *Defence of Madrid*, London 1937, Dunedin 2006

——— *The Race for Trieste*, Christchurch 1977

——— *Eyewitness*, Dunedin 1999

Crossman, Richard (ed.), *The God that Failed* — see Koestler

Cull, Mervyn, *After Me Came the Berlin Wall*, Auckland 2006

Davin, Anna, *Growing Up Poor*, London 1996

Davin, D.M., *For the Rest of Our Lives*, London 1947

———— "Bernard Freyberg" (essay) in Carver, Michael, *The War Lords*, London 1976

———— *Selected Stories*, London & Wellington 1981

Dobson, Christopher, & Payne, Ronald, *The Dictionary of Espionage*, London 1984

Elliott, Geoffrey, & Shukman, Harold, *Secret Classrooms*, London 2002

Fitzgerald, Penelope, *The Knox Brothers*, London 1977

Fox, Ralph, *A Writer in Arms*, London 1937

Freyberg, Paul, *Bernard Freyberg, V.C.: Soldier of Two Nations*, London 1991

Gilbert, Martin, *Road to Victory: Winston S. Churchill, 1941-1945*, London 1986

Gladkov, Alexander, *Meetings with Pasternak*, ed. & transl. by Max Hayward, London 1977

Griboyedov, A.S., *Gore ot Uma*, in *Four Russian Plays*, London 1972, 1990

Hingley, Ronald, *Pasternak, A Biography*, London 1983

Hobsbawm, Eric, *Interesting Times*, a Twentieth Century Life, London 2002

Ignatieff, Michael, *Isaiah Berlin: A Life,* London 1998

Kiernan, Victor, "Herbert Norman's Cambridge" (essay), in *E.H. Norman: His Life & Scholarship*, ed. Roger Bowen, Toronto 1984

King, Michael, *The Penguin History of NZ*, Auckland 2003

Kippenberger, Howard, *Infantry Brigadier*, London 1949

———— (ed.) "The Other Side of the Hill", in *New Zealand in the Second World War* series, Wellington 1952

Knight, G. Wilson, *Jackson Knight, A Biography*, Oxford 1975

Knightley, Phillip, *Philby: KGB Masterspy*, London 1988

Koestler, Arthur, in *The God That Failed: Six Studies in Communism* (essays), ed. Richard Crossman, London 1950, New York 2001

Greene, Graham, *The Human Factor*, London 1978

Hyde, Montgomery, *George Blake Superspy*, London 1987

Lengyel, Olga, *Five Chimneys: A Woman Survivor's True Story of Auschwitz* Academy Publishers Chicago, 1995, 2003 (originally publ. 1946, translated from the Hungarian, as *Souvenirs de l'au-delà*)

Litvinoff, Emanuel, *Journey Through a Small Planet*, London 1972, 1993

McClymont, W.G., *To Greece*, Wellington 1959

McGibbon, Ian (ed.), *Undiplomatic Dialogue: Letters between Carl Berendsen & Alister McIntosh 1943–1952*, Auckland 1993

———— (ed.) *Unofficial Channels: Letters between Alister McIntosh & Foss Shanahan, George Laking & Frank Corner 1946-1966*, Wellington 1999

———— (ed.) *The Oxford Companion to New Zealand Military History*, Auckland 2000

McNeish, James, *Dance of the Peacocks: New Zealanders in Exile in the Time of Hitler & Mao Tse-tung*, Auckland 2003

Macswan, Norman, *The Man who Read the East Wind: A Biography of Richard Hughes*, NSW 1982

Modin, Yuri, *My Five Cambridge Friends*, London 1994

Monro, Hector, *Fortunate Catastrophes: An Anecdotal Autobiography*, Melbourne 1991

Ovenden, Keith, *A Fighting Withdrawal: The Life of Dan Davin*, Oxford 1996

Overy, Richard, *Russia's War*, London 1998

———— *Interrogations: The Nazi Elite in Allied Hands, 1945*, London 2001

Pasternak, Boris, *Fifty Poems*, transl. by Lydia Pasternak Slater, London 1963

Paton, Harold, *Private Paton's Pictures: Behind the Lines with Kiwi Soldiers in North Africa*, 1941-3, Auckland 2003

Pincher, Chapman, *Their Trade is Treachery*, London 1981

———— *Too Secret Too Long*, London 1984

Poulsen, Charles, *Scenes from a Stepney Youth*, London 1988

Powell, Dilys, *The Villa Ariadne*, London 1973

Richardson, W.F. & Crawley, L.W.A., *Classics in Auckland*, Auckland 1983

Robertson, Geoffrey, *The Justice Game*, London 1998

Shirley, Henry, *Just a Bloody Piano Player*, Auckland 1971

Sinclair, Keith, *Walter Nash*, Dunedin, 1976

———— *A History of the University of Auckland, 1883–1983*, Auckland 1983

Snelling, O.F., *Rare Books and Rarer People*, London 1982

Stansky, Peter & Abrahams, William, *Journey to the Frontier: Julian Bell & John Cornford, their lives & the 1930s*, London 1966

Stone, R.C.J., *The Making of Russell McVeagh, 1863–1988*, Auckland 1991

Straight, Michael, *After Long Silence*, London 1983

Synge, J.M., *The Aran Islands*, Dublin (Maunsel edn.) 1906 (republished UK & USA, various editions)

Templeton, Malcolm, *Top Hats Are Not Being Taken: A Short History of the NZ Legation in Moscow 1944–1950*, Wellington 1988

———— (ed.), *An Eye, An Ear & A Voice: 50 Years in NZ's External Relations*, Wellington 1993

The Other Side of the Hill (monograph), in *New Zealand in the Second World War* series, Official History, ed. Howard Kippenberger, Wellington 1952

Trembath, K.A., *Ad Augusta: A Centennial History of Auckland Grammar School, 1869–1969*, Auckland 1969

Walker, Martin, *The Cold War,* New York 1993

Weir, Jim, *Russia Through New Zealand Eyes,* Wellington 1996

West, Nigel, *Seven Spies Who Changed the World*, London 1991

West, Rebecca, *The Meaning of Treason*, London 1982

Whitemore, Hugh, *A Pack of Lies* (play), London 1983

Wilson, A.C., *New Zealand & the Soviet Union 1950–1991: A Brittle Relationship*, Wellington 2004

Wilson, Janet (ed.) *Intimate Stranger: Reminiscences of Dan Davin*, Wellington 2000

Glossary

Chinar Oriental plane tree. The chinar tree (*P. orientalis*) of Asia Minor, Kashmir and the Old Testament

CIA Central Intelligence Agency

Demi-sezonny overcoat Russian for spring or autumn coat (demi-saison)

Dezhurny band or armlet, meaning "duty officer"

Doppelgänger literally, double-goer. A double or ghostly replica

G2 (Ops) General Staff Officer (Operations)

G3 (I) General Staff Officer (Intelligence)

Gopak spirited Ukrainian dance

KGB Soviet Intelligence Service (previously, 1917-1954, NKVD)

Lamington Chocolate and coconut-coated cube of sponge cake peculiar to New Zealand and Australia

LCV Light carrying vehicle

MI5 British Security Service

MI6 SIS (British Secret Intelligence Service)

NZEF New Zealand Expeditionary Force

NKVD see KGB

Pioneers Children's version of the Young Communist League

Quinsy tonsilitis

Samizdat unofficial (usually typed) manuscript, circulated clandestinely by hand

Shashlyk Georgian dish of grilled mutton and rice

Shtetl small town or village in Jewish districts of Eastern Europe, especially Russia

Sitrep Situation report

Spahis French Moroccan, or French Algerian mounted troops

Toheroa Shellfish delicacy, peculiar to New Zealand

Toughs Cambridge term for what Oxford calls "hearties"

Tsinandali local wine, named for a village in the Caucasus

Yasnaya Polyana Tolstoy's family estate 180 km south of Moscow, where he was born and where he wrote *War and Peace* and *Anna Karenina*

Index

PC is the abbreviation for Paddy Costello; Bil is the abbreviation for his wife, Bil Costello (Bella Lerner)

21st Battalion
  in Battle of Tempe 92–98
  escape to Crete 100–103
  ordered to engage enemy at Tempe 20
  saved ship at Piraeus 89
  unluckiest in the Division 338

agent of influence 356
Airey, Deirdre 289
Airey, Willis 289
Akhmatova, Anna 180, 185, 204, 375–376
Alamein offensive 110, 117
Alison, Jean 44
Allen, Brigadier 338
American ambassador to New Zealand 261, 372
American analysis of Molotov's speech 215, 222
American FBI dossier on PC 306
American foreign policy 351–352, 359
American nuclear monopoly 215, 359, 370
Andrew, Christopher 15–16, 241, 364–365
Angleton, James Jesus 179
Animal Farm (Orwell): *Imro* an answer to 199, 201, 204
anti-Americanism 180, 351–352
Aran island: holiday at 299–300, 385
The Aran Islands (Synge) 299–300
Armia Krajowa (AK) 348
Astrakhan: holiday in 186
Athens: PC's life as a sybarite in 48
atomic bomb, Soviet *see* Soviet atomic bomb
Auckland University 24–26
Auschwitz (concentration camp) 163–165, 316–318

balance-of-terror theory 370
Balck, Colonel 91, 98, 338
Bartlett, Jean 332
Bartlett, Peter 241
Batterbee, Sir Harry Fagg 179, 182, 261
Battle of Tempe 17–20, 92–98, 338
Behar, George 111
Bell, Julian 37
Bennett, Alan 273
Bennett, Jack 25–26
Berendsen, Carl August 231–233, 352, 362, 374
Beresford, Maureen 273, 274
Beresford, Michael 296–297
Berlin, Isaiah 174, 180, 278, 350, 375–376
Berlin: visit to 48–49
Berndt, Elisabeth 371–372
Bertram, James 25–26, 242, 365
Bethnal Green upbringing 53, 54, 58, 381–382
binge drinking 288–290
Birmingham Chair in Russian 246, 247, 248, 254, 264
Bishop, Terry 237
black eye 283, 284, 285
Blake, George 111
The Blind Owl (Hedayat): PC's translation 245, 279, 280, 281
Blok, Alexander 185
Blunt, Anthony
Blunt-Burgess ring 38
  at Cambridge 31, 36
  likened to PC 27
  reported allegation about PC 15, 307
  visit to Russia 49
Bolsover, George 258
Boswell, Charles
  attempt to learn Russian 175, 350–351
  head of N.Z. Legation in Moscow 153, 156
  lack of enthusiasm for Moscow 175
  meeting with Clark Kerr 157
  parsimony 350
  recall to N.Z. 209
  slide into Russophobia 154
  sought appointment as head of Paris Legation 228

Boswell, Jean 173, 200, 375
Brasch, Charles 49, 292–293
Bratislava Bridgehead 189–192, 354–355
British analysis of Molotov's speech 215, 222
British Communist Party *see* Communist Party of Great Britain
British diplomatic mission into Poland 157–158, 160–165, 314
British domestic Intelligence service
  believed to be behind PC's downfall 261
  file available on PC's pre-war affiliations 79
  file on PC's pre-war affiliations 260
  files references to PC as a traitor 176
  opposition to McIntosh 374
British Embassy in Moscow: N.Z. Legation's relationship with 184
British Foreign Office 179
British GHQ 106, 108–109, 111–112
British Government
  not prepared to deal with PC in Paris Legation 244
  policy on non-intervention in Spanish Civil War 71
British IB (Indian Intelligence Bureau) 72
British prisoners of war 158, 162, 166
British School in Athens 46, 47–48
British security authorities
  alleged evidence of PC as a Soviet agent 367, 375–376
  file on PC 182
  PC under surveillance by 241
  on PC's assignment to India 71
  British security: penetrated by Krogers 251–252
Burgess, Guy
  contemporary at Trinity College 31
  defection 370
  discussion with Churchill 79
  guest at Straight's parties 35
  introduced to Philby by Robertson 33
  in November 1933 peace demonstration 37
bursaries in Paris 241
Caesar, Julius 23, 257, 326–327
Cairo: wartime base 106, 108–110
Cambridge Union 37
Cambridge University
  hit by Marxism 36
  hotbed of political fervent and controversy 32
  PC's reason for choosing 34
  response to PC on academic post 219
  right-wingers at 33
  Socialist Society 33, 38
  Trinity College *see* Trinity College, Cambridge
Campbell, R.M. 372
Cassino: war service outside 125–133
Chekhov, Anton: *Three Sisters* 144, 169, 287
China as a world power 359
Christian, Reginald 292, 294
Churchill, Winston 157–160, 166
Clark, Kate 382–383
Clark Kerr, Sir Archibald 157, 179, 184
Cleghorn, Tony 119–120, 126, 127
Clementis, Vladimir 190–191, 277
Closing Times (Davin) 291–292
Cobb, Richard 248, 367
Cohen, Morris and Lena: real name of Krogers 251, 370
Cold War Joint Services School for Russian linguists 273
Collins, Richard Gray (Dick) 262, 372–373
Commonwealth prisoners of war 158, 162
Commonwealth Secretary-General 373–374
Communist Party of Great Britain
  Bil's membership 58, 71, 182, 183
  Cornford's membership 54
  Cox's consideration of joining 147, 344
  donation to Indian Communist Party 71
  Kiernan's membership 331
  Michael Costello's membership 297, 308
  PC's membership 61–62, 182
Communist Party of India: money delivered to 71–72

communist suspicions: fanned by McCarthyism 79, 261
communist sympathiser: PC as a 202–204, 276
concentration camps report 162–166, 313–318
Conference of Paris 186–195
Corner, Frank 176, 187, 188, 191, 374
Corner, Lyn 188, 191, 353
Cornford, John
on death of Maclaurin 70
fought and died in Spanish Civil War 37, 67, 69–70, 334
friendship with PC 37, 38
poem written to Heinemann 70, 135
transformed initial communist cell at Trinity 36–37
transformed into a demi-god 71
Costello, Bil (née Lerner)
Anna Davin's perception of 284, 381–382
on assuming the name Bil 57, 59
a background figure in Paris 248
Bethnal Green upbringing 53–54, 58, 60, 381–382
carried photo of Cornford and Heinemann 70
committed communist 201, 276, 285, 309
Communist Party membership 58, 182, 183
compass for PC's attitude to life 278
considered liability for PC's Moscow appointment 148
death 308
faced consequences of PC's drinking 288
family life after PC's death 382
forbade PC to go to Spanish Civil War 69
joined PC at Paris Peace Conference 188
joined PC in Moscow 169–170
Lerner family and early life 53–54, 331–332
Maclaurin's Bookshop assistant 52
marriage 56
message to Maclaurin 66–67
munitions factory work 127, 141, 143
objection to PC enlisting for war service 79
on PC's wartime leave 147–148
physical appearance and interests 59
qualities in the family environment 298
reaction to PC's death 305
relationship with PC 55, 57, 309
relief work during Spanish Civil War 71
translation assistant to PC 301, 387
translator of *Nikolai Negorev* 387
translator of *The Marriage* (Gogol) 387
translator of *The Murder of Rasputin* (Purishkevich) 309, 387
tutor at Manchester 278, 305, 382
visit from Davin in 1943: 127
Costello, Christopher (Kit) (PC's son)
birth 245
at boarding school in 1963: 297
holiday at Inis Mor 299–300, 385
living in Munich 308
PC's enjoyment as father to 248
PC's involvement in education of 298
reaction to PC's death 305–306, 386
scholarship to Shrewsbury 305, 382
taught to swim by PC 302
Costello, Christopher (PC's father) 26, 27, 28–29, 288
Costello Condition 28, 29
Costello, Desmond Patrick *see* Costello, Paddy
Costello, Frank (PC's brother) 43
Costello, John 364
Costello, Josie (PC's daughter)
college lecturer 308
contracted tuberculosis 245
education in Moscow 197
experience of PC's tough love in Moscow 170–171
on family life at Viroflay 244–245
fluency in Russian 171
on Metrostroevskaya 21: 217
on parents' discussion on collectivisation 276
on PC as a father 198
on PC's grave 309
teaching in Paris 297

theatre visits 217–218
as three-year-old 142
translated for VIPs from Leningrad 297
Costello, Katie (PC's daughter)
birth 163
on family settled at Withington 272
fluency in Russian 171
gave PC a pipe 286
grew up monolingual Russian 197, 285–286
holiday at Inis Mor 300
at home in 1963: 297
interpreter and translator 308
at kindergarten in summer pastures 177–178
on PC's death 302
on PC's drinking 288
on PC's educational standards 297
re-learning Russian 382
theatre visits 217–218, 244
tutored by PC in French and English 245
Costello, Kit *see* Costello, Christopher (Kit) (PC's son)
Costello, Mary (PC's mother)
born into the Irish Woods family 28
family characteristics and appearance 29
with PC on last visit 229, 237
PC's competitive genes inherited from 28
remarriage and death 298–299
singing ability 26
trained as teacher 24
Costello, Michael (PC's son)
birth 62
businessman and student 308
coached in English by Lawlor-Bartlett 264
on discussion with PC on Stalin and Soviet Union 277
education from PC 286
education in Moscow 197, 198
experiences PC's tough love in Moscow 170–171
fluency in Russian 171
on Hungarian press's vilification of PC 192
on Louis' arrest by KGB 173
married and living in Manchester 297
on PC and Moishe Lerner 59–60
PC questioning him on labour camps 204
on PC's assignment to India 72
on PC's happiness at Stalin's praise 355–356
on PC's purported admiration for Stalin 201
on PC's rejection of Klugmann 379
on PC's view on Polish situation 347
on radio discussion with von Senger 282
as seven-year-old 142
on unchanging behaviour of PC 180, 247
watched Soviet satellite 272
Costello, Nicholas (PC's son)
diplomat 308
at home in 1963: 297
a Maoist 382
member of European Commission 273
on PC growing up in a shop 27–28
on PC's death 302–303, 386
PC's involvement in education of 298
on priority given by PC to books 377
scholarship to Winchester 305
watched Soviet satellite 272
Costello, Paddy
on being known as Paddy 40
Athens interlude: activities on studentship 46–51
Auckland student: activities and contemporaries at University 25–26; graduation and departure for Trinity 30; linguistics and classics student 24; scholarships awarded 24, 27, 30
birth and childhood: altar boy 26; birth and family homes 24, 27; confirmation name 23, 257, 326–327; father's businesses 26, 27; interest in scholarships 28; school essay on Xerxes 23, 90
books and reading: antikvari in Moscow 174; Bolshevik literature 48; bought with Greek prize 48; *Doctor Zhivago*: opinion of and writing on 292–294; habit of a lifetime 264–266; Housman poetry 28; *Jane Eyre* 66, 67; Lemprière's *Classical*

Dictionary 24; priority given to books 377; Thucydide's history of the Peloponnesian war 100

Cambridge years: advantages of Trinity 39; graduation from Trinity 46; help for 1933 hunger marchers 37; Housman's lecture 34–35; initial disappointment 31, 32–33; John Stewart of Rannoch Scholarship 40–41; on quality of Cambridge classics students 35, 329; switch from economics to classics 33

careers considered: in academia 218-220, 246–247; after the war 142–143; as a graduate 51, 56; in an international organisation 255, 263; as a writer 143–144, 200–201

Davin friendship: in Cairo 109–111; Davin's unfinished writing on PC 292; first meeting 105, 106–107; intellectual tussles 281; intensity of 282–285, 292, 381

death: burial 306, 309–310; cause of death 287–288; Christmases as a resurrection of 386; circumstances of 301–303, 386; events consequent on 306, 309–310; obituary written by Davin 306, 319–321; preoccupation with 378

drinking: abstention from 267; arrest for drunkenness 236–237, 244, 261; a binge drinker 288–289; in Cairo 110; cure for hangovers 365; episodes of fighting and 283; lack of tact as a result of 180; as a liability in a spy 376; problem with 285, 286; Windsor Castle episode 291

Exeter: suspended from Exeter over Fyrth case 77–78, 336; University lecturer 62, 64–65, 66, 68, 74–75

fatherhood: abundance of his company 298; activities in Paris 244–245; birth of children 62–64, 78, 163, 245; strict encouragement of 198

friends and acquaintances *see also* **Davin friendship**: in Cairo 111; contemporaries at Auckland University 25–26; contemporaries at Trinity College 31, 39; Cornford 37, 38; Cox 69, 147, 148; Curiel 111; Freyberg 290–291; Gow 34; Klugmann 379; Maclaurin 39, 43–47, 51; R.A.K. Mason 26; McIntosh 183–184; McKenzie 237, 239, 240, 267, 377; Murray 75; Pahlavi 72; Pasternak 174–175, 180, 196–197, 350; Sollohub 33; visitors to home in Paris 247–248

Fyrth episode: consulted by Fyrth over offence under Official Secrets Act 76–78; factual blot on his record 260; feelings about Fyrth case 79; an issue for his safety and security 179; McIntosh unaware of 182; N.Z. Government acceptance of his version 76

health and physique: eyesight 18, 326; health prior to death 287–288, 299; nervous storms 142–143; physical appearance after war service 141–142; starost ne radost/growing old isn't much fun 266; stature 24–25; suffering from cafard (depression) 127

holidays and travels: Astrakhan 186; Berlin 48–49; early attempts to visit Russia 49, 56–57; France 46; Greece 47–48; Griboyedov's tomb 211–212; Inis Mor 299–300, 385; N.Z. 220, 227, 229–230, 235–237; Sicily 254; Soviet Union 177–178; Sparta 50; Stockholm 167–168; Tripolis (Greece) 50

homes and family life: in Moscow 169–170; at Rathen Road 267, 271–272, 278; at Viroflay 244–245, 247–248, 263, 264

influences and interests: the Ancient World 23–24; gardens 296, 301; Griboyedov 171–172, 238; likened to Blunt 27; poetry his real love 281; radio discussion with von Senger and Davin 282; singing 26–27, 32, 285; theatre 172–173, 209, 217–218, 244, 278, 286

Irish connection: ancestry 26; returned to study in vacations 35–36; trips to west of Ireland 278; visited family in

Ireland 31–32, 238; Woods relations 29
languages *see also* **Russian language**: ability in all used at Peace Conference 186; acquired while in Auckland 24; adult interest 27; approach to 280–281, 380; Arabic 108; Gaelic 24, 30, 299; Persian 212, 245, 280, 380; Sanskrit 380; those spoken and written 379–380; as a translator 281; Yiddish 24, 60
Manchester years: Chair in Russian 264, 266; contentment 278; dedication to teaching and examining 295–296, 378, 382–383; linguistic panache of master classes 281; move from Paris to Manchester 267; plaudits as a teacher 274–275; professor and head of school 271–272, 296–297
marriage: accusations arising from having a Russian wife 57; to Bil 56; Bil as the centre of his universe 143; Bil's influence 57; going alone to Moscow 148; importance placed by Bil on 285; met Bil 52, 55, 278; on relationship with Bil 309
Moscow diplomatic service: achievements of 215; on Boswell 156; Bratislava Bridgehead controversy 188–192, 354–355; closed Legation 219–220; clothing 149–150; colleagues 155; Cox's reservations on PC's appointment 146–147; decision to resign 214, 218; disclosure of Soviet atomic bomb 215, 259; effective running of the Legation 153; enthusiasm for Russian life and culture 175–178; excursion into forbidden zone 177–178; feted in Czechoslovakia 194–195; Freyberg's telegram about appointment 144–145; German Extermination Camps report 164–165, 313–318; influence of Moscow on 168, 185–186; interviewed by Fraser for position 147; leader of British diplomatic mission into Poland 158, 160–164; Paris Peace Conference attendance 186–195; promoted to First Secretary 197; relationship with British Embassy 184; restrictive rules of life in Moscow 180, 181; selected for position by McIntosh 146; tension over job offer 145; on underestimation of Soviet Union 359; views on Polish situation 347–348
Paris diplomatic service: accompanied Holland around Europe 243–244; alleged activity as Soviet agent 241; appointment 228, 238; discontented in role 246; farewell party 267; put on notice by Mcintosh 244, 246; resignation 243, 254, 255, 260; under surveillance by British 241, 247
personal qualities: as an academic 382–383; analytical and predictive skills 215–216, 359; attitude to life 278; Brigid Davin's memories of 285; brilliance 279–280, 379; Byronic persona 357; certainty provided by Bil 381; competitiveness 28; Griboyedov as doppelgänger 207–208; handwriting 209–210, 358; his monkish self 281; infidelities 109, 111, 143; journeyman-scholar 49–50; likened to Sutch 146; outsider 26, 39, 207, 357; overcoming fear 115–117; in persona of a diplomat 177, 218–219; renounced making money and getting on 36, 329; restored to being a New Zealander 117; as revealed through his diaries 181; romantic nature 29; talk about being depressed 127
political beliefs and associations: anti-Americanism 180, 351–352; assignment to Communist Party of India 71–72; categorisation 202, 356; Communist Party membership 61–62; course at Karl Marx House 56, 62; debate with Strachey 62; denounced to Fraser government as a communist 261; description of at Cambridge 38–39; lacking qualities of a communist 201; not part of Trinity communist cell 36; in November 1933 peace demonstration 38; purported admiration for Stalin

201–203, 355–356; raised funds for Republican cause in Spain 70–71; shift in attitude to Soviet communism 276–277; supporter of Marxism 281–282, 380–381; supposed student radical 25, 29

Russian language: asset in Moscow Legation 155; dictionary purchased 48; factor in Moscow appointment 146; interpreter for Red Army Generals 131, 146; knowledge of rules 264; largely self-taught 266; lessons taken in Cairo 112; Louis as teacher 173; as the most useful to know 122; privileged position as an outcome 176; progress with speaking 168, 173; reading *Three Sisters* in Russian 144; selection for Polish mission on basis of 158; teacher to army colleagues 119; teacher to Moscow diplomats 175

spy allegations/security issues: alleged by Blunt to have been a Soviet agent 307; alleged evidence as a Soviet agent 248, 368, 375–376; blame for Kroger passport affair 253, 364–365, 368, 370; engineers of his downfall 261; FBI dossier 306; Moscow activities questioned 181–182; NZSIS file as a student radical 24–25, 29, 331; NZSIS file on Athens studentship 47–48; NZSIS file on Moscow appointment 141; perceived reasons for being forced to resign 258–259; perception as villain in purges of state servants 263; pre-war affiliations 76–78, 258, 260; questions of his safety and suitability 179; reaction to accusations from Intelligence agencies 180; supposed links with Soviet intelligence service 176; whereabouts during Kroger passport affair 250

war service: Cornford poem 70; Day Lewis poem 116; enlisted with N.Z. Fifth Brigade 79; home leave 125–126, 141–144; myth of his immunity 132; private in 29th Battalion 83; reason for being a soldier 89, 100; volunteered for the Spanish Civil War 68–69; volunteered to enlist in 1939: 75, 182; wearing of his medals 242, 365

war service: Tempe to Crete: battalion ordered to hold Tempe pass 91; Battle of Tempe 92–98, 337; excitement of being back in Greece 90; initiation into war 17–20; led 21st's escape to Crete 100–103; reconnected with Xerxes' essay 23, 90

war service: Cairo and North Africa: in Alamein offensive 114–120; interlude in Syria 113; Italian army handbook 109, 112, 115, 144; officer training 106–108; outbreak at Minqar Qaim 113–114, 341; reaction to Nathan's injury 342; secondment to British GHQ 108–109, 111–112; trip with Davin from Enfidaville 110

war service: Cassino: accompanied Soviet delegation 131, 146; with Army Movement Control 133; assigned to Long Range Desert Group 107–108; confidence in Red Army prevailing 118–120, 359; Freyberg's divisional Intelligence officer 112, 114, 123; leave granted by Freyberg 128–129, 132–133; promoted to Captain 118; relationship with Freyberg 117–118, 130; revelry in truck 126–127; Russian language lessons given 119–120; waiting outside Cassino 125–133

writings: *The Blind Owl* (trans.) 245, 279, 280, 281; *Gore ot Uma* (trans.) 206, 207, 219; Imro (unpublished novel) 199–200, 203–204; Moscow Assignment (unfinished novel) 204, 356; *Nikolai Negorev* (trans.) 296, 301, 309, 387; *The Oxford Book of Russian Verse* 186–187, 196–197, 206; *Oxford Russian-English dictionary* (contributor) 296, 384; passion to be a writer 143–144, 200–201; projects in progress at death 295–296, 384–385; reviews 296; *Russian Folk Literature* (ed.) 281, 296; *Russian Grammar* (trans.: unfinished) 245, 366,

384; as a translator 387; "Zhivago Reconsidered" (essay) 294, 295, 384
Costello, Phil (PC's brother) 24, 34, 62
Council of Europe 243, 245
Counter-Intelligence 180, 261, 262
Cox, Geoffrey
considered joining Communist Party 147, 344
dinners with PC 148, 290
explained Maclaurin's death 69–70
introduced PC to Davin 105, 106
journalist and author 105–106, 200
McIntosh's first choice for Moscow position 145–146
on PC and Davin's friendship 381
recalled to N.Z. Division by Freyberg 111
The Red Army Moves 118
reservations on PC for Moscow position 144, 146–147
trained for Freyberg's Intelligence staff 106
visit to Russia 49
working for British GHQ in Cairo 109
Crete: 21st Battalion's escape to 102–103
Croft, Don 96
Crossman, Richard 277–278
Crowe, Marshall 175, 184, 202
Crusader operation 108–109
Cull, Mervyn 369
Curiel, Henri 111, 247–248, 340
Curran Street primary school 28
Currie, Colin 116–117
Czechoslovak-Hungarian border dispute 189–192, 354–355
Czechoslovakia: PC feted in 192, 194–195

Daily Worker 73, 75–77, 277, 297
Dance of the Peacocks (McNeish) 110, 261–262
Dartington Hall 35, 212, 380
Davin, Anna 283, 284, 285, 381–382
Davin, Brigid 283, 285
Davin, Dan
on 21st Battalion after Battle of Tempe 98
account of aerial assault on Crete 106
awareness of PC's discontentment 246
behaviour with PC in Cairo 109–110
Closing Times (Davin) 291–292
creator of rumour of PC as a saviour 103
cure for hangovers 365
death 292
dinner in London with Freyberg, PC and Cox 290
employment at Oxford University Press 16, 185, 206–207, 282
experience of comradeship in Italy 117
failure to find publisher for Imro 199–200
family home in Oxford 284–285
first meeting with PC 104, 105, 106–107
For the Rest of Our Lives 111
fourth daughter 371–372
on holiday with PC at Inis Mor 300
impact of PC's death on 306–307
intellectual tussles between PC and 281
in Intelligence section of British GHQ 106, 109, 115
intensity of friendship with PC 282–285, 292, 381
invited, with PC, to Windsor Castle 290–291
obituary of PC 306, 319–321
on PC's downfall 263
published author 200
radio discussion with PC and von Senger 282
recalled by Freyberg to N.Z. Division 111
Rhodes Scholar and Lieutenant 99–100
Soldiers and Scholars: unfinished book 292, 383
solicited for a trust fund for education of PC's children 305
support for PC's Manchester application 266
took over PC's Intelligence role 128–130
trip with PC from Enfidaville 110
unfinished writing on PC 291–292
visited Bil while on leave 127
wartime leave in Britain 125–126, 127–128
wounded on Crete 105–106

Davin, Delia 283, 284, 285–286
Davin, Patty 371–372
Davin, Tom 228
Davin, Winnie 282, 283–284, 300, 372
Day, Cecil 166
Day Lewis, C. 116
de Carbinnel, M. 177
de Guingand, General Sir Frederick 131
Department of External Affairs (N.Z.) 229–230, 258–259, 261–262, 313–318, 374–375
Deutscher, Isaac 277
diplomatic service, New Zealand 152–153
Dobb, Maurice 36
Dobbs, Alfred 202
Doctor Zhivago (Pasternak) 292–294, 350
Doidge, Frederick 231, 233–234, 237, 256
Dominions Office (Great Britain) 179
doppelgänger: Griboyedov as PC's 207–208
Dumbreck, Professor John 384
Dutton, Captain 102

Eden, Anthony 158
Edmonds, Ernest 232, 362–363
education
 as an accelerant to life 170–171
 importance placed on by PC 286, 297–298
 perception of N.Z. 35
 quality in Russian schools 197–198
Eighth Army General Headquarters (GHQ) 106, 108–109, 111–112
Elliott, Geoffrey. *Secret Classrooms* 273
Elwood, Sir Brian 367
espionage literature 16, 38, 247, 253, 307
Eugene Onegin (Pushkin) 172, 357
Exeter 66, 142
 see also University College of the South West, Exeter
Exeter city police 72–73, 74, 79, 179
Exeter College Council 77–78, 336
Exhibition scholarship 33
Extermination Camps report 162–166, 313–318

External Affairs Department (N.Z.) 229–230, 258–259, 261–262, 313–318, 374–375

FBI dossier on PC 306
Fifth Brigade (N.Z.) 79
Fifth Columnism 76
A Fighting Withdrawal (Ovenden) 110, 381
The Flap 114
Floyd, Flying Officer David
 accompanied PC on Polish mission 160
 German Extermination Camps report 316, 318
 objectivity on Polish mission 347–348
 on Polish support for Russia 162
 on supporters of London Poles 161
Foote, Paul 263, 281, 296
For the Rest of Our Lives (Davin) 111
forbidden zones in Soviet Union 177–178
forged documents for passports 251, 369
France: visit to 46
Fraser, Peter
 action on German Extermination Camps report 165–166
 Batterbee's visit reported to 183
 Boswell chosen for Legation in Moscow 152–153
 interviewed PC in London 147
 Moscow diplomatic post created 145, 151
 position taken on Bratislava Bridgehead 188–190
 replaced Berendsen with McIntosh 362
Frayn, Michael 273
Freeborn, Richard 299
French francs 231–233
Freyberg, Barbara 247, 291
Freyberg, General Bernard
 assigning of PC to divisional Intelligence 123
 bombardment of Monte Cassino 131
 dinner in London with PC, Davin and Cox 290
 helped PC overcome his fear 116–117
 immunity from death in battle 132
 interest in the Russian front 120, 129–130

invited PC and Davin to Windsor Castle 290–291
on Macky's performance at Tempe 97, 98
recalled PC, Davin and Cox to N.Z. Division 112
relationship with PC 117–118, 120
reluctance to approve PC's leave 128–129, 132
selection of PC to be trained for a commission 103–104
a subject of Davin's unfinished book 292
support for PC's Manchester application 266
telegram to PC re Moscow appointment 144–145
thwarted intellectual 130
wounded at Minqar Qaim 114
Freyberg, Paul 108
Fuchs, Klaus 370
Fulton speech (Churchill) 160
Fyrth, Hubert 75–77, 260
Fyrth, Patrick 75–76, 77

Garrone, Judge Alessandro Galante 245, 248, 367
George VI, King 166
German Extermination Camps report 162–166, 313–318
Germany: as most important European country 352
Gilbert, Brigadier Sir William 252, 368
The God that Failed (Koestler) 61
Gogol, Nikolai. *The Marriage* (Bil translation) 387
Gore ot Uma (Griboyedov) 171–172, 206–207, 208, 212, 219
Gow, Andrew 34, 386
Greece: visit to 47–48
Greene, Graham 49, 251, 264
Griboyedov, Alexander Sergeyevich
see also *Gore ot Uma* (Griboyedov)
accused of treason 357
appointment to Persia 357
diplomatic career and death 210–211
influence on PC 171–172
marriage 358
PC as doppelgänger of 207–208
PC's research on his murder 238
tomb in Tiflis 211–212, 221
Growing Up Poor (A. Davin) 381

Harriman, Kathleen 158–159
Hayward, Max 293, 384
Healy, Miss 220
Hedayat, Sadegh 280, 281, 301
Heenan, Sir Joseph 238–239, 363
Heinemann, Margot 37, 70, 135, 309
Hill, Christopher 383
Hill, Elizabeth (Liza) 247, 258, 273–274
Hill, Inez 306, 386
Hobsbawm, Eric 53, 204, 331
Holland, Sidney
American demand that he dismiss PC 261
cultural abjectness 230
importance of Paris Legation 241
instructed McIntosh to remove PC 244, 263
N.Z. Legation in Moscow closed by 214
PC reprimanded by 236–237
philistine party politician 242–244
visit to England and Europe 242–244
Holyoake, Sir Keith 374
Hooray-fuck slogan 114, 168
Hopkins, Harry 160
Housman, A.E.
"An asylum, in more ways than one" 31
luminary at Trinity College 31
PC's reason for choosing Cambridge 34
poetry lecture 34–35
poetry of assistance to PC 18
reactionary right-winger 33
A Shropshire Lad 29–30, 328
"To an Athlete Dying Young" 309–310
Hughes, Richard (Dick) 111, 248, 366–367
The Human Factor (Greene) 251, 264
Humphrey Rawlings scholarship 27
Hungarian-Czechoslovak border dispute 189–192, 354–355
Hungarian press 192
Hungary Commission 187, 188–192
hunger marchers 37

immunity myth 132
Imro (PC: unpublished novel) 199–200, 203–204
India: PC's assignment to 71–72, 182
Indian undergraduates: conversion to communism 39, 329
Inis Mor (Aran island): holiday at 299–300, 385
Intelligence circles: PC's reputation in 253
International Brigades 69, 70, 71, 334
Ireland: visits to 29, 31–32, 35–36, 238
Irish ancestry 26, 30
Iron Curtain 160
Italian army handbook 109, 112, 115, 144

Jewish background: of Lerner family 53–54, 57–58, 381
John Stewart of Rannoch Scholarship 40–41
Jones (PC's batman) 117, 119, 131–132
Jordan, Bill 185, 187, 188, 353
Journey Through a Small Planet (Litvinoff) 58
Julius: confirmation name 23, 257, 326–327

Karl Marx House course 56, 62
Kasr el Nil barracks 106
Keenan, George 216, 359–360
Kekushev's Mansion 217
Kelly, David 216
Kelly, Lady 346
KGB
  alleged file on Costello codenamed LONG 16, 241, 365, 376
  importance of Krogers to 251–252
Khadzhi Murat (Tolstoy) 275, 378
Khokhlovsky apartment 170–171, 196
Kiernan, Victor
  Communist Party membership 331
  contemporary at Trinity College 38
  inherited stock of Maclaurin's Bookshop 55
  on Maclaurin 332, 333–334
  took over group recruiting Indians 72
King, Michael 254, 261–262, 373–374
Kippenberger, Major-General Howard
  candidate for Davin's unfinished book 383
  on incident at Minqar Qaim 114
  loss of both feet 129, 137
  on numbers of the 21st reaching Crete 102
  played chess with PC 126
  thwarted intellectual 130
Klugmann, James 34, 36–37, 379
Knight, Jackson 74
Knightley, Phillip 307
Knox, Dilwyn 34
Koestler, Arthur 61
Konovalov, Professor Serge 219, 246, 258, 266
Kroger, Helen Joyce (née Hale) 251–252, 326, 369–370
Kroger, Peter John 16, 249–252, 325–326, 369–370
Kushchevsky, Ivan 296, 301, 309, 387

labour camps 204
Lake, Douglas
  alleged indoctrination by PC 263
  analysis of Molotov's speech 215, 222
  on Churchill and Stalin 158
  marriage to Macky 172, 214
  on Moscow temperatures 169–170
  on PC's prescience about China 359
  post-External Affairs career 375
  resignation 259, 262, 374–375
  return to N.Z. from Moscow 172
  on Soviet copying of cipher books 376
  on staff of N.Z. Legation in Moscow 155
  taught Russian by PC 175
Lake, Harry 375
Lake, Ruth (née Macky)
  alleged indoctrination by PC 263
  language polisher in Beijing 375
  marriage to Douglas Lake 172, 214
  pro-Soviet pamphlet 374–375
  return to N.Z. from Moscow 172
  Russian language skills 173, 175
  on staff of N.Z. Legation in Moscow 155
Lake, Sarah 172

Laking, Sir George
British Intelligence's pursuit of PC *title page*
on Collins 372–373
establishment of Paris Legation 227, 230, 231
PC's whereabouts during passport affair 250
reason for PC's dismissal 261
successor to McIntosh 262
Larkin, Tom 362, 372–373
Lattimore, Owen 16
Lawlor-Bartlett, Margaret 264, 267
Lawrence, Sue 250–251
Lengyel, Olga 163–164, 166, 349
Lequeux, Maurice 163, 166
Lerner, Abba (Bil's brother) 54, 332
Lerner, Arthur (Bil's brother) 60, 68, 69
Lerner, Bella *see* Costello, Bil (née Lerner)
Lerner, Doris (Bil's sister) 59, 60–61, 289
Lerner family
with Bil in Exeter 142, 143
experience as Russian Jewish emigrants 53–54, 57–58
PC thoughts of at Maidanek 163
PC's meeting with 60
Lerner, Jack (Bil's brother) 68, 73
Lerner, Moishe (Bil's father) 53–54, 60, 289
Lerner, Nat (Bil's brother) 60
Leys Institute 24, 28
Liberation of Bratislava (medal) 195
Lissie Rathbone Scholarship 24
Litvinoff, Emanuel 58
London-based Polish government-in-exile 161, 348
LONG: alleged KGB file codename for PC 16, 241, 365, 376
Louis, Victor 173, 349
Lublin
British diplomatic mission to 160–161
British ex-prisoners-of-war repatriated from 166
site of Maidanek concentration camp 162–163, 314–316
Macky, Colonel Neil Lloyd
escape to Crete 100–103, 339
military career 93
performance at Battle of Tempe 95, 97, 338
sacking and post-service career 98, 104
Macky, Ruth *see* Lake, Ruth (née Macky)
Maclaurin family 67–68
Maclaurin, Griffiths Campbell
bookseller 51, 54–55
Cambridge results 45, 46, 330
Communist Party membership 54
fought and died in Spanish Civil War 66–70, 333–334
friendship with PC 39, 43–47
marriage 69
teaching at St. Peter's School, York 51, 54, 332
unofficially engaged to Bil 55
Maclaurin, Richard Cockburn 44
Maclean, Donald 36, 37, 370
MacNeice, Louis 36, 285
Magyars: displacement of 189, 354–355
Mahon, Harold James de Monte 42
Mahoney, James Joseph 176–177
Maidanek (concentration camp) 162–163, 314–316
Manchester Chair in Russian 264, 266, 274
Mandelstam, Osip 185
The Marriage (Gogol): Bil translation 387
Marshall, John 372–373
Marx House course 56, 62
Marxism
as believed by PC 280–281
at Cambridge 36, 37
Doctor Zhivago as a rejection of 292–294
PC's ambivalence as a follower of 202
scholarship based on 380–381
Masaryk, Jan 190–191
Mason, R.A.K 26, 187–188
Mason, Wyn 240
Mather Chair of Russian Studies 266
Mayhew, Christopher 49
McCaffery, Leo 83–84
McCarthyism 78, 261
McCulloch, Martha 266, 306, 386

McCullough, Edward 306
McDonald, Alex (A.H.) 25, 39, 379, 384
McIntosh, Sir Alister
  action on Extermination Camps Report 164–165
  belief that British behind PC's downfall 261
  campaign to undermine his department 261–262
  Commonwealth Secretary-General nomination 373–374
  description of PC as brilliant 379
  discovery of windfall of French francs 233
  External Affairs set-up 229–230
  impact of PC's resignation on 260, 263
  on informant in Vegetable Club 373
  instructed by Holland to remove PC 244, 246
  on Masaryk 191
  Moscow diplomatic post closure 213, 218
  Moscow diplomatic post establishment 145–146, 151
  Paris Peace Conference attendance 188
  PC's arrest reported to 235–236
  PC's resignation received 255
  qualities 152
  quandary on PC's future after Moscow 227
  questioned about PC's activities in Moscow 181–182
  recruitment policy for diplomats 152–153
  replacement for Berendsen 362
  stance on PC 183–184
  victim of whispering campaign 262
McKenzie, Jean
  background and style as a diplomat 233–234, 238–239
  correspondence from McIntosh on PC 228
  as the N.Z. Pearl Mesta 363–364
  opened Paris Legation 228–229
  processed Kroger's passport application 250–253
  reaction to PC's enforced resignation 259
  relationship with PC 237, 239, 240, 267, 377
  vulnerability in Paris Legation 241–242
McMorris, Dr. 177, 212
McNeish, James 110, 261–262
Memories of Another Land (Lengyel) 166
Metrostroevskaya 21: 171, 186, 217
MI5 *see* British domestic Intelligence service
Ministry of Foreign Affairs and Trade (N.Z) 252–253, 368, 370–371
Minqar Qaim: break-out at 113–114, 341
The Minstrel Boy (song) 267
The Misfortune of Being Clever (Griboyedov): PC translation 206, 207, 291
The Mitrokhin Archive (Andrew) 16, 241, 364–365
Molotov, Vyacheslav 215, 222
Monte Cassino 131, 133, 282
Moore, Percy 84
Moorehead, Alan 111
Morris, Guy 264, 376–377
Moscow
  antikvari (secondhand bookshops) 174
  diplomatic colony cowed by paranoia and suspicion 180–181
  life pervaded by paranoia and suspicion 180
  PC's apartment in 169–171
  PC's wanderings around 175, 176, 177–178
  postwar conditions 154, 346
  restrictions on life 176–178
  shabbiness a disguise 359
  theatre visits 172–173, 217–218
Moscow Assignment (PC: unfinished novel) 204, 356
Moscow Legation *see* New Zealand Legation in Moscow
Mulgan, John 25–26
Mullinavat (Ireland) 31–32
The Murder of Rasputin (Purishkevich): Bil translation 309, 387
Murdoch, David 382
Murray, John 72, 75, 77–79, 182

Nash, Walter 372
Nathan, Lawrence (Laurie) 119, 127, 342, 380
National Hotel: N.Z. Legation in Moscow located at 154–155, 169
National Service training courses 273–274
naval secrets: relayed by Krogers to Moscow 251
Nazi Holocaust against the Jews 165, 166
New Zealand Division
commanded by Freyberg 291
commanded by Kippenberger 129
effect on PC on immersion in ranks of 117
Hooray-fuck slogan 114
in operation Crusader 108
PC recalled to 112
Stalin's praise of 356
New Zealand Government
acceptance of PC's version of Fyrth episode 76
diplomatic service 152–153
establishment of Moscow diplomatic post 145–146
foreign policy under Berendsen 362
PC's assessments of Soviet Union put to 359
Soviet atomic bomb disclosed by PC to 215
wartime support to Tahiti 231–233
New Zealand Legation in Moscow
closure 214–215, 216, 218, 219–220, 361
furniture 150–151, 216, 360
German Extermination Camps report 313–318
inspection by British security 376
located at Hotel National 154–155, 169
rationale for establishment 145
relationship with British Embassy 184
staffing 197
trade deals 197, 355, 360–361
travel limitations on members 176–177, 198–199
value of 215
New Zealand Legation in Paris
closure sought on financial grounds 241–242
Doidge's support secured 233–234
farewell party for PC 267
fate of consular papers 368
French francs behind establishment 231, 233
Krogers' passports issued by 249–252, 365, 369
in rue Léonard de Vinci 228–229
staffing 240–241, 242
uncertainty over 230–231
New Zealand Police Special Branch 367
New Zealand Security Intelligence Service
alleged evidence of PC as a Soviet agent 248, 367–368, 375–376
documents on Kroger passport affair 250, 252, 367–368, 371
file on PC as a student radical 24–25, 29, 331
file on PC on Athens studentship 47–48
file on PC's appointment to Moscow 141
formation 262
informant planted in Vegetable Club 373
original Kroger certificate 369
references to PC as a traitor 176
Nicholson, Michael 273, 274–275, 301
Nikolaevna, Yelena 211
Nikolai Negorev (Kushchevsky) 296, 301, 309, 387
Nobel Prize for *Doctor Zhivago* 292
Norman, Herbert 39, 72, 176, 180, 307
November 1933 peace demonstration 37–38

obituary: of PC 306, 319–321
Official Secrets Act 75–78, 182
Old Bailey trial of Krogers 251–252, 370
O'Leary, Trevor 29–30
Orwell, George 176, 199, 201, 204
Oswiecim (concentration camp) 163–165, 316–318
outsider figures in literature 207, 357

Ovenden, Keith
Bil's avoidance of opening up papers to 308
on Davin's Oxford home 284–285
on Davin's reaction to PC's death 306
on Davin's unfinished portrait of PC 292
on Enfidaville to Cairo trip 110
on PC and Davin's friendship 106, 282, 381
The Oxford Book of Russian Verse (PC) 186–187, 196–197, 206
Oxford Russian-English dictionary (PC: contributor) 296, 384

Pahlavi, Mohammed Reza 72
Paris Legation *see* New Zealand Legation in Paris
Paris Peace Conference 186–195
pass of Tempe 23, 90–91
passports issued to Krogers 249–253, 365, 369–370, 371
Pasternak, Boris
asked PC to translate *Doctor Zhivago* 293
death 294
Doctor Zhivago 292–294, 350
out of town when PC visited Moscow 292
PC as courier for 283
PC's friendship with 174–175, 180, 196–197, 350
in PC's Russian poetry anthology 185
Pasternak Slater, Lydia 283
Paterson, Professor 24
Patrick, R.T.G. 150–151, 155, 345
Patsalidis, George 111
"Paula" (PC's Russian emigrée mistress) 109, 111
Peace Conference 186–195
peace demonstration in Cambridge 37–38
Peace, Richard 207, 385
Pendelbury, John 47
Penguin History of New Zealand (King) 261–262
Perry, Ray 155
Peter, Prince of Greece 126–127
Peterson, Sir Maurice 184
Petrov affair 375
Philby, Kim 31, 33, 36
Pincher, Chapman 15, 253, 307, 364, 368
Platamon castle 19, 90
Poland: British diplomatic mission into 157–158, 160–162
police: responsibility for N.Z. security 261, 262
Polish resistance to Soviet domination 161
Pollitt, Harry 66
Ponsonby shop of Costello family 27–28
Portland naval spy ring 251
Potter, Dennis 273
Poulsen, Charles 58–59
Prior, Martin 300–301
Proctor, Josephine *see* Costello, Josie (PC's daughter)
Proctor, Patrick 386
Pugsley, Christopher 338
purge of state servants 258–259, 262
Pursihkevich, V. M. *The Murder of Rasputin*: Bil translation 387
Pushkin, Alexander 172, 208, 210, 281, 357

Queen Street riot 29
Quilty, Patrick (nom-de-plume) 199

Rathen Road home 267, 271–272, 278
Rawlings scholarship 27
Red Army
confidence in strength of 118–120, 359
delegation of generals 131, 146
The Red Army Moves (Cox) 118
Robertson, Dennis 33
Roche, Bill 123–124
Rogers, Bertie 285
Roosevelt, President Franklin D. 160
Rosenberg ring 251, 370
Ross, Margot 291
Russia *see* Soviet Union
Russian advance on Berlin 352
Russian education system 197–198
Russian Folk Literature (PC and Foote) 281, 296
Russian generals delegation 131, 146

Russian Grammar (PC: unfinished) 245, 366, 384
Russian-Jewish background: of Lerner family 53–54, 57–58
Russian language: difficulty of learning and speaking 173, 275
Russian life and culture 175–178, 180
Russian poetry anthology 186–187, 196–197, 206
Russian propaganda 201–202
Russian studies 273, 274–275
Russophobia 145

Samuels, Ralph 381
Scenes from a Stepney Youth (Poulsen) 58
Scotland Yard's Black Museum 252, 371
Scott, John 359
Scotten, Robert 261, 372
Secret Classrooms (Elliott and Shukman) 273
Security Intelligence Bureau (N.Z) 367
Security Intelligence Service (NZSIS) *see* New Zealand Security Intelligence Service
security: responsibility of N.Z. police 261, 262
Service, Jack 16
Seven Spies Who Changed the World (West) 249
Shanahan, Foss 235–237, 239
Shankar, Uday 212, 380
Sheehy, Rev. 101, 102
A Shropshire Lad (A.E. Housman) 29–30, 328
Shukman, Harold. *Secret Classrooms* 273
Sicily: holiday at 254
Sidey, Murray 130
Sinclair, Keith 372
singing 26–27, 32, 285
Sir William Mather Chair of Russian Studies 266
Sisam, Kenneth 383
Skhodnya: excursion into 177–178
Slater, Lydia Pasternak 283
Smith, Arnold 373
Smith, General Walter Bedell 189–190, 192, 355
Smuts, General 189
socialism: PC's ongoing belief in global 277
Socialist land 48
Socialist Society (Cambridge University) 33, 38
Soldiers and Scholars (Davin: unfinished) 292, 383
Sollohub, Count 33
Souvenirs de l'au-delà (Lengyel) 166
Soviet agent: allegations against PC as a 241, 247, 307
Soviet atomic bomb
  1949 news coverage of 222
  America's fallacious position on 359
  Krogers' role in development of 370
  PC's 1947 disclosure of 16, 215, 259
  speculation on quantity and use 258
Soviet satellites 272–273
Soviet Union
  Berendsen's position on 362
  diplomats regarded as spies 180–181
  excluded from PC's 1935 travel plans 49
  importance of Krogers to 251–252
  intentions in Poland 157–158, 160–162, 347–348
  purge of unreliable Spanish Civil War volunteers 71
  rationale for N.Z. diplomatic post in 145
  the reason for PC's privileged relationship with Freyberg 118
  resources invested in armaments 370
  second abortive attempt to visit 56–57
  shift in PC's attitude to communism in 276–277
  travels in 177–178
  underestimation of 359
  views on 168
Spanish Civil War 66–71, 333–334
Sparta: visit to 50
spies
  allegations against PC 241, 247, 307
  Blunt's confession 302
  Cold War Joint Services School as school for 273
  Davin's inability to rebut PC being 292, 307

government brought down by scandals 252
Krogers' operations 251–252
measure of success 16
Moscow diplomats regarded as 180–181
N.Z. passports as cover 370
Pincher's claim of PC's recruitment 253
Spycatcher (Wright) 307
Stalin, Joseph
meetings with Churchill 159–160
PC's purported admiration for 201–202
praise of N.Z. troops 356
regarded diplomats as spies 181
shift in PC's attitude to policies of 276–277
State Department biography of PC 192
state servant purges and denunciations 262
Stewart, Ian 252, 369, 371
Stitches in Time (A. Smith) 373
Stockholm: visit to 167–168
Stopford, Professor 266
Strachey, John 62
Straight, Michael 35, 278
Stubbs, Hugh 78, 79
student bursaries in Paris 241
student radical: PC associated with being 24–25, 29, 331
The Successful Russian (Kushchevsky) 296, 301, 309
Suez crisis messages 374
Sullivan, John 378, 385
Sutch, William Ball 146
Sweden: views on 167–168
Syme, Ronald
at Brasenose College 282
candidate for Davin's unfinished book 383
support for PC's Manchester application 264, 266
visitor at Viroflay 248, 367
visitor to Moscow 257
Synge, J.M.: *The Aran Islands* 299–300

Tahiti: N.Z.'s wartime support to 231–233
Tempe 23, 90–91
Tempe, Battle of 17–20, 92–98, 338
Templeton, Malcolm 145, 149, 152, 379
Tennant, Gray 83
Their Trade is Treachery (Pincher) 253, 307
Thomas, Dylan 285
Thornton, Lieutenant-General Sir Leonard 126, 128
Three Sisters (Chekhov) 144, 169, 287
Thucydide's history of the Peloponnesian war 100
Tiflis (Tbilisi): visit to 211–212
The Times obituary of PC 306, 319–321
"To an Athlete Dying Young" (Housman) 309–310
Tolstoy, Leo 275, 378
Tongue, S.M. 332
Tongue, Walter 17–19
Top Hats Are Not Being Taken (Templeton) 145, 149, 152, 379
trade deals: between N.Z. and the U.S.S.R. 197, 355, 360–361
traitor: perception of PC as a 16, 147, 176
Trinity College, Cambridge
communist cell 36
initial disappointment with 31, 32–33
record of PC's life held at 306, 386
scholarship to attend 30
Tripolis (Greece): visit to 50
Trofimov, Professor 274, 378
Truman, President Harry 191, 351
Tsvetaeva, Marina 185
Tunnicliffe, Shirley 248

Unbegaun, Boris 384
UNESCO 245, 255
United Nations General Assembly 245
University College of the South West, Exeter
Murray principal 72
PC's lectureship 62, 66, 68
PC's performance as a teacher 74–75
suspended PC 77–78
university communism 32–33

Vale of Tempe 23, 90–91
Vegetable and Political Club 229, 262, 361, 373

Venturi, Franco 175, 367
Vertinsky, Alexander 175
Viroflay home 244–245, 247–248
von Senger und Etterlin, Fridolin 282
Vyshinsky, Andrei 187

Wallace, Lieutenant 93, 94
Waller, Michael 265–266, 274, 275, 277
war debt funding of Paris Legation 231, 241
Webb, Clifton 236–237, 263, 266
West, Nigel 249, 364
West, Rebecca 251
Wheeler, Marcus 384
Williams, Bill 144
Wilson, J.V. 165, 237
Windsor Castle drinking episode 290–291
Withington home 267, 271–272, 278
Wittgenstein, Ludwig 31
Wolfenden, Jeremy 376
Woods, Betty 36
Woods, Mary *see* Costello, Mary (PC's mother)
Woods, Richard 367
Wordie, James 45, 332
Wright, Peter 307, 387

Xerxes: subject of school essay 23, 90

Yates, Gus 83
Young, Bruce 235

"Zhivago Reconsidered" (PC essay) 294, 295, 384
Zohrab, Douglas
evacuation from the bay of Volos 364
on food available to Muscovites 346
joined N.Z. Legation in Paris 240
on life under Stalin 181
military and diplomatic career 364
mistaken by British Minister for PC 206
at Paris Peace Conference 187–188, 353
at PC's Paris farewell 267
on staff of N.Z. Legation in Moscow 220
on trade with Soviets 360–361
whereabouts during passport affair 250, 252

McNeish is the wild card among New Zealand writers.

— *Lawrence Jones*

It is impossible for James McNeish to write a book which does not betray his commitment.

— *David Lange*

His writing is unforgettable.

— Norman Lewis in the London *Sunday Times*

James McNeish is a civilised urban writer, with a greater cosmopolitan sense of people's global inter-action than many other New Zealand writers.

— Agnes Mary Brooke in *The Press*

James McNeish is a marvel.

— Ted Reynolds in *The Listener*

Praise for James McNeish's last book, *Dance of the Peacocks: New Zealanders in Exile in the time of Hitler and Mao Tse-Tung*

The fascinating story of a group of Rhodes scholars, five young men — James Bertram, Geoffrey Cox, Dan Davin, Ian Milner, John Mulgan — caught up in the turmoil of their times: Spain, Hitler's Germany, Greece and North Africa, Eastern Europe, China. They left New Zealand in the thirties for "the dreaming spires" of Oxford. War intervened. Only one returned.

Not one Colossus of Rhodes, but five of them, and the brilliance of this work by James McNeish is to weave their stories into one compelling readable tale . . . This is a work of scholarship equal to the academic virtues it unashamedly celebrates. There are signposts aplenty here on the road map to a fledgling cultural identity.

— Simon Cuncliffe, *The Press*

. . . leaves one thirsting for more. *Dance of the Peacocks* is one of the most richly fascinating New Zealand non-fiction books for many years.

— Iain Sharp, *Sunday Star Times*

Dance of the Peacocks is the work where all of McNeish's gifts come together. The novelist, the biographer and the political journalist combine in this account of five New Zealanders who went to Oxford in the 1930s and became embroiled in the international political maelstrom of those times. In both general concept and concrete evocation, in pattern and detail, this is a remarkable book.

— Lawrence Jones, *Otago Daily Times*

Such is McNeish's skill that the book hangs together with, yes, the shape of a novel and the grip of a thriller. McNeish has walked a lone trail in New Zealand writing for 45 years. The young journalist who did six years on the *New Zealand Herald* in the '50s before becoming a fulltime writer in 1964 has travelled widely, carrying out what you might call a McNeish market of his own, while remaining, as Iain Sharp remarks, "private, elusive, inviolable".

Denis Welch in *NZ Listener*

. . . a thoroughly absorbing book: a rare combination of drama, group and individual biography, social, political, war and institutional history, part espionage thriller, part personal tragedy.

— John Hood, *Vice-Chancellor, University of Oxford*

It made me unbearably homesick.

— Denis Feeney, *Professor of Classics, Princeton, (USA)*

I think multiple biography is one of the hardest of all historical genres, and I admire the way you keep the reader fascinated throughout . . . Indeed I admire almost everything in the book.

— Sir Anthony Kenny, *Pro-Chancellor and former Master of Balliol, University of Oxford*

[McNeish's] ambition in taking on so unwieldy and complex a task as a group biography would seem to merit due recognition to start with, but it's hard to think of a book since Kenner's *The Pound Era* which could rival this one for thorough scholarship *combined* with entertainment value . . . If a better New Zealand biography comes out of this decade, I'd like to see it.

— Jack Ross, *World Literature Written in English (UK)*